POPE AND BISHOPS

THE MIDDLE AGES
a series edited by
Edward Peters
Henry Charles Lea Professor
of Medieval History
University of Pennsylvania

POPE AND BISHOPS

THE PAPAL MONARCHY IN THE TWELFTH AND THIRTEENTH CENTURIES

KENNETH PENNINGTON

UNIVERSITY OF PENNSYLVANIA PRESS

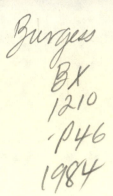
DESIGN BY CARL GROSS

Library of Congress Cataloging in Publication Data

Pennington, Kenneth.
  Pope and bishops.

  (The Middle Ages)
  Bibliography: p.
  Includes index.
    1. Papacy—History—To 1309. 2. Catholic Church—
Bishops—History. 3. Church and state—Catholic Church—
History. I. Title. II. Series.
BX1210.P46   1984   262'.13'09022   83-21799
ISBN 0-8122-7918-2

Printed in the United States of America

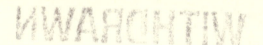

ERRATA for Kenneth Pennington, *Pope and Bishops*

A printer's omission of footnotes 124 and 125 occurs on page 114. They are listed below:

124. Ibid., X 1.9.10, v. *humiliter obedire*, fol. 91v-92r.

125. Ibid., v. *indubitanter* and *tu quomodo scis*, fol. 93r.

filiis carissimis

CONTENTS

ACKNOWLEDGMENTS

I first encountered the constitutional thought of the medieval lawyers and publicists in the seminars of Brian Tierney at Cornell University, where I learned the importance of medieval canon law for the history of political theory. This book owes much to his influence which cannot be fully acknowledged in the notes, and he will undoubtedly recognize some of his ideas that I have fitted out as my own. The paternity of other notions in this book he may be less ready to claim. I hope he realizes that almost all superb teachers share this experience to some extent. Professor Tierney has criticized my work with wit and patience over the last dozen years, and I am deeply indebted to him.

Many other friends and organizations made significant contributions to this project. Most of the writing was done during a sabbatical leave in 1980/81. Grants from the American Council of Learned Societies, funded by the National Endowment for the Humanities, and the Syracuse University Senate Research Fund made the leave possible. Stephan Kuttner at the Institute of Medieval Canon Law in Berkeley provided warm support, a space in which to work, and materials for my research. The members of the Institute and the librarians of the Robbins Collection in the Law School were unstinting in their efforts on my behalf. I would also like to express my appreciation to the librarians at Syracuse University, the Vatican Library, and the Biblioteca Nazionale in Florence for their assistance. And I am grateful to the Medieval Academy of America for permission to use a section in Chapter 4 that appeared earlier in the pages of *Speculum*.

A number of people read this manuscript at various stages, and their comments have made the book much better than it otherwise would have been. Brian Tierney, James Brundage, Robert Brentano, and James Powell read it in rough and early stages, and I am grateful for their criticism and forbearance. My colleagues in the history department, Joseph Levine, Samuel Eddy, and Edward Muir, helped me to sharpen its structure and argument and to improve its style. Robert Benson read the completed manuscript with care and offered a number of useful suggestions and corrections. Their collective efforts have spared readers much discomfort and made me appear more learned than I am.

This book is dedicated to my children. They will probably never enjoy reading it, but they brightened my life as I wrote it.

ABBREVIATIONS

Innocent III, Register I   *Die Register Innocenz' III.:* 1. *Pontifikats-*
                            jahr. Ed. Othmar Hageneder and Anton
                            Haidacher. Graz-Köln: 1964.
Innocent III, Register II   *Die Register Innocenz' III.:* 2. *Pontifikats-*
                            jahr. Ed. Othmar Hageneder, Werner
                            Maleczek, and Alfred Strnad. Graz-Köln:
                            1979.
Pressutti   *Regesta Honorii Papae III.* Ed. P. Pressutti.
                            2 vols. Rome: 1885–95.

LEGAL CITATIONS

a.c.   Dictum of Gratian before chapter
C.   Causa (division of the second part
                   of Gratian's Decretum)
c.   chapter
Cod.   Code of Justinian
1 Comp.   Compilatio prima
2 Comp., etc.   Compilatio secunda, etc.
D.   Distinctio (division of the first part
                   of Gratian's Decretum)
Dig.   Digest of Justinian
Instit.   Institutes of Justinian
p.c.   Dictum of Gratian after chapter
q.   quaestio (division of a Causa of Gratian's
                   Decretum)
VI   Liber Sextus of Boniface VIII
X   Liber Extra or Decretals of Gregory IX

For 1 Comp., 2 Comp., Cod., Dig., Instit., VI, and X, the numbers that
follow the abbreviation refer to book, title, and chapter in a work, and, in
some cases, a fourth number refers to paragraph.

A NOTE ON THE TRANSCRIPTIONS OF TEXTS FROM MANUSCRIPTS

I have followed the style of the Institute of Medieval Canon Law outlined in *Traditio* 15 (1959): 452–64 for the presentation of medieval legal texts. Whenever possible I collated two or more manuscripts of a work, basing my transcription on the best manuscript. Still, a manuscript's quality may vary in different sections, or the text may be corrupt in a particular place. Thus I have sometimes based my transcriptions of a work on different manuscripts. It is especially difficult to establish a good text for Huguccio's *Summa*. I relied on three manuscripts and consulted the texts of three others to establish a readable, if not critical, text; however, I am not entirely confident that I have always presented what Huguccio originally wrote. The various recensions of Tancred's *Apparatus glossarum* present almost as many problems as Huguccio's work. I have learned from my work on the *Apparatus* of Johannes Teutonicus that the text of a glossator's work can be established only after a thorough investigation of the manuscripts. Unfortunately, legal historians have not as yet made such studies of canonistic manuscripts, and so we are still prone to use the manuscripts which are conveniently at hand.

I have simplified the apparatus of the texts that I have included in the notes; consequently, I have not burdened the notes with meaningless variants from either the base manuscript or those I collated.

Vae qui condunt leges iniquas,
et scribentes injustitiam
scripserunt,
ut opprimerent in judicio
pauperes.

Isaias 10:1–2

Lex est ratio summa insita in
natura,
quae iubet ea, quae facienda
sunt,
prohibetque contraria.

Cicero De legibus 1.18

INTRODUCTION

Ernst Kantorowicz described the dualities of medieval political theory in luxurious detail in a book that has become a classic.[1] The theme that Kantorowicz explored, the king's public and private body, is a telling example of how medieval lawyers reconciled two opposing theories of monarchy. The first, derived from Germanic custom, subjected the prince to the law and restricted his authority to act without the consent of his subjects. The second, taken from Christian theological thought and classical jurisprudence and philosophy, placed the prince above the law, patterned his office after that of the deity, and emphasized the divine origins of political power. Kantorowicz showed how the irreconcilable tensions created by these two antithetical visions of political authority led medieval lawyers to distinguish between the prince's private body, which was subject to the law and bound to obey it, and his public body, which was above the law and beyond the reach of any other man.

These two contradictory conceptions of monarchy permeated all medieval thought; no medieval thinker ever evolved a thoroughly coherent system incorporating both sides of the prince's juridical personality. To modern critics who found this conception of kingship implausible, "scholastic and unworkable," and hardly worthy of the name of political theory, Kantorowicz answered:

John of Salisbury, Frederick II, or Thomas Aquinas . . . considered . . . those contradictions less unworkable and scholastic than the modern critic. . . . We may wonder whether those self-contradictions were not conditioned, directly or indirectly, also by the divine model of medieval kings who, being extra legally God and man at the same time, were likewise above and below the Law.[2]

Indeed, this dualistic conception of medieval kingship may be ultimately

---

1. Ernst H. Kantorowicz, *The King's Two Bodies: A Study in Mediaeval Political Theology* (Princeton: 1957).

2. Ibid., 143–44.

I

contradictory and logically unsatisfactory, but the fact remains that an understanding of these contradictions remains fundamental for studying western constitutional thought.[3]

The subject of this book is not the king's body, but the pope's. From the time the church shaped its governmental hierarchy to conform to the structure of the late Roman Empire, its constitution has been monarchical. For centuries the church's constitution did not come under serious scrutiny. However, during the eleventh century, the proper role of the church in society became a subject of intense debate, generating a vast literature of fiercely polemical tracts, and the pope's rights and duties began to be examined with unprecedented precision.

Although the early church borrowed its structure from the secular state, ecclesiastical government is particularly important for any study of medieval constitutional thought because secular kingdoms began to adopt the governmental practices of the church in the high Middle Ages. Further, the relationship of the church and state became tortured and complex. The place of the church in society changed dramatically between the eighth and the thirteenth centuries. In the eighth century the church was, by and large, subject to secular princes. Its organization centered around the king and his bishops.[4] In the thirteenth century, the church became independent of secular rule but was subject to the bishop of Rome. It had its own legal system, a sophisticated juridical organization, and an intricate network of relationships among members of the ecclesiastical hierarchy. Many even claimed that the church had the right to exercise temporal authority. By the end of the twelfth century, the church had generally achieved jurisdictional immunity from secular princes. The clergy was exempt from secular courts, but ecclesiastical courts exercised jurisdiction over both clergy and laymen in a range of matters. The result of these developments was that the question of political authority centered no longer on just the proper relationship between the church and state, but also on the proper relationship between the pope and the rest of the church.

As the church threw off the bonds of lay control, conflict between secular princes and the church became inevitable. Over the last forty years

---

3. Brian Tierney surveys the problem in "Medieval Canon Law and Western Constitutionalism," *The Catholic Historical Review* 52 (1966): 1–17, reprinted in *Church Law and Constitutional Thought in the Middle Ages* (London: 1979).

4. Horst Fuhrmann, "Das Papsttum und das kirchliche Leben im Frankenreich," *Nascita dell'Europa ed Europa Carolingia: Un'equazione da verificare*, Settimane di studio del Centro italiano di studi sull'alto medioevo 27 (Spoleto: 1981), 419–56, discusses the relationship of the Frankish church, the king, and the pope in a wide-ranging essay.

historians have deepened our understanding of these events and their significance.[5] The tensions created by the great disputes of church and state were eased and accommodated by a system of checks and balances linking each. Brian Tierney has described these disputes as having unexpected but salutary results:

There remained always two structures of government, ecclesiastical and secular, intricately interlinked but dedicated ultimately to different ends, often in conflict with one another, each constantly limiting the other's power. Evidently, the very existence of such a situation would enhance the possibilities for the growth of human freedom.[6]

The vivid personalities of the participants, Gregory VII, Thomas Becket, Innocent III, Frederick II, have continued to fascinate each new generation; their stories create some of the most important and colorful themes of medieval history.

Less colorful, less significant for the progress of human freedom, but just as important for the development of political theory and institutions of government, was the growth of ecclesiastical government during the twelfth and thirteenth centuries. Here too we find dualities, conflicts, and tensions that stimulated searching examinations of the church's constitution. The canonists who interpreted the growing mass of decretal legislation exalted the pope's authority and minutely described his power to legislate and render judicial decisions. They rummaged through classical Roman law for maxims with which they defined his position. The description of the Roman emperor they found in Justinian's *Corpus iuris civilis* provided a model of monarchical power, and the language of papal authority became virtually indistinguishable from that of imperial authority.

The writings of the canonists abound with statements describing the pope's supreme and undisputed authority within the church. However, they

---

5. The literature touching upon the conflict of church and state in the Middle Ages is enormous. Walter Ullmann's *Medieval Papalism: The Political Theories of the Medieval Canonists* (London: 1949) has pride of place. In this and his succeeding books, Ullmann argued that an understanding of papal monarchy was essential for tracing the development of western political thought, and he stimulated a generation of scholars to examine the problem in depth. The most recent summing up is Jürgen Miethke, "Geschichtsprozess und Zeitgenössisches Bewusstsein—Die Theorie des monarchischen Papats im hohen und späteren Mittelalter," *Historische Zeitschrift* 226 (1978): 564–99, with exhaustive references to the literature. Brian Tierney's older, but still-informative "Some Recent Works on the Political Theories of the Medieval Canonists," *Traditio* 10 (1954): 594–625, reprinted in *Church Law and Constitutional Thought in the Middle Ages* (London: 1979), should also be consulted.

6. Tierney, "Medieval Canon Law," 8.

also place limits on that authority. Canon law of the twelfth and thirteenth centuries did not simply support ecclesiastical absolutism. It also contained many "constitutional ideas" commonly found in medieval tracts on kingship.

Just as a king shared his authority with the great barons of the realm, the pope governed the church with his bishops. The canonists did not, perhaps could not, ignore the model of a king ruling with the consent of his barons. Consent played an important role in their thought even though bishops were not equated with feudal barons. Still, as Robert Benson has pointed out in his fine study of episcopal office, "the episcopate was, like monarchy, a universal governing institution throughout Latin Christendom."[7] Many bishops were secular as well as ecclesiastical princes. They ruled vast lands and exercised extensive secular and ecclesiastical authority. And although the practice became less frequent in the thirteenth century, it was not unusual for bishops to hold high secular and ecclesiastical offices simultaneously. Nevertheless power did not exempt them from divided loyalties and responsibilities. They discovered that vowing loyalty and obedience to more than one person was dangerous. They often found themselves caught between two masters, the pope and the king.[8]

Considered only as ecclesiastical princes, the bishops could be vulnerable to divided loyalties too. They were responsible for the well-being of their dioceses, and they had sworn to obey the will of the pope. They paid papal taxes. They provided benefices to papal candidates who arrived on their doorsteps armed with letters of provision. After the Roman curia developed its court system into a court of last appeal, bishops in far-flung corners of Europe were faced with the expense and trouble of carrying on court cases at the curia. They also had to contend with a system of papal law in which their jurisdictional prerogatives were being more precisely and, in some cases, more narrowly defined.

The troubled relationship, both legal and administrative, of magistrates to central authority is not peculiar to the Middle Ages or to bishops; it is a perennial problem of government. During the twelfth and thirteenth centuries, the canonists fitted the bishops into an increasingly juridical church. However, they never clearly defined the relationship between the bishops and the pope, and they were reluctant to subject the bishops completely to papal power. The complex relationship between the pope and his bishops is the central concern of this book.

---

7. Robert L. Benson, *The Bishop-Elect: A Study in Medieval Ecclesiastical Office* (Princeton: 1968), 3.

8. See the articles on bishop, the bishop's city, and the constitutional position of the bishop in *Lexikon des Mittelalters* (Munich: 1981), 2: 228–45.

The origins and character of episcopal jurisdiction had become a burning issue by the middle of the thirteenth century. The problem was minutely examined in the controversy between the mendicant and secular theologians. This dispute revolved around what may seem to be relatively insignificant issues. The bishops jealously guarded their right of granting permission to wandering priests to hear confessions and to say mass within their diocesan boundaries. The mendicant theologians argued that the pope's plenitude of power was the source of all jurisdiction and that the privileges the pope had granted to the mendicants released them from episcopal authority. The bishops' right to issue such permission was, they asserted, merely delegated to them by the pope.

The academic lawyers played a small role in this controversy. The most important thirteenth-century canonists who were working while the controversy raged, Pope Innocent IV, Hostiensis, and Guilielmus Durantis, wrote little about the issues involved.[9] There was, however, a brief, but strong statement of episcopal support in the Ordinary Gloss to the Decretals of Gregory IX.[10] Although two lawyer popes, Innocent IV and Boniface VIII, issued decretals limiting the privileges of the friars, there is no evidence that they favored the ideas of the secular theologians.[11] In chapter 5 I argue that there were two reasons for the canonists' reticence: they were not directly involved in the dispute as were the secular and mendicant theologians, and the canon law of privileges provided a satisfactory solution to the problem. The canonists' doctrine of privilege was based on a view of the church as a collection of rights or "liberties." The constitution of the church comprised liberties whose origins could be found in the primitive church of apostolic times, in customary usage, and in historical development. Every church and

---

9. Discussions did take place on canon 21 of the Fourth Lateran Council, later incorporated into the Decretals of Gregory IX at X 5.38.12.

10. Bernardus Parmensis to X 5.38.12 v. *alieno sacerdoti:* "Sed ecce si praedicatores et fratres minores vel alii religiosi non habentes populum habent privilegium ut alienos parochianos possint recipere ad poenitentiam, numquid sufficit privilegium, ut parochianum alterius possint recipere ad poenitentiam sine licentia proprii sacerdotis? Dicas quod non." See Ludwig Hödl, "Dienst und Vollmacht der Presbyter im mittelalterlichen Ringen um das theologische Verständnis der Kirchenverfassung," *Collectanea Stephan Kuttner,* SG 11 (Bologna: 1967), 1: 545–46. Hostiensis agreed with Bernardus, *Commentaria* (Venice: 1581), vol. 2, fol. 102v to X 5.38.12 v. *a proprio sacerdote.*

11. Yves-M. Congar, "Aspects ecclésiologiques de la querelle entre mendiants et séculiers dans la seconde moitié du XIIIe siècle et le début du XIVe," *Archives d'histoire doctrinale et littéraire du moyen âge* 25 (1961): 45–50 (see n. 18). Boniface VIII restricted the privileges of the friars. Before his pontificate, however, as a papal legate, he had vigorously rebuked Henry of Ghent and the secular masters of Paris.

prelate possessed rights that were inviolable.[12] The canonists built all their theories of authority on this assumption.

The secular-mendicant controversy was an important turning point in the history of political thought. Before the dispute, the canonists had never portrayed the church as a simple network of jurisdictions emanating from Rome. Brian Tierney has recently written:

> The dispute took a new turn in 1256 when a Franciscan, Thomas of York, declared that one supreme hierarch existed in the church, the pope, from whom all power descended to lesser prelates; and that, accordingly, whatever privileges the pope granted to friars, bishops had no right to protest since all their own jurisdiction was derived from the papacy. This "derivational" theory was not new in itself, but it had never been asserted so trenchantly and in such a sensitive context. In the explosive atmosphere of 1256 it transformed what had been a vague grumbling about the activities of the friars, based largely on the jealousy of the secular masters, into a great debate about the proper constitution of the church.[13]

Although the canonists described many legal relationships in purely jurisdictional terms—for example, legates and procurators—they did not use jurisdiction to elucidate the rights and prerogatives of local ecclesiastical officials. To support the claims of the friars, the mendicant theologians turned away from a theory of rights to a theory of jurisdiction to explain the right ordering of the church. If the pope was the source of all jurisdiction, he could grant or take away ecclesiastical rights and prerogatives on the authority of his office. This theory had the merit of simplicity and elegance.

By the end of the thirteenth century, stimulated by the secular-mendicant controversy, secular and mendicant theologians regularly discussed the origins of episcopal jurisdiction. Some of the most extreme statements of papal primacy came from the pens of the mendicants. Both the Dominican, Thomas Aquinas, and the Franciscan, St. Bonaventura, argued that the bishops derived all their jurisdiction from the pope. Later Franciscan and Do-

---

12. I. S. Robinson, " 'Periculosus homo': Pope Gregory VII and Episcopal Authority," *Viator* 9 (1978): 103–31, has described the bishops of the eleventh century as viewing the church as a "rigid hierarchy of inviolable jurisdictions." This view of the church was not peculiar to the eleventh century. It had been and would continue to be an important element of ecclesiological thought.

13. Brian Tierney, *Religion, Law, and the Growth of Constitutional Thought, 1150–1650* (Cambridge: 1982), 61. For examples of the derivational theory of jurisdiction, see Charles Zuckerman, "Some Texts of Bernard of Auvergne on Papal Power," *Recherches de théologie ancienne et médiévale* 49 (1982): 174–204.

minican theologians followed their lead.[14] In contrast, the secular theologians maintained that the bishops received at least a part of their jurisdiction from sources other than the pope. Guilielmus Durandus Junior provides a good example of the episcopalist position. He wrote that all episcopal power and honor came from God, for God placed the apostles and their successors, the bishops, in their offices.[15] Later, in the fourteenth century, Augustinus Triumphus emphasized the importance of St. Peter in his papalist ecclesiology. Christ granted the powers of order to all the apostles. However, he bestowed judicial power only on Peter. The prelates and bishops of the church derive their powers of jurisdiction from the pope.[16] Although there were variations on this theme, the adherents of the episcopal position generally insisted that bishops, too, were the vicars of Christ and the immediate successors of the apostles. This idea was not new. When Innocent III called bishops "vicars of Christ," he was echoing older formulas.[17]

The status of bishops remained a problem throughout the later Middle Ages. Two theories of authority, one stressing rights and the other jurisdic-

---

14. On the mendicants' ecclesiology see, Congar, "Aspects ecclésiologiques," 88–100 (see n. 11) and the penetrating analysis of Jürgen Miethke, "Die Rolle der Bettelorden im Umbruch der politischen Theorie an der Wende zum 14. Jahrhundert," *Stellung und Wirksamkeit der Bettelorden in der städtischen Gesellschaft,* ed. Kaspar Elm, Berliner Historische Studien 3 (Berlin: 1981), 119–53, with rich bibliographical references. Also see Michael Wilks, *The Problem of Sovereignty in the Later Middle Ages: The Papal Monarchy with Augustinus Triumphus and the Publicists* (Cambridge: 1964), 382; Brian Tierney, "Grosseteste and the Theory of Papal Sovereignty," *Journal of Ecclesiastical History* 6 (1955): 1–17, reprinted in *Church Law.* Thomas Izbicki, *Protector of the Faith: Cardinal Johannes de Turrecremata and the Defense of the Institutional Church* (Baltimore: 1981) is a study of late medieval ecclesiology.

15. Guilielmus Durandus, *Tractatus de modo generalis concilii celebrandi* (Paris: 1671), 34: "Cum itaque pateat ex praemissis quod episcopi potestatem et honorem suum receperunt a Deo, a quo ordo praelationis institutus est, et a quo episcopi in loco apostolorum constituti sunt in singulis civitatibus et diocesibus." On the purpose and structure of Durandus' work, see Constantin Fasolt, "A New View of William of Durant the Younger's 'Tractatus de modo generalis concilii celebrandi,' " *Traditio* 37 (1981): 291–324. William of Saint Amour was one of the earliest, if not the earliest, secular master to state that the bishops received their authority and jurisdiction from Christ through their predecessors, the apostles. See James D. Dawson, "William of Saint-Amour and the Apostolic Tradition," *Mediaeval Studies* 40 (1978): 223–38. Also see M. -M. Dufeil, *Guillaume de Saint Amour et la polémique universitaire parisienne* (Paris: 1972).

16. Wilks, *Problem of Sovereignty,* 532 n. 1.

17. Innocent III, *De sacro altaris mysterio libri sex* I c. 9 (PL 217.779–80): "Verum tamen et maiores et minores sacerdotes communiter in quibusdam vices gerunt summi pontificis, id est Christi, dum pro peccatis obsecrant, et peccatores per poenitentiam reconciliant." See Michele Maccarrone, *Vicarius Christi: Storia del titolo papale* (Rome: 1952), 110.

tion, commingled in later medieval thought. Neither theory became dominant. Walter Ullmann has written that the constitutional position of the bishops was "and still is, one of the trickiest ecclesiological problems." Although most thinkers conceded that the episcopal power of order *(potestas ordinis)* was given to bishops and priests directly by God, some thought that the pope was the sole source of jurisdiction *(potestas jurisdictionis)*.[18]

Since Vatican Council II, contemporary Catholic lawyers and theologians have struggled once again with the constitutional position of the bishops.[19] The official decrees of the church have always skirted the issue. At the Council of Trent in the sixteenth century and at Vatican Council I in the nineteenth, churchmen debated the role of the bishop and the relationship of his office to papal authority. The arguments were often subtle, sometimes forceful, and always lengthy.[20] In the end, both councils issued decrees in which episcopalists and papalists compromised. As might have been expected, this resulted in the question being left unresolved. A section from the final decrees of Vatican Council I, *Pastor aeternus,* illustrates this ambiguity quite well:

We teach and declare therefore that God ordained that the Roman church obtained *principatus* of ordinary power over all others, and this power of jurisdiction which the Roman pontiff has is truly episcopal and immediate. Whence as the pastors and

18. Walter Ullmann, "Eugenius IV, Cardinal Kemp, and Archbishop Chichele," *Medieval Studies Presented to Aubrey Gwynn, S.J.,* ed. John A. Watt et al. (Dublin: 1961), 377, now reprinted in *The Papacy and Political Ideas in the Middle Ages* (London: 1976). Zuckerman, "Bernard of Auvergne," 187–89, notes that Bernard was one of the few theologians (p. 189 n. 42) who wrote that bishops received their sacramental powers from the pope.

19. The literature on ecclesiology has grown since Vatican Council II focused attention on the status of bishops in the church. Some of the work produced by the church's renewed interest in its constitutional structure is very good history, especially Congar, "Aspects ecclésiologiques," 35–151. Other work of value is J. Lecuyer, *Etudes sur la collégialité épiscopale* (Le Puy-Lyon: 1964): Guiseppe Alberigo, *Lo sviluppo della dottrina sui poteri nella chiesa universale: Momenti essenziali tra il XVI e il XIX secolo* (Rome-Freiburg-Vienna: 1964): K. Morsdorf, "Die Regierungsaufgaben des Bischofs im Lichte der kanonischen Gewaltenunterscheidung," *Episcopus: Studien über das Bishofsamt* (Regensburg: 1949), 257–77: Yves-M. Congar and B.-D. Dupuy, eds., *La collégialité épiscopale: Histoire et théologie,* Unam Sanctam 52 (Paris: 1965) and *L'épiscopat et l'eglise universelle,* Unam Sanctam 39 (Paris: 1964); Yves-M. Congar, *L'Eglise de saint Augustin à l'époque moderne* (Paris: 1970) and *L'ecclésiologie du haut Moyen Age: De saint Grégoire le Grand à la désunion entre Byzance et Rome* (Paris: 1968). Jean Gaudemet has written an excellent survey of episcopal government, *Le gouvernement de l'église à l'époque classique,* II: *Le gouvernement local,* Histoire du Droit et des Institutions de l'Eglise en Occident 8.2 (Paris: 1979).

20. See Alberigo, *Lo sviluppo della dottrina,* chapters one and five, in which he describes the various shades of opinion about episcopal authority at Trent and Vatican I.

the faithful of every rite and dignity, as much separately as together, are bound to the office of hierarchical subordination by true obedience. . . . It is far from true that this power of the supreme pontiff may hinder the ordinary and immediate power of episcopal jurisdiction as the bishops were established by the Holy Spirit in place of the apostles.[21]

This definition leaves many questions unanswered. If the bishops are subordinated to the pope, is their power merely delegated? Do the bishops receive their jurisdiction from the pope directly or from Christ and the Holy Spirit? What is the legal relationship of papal to episcopal power? *Pastor aeternus* skillfully avoids these knotty problems.

The study will explore ecclesiastical authority in the twelfth and thirteenth centuries by focusing on developing definitions of papal monarchy and the formation of doctrine that governed the relationship of the popes and lesser prelates. This period produced the concepts and the language that would provide a skeleton for the sophisticated polemics of the later Middle Ages. Putting aside problems of church and state, I shall concentrate on the pope's relationship to his episcopal colleagues. I shall also forego any analysis of the Roman curia's constitution. Brian Tierney, John Watt, and others have studied the role of the general council and the status of the college of cardinals in the governance of the church and have indicated the significance of these institutions for the development of constitutional thought and political theory.[22]

I have not ventured to write a comprehensive history of papal and episcopal relations in the twelfth and thirteenth centuries. Nor have I written

---

21. The text of *Pastor aeternus* is conveniently printed in *Conciliorum Oecumenicorum decreta*, ed. G. Alberigo et al. 3rd ed. (Bologna: 1972), 811–16. The quoted text reads: "Docemus proinde et declaramus, ecclesiam Romanam, disponente Domino, super omnes alias ordinariae potestatis obtinere principatum, et hanc Romani pontificis jurisdictionis potestatem, quae vere episcopalis est, immediatam esse. Ergo quam cuiuscumque ritus et dignitatis pastores atque fideles, tam seorsum singuli quam simul omnes, officio hierarchicae subordinationis, veraeque obedientiae obstringuntur. . . . Tantum autem abest ut haec summi pontificis potestas officiat ordinariae ac immediatae illi episcopalis jurisdictionis potestati, qua episcopi, qui positi a Spiritu Sancto in apostolorum locum successerent." On Vatican I see Jean-Pierre Torrell, *La théologie de l'épiscopat au premier concile du Vatican* (Paris: 1961) and Gustave Thils, *Primauté pontificale et prérogatives épiscopales* (Louvain: 1961). The question was discussed again at Vatican II. The resulting canon, *Lumen gentium* (Alberigo, op. cit., 849–55) was just as imprecise as its predecessor.

22. Brian Tierney, *Foundations of the Conciliar Theory: The Contribution of the Medieval Canonists from Gratian to the Great Schism* (Cambridge: 1955) and the works of Tierney, Watt, and others cited in Chapter 2, n. 90 on the College of Cardinals. Tierney has recently discussed the importance of canon law on constitutional thought in *Religion, Law, and the Growth of Constitutional Thought*.

a detailed history of canonistic thought about papal monarchy. The canon-ists of this period are numerous and their writings voluminous. If I had discussed each important lawyer in detail, this book would have become unwieldy. Instead, I sketch the development of canonistic thought for the topics covered in broad strokes and do not attempt to present subtle nuances of opinions that were essentially in agreement. Consequently there may seem to be a chronological imbalance in some of my discussions. This imbalance reflects, I hope, the actual importance of particular canonists for the devel-opment of certain ideas. If a lawyer simply repeated the ideas of his prede-cessors, I generally do not present his thought. Although I treat the years from roughly 1180 to 1270, the solutions to all problems were not resolved at the same time and not all important canonists of the period made signifi-cant contributions to all areas of canonistic thought.

In Chapters 1 and 2, I focus on the development of the doctrines and theories of papal monarchy that defined papal and episcopal relations in the twelfth and thirteenth centuries. This was a particularly fertile period for the growth of both the theory and the practice of papal monarchy. Historians have traditionally marked off the pontificate of Innocent III as beginning the transformation of the church from a decentralized, "feudal" church into an absolute monarchy. As with any generalization, it is not perfect, but it does have a core of undeniable truth. In Chapters 3, 4, and 5, I explore three topics in which the papacy exercised jurisdiction in the affairs of bishoprics: (1) episcopal translations, abdications, and depositions; (2) papal provisions; (3) papal privileges of exemption. These chapters attempt to illustrate the strengths and limitations of the medieval papal monarchy.

I have tried to draw some connections between theory and practice and in spite of the difficulties presented by the sources, I have attempted to use anecdotal evidence to illustrate legal problems. I have also paid close atten-tion to the events that generated the theory we find in papal letters and in the glosses of the canonists. The letters reflect disputes in which theory was often only a secondary consideration of the participants, but the events help us to put theory and practice into perspective.

The main characters who appear in the following pages are the canon-ists and Pope Innocent III.[23] I have normally limited myself to canonists who wrote between Huguccio of Pisa (1180–90) and Henricus de Segusio (1250–

---

23. For a brief introduction to the canonists with further bibliography, see Benson, *Bishop-Elect*, 10–20, 387–90. Tierney, *Foundations*, 254–63 appended a short biographical dictionary of the major canonists.

71), or Hostiensis, although I have at times cast a wider net. Innocent III plays a much more important role in this book than I had originally anticipated or intended. After I began to write, it became clear to me that Innocent had upstaged all his fellow pontiffs of the period and most of the canonists. Perhaps only Hostiensis was his equal in inventiveness. As I wrote these chapters, I came to realize that Innocent had a preeminent place in the theory and practice of papal monarchy. He demanded center stage.

Pope Innocent III's pontificate marked the beginning of a new era.[24] He injected style and vigor into the decretals in which he discussed the papal office, and he impressed his contemporaries, particularly when they compared him to his predecessor, the aged Celestine III. Celestine's last years had been marked by bad luck and turmoil—bad luck because his leadership was uncertain and faltering[25] and turmoil because he lacked judgment and ability. He created a spectacle when he tried to abdicate in favor of John Cardinal of St. Paul. He caused confusion in the curia by his arbitrary and unskillful handling of judicial affairs. Even a canonist, Laurentius Hispanus, commented rather unkindly on Celestine's legal learning in a Parisian manuscript: "You may say that the prince has all laws within his breast as far as interpretation of the law, not, however, as far as the memory of the law. It is said of Celestine that he was not very learned in the law; whence it could be said to him that 'so saith the law.' "[26] Significant numbers of Innocent III's decretals from his first and second pontifical years were devoted to rectifying his predecessor's judgments.[27]

Celestine, however, cannot be blamed because his young successor was a pope of genius and vision. Innocent would have dwarfed most men. Contemporary chroniclers noted his unusual mental gifts. Although a few despaired of his youth or his policies, their opinions of Innocent were generally favorable. Innocent immediately used his decretal letters as a tool to shape his conception of papal monarchy. Within the first four years of his pontifi-

---

24. On Innocent's importance, see the perceptive remarks of Miethke, "Geschichtsprozess und Zeitgenössisches Bewusstsein," 581–87.

25. See Volkert Pfaff, "Der Vorgänger: Das Wirken Coelestins III. aus der Sicht von Innozenz III." ZRG Kan. Abt. 60 (1974): 121–67.

26. Laurentius Hispanus? to C. 25 q. 2 p.c. 16 v. *sive in iuris,* Paris, B.N. 15393, fol. 208v: "Dic quod princeps omnia iura habet in suo pectore quoad interpretationem . . . non autem quoad memoriam . . . sicut dicitur de Celestino quod non erat multum peritus in iure unde potuit ei dicere, quod ita dicebat ius. la." I am grateful to Stephan Kuttner for bringing this passage to my attention.

27. Pfaff, "Vorgänger," 155–57.

cate, we find almost all the famous similes, metaphors, and biblical figurae with which he gave sinew to the muscular prose encasing his thought. He has been called the greatest pope of the Middle Ages, and with Innocent we shall begin.

CHAPTER ONE ‹ INNOCENT III AND THE DIVINE AUTHORITY OF THE POPE

Pope Innocent III (1198–1216) transformed the theory of papal monarchy and, to a lesser extent, changed the practice of papal government during his pontificate. He pushed the papacy in new directions, created new justifications for the exercise of papal authority, and used older justifications in new ways. Innocent combined hardheaded practicality with an intellectual's interest in the power and importance of ideas. Ideas could shape the world, and Innocent used them as effectively as any pope, before or since.

The author of the *Gesta Innocentii* understood the duality of Innocent's talents. At the beginning of his account, he listed Innocent's attributes as a series of contrasts:

He was a man who was learned in both literature and scripture . . . neither prodigal nor covetous . . . harsh with the inobedient and the obstinate, but kind to the humble and loyal . . . humble in prosperity and patient in adversity, a little prone to anger, but quick to forgive.[1]

Although the list contains platitudes that might have been taken from any handbook of *Ars dictaminis,* it rings true, particularly the reference to Innocent's volatile temper.

Both sides of Innocent's character were important. One side did not dominate the other. Shortly after ascending the papal throne, he reformed the papal curia, reorganized the government of the City of Rome, reunited

---

1. *Gesta Innocentii papae III*, PL 214.xvii: "in divinis et humanis litteris eruditus . . . medius inter prodigalitatem et avaritiam . . . severus contra rebelles et contumaces, sed benignus erga humiles et devotos . . . humilis in prosperis, et patiens in adversis; naturae tamen aliquantulum indignantis, sed facile ignoscentis" [Vat. lat. 12111, fol. 1r].

the papal states, and restructured the Roman chancery. At the same time, he demonstrated his keen appreciation of the power of language and ideas in his decretals, using them to bridge the chasm between papal rights and papal claims. Indeed his greatest contribution to the ideology of papal power may have been the mellifluous language with which he exalted the office of pope.

The language of his decretals influenced the rhetoric of the canonists. As they glossed his decretals, they began to describe papal authority in words and phrases redolent of Innocent's language and stamped with his spirit. This development cannot be entirely coincidental. Although such language was a common feature of the age, the canonists reacted to Innocent's rhetoric by embracing hyperbole and florid—sometimes ironic—prose on an unprecedented scale.[2] While the resulting works provide difficulties for modern historians, they also misled men of the Middle Ages. Contemporaries of Innocent were often confused and dismayed by the extravagant language with which the pope and the lawyers defined papal prerogatives.

The canonists and the jurisconsults of the Roman Empire had much in common. Their roles and functions in their respective legal systems were similar. Like the jurisconsults, the canonists interpreted canon law and produced detailed commentaries on papal judicial decisions. By the beginning of the thirteenth century, popes were sending individual decretals and entire collections to Bologna for "reception" in the law school.[3] The canonists were independent of the papacy but connected to it in a fruitful relationship that was like an intricate musical counterpoint. The papacy produced a melodic line to which the canonists responded, sometimes forcing Rome to reconsider the structure and rhythm of the piece. At times, the process became visible. For example Innocent III wrote a decretal to the doctors of the Decretum at Bologna in which he explained under what circumstances it was permitted to have contact with an excommunicate. In this decretal Innocent provided an answer to problems of interpretation that had arisen in the schools because an earlier decretal was not as precise as it should have been.[4] The questions canonists raised in the classroom

---

2. Christopher R. Cheney, *Pope Innocent III and England*, Päpste und Papsttum 9 (Stuttgart: 1976): 1–11; K. Pennington, "Pope Innocent III's Views on Church and State: A Gloss to *Per venerabilem*," *Law, Church, and Society: Essays in Honor of Stephan Kuttner*, ed. K. Pennington and Robert Somerville (Philadelphia: 1977), 49–67; Robert Lerner, "Joachim of Fiore as a Link between St. Bernard and Innocent III on the Figural Significance of Melchisedech," *Mediaeval Studies* 42 (1980): 471–76.

3. K. Pennington, "The Making of a Decretal Collection: The Genesis of *Compilatio tertia*," *Proceedings of the Fifth International Congress of Medieval Canon Law*, ed. Stephan Kuttner and K. Pennington, MIC, Series C, 6 (Città del Vaticano: 1980), 67–92.

4. Po. 1107; 3 Comp. 5.21.4 (X 5.39.31), dated 1200.

prompted Innocent to issue a clarification of the earlier law.

Innocent had rapidly established the issues he considered to be special prerogatives of the papacy: the renunciation, deposition, and translation of bishops were, for him, signposts of papal supremacy within the church.[5] To judge from Innocent's attention to the issue in the first two years of his pontificate, the exclusive right of the pope to transfer bishops from one bishopric to another may have been the most important of the three.

I shall discuss the prerogatives the papacy claimed over episcopal translations in Chapter 3. For now, let me note that the popes and the lawyers of the twelfth century had not established firm rules governing the transfer of bishops and had not established that the pope had the exclusive right to authorize and approve the translation of a bishop from one see to another.[6]

In the first two years of his pontificate, Innocent seized the chance to rule on several cases of unauthorized episcopal translations. The canonists did not immediately see the importance of Innocent's resolve to reserve the matter for the pope. Rainer of Pomposa, who was undoubtedly closer to Innocent than any other canonist we know of during the early years of his pontificate, was the first compiler to place three of Innocent's letters under a title that treated the transfer of bishops.[7] Other canonists did not imitate Rainer and may have wondered whether papal approval was necessary for translations. After Rainer of Pomposa, the collections of Gilbertus (1203) and Alanus (1206) ignored the title and most of the pertinent decretals even though a few ancillary decretals touching related issues were placed under other titles. Only in Bernardus Compostellanus' *Collectio Romana* (1208) and Petrus Beneventanus' *Compilatio tertia* (1209/10) did Innocent's decretals enter canon law under their proper title, *De translatione episcopi et electi*.[8]

For translations and the language of papal power, the most important decretal in the canonical collections was *Quanto personam*. Innocent sent the decretal to five bishops of Germany and ordered them to excommunicate Conrad of Querfurt if he failed to obey papal mandates within twenty days.[9] Conrad had been bishop of Hildesheim. He left Hildesheim for Würzburg without papal permission after having been elected by the canons at Würzburg to their episcopal see.

---

5. Cheney, *Pope Innocent III*, 50–79.

6. Ibid., 71–72.

7. Ibid., 73.

8. Ibid.

9. 3 Comp. 1.5.3 (X 1.7.3); Bern. 1.7.3; Coll. Fuld. 1.5.13; Po. 352. Innocent III, Register I, 495–97, no. 335.

In contending that a bishop is married to his church, a metaphor that had become commonplace during the twelfth century, Innocent compared the bond of marriage to a bishop's tie to his church and claimed that the pope had the sole authority of approving episcopal translations.[10] Since only God may dissolve the bond of marriage, Innocent argued that only God has the power to break the bond between a bishop and his flock. This authority was a special privilege that Christ had granted to St. Peter and his successors. Early statutes of the fathers, concluded Innocent, supported his interpretation. Therefore, only the pope possessed the authority to dissolve episcopal marriages, and only he could translate bishops:

God, not man, separates a bishop from his Church because the Roman pontiff dissolves the bond between them by divine rather than by human authority, carefully considering the need and usefulness of each translation. The pope has this authority because he does not exercise the office of man, but of the true God on earth [*non puri hominis, sed veri Dei*].[11]

In this letter, his sermons, and other decretals, Innocent introduced the title "vicar of Christ" or "vicar of God" into the vocabulary that the pope and the curia used to describe the papal office.[12] His verbal images suited contemporary ideas and taste. That the pope's power was derived from Christ was not a new idea. This had been a basic argument for papal monarchy from patristic times. Innocent's genius lay in selecting a commonplace idea—that Christ granted the pope his authority—and using it to establish the belief that the pope could also exercise certain prerogatives permitted only to Christ and his vicar.

The pope was Christ's legal representative on earth. The canonists were familiar with the jurisdictional distinction between a prince and his representative and made it regularly when they discussed the authority of papal legates. They constructed long lists of powers that a legate could not wield and distinguished between the authority that a legate could exercise with a special mandate and his ordinary powers. Bishops, however, were not legates, and the relationship between the pope and bishops was different from that of a prince and his representative; indeed the issue was a delicate constitu-

---

10. Benson, *The Bishop-Elect*, 121–24, 126–28.

11. 3 Comp. 1.5.3: "Non enim homo, sed Deus separat, quos Romanus pontifex, qui non puri hominis, sed veri Dei vicem gerit in terris, ecclesiarum necessitate vel utilitate pensata, non humana, sed divina potius auctoritate dissolvit." See Innocent's language in an earlier letter, Register I, 472–74, no. 326.

12. Maccarrone, *Vicarius Christi*, 109–18. In *Quanto personam* Innocent wrote that Christ bestowed power on St. Peter, "vicario suo."

tional problem. A bishop's bond to his church was not to be broken or tampered with lightly. Thus in order to establish his authority over bishops, in particular to determine the pope's absolute prerogative to translate and depose bishops, Innocent needed to give a particularly persuasive justification of the pope's right to regulate episcopal affairs.

His solution was truly brilliant. The pope had the extraordinary right to exercise divine authority on earth in certain cases, a right that had been specially mandated to the pope by Christ. Later in the thirteenth century, Hostiensis adapted Innocent's idea and called this papal power "potestas absoluta."

Innocent's thought may not have been clear and lucid. He may have been only partially aware of the implications of his arguments. Nevertheless he established an important tradition of political thought in which the prince's authority was categorized into two types: those powers that were human, "ordinary," and those that were special, in Innocent's words, "divine." This division of papal authority had its roots in Christian political thought that had long contained strong dualist elements. For example, the Christian church was called the body of Christ. Like Christ, the church had a spiritual and a material nature. It also had heavenly and earthly powers. The pope derived his authority from Christ and his human vicar, St. Peter.[13] In *Quanto per-sonam*, Innocent implied that the pope had two types of authority. In the ordinary exercise of his office, the pope did not rely on extraordinary prerogatives; his powers were those of any prince and were circumscribed by custom, law, and tradition. However, when he exercised the prerogatives that he shared with Christ, he could do much more.

The canonists of Bologna found *Quanto personam* a challenging text and reacted to it in several distinct ways. The first glosses to *Quanto per-sonam* were written about twelve years after Innocent sent the letter to Germany. One of the first glossators of *Compilatio tertia*, Laurentius Hispanus, was attracted to Innocent's formulation that the pope had acted from the office "not of man, but of the true God on earth." He wrote:

Hence [the pope] is said to have a divine will . . . and O, how great is the power of the Prince. He changes the nature of things by applying the essences of one thing to another . . . he can make iniquity from justice by correcting any canon or law; for in these things that he wishes, his will is held to be reason [*est pro ratione voluntas*] . . .

---

13. Walter Ullmann's *The Growth of Papal Government in the Middle Ages: A Study in the Ideological Relation of Clerical to Lay Power*, 2nd ed. (London: 1962) is an extended discussion of the duality in Christian political thought.

and there is no one in this world who would say to him, why do you do this? He is held, nevertheless, to shape this power to the public good.[14]

Laurentius' words, "est pro ratione voluntas," were based on Juvenal's *Satires* (6.223). Gaines Post has shown that both Roman and canon lawyers began to use this aphorism in their writings at the end of the twelfth century. Although the commentators on Roman law were slow to use the phrase as a description of the prince's powers, the canonists used the phrase frequently during the pontificate of Innocent III.

Post argued that when they quoted Juvenal's phrase the canonists were intending to characterize papal power according to commonly accepted medieval constitutional ideas. The pope's actions should not be arbitrary and could not depart from justice. Post thus concluded that when a medieval canonist wrote or read that "a prince's will is held to be reason," he did not assume that the prince could legislate arbitrarily. The canonists were not advocating absolutism.[15]

Post is certainly correct; however, the glosses to *Quanto personam* are important not only because they embody conventional ideas of "medieval constitutionalism," but also because they are careful and sophisticated definitions of papal legislative and judicial prerogatives.

While glossing *Quanto personam*, the canonists examined several hitherto untouched concepts of political theory. They did not adopt Innocent's new formulation of bifurcated papal authority. Instead, they explored the problem of princely power and authority in much more general terms, not-

---

14. Laurentius Hispanus, 3 Comp. 1.5.3 v. *puri hominis*, Admont 55, fol. 110r [Karlsruhe Aug. XL, fol. 128v]: "Vnde et dicitur habere celeste arbitrium, C. de summa trin. l.i. in fine, et o quanta est potestas principis quia etiam naturas rerum immutat substantialia huius rei applicando alii, arg. C. commun. de leg. l.ii. et de iustitia potest facere iniquitatem corrigendo canonem aliquem uel legem, immo in his que uult, est pro ratione uoluntas, arg. instit. de iure naturali § Set quod principi [Instit. 1.2.6], non est in hoc mundo qui dicat ei, cur hoc facis, de pen. di. iii. § Ex persona. Hanc tamen potestatem tenetur ipse utilitati publice conformare (K: conformitare), extra. de foro compet. Licet legalis (A and K: regalis) [Bern. 2.2.6]." On Laurentius, see Antonio García y García, *Laurentius Hispanus: Datos biográficos y estudio crítico de sus obras* (Madrid-Rome: 1956).

15. Gaines Post, "Vincentius Hispanus, 'Pro ratione voluntas,'" and Medieval and Early Modern Theories of Sovereignty," *Traditio* 28 (1972): 159–84. Although the following pages differ from Post on a number of points, my debt to his article will be obvious. On the glosses to *Quanto personam*, see Brian Tierney, *Origins of Papal Infallibility, 1150–1350: A Study on the Concepts of Infallibility, Sovereignty and Tradition in the Middle Ages* (Leiden: 1972), 26–28; and Ernst Kantorowicz, "The Sovereignty of the Artist: A Note on Legal Maxims and Renaissance Theories of Art," *Essays in Honor of Erwin Panofsky*, ed. Millard Meiss (New York: 1961), 267–79.

ing a number of interesting discrepancies between accepted ideas about law and the relationship of the monarch to law. Every medieval thinker assumed two things about law: it must be just, and it must be reasonable. Intrigued by Innocent's claim that he exercised the office of the true God on earth, the canonists probed the anomalies and paradoxes of monarchical power.

In their discussions of these issues, the canonists noticed, for the first time, a serious difficulty in defining the relationship of the prince and positive law. They cited Juvenal's aphorism, "pro ratione voluntas," to define the prince's will as being the source of positive canon law. But while exploring the implications of the maxim, they discovered that the prince's will could be distinguished from the content of law. The exercise of authority carried with it obligations and was subject to moral judgments, but the prince's will, as the source of positive law, could be considered separately from issues of morality.

Laurentius was the first to apply Juvenal's phrase to the pope's legislative authority, and the aphorism is embedded in a tissue of ideas with which Laurentius described the pope as law-giver and judge. His gloss is quite different from earlier canonistic glosses discussing papal authority. Twelfth-century descriptions of papal prerogatives were generally utilitarian descriptions of princely authority based on Roman law. Inspired by Innocent III's language, Laurentius inaugurated a tradition of high-flown and exaggerated language which became a characteristic feature of later canonistic discussions of the papal office.

The beginning of Laurentius' gloss is a conscious echo of Innocent's thought and language in *Quanto personam*: "[The pope] is said to have a divine will: O, how great is the power of the Prince."[16] Laurentius then composed a series of paradoxical descriptions of papal power beginning with "he changes the nature of things by applying the essences of one thing to another." At first glance, the statement seems to violate both logic and science. Nevertheless, Laurentius did not offend God or nature. His citation to Justinian's Code makes clear that Laurentius had a specific legislative power of the prince in mind: the prince may change the meanings of legal terms without changing the words themselves. Laurentius cited a law of Justinian in which the emperor had emended the rules concerning testaments so that a "legatum" and a "fideicommissum," originally two different acts in Roman testamentary law, became the same.[17] Justinian had made the essence of two things the same while allowing their superficial appearances,

---

16. The term "celeste arbitrium" is taken from Roman law, Cod. 1.1.1.1.
17. Cod. 6.43.2.

the words themselves, to remain different. Thus, Laurentius was not granting unbridled legislative authority to the pope when he wrote that he may change the nature of a thing. Rather, every legislator has the authority to enact such legislation.

Laurentius' next statement seems even more paradoxical than the first. The pope can make iniquity out of justice by correcting any canon or law. The canonists had a keen sense of the justness of their texts and often argued that even when a law was superseded, the reason (*ratio*) of the law would remain. They believed that all law must ultimately be founded on reason. For them reason and justice were closely related. How then could the pope make injustice out of justice? A theologian might argue that even God could not do that.

The ordinary glossator of the Decretals of Gregory IX, Bernardus Parmensis, felt so uncomfortable with the idea that good laws could ever, in their essence, be unjust, that he altered his version of the gloss to read: "the pope can make justice from injustice," a more seemly formulation.[18] The legal point Bernardus made, however, was the same as Laurentius': the pope may change law. What was defined as just, he could make unjust through new legislation. Laurentius supported his statement with the famous passage from Justinian's *Institutes*, "What pleases the prince has the force of law" ("Sed et quod principi placuit, legis vigorem habet" Instit. 1.2.6). Brian Tierney has persuasively demonstrated that for the Roman lawyers this maxim was not a mandate for the absolute authority of the prince.[19] Nor was it for the canon lawyers.

A few years later, Tancred copied the gloss of Laurentius and gave a concrete example. To justify the pope's making injustice from justice, Tancred cited two Fourth Lateran constitutions, *Ut debitus* and *Non debet*.[20]

---

18. X 1.7.3 v. *veri Dei vicem*. Post was misled by Bernardus' emendation and conjectured that the original wording of the gloss was the same as Bernardus' but that the earlier texts had been corrupted by scribal errors ("Vincentius Hispanus," 170–71).

19. Brian Tierney, " 'The Prince Is Not Bound by Law': Accursius and the Origins of the Modern State," *Comparative Studies in Society and History* 5 (1963): 378–400, reprinted in *Church Law*.

20. Tancred's gloss has been printed many times and is almost identical to Bernardus Parmensis' in the Ordinary Gloss to X 1.7.3 v. *veri Dei vicem*. The key words are: "Item quia de iustitia potest facere iniustitiam, ut in const. domini Innocentii iii. Vt debitus et c. Non debet" [4th Lat. c. 35 (4 Comp. 2.12.3 = X 2.28.59) and c. 50 (4 Comp. 4.33.3 = X 4.14.8)]. For the texts of the constitutions and contemporary glosses to them, see *Constitutiones Concilii quarti Lateranensis una cum commentariis glossatorum*, ed. Antonio García y García, MIC, Series A, 2 (Città del Vaticano: 1981), 78, 90–91. For the text of Tancred's gloss and Post's discussion of it, see "Vincentius Hispanus," 171.

The two constitutions demonstrate both sides of a prince's legislative power. In *Ut debitus* the pope and council forbade appeals before a case had been decided in a lower court unless there were unusual circumstances. Before this canon, valid appeals had been permitted even before an inferior court had rendered a judgment. Thus the pope converted what had formerly been a just act into an unjust one. *Non debet* made the opposite point. In this canon Innocent changed the number of degrees of consanguinity permitted in marriage from seven to four. Consequently, consanguinity to the fifth degree was now permitted. The pope made what had been unlawful, lawful. He made justice from injustice. It is clear that Laurentius and Tancred did not consider the pope's authority to change "justice to injustice" an extraordinary exercise of authority. They were simply describing the power of every legislator, whether absolute or constitutional.

At this point in his gloss, Laurentius quoted Juvenal: "For in these things that he wishes, his will is held to be reason." "These things" are the two examples of the pope's authority to enact legislation that seem to be contrary to logic and reason. Normally reason and law are congruent. Sometimes, Laurentius observed, they diverge. In these unusual cases, the prince's will substitutes for reason. Laurentius did not mean that the prince's will was arbitrary but that sometimes law did not conform to reason or logic. Before Laurentius, lawyers had not distinguished between the reason of law (*ratio iuris*) and the will (*voluntas*) of the prince.

This new distinction challenged older ways of thought. The canonists believed that law must contain reason; this idea had been burned into their minds. Without reason, law was not valid, no matter who the source of the legislation was. Huguccio of Pisa, the greatest and most influential of the twelfth-century canonists, lived comfortably with a conception of law quite alien to modern ideas about legislative sovereignty: a legislator's will could always be thwarted by forces impervious to his authority. Law had at least two sources: the legislative authority of the prince and reason. Huguccio discussed this issue in a gloss to Gratian's *Tractatus de legibus* in the Decretum:

Certain canons cannot be abrogated by the pope, as for instance those promulgated concerning the faith and the general state of the church. . . . But cannot the clergy or people be compelled to do what the prince wills since the pope has the fullness of power, and all power is given to the prince? I believe they can if they deviate from reason or the faith, otherwise not. Again, can the pope promulgate something without or contrary to the will of his cardinals, or the emperor against the will of his barons? I think not, if he can have their assent; otherwise he can, provided it was not contrary to reason and the Old and New Testaments. But in any case, if they establish [a law] that is just, it will be valid and others are bound to obey. The people bestow the right of granting all laws and canons on the emperor, the church to the Holy See. Hence, both are understood to have "fullness of power."[21]

Huguccio could not envision a valid law that could be contrary to reason. His "reason," of course, was very different from the simple reason that Laurentius found missing in certain canons and laws. Huguccio's *ratio* was metaphysical, embracing first principles of medieval political theory and law and transcending simple logical coherence.

Laurentius, nevertheless, was not insensitive to Huguccio's *ratio*. At the end of his gloss he wrote that the prince's will must always incorporate the public good, even in those cases in which his will did not embody reason. Both Huguccio and Laurentius thought of *ratio* as being much more than simple "reason": it was morality, the public good, custom, and divine law. The Spaniard, however, was the first medieval lawyer to distinguish between *ratio iuris* and *voluntas principis*. By separating reason from will, Laurentius laid the groundwork for a conception of authority in which the prince or the state might exercise power "unreasonably" but legally.

Up to this point, Laurentius' imagery and thought were fresh and new. Only the last section of his gloss in which he asked "who would say to him, 'why do you do this?'" is shaped and fashioned from earlier glosses. The question was not just rhetorical, for it touched the core of the pope's juridical authority within the church.

In the last half of the twelfth century, the decretists placed the pope at the apex of the juridical hierarchy of the church. Gratian had given the pope exclusive judicial and legislative primacy in his Decretum. By granting the pope great authority, Gratian followed the thrust of canonical jurisprudence

---

21. Huguccio, D. 4 p.c. 3, v. *abrogate*, Admont 7, fol. 6vb [Klosterneuburg 89, fol. 6va]: "Set nota quod nec papa quidam canones possunt abrogari: puta de articulis fidei uel de generali statu ecclesie editi. . . . Set nonne clerus uel populus posset compelli ut impleret quod papa uel princeps uult, cum papa habeat plenitudinem potestatis, et omnis potestas sit in principe collata? Credo quod posset si a ratione uel fide uellet deuiare, ut di. lxii. Docendus [c. 2] alias non deberet. Item posset papa, preter uel contra uoluntatem suorum cardinalium aliquid statuere, uel imperator preter uel contra uoluntatem suorum baronum? Respon. Non deberet si eorum consensum posset habere. Alias posset, dummodo non sit contrarium rationi uel ueteri uel nouo testamento. Set quicquid dicatur, si sic aliquid quod sit iustum constituunt, ratum erit, et alii tenebuntur obedire. Omne ius condendi leges uel canones populus [MSS: p̄p̄] contulit in imperatorem, ecclesia in apostolicum. Vnde intelligitur uterque plenitudinem potestatis habere quo ad hec." See Brian Tierney, " 'Only the Truth Has Authority': The Problem of 'Reception' in the Decretists and in Johannes de Turrecremata," *Law, Church, and Society: Essays in Honor of Stephan Kuttner*, ed. K. Pennington and R. Somerville (Philadelphia: 1977), 69–96, reprinted in *Church Law*. Also Luigi de Luca, "L'accettazione popolare della legge canonica nel pensiero di Graziana e suoi interpreti," SG 3 (1955): 193–276, prints most of the gloss at 233 n. 74.

predominant since the Gregorian reform movement.[22] All theorists of monarchical government have to ask themselves, once the monarchy is established, "who may judge the prince."[23] Although the canonists devoted much ingenuity and thought to the problem of the pope who erred in the faith, the question of who could judge the pope in more mundane matters also intrigued them.[24] Most canonists felt that the pope's judicial decisions could not be questioned. Whatever the pope decided in his curia, other members of the ecclesiastical hierarchy could not question.

Some canonists did not demand absolute obedience to papal judicial decisions, but most denied emphatically that anyone could refuse to obey a papal judgment. Even with discretion, one could not act contrary to a papal command.[25] The canonists modeled the pope's role as supreme judge within the church after the prerogatives of the Roman emperor. An appeal to the pope invalidated all subsequent litigation; a papal judicial decision made law; a litigant could not appeal the pope's decision.

Huguccio of Pisa succinctly characterized the pope's supreme judicial position within the church by asking, "Who could resist the pope?"[26] This refrain, not new with Huguccio, was repeated in the works of the canonists

22. Stanley Chodorow, *Christian Political Theory and Church Politics in the Mid-Twelfth Century: The Ecclesiology of Gratian's Decretum* (Berkeley-Los Angeles–London: 1972), 178–86, discusses the place of the pope in Gratian's thought.

23. Brian Tierney, "Bracton on Government," *Speculum* 38 (1963): 295–317, reprinted in *Church Law*, is a masterly discussion of the problem in the work of the thirteenth-century writer known as Bracton. Also see Gaines Post, "Bracton as Jurist and Theologian on Kingship," *Proceedings of the Third International Congress of Medieval Canon Law*, ed. Stephan Kuttner, MIC, Series C, 4 (Città del Vaticano: 1971), 113–30.

24. See Tierney, *Foundations* 56–67.

25. For a discussion of the legal force of various papal commands, see Othmar Hageneder, "Mandatum and Praeceptum im politischen Handeln Papst Innocenz' III." to appear in the *Proceedings of the Sixth International Congress of Medieval Canon Law, Berkeley*, MIC, Series C, 7 (Città del Vaticano: 1984).

26. Huguccio, C. 11 q. 1 c. 39 v. *despectis,* Admont 7, fol. 223r [Klosterneuburg 89, fol. 195r]: "Si tamen papa hoc faciat, quis resistit ei?" Discussed by M. Ríos Fernández, "El primado del romano pontifice en el pensamiento de Huguccio de Pisa decretista," *Compostellanum* 6 (1961): 47–97; 7 (1962): 97–149; 8 (1963): 65–99; 11 (1966): 29–67, at vol. 8, p. 97. In another gloss, Huguccio illustrated the obverse of canonistic thought: if the pope did something unjust, he sinned. C. 16 q. 1 c. 52 v. *uentiletur,* Admont 7, fol. 277r [Klosterneuburg 89, fol. 239r]: "Ex hoc aperte (A: cap. ex parte) probatur quod papa potest unam ecclesiam alii subtrahere, similiter potest clericum et monachum eximere a potestate sui prelati, ut viiii. q.iii. Per principalem. Cuilibet clerico etiam potest subtrahere ecclesiam et prebendam suam ex iusta causa, ut fecit Corado archiepiscopo Magutino Alex. iii., set si hoc facit sine causa peccat, set non est qui ei resistere ualeat, cum plenitudinem habeat potestatis, ut ii. q.vi. Decreto, Qui se scit, nam qui eum iudicat dominus est, ut viiii. q.iii. Aliorum" (Ríos Fernández, "El primado," 8:90).

throughout the thirteenth century. In his formulation of the same idea, Laurentius asked, "Who would say to him, why do you do this?"[27] and referred to the ringing cry of St. Augustine in the Decretum of Gratian: "Who dares to say to God, why this man . . . ?"[28]

When Laurentius asked "who would say to him, 'why do you do this?' " he had the pope's judicial authority in mind. His next allegation, in which he cited *Licet quod legalis sanxit auctoritas,* a decretal that appeared only in Bernardus Compostellanus' *Collectio Romana,* confirms this interpretation.[29] The decretal discussed the judicial prerogatives of the papacy, and in it Pope Innocent III stated that the pope's judicial power should conform to the "public good."[30] Laurentius repeated Innocent's words, making clear that he was describing the pope's judicial authority: "There is no one in this world who would say to him, why do you do this? He is held, nevertheless, to shape this power to the public good."

Two points become evident after a careful analysis of Laurentius' gloss: he was the first canonist to envelope papal authority in the grandeur of hyperbole, and his hyperbole did not contain within it the substance of papal absolutism, but rather defined papal authority more accurately and, for the first time, separated the source of law from the "morality" of law. Laurentius' contribution to the history of political thought was to clothe sovereignty in language that preserved decorem but attracted notice.

After Laurentius, few canonists passed *Quanto personam* without trying to add something to the Spaniard's thought or rhetoric. Vincentius Hispanus began his gloss by repeating Laurentius' central point: the prince's will is the source of all law:

Note how great is the power of the prince; his will is held to be reason, as in the Institutes "what pleases the prince has the force of law." No one may say to him,

---

27. For the antecedents of "cur ita facis," see Peter Cantor, *Verbum abbreviatum* c. 44, PL 205.139d. Gerhoh of Reichersberg, De inv. antichristi 1.58, MGH Libelli de lite 3.372 lin.12. Ullmann, *Growth of Papal Government,* 411 n. 2; Kantorowicz, "Sovereignty of the Artist," 272 n. 28; Heinrich Singer, "Beiträge zur Würdigung der Dekretistenlitteratur," AKKR 69 (1893): 369–447. I am grateful to Stephan Kuttner for these references.

28. Laurentius cited Augustine's text from the Decretum, de pen. D. 3 c. 22. See Post, "Vincentius Hispanus," 164 n. 20, 172 n. 49.

29. Bern. 1.7.2, Modena, Bibl. Esten. lat. 968, fol. 132v. The text of the decretal is printed by Heinrich Singer, *Die Dekretalensammlung des Bernardus Compostellanus antiquus,* Sitzungsberichte der kaiserlichen Akademie der Wissenschaften phil.-hist. Klasse, Wien 171.2 (Vienna: 1914), 56–57.

30. Ibid.: "potentiam suam publice utilitati conformet."

"why do you do this." . . . However he must shape his will to public utility.[31]

Vincentius did not repeat Laurentius' example of the prince's will substituting for reason, but he gave a shortened version of his countryman's gloss, making one significant change in Laurentius' allegations. Instead of citing *Licet quod legalis,* which had not become part of the accepted corpus of canon law, Vincentius turned to Roman law and referred to *Digna vox,* a text in which the Roman emperor declared that he had a duty to submit himself to the law.[32]

Digna vox was a critical text in Justinian's Code for medieval ideas about the relationship of a ruler and the law. Brian Tierney has argued that the lawyers, in particular Accursius, the ordinary glossator of the *Corpus iuris civilis,* interpreted *Digna vox* as being a statement of the prince's fidelity to law.[33] Vincentius underlined the contrast between the pope's position as supreme judge in the church and his duty to preserve and care for his Christian flock by referring to another decretal of Innocent III, *Cum instantia.*[34] In this decretal Innocent had written that the pope may never cease exercising his pastoral duties on behalf of all churches. Vincentius quoted the famous image of Justinian, "for the public good, the emperor spends sleepless nights," in his gloss to the decretal and applied the image to the pope's care of the universal church. The pope's pastoral duties demand that he be faithful to the constitution of the church.[35]

Vincentius had a long career. He was the only decretalist who wrote glosses to the *Compilationes antiquae* between 1210 and 1220 and also

---

31. Vincentius Hispanus, 3 Comp. 1.5.3 (X 1.7.3) v. *uicem gerit in terris,* St. Gall 697, fol. 17v: "Nota quanta est potestas principis, ut in eo sit uoluntas pro ratione, instit. de iure naturali §Set quod principi [Instit. 1.2.6], nec est aliquis qui dicat contra hoc facis, de pen. iii. §Ex persona. Hanc tamen potestatem tenetur ipse reformare [MS: refrenare *ante corr.*] utilitati publice, C. de leg. Digna et infra de censibus, Cum instantia." Vincentius repeated this gloss in his Commentary to X 1.7.3 v. *ueri Dei uicem,* Paris B.N. lat. 3967, fol. 30v. Post, "Vincentius Hispanus," 164, prints his gloss from Bamberg, Staatsbibl. can. 20, fol. 104v which has several errors. Vincentius stated that the pope must conform to the public good in a gloss at the beginning of the Gregoriana printed in an Appendix by Stephan Kuttner, "Universal Pope or Servant of God's Servants: The Canonists, Papal Titles, and Innocent III," *Revue de droit canonique* 32 (1981): 123. See Javier Ochoa Sanz, *Vincentius Hispanus canonista boloñes del siglo XIII.* (Madrid-Rome: 1960).

32. Cod. 1.14.4.

33. Tierney, "The Prince," 389–95.

34. 3 Comp. 3.37.2 (X 3.39.17).

35. Vincentius Hispanus, 3 Comp. 3.37.2 [Cum instantia] v. *sollicitudo,* St. Gall 697, fol. 111v [Karlsruhe Aug. XL, fol. 282r]: "et pro re publica imperator noctes ducit insompnes." The entire gloss is printed by Post, "Vincentius Hispanus," 168.

produced a full apparatus of glosses to the Decretals of Gregory IX shortly after they appeared in 1234. In his gloss to *Quanto personam* in the Decretals, Vincentius added a series of aphorisms to the close:

In this the [pope] exercises the office of God, because he makes something out of nothing. . . . Likewise in this he has plenitude of power in ecclesiastical affairs. . . . He dispenses from the law . . . Johannes.[36]

Vincentius borrowed this passage from Johannes Teutonicus, who had expanded the first part of Laurentius' gloss which Vincentius had originally omitted.[37] Johannes' formulation of papal prerogatives, along with additional parts of Laurentius' and Vincentius' glosses, was later inserted into the Ordinary Gloss to the Decretals of Gregory IX by Bernardus Parmensis.

Johannes' gloss has not always been properly understood. One modern historian has interpreted his words to mean that the pope could work miracles.[38] Even in the sixteenth century, the *correctores Romani,* who were responsible for the editing of the official edition of the *Corpus iuris canonici* and its glosses, knew that the gloss was difficult to understand. "This entire gloss," they said, "scarcely explains anything in its own terms."[39] Today we

---

36. Vincentius Hispanus, X 1.7.3 v. *ueri Dei uicem,* Paris B.N. 3967, fol. 30v: "In hoc gerit uicem dei quia de nichilo facit aliquid, ut iii. q.vi. Hec [MS: Hoc] quippe. C. de rei uxor. act. l. una, in principio. Item in hoc quod plenitudinem potestatis habet in rebus ecclesiasticis, ii. q.vi. [MS: q.v.] Decreto. Item in hoc quod supra ius dispensat, ut infra de concess. preb. non uac. Proposuit. jo."

37. Johannes Teutonicus, 3 Comp. 1.5.3 (X 1.7.3) v. *set ueri dei, Apparatus glossarum in Compilationem tertiam,* ed. K. Pennington, MIC, Series A, 3 (Città del Vaticano: 1981), 43: "In hoc gerit uicem dei, quia de nichilo facit aliquid, ut iii. q.vi. Hec quippe, C. de rei uxor. act. 1. una, in principio. Item in hoc quod habet plenitudinem potestatis in rebus ecclesiasticis, ut ii. q.vi. Decreto. Item in hoc quod supra ius dispensat, ut infra de conces. preb. non uac. c.i. ut ibi dixi." A number of problems forced the lawyers to examine the historical development of law; they were not blind to history. For a particularly interesting example of their combining law and the past, see Edward Peters, *The Shadow King: Rex inutilis in Medieval Law and Literature, 751–1327* (New Haven: 1970).

38. Wilks, *The Problem of Sovereignty,* 371 n. 4.

39. The *correctores Romani* were the scholars who edited the *Corpus iuris canonici* in the sixteenth century. The result of their labors was the Roman edition of 1582 that became the official text of the *Corpus* upon which later editions were based. They observed about the language of the gloss to X 1.7.3: "tota haec glossa vix aliquid explicat propriis verbis. Quod si bene intelligatur vera astruit, nam de nihilo aliquid facere est ius novum condere et de iniustitia iustitiam, intellige per constitutionem iuris, et immutare substantiam rerum accipi debet in his quae sunt iuris positivi et ita loquuntur iura quae citantur." Cf. John A. Watt, *The Theory of Papal Monarchy in the Thirteenth Century: The Contribution of the Canonists* (London: 1965), 87 n. 42; and Tierney, *Origins of Papal Infallibility,* 27.

cannot understand the constitutional thought of the canonists unless we grasp the substance that lies beneath their rhetorical froth.

When Johannes added more examples of the pope's will substituting for reason, he included one phrase that is particularly difficult to understand: "He can make something out of nothing." This is a conundrum that seems to exalt the power of the pope to the level of the Creator himself: an idea tainted with heterodoxy and certainly with hubris.[40]

The legal references which Johannes cited to support his claim of papal creativity are not very helpful at first glance: a chapter of the Decretum in which the pope tolerated the illegal deposition of a bishop,[41] and a section from the Code in which Justinian stated that if a "stipulatio" of a marriage contract was invalid for some reason, the prince or judge could validate it.[42] Neither of these texts explains how, juridically, the pope could make something out of nothing. Other glosses, however, offer clues. In a gloss to *Compilatio quarta* Johannes wrote:

Again here you have a case in which a judgment can be held to be valid by the prince, which is invalid (*nulla*) by law. . . . But this can only be done by the prince, for a judgment or fact which is invalid can be validated by the prince . . . because the prince changes the substance of a thing, as in the Code.[43]

Later canonists who wrote about papal plenitude of power combined the phrase "the pope can make something out of nothing" with "he may change the substance of a thing," and brought Johannes' and Laurentius' glosses together.[44] However, Johannes' thought is quite simple: when the prince validates an invalid judgment, he can be said to have changed the substance of a thing.

Another gloss from *Compilatio tertia* further clarifies Johannes' point:

---

40. Kantorowicz, "Sovereignty of the Artist," 273–74, demonstrates that the phrase "ex nihilo facere" was inspired by a text of St. Ambrose in Gratian's Decretum, de con. D. 2 c. 69. See the gloss of Johannes Teutonicus to this chapter v. *minus:* "dicit imperator quod cum nobis consentaneum est ubi nulla est stipulatio interposita, intelligi eam adhibitam. Multo fortius ubi inutilis fuit ab initio, per nos validam effici, ut C. de rei uxor. act. l.i. circa prin. (Cod. 5.13.1)."

41. C. 6 q. 6 c. 10.

42. Cod. 5.13.1.

43. Johannes Teutonicus, 4 Comp. 5.1.3 v. *facta fides,* Admont 22, fol. 264v [ed. Antonio Agustín (Ilerdae: 1576)]: "Item habes hic quod sententia que nulla est ipso iure rata potest haberi a superiori ut patet ex predictis capitulis, set hoc a solo principe potest fieri, ut sententia que nulla est uel factum, quod ipso iure nullum est, possit a principe ratificari, ut xvi. q.v. Si episcopum, et hoc ideo quia ipse mutat substantiam rei, ut C. de rei uxor. act. in principio. jo." See also Ullmann, *Medieval Papalism* 51–52.

44. Bernardus Parmensis to X 1.7.3 v. *Dei vicem.*

The pope, however, can suspend the effect [of excommunication] . . . for he makes a valid from an invalid judgment, as in the Decretum. It is greater to make something from nothing than to change something into another thing or to make something nothing.[45]

It is clear from this gloss and his gloss on "plenitudo potestatis" that Johannes was punning on the word "nulla." "Nulla" can mean nothing or invalid. When Johannes wrote that the pope can make something out of nothing, he was not claiming miraculous powers for the pope, but only that the pope could validate any invalid judgment or judicial decision rendered by an episcopal court. The chapter he cited from the Decretum stated that the pope could recognize the deposition of a bishop by a court even though the deposition was invalid because the court did not have jurisdiction over the deposition of bishops, a matter that Pope Innocent III and the canonists of the late twelfth century reserved to papal judgment.

Canonists did not develop the ideas of Laurentius, Vincentius, and Johannes Teutonicus any further. Bernardus Parmensis gave their thought its final form. He wrote a gloss that combined sections from the earlier glossators and produced a statement of papal power that the *correctores Romani* found florid and hyperbolic. Like his predecessors, Bernardus did not describe an absolute monarch, but rather a judge and legislator who had the prerogatives of every supreme judge and chief legislator.

Although one may argue that the canonists' extravagant language helped to destroy the accepted paradigm of "medieval constitutionalism," the thirteenth-century canonists had no thought of creating a pattern of legal maxims that would support autocratic power. Such ideas were far from their original intent. They were merely seeking to define the prince's will as the source of legislation and his juridical position in the church more precisely than had their predecessors. Their language has obscured their purpose.

Only one canonist wrote plainly when he glossed *Quanto personam.* In his apparatus to the Decretals of Gregory IX, Goffredus da Trani transformed the language of his predecessors into comprehensive statements of papal judicial prerogatives:

[The pope is] the vicar of God, Jesus Christ, because he has the fullness of power on earth. . . . He changes the substance, the quantity, or the nature of things. . . . He

---

45. Johannes Teutonicus, 3 Comp. 2.19.13 (X 2.28.55) v. *suspendendum,* ed. Pennington, 359: "Papa tamen posset eius effectum suspendere, ut infra de sent. excomm. Si uere, qui de nulla sententia facit aliquam, ut iii. q.vi. Hec quippe. Maius enim est de nichilo aliquid facere, quam de aliquo aliud uel nichil, de con. di.ii. Reuera."

makes a secular canon from a monk . . . and just like the emperor, he changes the nature of an action . . . and like the emperor, he makes two things one, as "legatum" and "fideicommissum." . . . The pope makes two churches one. . . . By binding and loosing, he holds the office of God on earth. . . . The pope is above the law . . . dispenses from the rules of the Apostle . . . he is above any council.[46]

Goffredus retained his predecessors' outline of papal prerogatives, but the language of his gloss is straightforward and matter-of-fact. The last three listed attributes of the pope—the pope is above any council and law and can dispense from the rule of the Apostle—are not extraordinary powers but common papal legislative powers. Brian Tierney has written that "we must distinguish (as did the canonists) between the eternal principles of faith and changing rules of church discipline. Not every precept of Holy Writ was meant to be observed literally forever."[47] The pope, through his legislative authority, could alter a rule of ecclesiastical discipline found in the Scriptures; he could change any positive law or alter any conciliar decree. No canonist ever dissented from this.

The canonists did debate issues on the boundary between positive law and divine law: Could the pope dispense from a vow of chastity? Could he transform a monk into a secular canon as Goffredus alleged above? Could he alter divine law to the extent of expanding the number of degrees of consanguinity permitted in marriage. The canonists differed on these issues. They all concurred, however, on one point: the pope could not change or alter a central article of the Christian faith. It is indicative of the temper of the age that other canonists did not use Goffredus' straightforward catalogue of papal prerogatives but preferred the words of Laurentius, Vincentius, and Johannes.

There is a well-known parallel to the glosses of *Quanto personam* which is another illustration of the lawyers' infatuation with language. Again,

46. Goffredus da Trani, X 1.7.3 v. *uicem gerit*, Paris B.N. 15402, fol. 19v: "Vicarius dei ihesu christi quia plenitudinem potestatis habet in terris, ut ii. q.vi. Decreto [c. 11], infra de usu pal. Ad honorem. Item mutat substantiam (MS: substantialem), qualitatem, siue naturam, ut infra qui filii sint legit. Per uenerabilem. De monacho facit canonicum secularem, ut lxxiiii. di. Quorumdam et iv. di. Priscis, sicut et imperator mutat naturam actionis, ut C. de re uxor. act. l. una, in prin. et satis imperator facit utrumque unum, sic legatum et fideicommissum, et C. commun. del. l.ii. sicut et papa facit duas ecclesias unam, ut xvi. q.i. Et temporis qualitas. Item quia in ligando et soluendo locum dei tenet in terris, ut infra ut benefic. eccles. sine dimin. confer. Vt nostrum. xxiiii. q.i. Quodcumque ligaueris. xi. q.iii. Nemo contempnat. Item papa est supra ius ut <infra> de concess. preb. uel eccles. non uac. Proposuit, in fine. Ipse dispensat contra apostolum, ut xxxiiii. di. Lector. lxxxii. di. Presbyter. Ipse est supra omne concilium, ut supra de elect. Significasti. G."

47. Tierney, *Origins of Papal Infallibility*, 27–28.

in this instance, they sacrificed clarity and understanding for style.

Johannes Teutonicus wrote a colorful description of the pervasive power of the emperor in his gloss to the decretal *Venerabilem*.[48] The gloss is a short outline of imperial authority culled from texts in Justinian's *Corpus iuris civilis*. The emperor was, Johannes observed, the lord of the world and all nations were under him. All things were in the power of the emperor; he was the overlord of all kings. Bernardus Parmensis put Johannes' gloss, almost word for word, into his Ordinary Gloss.[49] Johannes and Bernardus were not imperialists, and they did not claim extreme prerogatives for the medieval German emperor. They simply described the powers of the emperor as they found them set out in Roman and canon law. As in the glosses to *Quanto personam*, the language was high flown—more sustained rhetorical analogy.

With that said, we misread the canonists' glosses if we think that they believed their descriptions of imperial prerogatives to be literally true. They knew quite well that all kings did not submit themselves to the emperor. Pope Innocent III himself had written in a famous passage of a decretal they all knew that the Kingdom of France was not subject to higher temporal authority.[50] Later, when Innocent accepted England from King John as a papal fief, he tacitly denied that European monarchs held their authority from the emperor.[51]

The canonists described the "ideal" picture of imperial authority they found in Roman law. Their image was not historical and certainly did not reflect contemporary German imperial authority. Like those to *Quanto personam*, these glosses are good examples of how much the canonists—and the Roman lawyers—enjoyed writing descriptions that were paradoxical and, to us today, challenging.

We have no way of knowing today how much historical understanding the canonists had of the changes that had transformed the papal and imperial offices over the centuries. Did they view the emperor they found in the pages of the *Corpus iuris civilis* as larger than life, and at the same time insubstantial, diaphanous, and, in Vinogradoff's happy phrase, ghostly? They

---

48. Johannes Teutonicus, 3 Comp. 1.6.18 v. *in Germanos*, ed. Pennington, 84–85: "Est autem imperator iste super omnes reges . . . et omnes nationes sub eo sunt. . . . Ipse enim est dominus mundi. . . . Nec aliquis regum potuit prescribere exemptionem. . . . Immo omnes de capite suo dabunt imperatori tributum. . . . Omnia enim sunt in potestate imperatoris."

49. X 1.6.34 v. *transtulit in Germanos*.

50. Innocent wrote in *Per venerabilem*, X 4.17.13: "Insuper cum rex ipse superiorem in temporalibus mimine recognoscat, sine iuris alterius laesione in eo se iurisdictioni nostrae subiicere potuit et subiecit."

51. Cheney, *Pope Innocent III and England*, 326–56.

must have compared the description of imperial pretensions found in Roman law to the diminished imperial office of their own times. Still, we shall never know their thoughts. The Roman lawyers often wrote with what seems to have been a monumental disregard of the world they lived in. Their intention was to understand the law of Justinian, not to write a comparative history of law.

The canonists too might have sometimes been struck by differences between papal claims of jurisdiction and authority, and the realities of papal power. Popes often had to watch helplessly as their mandates were ignored or circumvented. The decretal *Quanto personam*, with which we began our discussion of the language of papal authority, is an illustration of this point.

The newly elected bishop of Würzburg, Conrad of Querfurt, did not obey Innocent III's stern and peremptory command in August 1198 to step down from his bishopric immediately. A few months later (February 1199), Innocent wrote to "Conrad, formerly bishop of Hildesheim, with salutations," and urged him to obey the papal mandate. He should abandon Würzburg, but not return to Hildesheim.[52] In May 1199, Innocent ordered the cathedral chapter of Hildesheim to elect a new bishop, and in October he directed the archbishop of Magdeburg, his suffragans, and the other bishops of Germany to excommunicate Conrad. He also annulled those benefices that Conrad had bestowed and gave the right of bestowal to the bishop of Mainz.[53]

In November Innocent wrote another letter that dealt with a further aspect of what had become a very complicated problem. Conrad had bound the canons of the cathedral chapter of Würzburg with oaths to elect the current bishop of Münster his successor. The canons had also promised to pay Conrad's family two thousand marks after he died. They had sworn not to obey the new bishop until this debt was paid. All these endeavors Innocent condemned.[54]

In January 1200, Innocent queried the bishop of Bamberg whether

---

52. Innocent III, Register I, 826–27, no. 568 (574). Helene Tillmann, *Papst Innocenz III.* (Bonn: 1954), 5, interprets a phrase of this letter, "licet olim dilectum nobis, cum in minori essemus officio constituti," as meaning that Conrad met Innocent in Paris during their student days. I think that "in minori officio" has a more technical meaning, i.e., when Innocent held a lower ecclesiastical office in Rome. Innocent might have met Conrad in 1194, when Conrad was the bishop-elect of Hildesheim. He made a long journey through Italy and wrote an epistolary description of the trip that is a splendid example of twelfth-century classical learning. The letter is preserved in Arnold of Lübeck, *Chronica Slavorum*, ed. I. M. Lappenberg, MGH, Scriptores in usum scholarum 14 (Hannover: 1868), 174–83. See also Roberto Weiss, *The Renaissance Discovery of Classical Antiquity* (Oxford: 1969), 5.

53. Innocent III, Register II, 97–100, no. 52 (54), 53 (55); 366–67, no. 192 (201).

54. Ibid., 403–404, no. 207 (216).

Conrad had obeyed his commands. If not, he ordered the bishop to inform the cathedral chapter at Würzburg that they must no longer obey Conrad.[55] The case went on. Between 1198 and 1202, twenty letters were enregistered concerning Conrad and his affairs.[56] Six found their way into the canonical collections.[57] As usual, there were probably a substantial number of letters we do not now know about. Conrad was a powerful figure in Germany, and he did not bend easily to papal threats. He had been the imperial chancellor to Emperor Henry VI and was still active in German politics.[58]

The outcome of the case is reported in the *Gesta* of Pope Innocent III. The author of the *Gesta* reports that Conrad was importuned by the bishops of Magdeburg and Mainz, and other German princes, to submit himself to apostolic judgment. Innocent arranged what was probably a compromise, and Conrad was persuaded that Innocent wanted his submission, but did not intend to destroy his career. In the end, Conrad was assured that if he would recognize papal authority, the pope would restore him to his see. Conrad journeyed to Rome and, renouncing Hildesheim and Würzburg and begging papal forgiveness, presented himself to Innocent as a humble supplicant. The author of the *Gesta* relished the drama and described how Conrad spread himself on the floor of the papal curia, his body taking the symbolic form of a cross.[59]

The delicacy of the negotiations is revealed by an anecdote in the *Gesta*.

---

55. Ibid., 516–19, no. 266 (278).

56. See the notes to these letters in Innocent III, Register II. Four letters are recorded in the lost registers, see Augustin Theiner, *Vetera monumenta Slavorum meridionalium historiam illustrantia* (Rome: 1863) 1: 49, no. 86, p. 57, no. 58, 59, p. 58, no. 95, p. 59, no. 124, p. 60, no. 167, 168, 169, 178, 179, 180.

57. 1. 3 Comp. 1.5.3 (X 1.7.3) = Bern. 1.7.3, Fuld. 1.5.13, Po. 352. 2. Rain. 20.2, *Miramur*, Po. 611. Innocent III, Register I, 826, does not note the letter in Rainer's collection. 3. Alan. W. 2.13.5 (V. 2.15.5), addition to Dunelm. IV 64, Fuld. 2.21.13, Po. 875. 4. 3 Comp. 1.5.4 (X 1.7.4) = Bern. 1.7.4, addition to Dunelm. IV 86, Fuld. 1.5.14, Coll. Rotomag. 54, Po. 942. 5. 3 Comp. 1.21.1 and 5.12.1 (X 1.33.5 and 5.27.5) = Bern. 5.14.1, Po. 1002. This letter is not in the registers, but was printed from an original by J. F. Schannat, *Vindemiae literariae*, 2 vols. in 1 (Fulda: 1723–24), 1.185. 6. Alan. 2.10.4 (V. 2.11.5), Fuld. 2.15.7, Po. 1412. Printed from Alan W. in H. F. O. Abel, *König Philipp* (Berlin: 1852), 279; Rudolf von Heckel noted several errors in Abel's transcription, "Die Dekretalensammlung des Gilbertus und Alanus nach den Weingartener Handschriften," ZRG Kan. Abt. 29 (1940): 249. Cf. Theiner, *Vetera monumenta* 1: 58, no. 95.

58. On Conrad, see Leopold von Borch, *Geschichte des kaiserlichen Kanzler Konrad, Legat in Italien und Sicilien, Bischof von Hildesheim und Wirzburg* (Innsbruck: 1882); and Alfred Wendehorst, *Das Bistum Würzburg*, I: *Die Bischofsreihe bis 1254*, Germania Sacra 1 (Berlin: 1962), 183–200.

59. *Gesta Innocentii tertii*, PL 214. lxxxvii–lxxxviii.

After swearing his oath to give up both sees, Conrad sent the pope gifts of beautiful silver vases. Innocent was perplexed. Should he refuse to accept them? Conrad might be hurt, or even worse, might misunderstand his refusal. Fearing, no doubt, that Conrad still suspected his intentions, the pope wrestled with this moral dilemma. In the end, he reluctantly accepted the vases, hoping thereby to assure Conrad of his goodwill. However, to demonstrate that the pope was not corruptible, Innocent gave Conrad an even more valuable present, a golden cup.[60] Subsequently, the cathedral chapter of Würzburg was informed that if Conrad were reelected and postulated to Rome, he would be recognized as their bishop. Conrad's fate was not, however, a happy one. In December 1202 he was assassinated for reasons connected with German politics, not with the problems surrounding his translation.[61]

The translation of Conrad of Querfurt from Hildesheim to Würzburg illustrates not only Innocent III's tenacity in pursuing what he thought were papal prerogatives but also the difficulties involved in coercing distant subjects to respect papal power. In *Quanto personam*, Innocent may have deposed Conrad with the authority of the true God whose office he exercised on earth, but the dispute was resolved through delicate negotiations and compromise.

The case was famous and its details and final outcome were doubtless known to the canonists. It would not be completely farfetched to speculate that when Laurentius Hispanus wrote the gloss to *Quanto personam* in which he elevated the language of papal monarchy to celestial levels, he was aware that the grandeur of his rhetoric clashed not a little with what he knew to have been the facts and ultimate resolution of the case.

The early thirteenth century was a key period in the development of the language of papal power. Prodded by a pope of genius and their own growing sophistication, the canonists shaped a description of papal authority that lasted to the end of the Middle Ages and beyond. Although their thought was traditional in many ways, and, as we have seen, their ideas did not reject or change traditional medieval ideas about the duty of a monarch to submit himself to the law, their language did prepare the way for more-authoritarian ideas of monarchical authority by the end of the thirteenth century.

---

60. Ibid., Vat. lat. 12111, fol. 13r–13v: "misitque munera quedam ipso domino pape, uasa uidelicet argentea, pulchra uisu; qui anima hesit paulisper, hesitans utrum deberet illa recipere, an potius refutare. Set, ne ille de gratia sua penitus desperaret, recepit ablata, et, ne putaret quod munerum posset donatione corrumpi, misit ei per honorabilem nuntium unam cuppam auream pretiosam, maioris quam illa essent uasa argentea uniuersa ualoris."

61. Wendehorst, *Bistum Würzburg*, 195–200; Tillmann, *Papst Innocenz III.*, 281–86.

To the nonlawyer, the language the canonists adopted remained offensive. Sometime during the final years of Pope Innocent III's pontificate (probably between 1212 and 1214), an anonymous poet wrote a vigorous defense of Otto of Brunswick's imperial claims against the pretentions of his newest rival, the boy Frederick II. He cast the poem in the form of a dialogue between the City of Rome and Innocent III, who had just recently withdrawn his support of Otto. The poem is propaganda and pulses with the passions of German imperial sentiment. Its author knew some law, for the legal arguments he used have many resonances in the law of the thirteenth century.

The figura of Rome was Otto's advocate, and she went right to the heart of the matter. With what right, she asked Innocent, had he deposed Otto? She reminded Innocent that there were only three reasons for deposing a monarch: the abandonment of his wife, damage to imperial honor, and heresy (*conjux dimissa, minutus imperialis honor, heresis*). Otto, said Rome, was innocent of all these crimes. Innocent had abandoned him unjustly:

> You have bound the innocent with the fetters of anathema, even without guilt; You have bound Otto in fact, but not in law. You have deposed him in fact, but not in law—you have violated the law. You rule in this world through your will, not reason; you produce effect without cause, punishment without guilt.[62]

Innocent acted, said the horrified poet, according to his will, not law.

Innocent grappled with Rome's accusations but, in the end, finished the debate by declaring, "If I have not convinced you with these reasons that I have the right to replace Otto with Frederick, let it be said, as I wish, so it is done, for my will substitutes for reason."[63] Innocent's words shocked Rome, even though they confirmed her worst fears about Innocent's willingness to exercise papal authority arbitrarily.

---

62. Gottfried Wilhelm Leibniz, *Scriptores rerum Brunsvicensium* (Hannover: 1710), 2: 525–32:
"Tu vero, culpa non persuadente, ligasti
Innocuum vinculis anathematis, ergo ligando
Illum de facto, sed non de iure ligasti,
Et deponendo de facto deposuisti,
Sed non de iure: Ius ergo per hoc violasti.
Ergo, regens mundum tua pro ratione voluntas
Effectum sine causa dat, poenam sine culpa."
63. Ibid., 531: "Si te
non moveant super hoc assignatae rationes,
Per quas Otoni Fredericus substituatur,
Sic volo, sic fiat, sit pro ratione voluntas."

At the poem's end, Rome appealed to a general council. Innocent, Rome alleged, wished to rule by his will alone, not by law. Quoting a law from Justinian's Code, Rome declared that law which punishes the authors of their crimes is most just.

The council answered that it did not have the right to depose the pope, but Rome should not despair. God can lay low the mighty and exalt the humble. Right demanded that the council should depose Frederick and restore Otto:

Faithful Rome, we may not depose the pope, but your righteous plaints move us. Take heed with us: He has deposed the mighty and exalted the weak. It is just that we depose Frederick and restore Otto.[64]

Many later writers echoed the poet's dislike for Juvenal's maxim. The fourteenth-century English chronicler Henry Knighton described in rhyme the depredations of papal legates sent to England by Pope Gregory IX:

What the pope did, he did not from reason,
but the plunderer seized whatever open lay,
and this was his justification: What I want,
I command, my will stands for reason.[65]

The notion that the pope could substitute his will for reason was and remained despicable to the popular mind. Salimbene de Adam described an evil prelate who plagued the church:

A scurrilous prelate does not believe that he can command obedience from a subject cleric unless he treats him arbitrarily and dishonorably. Such a prelate thinks that

---

64. Ibid., 532:
"Roma parens, non est nostrum deponere papam,
Sed nos in reliquis tua iusta petitio pulsat.
Nobiscum cave: deposuit de sede potentes,
Ac exaltavit humiles. Ius est Fredericum
Ut deponamus, et restituamus Otonem."

65. Henry Knighton, *Chronicon*, ed. J. R. Lumby, RS 92 (London: 1889), 1:226:
"Quod voluit papa non ex ratione fiebat,
Sed tamen invaluit rapiens quodcunque patebat.
Iuxta illud
Sic volo, sic jubeo, sit pro ratione voluntas."
I am grateful to Richard Spence for this citation.

what he commands is reasonable, according to the maxim: What I want, I command, my will stands for reason.[66]

Salimbene applied the maxim to prelates. It was not limited, however, to describing abuses of ecclesiastical authority.

The dialogue of a drama played out in Ferrara in 1264 is the clearest echo of contemporary secular reaction to the thought of the canonists. After the death of Azo VII, the citizens of Ferrara met and decided to grant the lordship of the city to Azo's illegitimate son, Obizo. An anonymous chronicler present at the ceremony described how the authority of the city was bestowed upon the new prince. A syndic was selected, and he conferred full lordship (*dominium plenissimum*) on Obizo, which permitted him to do all things, just and unjust, by the judgment of his will (*pro suae arbitrio voluntatis*). The language of the ceremony must have contained some phrases taken from the glosses of the canonists. If the syndic had been a lawyer, he would have quite naturally borrowed phrases from the glosses to *Quanto personam* to describe Obizo's judicial and legislative authority. The chronicler, however, was a better historian than lawyer, and he recoiled from the syndic's description of Obizo's power. He somberly noted that "the new prince then had more power than eternal God who cannot create injustice."[67] The chronicler did not recognize the mundane implications of the syndic's language. For his part, the syndic may have been more desirous of wishing to please the new prince with his rhetoric than with introducing the latest definitions of sovereignty to his listeners. It may have been due to a misunderstanding, but theologians and polemicists in the later Middle Ages often recognized only the rhetoric of papal power and ignored the limitations implicit in the thought of the early canonists.[68] To them, Juvenal's "pro ratione voluntas" represented the unbridled power of the prince.

---

66. Salimbene de Adam, *Cronica*, ed. O. Holder-Egger, MGH Scriptores 32.144 (Scrittori d'Italia 187–188 [Bari: 1942], 1: 207): "Aliquis vero maledictus prelatus, nisi malitiose insurgat contra subditum et furibunde et indignabunde ei precipiat, non credit quod possit eum sub dominio suo tenere, et quicquid ei precipit, rationabiliter precipere credit iuxta illud: Sic volo, sic iubeo, sit pro ratione voluntas."

67. *Chronica parva ferrariensis*, ed. L. Muratori (Milan: 1726), 8: col. 488: "Facto deinde silentio constituitur Syndicus ad conferendum dominium civitatis . . . Stipulatione facta, Syndicus constitutus ei Obizioni dominium defert plenissimum, ut omnia possit, justa, vel iniusta, pro suae arbitrio voluntatis. Plus potestatis tunc est illatum novo dominatori quam habeat Deus aeternus, qui iniusta non potest." See John Larner, *Italy in the Age of Dante and Petrarch, 1216–1380* (London–New York: 1980), 138.

68. Juvenal's maxim was well known in the late Middle Ages. Vincent of Beauvais, *Speculum historiale* (Duaci: 1624), 4: 321, quotes it in a florilegium of quotations from Juvenal.

Innocent himself may not have shared the canonists' enthusiasm for the maxim. His thought was ingenious, but not radically out of step with contemporary beliefs. Although the canonists cited Juvenal's aphorism to remind themselves that the ultimate source of positive law was the prince's will, not reason, the pope may not have appreciated the distinction.[69] In January 1201, Innocent wrote a letter to the ecclesiastical and secular princes of Germany lamenting the turbulent conditions in Germany, where violence and revolt had become prevalent:

In short, now evil deeds have taken the place of right; reason does not make law, but will. Some seem to think that whatever pleases them is permitted to them.[70]

If Innocent drafted this passage himself, he certainly did not believe that Juvenal's maxim should describe a prince's legislative authority. Rather, like Henry Knighton, Salimbene, and the chronicler of Ferrara, he instinctively concurred with most medieval thinkers who understood that reason must inform all law. They would have agreed with another lawyer, known as Henry Bracton, who wrote: "There is no rex where the will rules rather than the lex."[71] Unlike the canonists, Innocent and Bracton wished to describe the

---

For other uses of the aphorism, see Hans Walther, *Proverbia sententiaeque latinitatis medii aevi*, 5 vols. (Göttingen: 1963–67), no. 11083, 21053, 22413, 29559. For other examples of lawyers' using the maxim, see Ennio Cortese, *La norma giuridica* (Milan: 1964), 2: 217, 260, 277, 296, and his summary of the problem in "Norma Giuridica, Storia," *Enciclopedia del diritto* 28 (1978): 393–412.

69. Innocent's decretals are sprinkled with legal maxims; a study of their importance and function in his letters would be useful. Some examples can be found in: 3 Comp. 1.3.3 (X 1.4.4), 3 Comp. 1.6.5 (X 1.6.20), 3 Comp. 1.6.15 (X 1.6.30), 3 Comp. 1.5.2 (X 1.7.2), 3 Comp. 2.4.1 (X 2.10.2), 3 Comp. 2.6.1 (X 2.22.6), which contains two maxims.

70. *Regestum Innocentii III papae super negotio Romani imperii*, ed. Friedrich Kempf, Miscellanea Historiae Pontificiae 12 (Rome: 1947), 95–97, no. 31: "Et ut singula breuius perstringamus, iam sibi iuris locum iniuria uendicauit, et legem facit non ratio, sed uoluntas; ita ut quidam totum sibi licere reputent quod nouerint complacere." See Manfred Laufs, *Politik und Recht bei Innozenz III.: Rekuperationspolitik Papst Innozenz' III.* (Köln-Wien: 1980), 278, for a brief discussion of this passage from a different perspective.

71. Henry Bracton, *On the Laws and Customs of England*, ed. and trans. Samuel Thorne (Cambridge, Mass.: 1968), 2: 33: "Ipse autem rex non debet esse sub homine sed sub deo et sub lege, quia lex facit regem. Attribuat igitur rex legi quod lex attribuit ei, videlicet dominationem et potestatem. Non est enim rex ubi dominatur voluntas et non lex." Also see vol. 2: 305: "quod dicitur quod principi placet legis habet vigorem, quia sequitur in fine legis cum lege regia quae de imperio eius lata est, id est non quicquid de uoluntate regis temere praesumptum est, sed quod magnatum suorum consilia, rege auctoritatem praestante et habita super hoc deliberatione et tractatu, recte fuerit definitum." On this passage see Tierney, "Bracton on Government," 297 and Post, "Bracton as Jurist."

spirit that should infuse the source of legislative authority, not the source itself.

In spite of the disagreements "pro ratione voluntas" became a commonplace in political theory. In the fourteenth and fifteenth centuries, canonists invariably cited the tag when they discussed papal authority. The meaning of the maxim did not, however, change during the medieval period. The *correctores Romani* of the sixteenth century understood the aphorism and its associated glosses without difficulty: it defined the source of positive ecclesiastical law.

The maxim was used by political theorists until the seventeenth century. Historians of political theory in the early modern period have assumed that when applied to a monarch, it meant unlimited and arbitrary authority. They may not be right. As Gaines Post has written, more work will have to be done in order to determine whether the successors of the canonists followed or departed from the doctrine of their predecessors.[72]

Quanto personam was just one of many letters in which Innocent justified his new conception of papal monarchy. The pope derived his authority to exercise power over episcopal translations from Christ, and, although all papal jurisdictional rights could be said to have originated from Christ's mandate, Innocent distinguished between the pope's ordinary powers and those that granted him special authority over bishops. The marriage of a bishop to his church was a bond that Innocent could break only with an appeal to the pope's right to exercise Christ's authority on earth. He did not claim that his authority could be arbitrary. On the contrary, he wrote in *Quanto personam* that the pope must carefully consider the need and the usefulness of his actions. Although Innocent did not use the term "plenitudo potestatis" in *Quanto personam*, he certainly had "fullness of power" in mind. Just two weeks earlier, while writing to the bishop of Faenza about another unauthorized translation, Innocent had called his exercise of authority over translations "plena potestas."[73]

The canonists recognized *Quanto personam* as an example of papal *plenitudo potestatis*. Once the decretal was included in Innocent III's authenticated decretal collection, *Compilatio tertia*, they immediately perceived that it was a new and innovative statement of papal authority. Their reaction to Innocent's claim to have divine authority, to be the holder of the office of the true God on earth, not the holder of the office of any man, is very revealing and gives us an insight into the attitudes of the professors in the schools.

---

72. Post, "Vincentius Hispanus," 159–60.
73. Innocent III, Register I, 473, no. 326.

Innocent granted the pope a new justification of monarchical authority that no other bishop could possess. He took an old title, *vicarius Christi,* and injected it with new meaning. Since his conception of the papal office was rooted in traditions that reached back to the early church, the titles and terms he used were, for the most part, not new. He invented little. Rather he fitted older terminology, biblical texts, and titles together into such a luminous mosaic that no one could later speak or write about the papal office without invoking Innocent's spirit.[74]

What was new and innovative about his thought was his powerful and vivid grasp of papal purpose independent of the thought of the lawyers and theologians as well as of the historical development of the papacy. Innocent divined, intuitively, that if the pope was Christ's vicar (*vicarius Christi*) exercising the office of God on earth, each pope derived his authority from that crucial moment in history when Christ gave St. Peter lordship over the church.[75] The lawyers might argue about precedents, terminology, and issues of jurisdiction, but the vicissitudes of man's understanding of papal monarchy were not important. Innocent reduced the origins of papal authority to the essentials: the pope's right to exercise divine authority and his office of "vicarius Christi," vicar of Christ. One might unravel the knot of history to explain a particular papal prerogative, but such unravelings were irrelevant.

Innocent created a "cosmology" to explain papal authority. There were three stages in the creation of his universe. Before Christ, the priest kings of the Old Testament adumbrated both the coming of Christ and the establishment of papal monarchy. Melchisedech, a favorite *figura* of Innocent, represented this epoch.[76] In his time on earth Christ himself reigned over the second era. Before Christ left his earthly ministry, he established the right order of ecclesiastical government for the third stage. Innocent understood papal prerogatives and authority in relation to the pope's divine ministry. The pope acted on divine authority, not on the transient, ephemeral authority of a papal decretal or a conciliar canon. Ignoring the dynamics of historical development, Innocent conceived of the constitution of the church as static.

I have quoted Innocent's graphic justification of his prerogatives within the church several times in different contexts: "The pope had this authority

---

74. In an excellent piece of synthesis, Jürgen Miethke discusses Innocent's role in shaping papal thought; see "Geschichtsprozess und Zeitgenössiches Bewusstsein," 582–92.

75. Historians have long seen that the concept "vicarius Christi" was the most important of Innocent's titles. See the standard work of Maccarrone, *Vicarius Christi,* 135–40.

76. Innocent III and Joachim of Fiore looked at the history of the world in similar ways, even though their concerns were quite different. For an example of possible Joachite influence on Innocent's thought, see Robert Lerner, "Joachim of Fiore," 471–76.

because he exercises the office not of man, but of the true God on earth." Innocent, and popes before him, also used papal titles that showed a humbler conception of the pope's office. At the beginning of every letter, Innocent styled himself "servus servorum Dei," "servant of God's servants," a title that emphasized the pope's pastoral duties to his church, not the immensity of papal authority. Pope Gregory the Great introduced the title into papal correspondence. Stephan Kuttner writes:

Other bishops before him had occasionally used similar phrases, but Gregory's expression was perfectly coined in its conciseness to become a set chancery style and convey at the same time a strong spiritual message. Its sublime humility made a striking contrast with the proud title of "ecumenical patriarch."[77]

In contrast to Gregory's letters, Innocent's epistles are not steeped in humility, although they are certainly not devoid of spirituality.

The canonists eliminated the papal salutation from the letters they put into their decretal collections. The formal and complete salutation did, however, remain attached to the letter Innocent III sent to Bologna with *Compilatio tertia* when the collection was authenticated. The letter, *Devotioni vestrae*, introduced the new collection, and the canonists began to gloss the title included in the salutation, "servus servorum Dei."[78] It was almost inevitable that the canonists would compare the language of Innocent's decretals, especially *Quanto personam*, to the humility of his salutations. The earliest canonist to gloss the words could not refrain from a touch of sarcasm. An anonymous glossator quoted a line from Horace implying that the pope's servitude was due only to greed.[79]

Johannes Teutonicus was the first glossator to scorn Innocent's humility openly. Subtlety was not a striking part of Teutonicus' character. To the words "servus servorum Dei," he wrote:

Although you call yourself the servant of God's servants, you thunder from on high when you disdain to be called the vicar of Peter, as in the decretal *Quanto personam*; Jerome calls you the successor of the fisherman.[80]

---

77. Kuttner, "Universal Pope or Servant of God's Servants," 101.

78. Ibid., 117–27.

79. Ibid., 120.

80. Johannes Teutonicus, *Devotioni vestrae* v. *seruus*, ed. Pennington, 1: "Licet hic te appelles seruum seruorum dei, altius tamen intonas, cum dedignaris dici uicarius Petri, ut infra de translat. episc. Quanto et a Ieronimo appellaris successor piscatoris, xxiiii. q.i. Quoniam uetus." See Kuttner, "Universal Pope or Servant of God's Servants," 121–22, and my "Prolegomena" to the edition, p. xxii–xxiii.

Johannes had managed to touch a central concept of Innocent's ecclesiology. Innocent had not rested his claim in *Quanto personam* to absolve the spiritual marriage between a bishop and his see on the deeds or decrees of any earlier pope. His authority stemmed solely from the special mandate bestowed on him by Christ. Johannes objected to Innocent's "deification" of the papal office. Innocent also violated his sense of how the church should be governed.[81]

If the pope did, indeed, act only on divine authority, who could resist him? To have been the vicar of Peter would have limited the pope to time and history. Instead, Innocent elevated the papacy beyond the confines of human understanding and law. When Johannes glossed *Quanto personam*, he took pains to observe that the pope was sometimes called the "successor of the fisherman."[82] This section of Johannes' gloss was omitted from most manuscripts, since many contemporary canonists found Johannes' invective repugnant.

Some canonists, with less bombast and more reason than Johannes, undercut the force of Innocent's argument. Laurentius Hispanus wrote that every bishop was the vicar of Christ, for the bishops were the successors of the apostles and of Christ.[83] Johannes Galensis insisted that the pope was, in spite of Innocent's assertion, the vicar of Peter "because the heir of the heir of the testator is an heir."[84] Later episcopalists would build their ecclesiology on the apostolic origins of the episcopate. However, no canonist in the thirteenth century expanded this idea systematically.

In *Quanto personam* and its glosses, Innocent and the canonists make an interesting contrast. The pope created one duality, the pope's ordinary

---

81. We shall encounter Johannes' opposition to Innocent's policies several times in the following chapters. For a gloss in which Johannes takes Innocent to task, see C. 35 q. 10 c. 1 v. *permanere.*

82. Johannes Teutonicus, 3 Comp. 1.5.3 (X 1.7.3) v. *set ueri dei,* ed. Pennington, 43: "Alibi tamen appellatur successor piscatoris, ut xxiiii. q.i. Quoniam uetus." See also the apparatus criticus.

83. Laurentius, 3 Comp. 1.5.2 (X 1.7.2) v. *uicarium,* Admont 55, fol. 109r: "Licet successor piscatoris, xxiiii. q.i. Quoniam uetus, similiter quilibet episcopus est uicarius Christi, xxxiii. q.v. Mulierem, et episcopi sunt successores apostolorum, lxviii. Quorum uices. laur." Goffredus da Trani [Paris, B.N. lat. 15402, fol. 19r] and Bernardus Parmensis in the Ordinary Gloss repeated Laurentius' gloss.

84. Johannes Galensis, 3 Comp. 1.5.2 (X 1.7.2) v. *uicarium,* Munich, Staatsbibl. 3879, fol. 157r: "Nichilominus tamen est Petri uicarius, ut supra di. xcvi. Constantinus. i. q.vii. Quotiens, quia heres heredis testatoris est heres, C. de hered. inst. l.ult." and his gloss to 3 Comp. 1.5.3 (X 1.7.3) v. *qui locum,* Munich, Staatsbibl. 3879, fol. 157v: "Idest Petri, ut supra di. lxxxvi. [*sic*] in illa palea Constantinus, ubi Petri uicarius dicitur; uel uicarius eius, idest Christi, ut supra c. proximo. Alibi primus homo uicarius Christi dicitur, xxxiii. q.v. Hec imago."

and divine authority. The canonists fashioned distinctions between the will of the pope and reason, and between the pope's supreme authority and his obligation to submit himself to the law. Both arguments enhanced papal authority and defined fundamental concepts of government. Innocent established the sole right of the pope to govern the transfer of bishops—which had not been firmly established by earlier ecclesiastical custom and practice—and the canonists demonstrated that when the pope promulgated positive law, he could violate—in certain circumstances—a long-accepted truth: law must embody reason. Both broke new ground. *Quanto personam* left one fundamental question unanswered: What was the relationship of the pope's divine authority and his *plenitudo potestatis?* In the next chapter we shall turn to Innocent's definition of *plenitudo potestatis* and trace the acceptance of his thought into canonistic theory.

CHAPTER TWO · PAPAL
FULLNESS OF POWER

Although Innocent III and the canonists created new definitions of papal authority, their approaches were quite different. Much of Innocent's vision of papal monarchy was theological: "The pope does not exercise the office of man, but of the true God on earth." He placed the pope well above man and, perhaps, just slightly below the angels. For their part, the canonists sharpened their definitions of the pope's authority by carefully describing his prerogatives as judge and legislator.

The canonists were struggling with legal concepts and ideas that they were just beginning to understand clearly. Although Roman law provided them with many definitions, the classical jurists had never discussed legislative authority, jurisdiction, or delegated authority in any systematic fashion. Medieval lawyers had to work out a coherent theory for themselves. Their task was complicated by the weight of traditional ideas and values they had received from Germanic custom, which emphasized the sanctity of law and the ruler's responsibility to preserve the law. Reconciling the prince's authority to change law—through his will—with the demand that law must also be just, embody reason, and represent the will of the people was the task of the twelfth- and thirteenth-century lawyers.[1]

Following in the footsteps of their predecessors, Innocent and the canonists called the pope's power within the church, "plenitudo potestatis," "fullness of power." By this term they distinguished his authority from that of patriarchs, bishops, and priests. Fitting well with the rhetoric that the pope and canonists were developing, "plenitudo potestatis" described the vastness of papal power and the pope's supreme position within the church.[2]

---

1. The best introduction to early medieval ideas about law is still Fritz Kern, *Kingship and Law in the Middle Ages,* trans. S. B. Chrimes (New York: 1956).

2. On "plenitudo potestatis" see Watt, *Theory of Papal Monarchy,* 75–92, with the older bibliography he cites.

Innocent made "plenitudo potestatis" the most important element in the vocabulary of his decretal letters.[3]

The term itself dates back to the early Middle Ages. It had lain dormant before flowering in the twelfth century, when it became the single most important definition of papal power. At first "plenitudo potestatis" did not define just papal authority. In the twelfth century, archbishops were sometimes described as having "plenitudo potestatis" or "plenitudo pontificalis officii" after they accepted their pallium. It was thus "a technical term for the increment of priestly and jurisdictional power which accompanied the pallium."[4]

Another similar, but legally quite distinct technical term developed at this time was "plena potestas." The popes and canonists used "plena potestas," "libera potestas," or "potestas" to define an unrestricted grant of authority—within the specific terms of the mandate—to a legate or procurator. "Plena potestas" was a concept borrowed from Roman private law and normally meant delegated authority or jurisdictional power given to a representative.[5] Sometimes even the pope was described as having "plena potestas" after his election, and Innocent III occasionally called "fullness of power," "plena potestas."[6]

Later, publicists applied the concept of "plenitudo potestatis" to the emperor and other temporal princes.[7] For lawyers of the later Middle Ages,

---

3. Klaus Schatz, "Papsttum und partikularkirchliche Gewalt bei Innocenz III. (1198–1216)," *Archivum Historiae Pontificiae* 8 (1970): 61–111, is a fine study of Innocent's use of the term.

4. Benson, *Bishop-Elect,* 169–73. The following letters are important examples of Innocent III's use of the term "plenitudo potestatis": Innocent III, Register I, 567–68, no. 374; 627–29, no. 419; Register II, 320–21, no. 165 (174); 326–33, no. 169 (178). Innocent continued to describe the authority a bishop received with his pallium as "plenitudo pontificalis officii."

5. Innocent III, Register I, 472–74, no. 326. Text is cited below, Chapter 3, n. 6.

6. Tierney, *Foundations,* 143 n. 2, cites several examples of "plena potestas" being used to describe papal power. On the Roman law origins of the term and its subsequent history, see Gaines Post, *Studies in Medieval Legal Thought: Public Law and the State,* 1100–1322 (Princeton: 1964), 61–162. Cf. Innocent III, Register II, 366, no. 191 (200); 367–68, no. 193 (202). For canonistic usage, see Antonio Padoa Schioppa, "Sul principio della rappresentanza diretta nel Diritto canonico classico," *Proceedings of the Fourth International Congress of Medieval Canon Law,* ed. Stephan Kuttner, MIC, Series C, 5 (Città del Vaticano: 1976), 107–31.

7. The canonists applied "plenitudo potestatis" to describe temporal power in the late twelfth century, Watt, *Theory of Papal Monarchy,* 83 (Huguccio); 112 (Hostiensis). Later, the emperor was commonly described as having "plenitudo potestatis." See Ernst Schubert, *König*

the term became synonymous with the supreme power of the monarch. In the last chapter we saw that when the canonists wrote that the pope's will was the source of law, they did not mean that he had arbitrary power. Likewise, they never conceived of papal "plenitudo potestatis" as a license for the irresponsible exercise of power by a monarch.[8]

In his decretal letters, Innocent discussed the origins of "plenitudo potestatis" and described its relationship to other powers within the church. The canonists also wrestled with the meaning of "plenitudo potestatis" and, during the thirteenth century, sharpened their definition of the term. At the beginning of the century, "plenitudo potestatis" was a general concept describing papal power. By the end of the century, the canonists distinguished between those occasions in which the pope acted through his "plenitudo potestatis" and those in which he acted through his ordinary power. In doing so, they established the basis upon which later thinkers would discuss the prerogatives of the prince and his ordinary and extraordinary powers. Gradually, the duality of papal authority that Innocent described in *Quanto personam* was given more precision.

"Plenitudo Potestatis" in Innocent III's Decretals

Innocent III was a Roman aristocrat who seems never to have felt the searching self-doubt some men endure while holding high office. He was supremely confident of his abilities; the rhythm of the phrase "plenitudo potestatis" must have pleased him. Again and again, Innocent cited the pope's "plenitudo potestatis" as a justification for his actions. Again and again, he described the bishops as exercising "pars sollicitudinis"—a share

---

und Reich: Studien zur spätmittelalterlichen deutschen Verfassungsgeschichte (Göttingen: 1979), 128–39. Schubert interprets the term to mean absolute, autocratic authority. See also Wilks, *The Problem of Sovereignty,* 318, 443; William D. McCready, "Papal *Plenitudo potestatis* and the Source of Temporal Authority in Late Medieval Hierocratic Theory," *Speculum* 48 (1973): 654–74 and "Papalists and Antipapalists: Aspects of the Church/State Controversy in the Later Middle Ages," *Viator* 6 (1975): 241–73 and his introduction to *The Theory of Papal Monarchy in the Fourteenth Century: Guillaume de Pierre Godin Tractatus de causa immediata ecclesiastice potestatis,* Studies and Texts 56 (Toronto: 1982), 3–33. The knight in the *Disputatio inter clericum et militem* (ca. 1300) bestowed "plenitudo iuris et potestatis" on his king, see Thomas J. Renna, "Kingship in the *Disputatio inter clericum et militem,*" *Speculum* 48 (1973): 675–93.

8. Tierney, *Foundations,* 56–67 and passim.

of responsibility—which in no way diminished papal fullness of power.[9] The common formula that he and the canonists used—"bishops are called by the pope to a share of responsibility, but not to fullness of power"—starkly contrasted the power of the pope and the bishops. The contrast demeaned episcopal authority and invited the development of jurisdictional theories that derived episcopal from papal authority.

There is some evidence that this language was also used in the curia during Innocent's pontificate. Thomas of Marlborough was an English monk at the abbey of Evesham who had been selected as the abbey's proctor to carry on the monks' litigation with Mauger, bishop of Worcester, in the Roman curia. The central question in this famous case was whether Mauger had the right to make a visitation of the abbey. Thomas wrote a vivid account of his experiences in Rome.[10] He was an entertaining, slightly unscrupulous, intelligent advocate who illustrates how important a lawsuit could be for the litigants who made the long, perilous journey to Rome to protect their rights. Thomas left his name to posterity by making his quest for justice the principal focus of his ecclesiastical career. His memory of conversations with Pope Innocent III may be distorted by a fecund imagination, but his description of the striking impression that Innocent's personality made on him allows us a glimpse of the pope's character. His interviews with Innocent, which he recorded so faithfully in his history, also let us hear the rhetoric of the curia that the protocol of the times demanded. At a particularly trying time during the proceedings of his case, Thomas wrote that he addressed Innocent: "Holy father, you have been called to fullness of power, and all things therefore are permitted to you."[11] Thomas followed his flattery with an objection to the procedure of Innocent's courtroom, but his exaggerated form of address is an indication that the pope's "plenitudo potestatis" had become a part of the curia's language.

By the time Thomas visited the papal curia, Innocent was using the

---

9. Schatz, "Papsttum und partikularkirchliche Gewalt," 64 n. 16, lists the letters in which Innocent used "plenitudo potestatis." Konrad Burdach, "Der Kampf Walthers von der Vogelweide gegen Innozenz III. und gegen das vierte lateranische Konzil," *Zeitschrift für Kirchengeschichte* 55 (1936): 445–522, describes the opposition of German bishops to Innocent's absolutism. I think that Burdach's thesis is not supported by the evidence he presents.

10. *Chronicon abbatiae de Evesham ad annum 1418*, ed. W. D. Macray, RS 29 (London: 1865).

11. Ibid., 191: "Pater sancte, in plenitudine potestatis vocati estis, et ideo omnia licent vobis." Some lawyers suggested that flattery of the judge in the courtroom could be advantageous to a case, see James Brundage, "The Ethics of the Legal Profession: Medieval Canonists and their Clients," *The Jurist* 33 (1973): 237–48.

term in his letters and sermons frequently, at least more regularly than his predecessors.[12] Innocent's letters were suffused with a self-conscious majesty that differed markedly from the tone of twelfth-century papal letters. In particular, the arengas—or introductions—of Innocent's decretals became dramatic statements of the pope's authority.[13] The rolling cursus of chancery style beats a solemn and stately march across the folios of Innocent's registers. Sound and meaning felicitously come together in Innocent's arengas to create an indelible impression on the minds of those who read or listened to them. In translation, they become stilted and lose their musicality:

Quia diversitatem corporum diversitas sepe sequitur animorum, ne plenitudo ecclesiastice iurisdictionis in plures dispensata vilesceret, sed in uno potius collata vigeret, apostolice sedi Dominus in beato Petro universarum ecclesiarum et cunctorum Christi fidelium magisterium contulit et primatum; que retenta sibi plenitudine potestatis ad implendum laudabilius officium, quod omnibus eam constituit debitricem, multos in partem sollicitudinis evocavit. [A diversity of intentions often arises from a diversity of people. Hence the Lord gave to St. Peter and the Apostolic See the magisterium and lordship of all the churches and all the faithful of Christ. He did this so that the fullness of ecclesiastical jurisdiction would not be debased by giving it to many people. Rather he gave jurisdiction to one so that it could flourish. Peter retained for himself a fullness of power in order that he might exercise his worthy pastoral office, for which he is beholden to all to exercise. He called many to a share of the responsibility.][14]

We can be fairly certain that Innocent wrote this and other similar arengas

---

12. Watt, *Theory of Papal Monarchy,* 85 n. 34 and his article, "The Use of the Term 'Plenitudo potestatis' by Hostiensis," *Proceedings of the Second International Congress of Medieval Canon Law,* ed. Stephan Kuttner and J. Joseph Ryan, MIC, Series C, 1 (Città del Vaticano: 1965), 161–87.

13. We cannot always know when Innocent "speaks" to us in his letters or when we are reading the words of a curial official. See Kenneth Pennington, "The Legal Education of Pope Innocent III," BMCL 4 (1974): 75–76. Innocent reformed the curia at the beginning of his pontificate. The *Gesta Innocentii,* c. 41 and c. 42, emphasized the changes he made in curial judicial procedure. He not only played a greater role in the courtroom than his immediate predecessors, but he also reformed the curial bureaucracy. I think the professional quality of his letters is due to these changes. However, in the present work I have carefully avoided the problem of Innocent's authorship of certain letters and the related question to what extent the letters embody his legal learning. Readers will note that I have cited evidence that would support both sides of the issue. See Brigide Schwarz, *Die Organisation kurialer Schreiberkollegien von ihrer Entstehung bis zur 15. Jahrhunderts* (Tübingen: 1972), 7–18.

14. Innocent III, Register II, 106, no. 57 (60) (3 Comp. 3.8.2 [X 3.8.5]).

himself. The style and content almost certainly preclude another's pen.[15] Though these introductions to Innocent's decretals contain graphic images of papal authority, they set the tone rather than the substance of canonistic thought. This arenga, from the decretal, *Quia diversitatem,* which will be discussed in Chapter 4, was excised by Raymond of Pennafort when he placed it in his edition of the Decretals of Gregory IX. The arengas, nevertheless, hammered out a new doctrine of papal authority.

Klaus Schatz has observed that after his tenth pontifical year, the arengas of Innocent's decretals no longer contained statements of papal authority or descriptions of "plenitudo potestatis." The characteristic arengas of his early years had almost disappeared.[16] No one has explained this change satisfactorily. Almost all of Innocent's ideas about ecclesiastical authority and papal power can be found in the letters and arengas of the first two years of his pontificate. Although most of these letters were not included in the canonical collections—and those that were had their arengas cut drastically or even eliminated by Raymond of Pennafort's editorial work in 1234—they influenced the canonists. After Innocent's pontificate, whenever a canonist wrote about papal authority, "plenitudo potestatis" inevitably became a central element of his commentary.

In his recent essay, Schatz argues that Innocent developed "plenitudo potestatis" for two reasons: first, to assert papal authority over the entire church, including the schismatic Eastern church; and second, to define the position of the bishops within the church. Schatz also believes that Innocent thought that the bishops derived their jurisdiction from the pope. Although Schatz has contributed much to our understanding of Innocent's thought, I think that he and other historians have underestimated the novelty and importance of a New Testament passage, John 1.42, for Innocent's justification of papal monarchy and have attributed too much clarity to Innocent's conceptions of papal and episcopal jurisdiction.

The letters and sermons in which Innocent treated the theme of papal authority cover a range of recipients and topics. Writing to the patriarch of Constantinople, Innocent lectured him on papal primacy and developed the image of the pope as "head" of the church.[17] In a slightly earlier decretal to

---

15. Tony Honoré has written an important essay on the role of the emperors in drafting legislation in the late Roman Empire. He has attempted to distinguish the individual contributions of those lawyers who wrote rescripts. No comparable work has been done for the legislation of the medieval papacy. See *Emperors and Lawyers* (London: 1981), chapters one, two, and three. See, however, the critical assessment of Honoré's methodology by Alan Watson, *Tijdschrift voor Rechtsgeschiedenis* 50 (1982): 409–14.

16. Schatz, "Papsttum und partikularkirchliche Gewalt," 64.

17. Innocent III, Register II, 382–89, no. 200 (209) [Nov. 1199].

the archbishop of Tours, he fashioned the same image but with less detail.[18] He expounded his doctrines of ecclesiastical power in letters to the king of Bulgaria, the king of Armenia, the bishops of France, the bishop of Skalholt and Holar in Iceland. He did not confine his teachings to churchmen or limit them geographically.[19] Topically, the decretals have a narrower range. The letters in which the theme of papal authority arose most frequently were those deciding disputes about or between bishops, particularly cases of episcopal translation or renunciation, and disputes between bishoprics over jurisdictional rights. As in *Quanto personam,* Innocent developed his theories of papal authority over bishops in the heat of practical affairs, not in the quiet of theoretical contemplation.

Although Innocent frequently used the traditional formula, "plenitudo potestatis" contrasted to "pars sollicitudinis," he expanded the number of images associated with it. The twelfth-century canonists had been content with a formula. Innocent added two metaphors to it: the sacramental image of anointing to represent the flow of authority to bishops; and the comparison of the church to a body, the head representing the pope and the limbs the bishops, the clergy, and the faithful. This anthropomorphic image of the church first appeared in the Apostle Paul's letters and the description of the church as a body (*corpus*), usually the body of Christ, had become a commonplace before Innocent's pontificate. Innocent made this image a powerful representation of the church's structure.

Innocent also expanded the traditional scriptural basis of papal authority. To the standard text of Matthew 16.18, he added John 1.42. Later theologians did not accept Innocent's interpretation of John 1.42, but his exegesis of the text illustrates an important element of his thought: his conscious return to Scripture to justify his vision of papal monarchy. By citing John 1.42, Innocent isolated the moment when Christ granted St. Peter "plenitudo potestatis." The pope had chosen this text carefully. John 1.42 was an important piece of evidence that Christ's mandate of authority to Peter had not included the other apostles.

Innocent expanded the theological and scriptural basis of papal primacy with some ingenuity. When he turned to the Bible, he was an inventive and original exegete.[20] His interpretations of biblical passages were sometimes untraditional; his ideas often seem untrammeled by earlier commentators. This is particularly true when he used Scripture to support his views

18. Innocent III, Register II, 150–71, no. 79 (82) [June 1199].

19. These letters are discussed below. Schatz, "Papsttum und partikularkirchliche Gewalt," lists every important letter in which Innocent discussed "plenitudo potestatis."

20. See Pennington, "Pope Innocent III's Views," 60–61.

of papal authority. He cited no new texts, but he combined old ones in strikingly new ways. In a letter written to the archbishop of Compostela during the second year of his pontificate, he described the scriptural foundations of papal monarchy:

Although the body of the Church is one, in which Christ is the head and all the faithful are the limbs, nevertheless Peter, who was called the rock by Christ [Matthew 16.18] was also called the head by Christ—who is also the Head—when he said "You shall be called Cephas" [John 1.42]. According to one interpretation, "cephas" means head. Thus, just as the fullness of the senses [*plenitudo sensuum*] abounds in the head, and some part of this fullness is drawn off to the limbs, so others are called to a sharing of responsibility; but only Peter received fullness of power [*plenitudo potestatis*]. Therefore, important cases [*causae maiores*] of the church should be justly referred to him as head, not so much by canonical constitution, but by divine institution.[21]

Theologians and canonists had long cited Matthew 16.18, "You are Peter and upon this rock I shall build my Church," as the scriptural justification of Peter's and his successors' preeminent jurisdictional position within the church. This passage of Matthew was the foundation of the Petrine doctrine upon which the authority of the bishop of Rome had been based. As Peter's successor—*vicarius Petri*—the pope was the "head of the Church, supreme exponent of the power of jurisdiction conferred on the Church, symbol of the Church's enduring faith."[22]

Matthew 16.18, however, had a potentially fatal weakness that made it vulnerable to anti-papal interpretations. The words of Christ to Peter, "Whatsoever you shall bind on earth shall be bound in heaven," upon which an important part of papal monarchy rested, were repeated by Christ when he addressed all the apostles in Matthew 18.18. Matthew 16.18 could justify papal monarchy, but, in context, together with Matthew 18.18, the passage

---

21. Innocent III, Register II, 247, no. 124 (133): "Licet unum sit corpus ecclesie, in quo Christus est caput et universi fideles sunt membra, ille tamen, qui a Christo petra dictus est Petrus, etiam a Christo capite vocatus est caput, ipso testante, qui ait: 'Tu vocaberis Cephas,' quod secundum unam interpretationem exponitur caput: quia sicut plenitudo sensuum abundat in capite, ad cetera vero membra pars aliqua plenitudinis derivatur, ita ceteri vocati sunt in partem sollicitudinis, solus autem Petrus assumptus est in plenitudinem potestatis, ad quem velut ad caput maiores ecclesie cause non tam constitutione canonica quam institutione divina merito referuntur." Although he alluded to the other definition of "cephas" here, Innocent noted "cephas" had two interpretations in his sermon for the feast of St. Peter and Paul, PL 217.552c: "Cephas enim licet secundum unam linguam interpretatur Petrus, secundum aliam dicitur caput."

22. Tierney, *Foundations*, 25–36 on the Petrine doctrine; passage quoted at 36. Also see Watt, *Theory of Papal Monarchy*, 80–83.

could also justify a collegial sharing of authority with the bishops, who were the successors of the apostles. Later papal theorists attempted to avoid this difficulty by citing John 21.15–17, "feed my sheep," in which Christ spoke only to Peter.[23] Much earlier, Innocent cited John 1.42 for the same purpose. If Innocent's interpretation of John 1.42 had been accepted, it could have become, as John 21.15–17 later became, a compelling and important justification of papal monarchy.

By coupling Matthew 16.18 with John 1.42, Innocent transformed the latter into an important witness of Christ's bestowal of authority and jurisdictional primacy on Peter. At first glance, the passage did not hold much promise. Christ had said to Peter (Simon), "You shall be called Cephas," and the author of John explained, "which means Peter" (in the Greek text PETROS). The Aramaic word from which "cephas" was derived meant rock.[24]

The early fathers of the church had been intrigued by Christ's naming of Peter. Augustine wrote in his commentary to John 1.42 that "Peter was from rock, the rock which is the Church. Therefore, the church is represented in the name of Peter."[25] Somewhat surprisingly, very few of the early biblical commentators took their exegesis of the passage one step further and identified "cephas" with "head," even though most of them knew Greek. The Greek word for head, transliterated CEPHALE, had identical beginning letters, more than enough evidence for medieval etymologists to establish a link between the Greek and Aramaic words. However, since the Gospel itself had already given its interpretation of "cephas," perhaps they were reluctant to give a second, figurative interpretation.

The earliest commentator who interpreted "cephas" as head was Optatus Afer (ca. 370). He noted that Peter was the head of the apostles, and for this reason Christ called him Cephas.[26] Later, Isidore of Seville adopted

---

23. Tierney, *Religion, Law, and the Growth of Constitutional Thought*, 63–64.

24. Rudolf Schnackenburg, *Das Johannesevangelium*, 1. Teil: *Einleitung und Kommentar zu Kap. 1–4*, 2nd ed. (Freiburg-Basel-Wien: 1967), 310–12. Schnackenburg notes that Matthew 16.18 is not a parallel text to John 1.42.

25. Augustine, *In Iohannis Evangelium tractatus CXXIV*, ed. D. R. Willems, CC 36 (Turnholt: 1954), 74: "Petrus autem a petra, petra vero ecclesia; ergo in Petri nomine figurata est ecclesia."

26. Optatus Afer, *De schismate Donatistarum*, book II, c. 2 [PL 11.947]: "Igitur negare non potes scire te in urbe Roma Petro primo Cathedram episcopalem esse collatam, in qua sederit omnium apostolorum caput Petrus, unde et Cephas appellatus est." Cf. Schatz, "Papsttum und partikularkirchliche Gewalt," 81–82. Yves-M. Congar, "Cephas-cephale-caput," *Revue du moyen âge Latin* 8 (1952): 5–42. See also Congar, "Aspects ecclésiologiques," 41–43.

this interpretation for his etymologies.[27] Their reading of John 1.42 entered the canonical tradition in the ninth century through a letter of Pseudo-Anaclet in the Pseudo-Isidorian Decretals.[28] The letter found its way into all the major canonical collections and eventually into Gratian.[29] Most of the twelfth-century canonists passed the reading in Gratian by without comment. Huguccio, however, asserted that "cephas" meant head and connected it with Peter's primacy over the other apostles.[30] I have found almost no later biblical commentators who followed Isidore of Seville or Pseudo-Isidore. It may be that this interpretation of John 1.42 can be found in the unprinted commentaries of the late twelfth century and would provide an as yet unknown source for Innocent's thought. Later, Thomas Aquinas wrote that Peter was the head of the apostles and the vicar of Christ, but stopped short of interpreting the passage as having granted papal primacy. He viewed John 1.42 as a prophecy of Christ's bestowal of authority on Peter in Matthew 16.18.[31]

---

27. Isidore of Seville, *Etymologiarum sive originum libri XX*, ed. W. M. Lindsay (Oxford: 1966), VII, c. 9: "Petra enim erat Christus, super quod fundamentum etiam ipse aedificatus est Petrus. Cephas dictus eo quod in capite sit constitutus apostolorum. KEPALE enim Graece caput dicitur, et ipsud nomen in Petro Syrum est."

28. *Decretales Pseudo-Isidorianae et Capitula Angilrammi*, ed. Paul Hinschius (Leipzig: 1863), 83: "Et licet omnes essent apostoli, Petro tamen a domino est concessum, et ipsi inter se idipsum voluerunt, ut reliquis omnibus praeesset apostolis, et Cephas, id est caput, et principium teneret apostolatus" (Congar, "Cephas," 7–9).

29. D. 22 c. 2 [Sacrosancta Romana]. Congar, "Cephas," 8 n. 10.

30. Huguccio, D. 22 c. 2 v. *cephas*, Admont 7, fol. 27v [Klosterneuburg 89, fol. 28r]: "idest capud. Vnde acepalum dicitur, idest sine capite, ut di. xxi. Sumitur et di. xciii. Nulla." Huguccio connected Cephas to Peter's primacy at D. 21 c. 2 [In novo testamento] v. *pari consortio*, Admont 7, fol. 26r [Klosterneuburg 89, fol. 26v]: "Item prefuit in appellatione quia ipse solus cefas, idest capud apostolorum dictus est, ut xxii. di. Sacrosancta." He only called Peter first in title on the basis of John 1.42; he did not interpret the passage as conferring authority on Peter. Huguccio had also connected "cephas" with head in his *Agiographia*, ed. Giuseppe Cremascoli (Spoleto: 1978), 163: "et dictus est Cephas a cephas, quod est caput, quia caput sit et princeps" (following the Venetian manuscript).

31. Congar, "Cephas," 8–9, found only one theologian who connected, very tentatively, "cephas" and "caput." He also notes the reluctance (pp. 12–14) of thirteenth-century theologians to interpret John 1.42 to mean "head." Thomas Aquinas to John 1.42, *Super Evangelium S. Ioannis lectura*, ed. Raphael Cai (Rome: 1952), 60: "Tertio vero quantum ad occulta futura; unde dicit 'Tu vocaberis Cephas, quod interpretatur Petrus,' et in Graeco caput. Et congruit mysterio, ut ille qui debet esse aliorum caput et Christi vicarius, firmitati inhaereret. Matth. XVI 18:'Tu es Petrus, et super hanc petram aedificabo Ecclesiam meam.' " ed. Angelico Guarienti (Rome: 1953), 1.162 and 2.353–54, where he quotes Bede, Augustine, Rabanus Maurus, and Alcuin. Also Matthew 10.2, *Super Evangelium S. Matthaei lectura*, ed. Raphael Cai (Rome: 1951), 128: "Petrus a petra dicitur propter eius firmitatem; et Cephas, quod syrum nomen est, non hebraeum." See also Thomas' comment to Matthew 10.2 and John 1.42 in *Catena aurea in quatuor Evangelia*, ed. Angelico Guarienti (Turin-Rome: 1953), 1:162 and 2:353–54.

In Innocent's mind, Matthew 16.18 and John 1.42 both granted Peter primacy in the church. Consequently, "important cases of the Church should be justly referred to him as head, not so much by canonical constitution but by divine institution." John 1.42 provided a sharp, definitive explanation of Christ's words in Matthew 16.18: Peter was the head of the church and was, as head, the sole judge of all important cases. In *Quanto personam*, Innocent had argued that only the pope could dissolve the bond between a bishop and his see. "God, not man, separates the bishop from his Church because the Roman pontiff dissolves the bond by divine rather than by human authority."[32] In order to set the papal office clearly apart from other episcopal offices, Innocent strengthened the pope's scriptural right to judge all cases involving bishops and expanded the scriptural foundations of the Petrine doctrine. Matthew 16.18 and John 1.42 were a well-suited tandem. Earlier papal decretals or conciliar canons that may have supported papal primacy were not important for Innocent. They may have reflected Christ's wishes, but the pope's jurisdictional primacy over bishops was not dependent on them.

According to Innocent, the pope received his authority to translate bishops from God, not from any man. The canonists did not normally make such a sharp distinction between human and divine authority. When they described the origins of ecclesiastical jurisdiction, they usually mixed the pope's human and divine offices. The pope was the vicar of Peter as well as the vicar of Christ. Each office gave authority to the pope. There were, nonetheless, exceptions. A contemporary canonist, perhaps Alanus, also emphasized the divine origins of papal power:

This is an argument that the pope receives his authority from the Lord and not from man. . . . Hence it can be seen that the pope may establish new canons without the consent of the cardinals and without a synod. Even if the entire church opposed the pope, his authority would still prevail.[33]

---

32. See Chapter 1 and Chapter 3 for a discussion of these texts.

33. Alanus? to C. 9 q. 3 c. 17 v. *Beatus Petrus apostolus Domini voce tenuit,* Vat. Ross. lat. 595, fol. 132v: "Arg. dominum papam dignitatem et potestatem habere ex domini auctoritate et non hominis, supra di. xvii. § Hinc contra. supra di. xxi. Queris, supra di. xxii. c.i. et c.ii. Vnde colligitur quod sine sinodo et absque consilio (MS: concilio) cardinalium possit novos canones condere, et si sinodus et cardinales et omnes generaliter essent ex una parte et ipse solus ex alia, eius auctoritas debeat preualere." I have not found this gloss in any other manuscript of Alanus. Although the glossator puts the argument forward as only a possibility, if this gloss does report Alanus' opinion, his rejection of shared authority is congruent with his other glosses. For the canonists' emphasis of the divine origins of papal authority after Innocent III, see Tierney, *Foundations,* 91.

Like Innocent, this canonist seemed to prefer a church ruled by a powerful monarch unfettered by shared authority or responsibility. Later canonists regularly underlined the divine origins of papal authority. Innocent had permanently shifted the focus of the discussion about ecclesiastical jurisdiction.

Innocent continued to link John 1.42 and Matthew 16.18 in his sermons and decretal letters. The last datable letter incorporating these passages is one addressed to the king of Bulgaria.[34] There is little evidence, however, that his decretals and sermons containing his exegesis of John 1.42 circulated very widely. His reply to the patriarch of Constantinople was included in two early canonical collections and in the *Gesta Innocentii*.[35] The *Gesta* also included his letter to the king of Bulgaria.[36] The *Gesta,* however, was not widely known in the Middle Ages, and since the letters were not included in *Compilatio tertia* or in the Decretals of Gregory IX, Innocent's interpretation of John 1.42 did not directly reach many later thinkers.

Innocent did, however, influence one later writer. James of Viterbo referred to Innocent's decretal to the patriarch of Constantinople as a "quaedam epistola," without citing his source for the decretal.[37] James adopted Innocent's interpretation of John 1.42 when he discussed the origins of Peter's office.[38] Most later writers who interpreted "cephas" as head and connected the passage with Matthew 16.18 rely on Pseudo-Anaclet's letter

---

34. VII 1, PL 215.279. Other letters and sermons citing John 1.42 are: Innocent III, Register I, 527, no. 353 [to the emperor of Constantinople]; Register II, 151, no. 79 (82); 383, no. 200 (209) [to the patriarch of Constantinople]; V 119, PL 214.1116–17; X 138, PL 215.1233; Sermo II, In consecratione pontificis maximi, PL 217.658a; Sermo XVIII, PL 217.517b; Sermo XXI, PL 217.552c; *De sacro altaris mysterio libri sex* I c. 8, PL 217.778–79. See Walter Ullmann, "John Baconthorpe as a Canonist," *Church and Government in the Middle Ages: Essays presented to C. R. Cheney,* ed. C. N. L. Brooke et al. (Cambridge 1976), 229, 232; and Schatz, "Papsttum und partikularkirchliche Gewalt," 81. Innocent did not always cite John 1.42, although he never omitted Matthew 16.18. In his letter to the Catholicus of Armenia, for example, Innocent left the passage out. Register II, 406–7, no. 209 (218). Congar, "Cephas," 10–12.

35. Rainer of Pomposa, *Collectio decretalium* 3.1 [PL 216.1186–91]: Bernardus Compostellanus, *Collectio Romana,* 1.2.1 [ed. Singer, 37–38]: *Gesta Innocentii,* c. 61 [PL 214.cxxiii]. On this letter, see Kuttner, "Universal Pope or Servant of God's Servants," 112–15. Also D. L. d'Avray, "A Letter of Innocent III and the Idea of Infallibility," *The Catholic Historical Review* 66 (1980): 417–21 and "Origins of the Idea of Infallibility: A Rejoinder to Professor Tierney," ibid. 67 (1981): 60–69 discusses the letter's importance for infallibility. I find d'Avray's interpretation of the decretal unconvincing.

36. *Gesta Innocentii* c. 73 [PL 214.cxxvi–cxxvii].

37. James of Viterbo, *De regimine Christiano (1301–1302): Etude des sources et édition critique: Le plus ancien traité de l'église,* ed. H. - X. Arquilliere (Paris 1926), 209.

38. Ibid., 214–15, 275. When James quoted John 1.42, however, he copied the words of Fr. Buonaccorsi which he attributed to Cyril of Alexandria; see Congar, "Cephas," 14.

in the Decretum. Pope John XXII cited John 1.42 in his condemnation of Marsilius of Padua and John of Jandun. "Peter is the head of the church, and he is called the head."[39] I have found a small number of writers who interpreted the passage similarly: John of Paris, Augustinus Triumphus, John Baconthorpe, John of Naples, Johannes Turrecremata, Nicholas of Cusa, and Domenico de' Domenichi.[40]

Still, most writers preferred to leave John 1.42 aside when they discussed papal primacy. From the early Middle Ages on, "cephas" was known to have been a "Syrian" word, and most biblical commentators were uncomfortable ascribing a Greek meaning to it.

In the sixteenth century, Martin Luther mounted a formidable attack against the authenticity of Pseudo-Anaclet's letter in the Decretum. Luther was convinced that the decretal was a forgery; he could not believe that Pope Anaclet would have made such a gross error of interpretation. Later, when editing Pseudo-Anaclet's letter the *correctores Romani* carefully described how "cephas" had been interpreted as head by some early commentators. The precision of the note betrays their uneasiness with Pseudo-Anaclet's definition.[41]

John 1.42 had another function in Innocent's thought on papal authority. Peter's "headship" introduced an anthropomorphic image of the church

---

39. The letter is conveniently printed in Odorico Raynaldo, *Annales ecclesiastici* (Coloniae Agrippinae: 1694), 15: fol. 326–331: "Sic igitur ex praedictis patet quod Petrus secundum predictum modum caput est ecclesiae et vocatur. Et hoc videtur Christus in impositione nominis designasse; dixit enim sibi, sicut legitur in Joanne: 'Tu vocaberis Cephas'; cephas autem Graece interpretatur latine caput." It may be significant that Pope Gregory IX quoted Innocent's words to the patriarch of Constantinople almost exactly, but left Innocent's definition of cephas-caput out. See Po. 8981: Mansi 23.56; cf. Congar, "Cephas," 11 n. 17.

40. John of Paris, *De confessionibus audiendis (Quaestio disputata Parisius de potestate papae)*, ed. Ludwig Hödl (München: 1962), 48; Augustinus Triumphus, see Wilks, *Problem of Sovereignty*, 62 n. 3, 383 n. 2; John Baconthorpe, see Ullmann, "John Baconthorpe," 229; John of Naples, *Quaestiones variae Parisiis disputatae* (Neapoli: 1618), 334. *Domenico de' Domenichi und seine Schrift "De potestate pape et termino eius,"* ed. Heribert Smolinsky (Münster: 1976), 225. On Turrecremata and Cues, see Congar, "Cephas," 18–19. John 1.42 reappears with Matthew 16.18 in *Pastor aeternus* of Vatican Council I. However, the text is not used as a justification for Peter's "headship." See *Conciliorum oecumenicorum Decreta* 812. Dante called Peter "Cefas": Paradiso 21.127.

41. Congar, "Cephas," 19–26, describes the Lutheran attack on the interpretation of cephas-caput and the Catholic concession of the point. The *correctores* wrote: D. 22 c. 2 v. *Cephas:* "In evangelio Ioannis c.1 Cephas (quae vox syriaca est) exponitur PETROS quod graece petram significat: idque docet etiam B. Hieronymus in comm. epist. ad Galatas cap. 2; neque credendum est ignorasse Anacletum, sed voluisse eam dictionem ad graecam linguam eo tempore notissimam referre."

into Innocent's discussion of papal primacy. The passage from John provided a natural transition from papal primacy to the *corpus ecclesiae*. Since Peter had been the head of the church, Innocent could use the metaphor of the human body to describe the relationship of the pope and the bishops.[42] The pope was the "head" which contained the "fullness of the senses." The bishops and other clergy were the limbs that received a "share of the responsibility."[43] In some letters, Innocent explained that even though the head would "distribute" or "divert" a share of the "senses" to the rest of the body, the head lost nothing.[44] When Innocent wrote to the king of Bulgaria, he used for the first—and last—time another metaphor to describe the relationship of the pope and other prelates: the sacramental anointing of the body. He also pinpointed the time when Christ first granted Peter "plenitudo potestatis" to the moment in which Christ spoke to Peter in John 1.42. In earlier texts, he had only implied that Christ granted Peter "plenitudo potestatis" when he addressed him in John 1.42. Here he was explicit:

Whence, after calling the others to a share of the responsibility, the Lord received Peter into a fullness of power when he said to him, "you shall be called Cephas," by which he meant both Peter and head, as he showed Peter to be the head of the Church. Just as the ointment from the head of Aaron flowed into his beard, Peter spread a share of the responsibility to the body, but without losing anything of it

---

42. The literature on the ancient metaphor of the church as a body is enormous. See Kantorowicz, *The King's Two Bodies*, 194–206; Tierney, *Foundations*, 132–41; Walter Ullmann, *Growth of Papal Government*, 442–46, and his "The Bible and Principles of Government in the Middle Ages," *Settimane di studio del Centro italiano di studi sull'alto medioevo* (Spoleto: 1963), 10: 216–21, reprinted in *The Church and the Law in the Earlier Middle Ages* (London: 1975): Pierre Michaud-Quantin, *Universitas: Expressions du mouvement communautaire dans le moyen-âge latin* (Paris: 1970), 59–64, who cites the important earlier literature at p. 60 n. 4. For Innocent's use of "corpus," see Schatz, "Papsttum und partikularkirchliche Gewalt," 80–85.

43. Sermo XIII, PL 217.517b: "Ei namque singulariter dictum est: 'Tu vocaberis Cephas,' id est caput. Sicut enim in humano corpore solum caput habet plenitudinem sensuum, caetera vero membra partem recipiunt plenitudinis: sic et in ecclesiastico corpore caeteri episcopi vocati sunt in partem sollicitudinis, sed supremus pontifex assumptus est in plenitudinem potestatis." Register II, 387, no. 200 (209): "Et secundum hanc acceptionem vocabuli ecclesia Romana non est universalis ecclesia, sed pars universalis ecclesie: prima videlicet et precipua veluti capud in corpore, quoniam in ea plenitudo potestatis existit, ad ceteras autem pars aliqua plenitudinis derivatur." Cf. n. 21 above. Schatz, "Papsttum und partikularkirchliche Gewalt," 84–85.

44. Schatz, *op. cit.* 82–83, especially Innocent III, Register I, 464–66, no. 320: "Ut ad eam velut capud alie sicut spiritualia membra respondeant, cuius pastor ita suas aliis vices distribuit, ut ceteris vocatis in partem sollicitudinis solus retineat plenitudinem potestatis."

himself, because the fullness of the senses thrives in the head, even though some part of them is diverted to the limbs.[45]

Schatz has indicated that this text is central to an understanding of Innocent's thought. He argues that the passage shows that bishops and lesser prelates receive their share of responsibility through the mediation of the head.[46]

Innocent was mixing his metaphors when he compared the anointing of the body to the sharing of the senses between the head and the body. His logic for the second metaphor may have been as follows. The head's senses of sight, sound, touch, smell, and faculty of reasoning were analogous to the pope's fullness of power. The head contained some senses the body did not, just as the pope exercised some powers that other prelates did not. Further, all the body's senses were directed by the head. For example, even though the head shared its sense of touch with other parts of the body, none of its sense was diminished by this sharing. The anointing metaphor has, I believe, the same rather simple logic. The ointment flowed, thought Innocent, from Aaron's head into his beard, but his head did not thereby lose any of the effect of the anointing.

Schatz believes that this text, taken together with other passages in which Innocent discussed the pope's distribution of ecclesiastical authority, shows that Innocent thought all ecclesiastical jurisdiction was derived from the pope.[47] I think we should be cautious in drawing this conclusion. First,

---

45. *Acta Innocentii PP. III (1198–1216)*, ed. T. Haluščynskyj (Città del Vaticano: 1944), 254 (PL 215.279): "Unde vocatis caeteris in partem sollicitudinis, hunc assumpsit Dominus in plenitudinem potestatis, cum inquit ad eum: 'Tu vocaberis Cephas' quod Petrus interpretatur et caput, ut Petrum caput ecclesiae demonstraret, qui sicut unguentum quod a capite Aaron descendit in barbam, in membra diffunderet, ut nihil sibi penitus deperiret, quoniam in capite viget sensuum plenitudo, ad membra vero pars eorum aliqua derivatur." The *Gesta Innocentii* c. 73, Vat. lat. 12111, fol. 24r–24v, has a medieval transcription of the letter that is almost identical with the letter as we have it in the register. In a letter to the clergy of Russia, Innocent wrote that Christ instituted Peter "magister" when he spoke to him in John 1.42, X 138, PL 215.233. A possible source of Innocent's anointing imagery is noted by Robert Charles Figueira, "The Canon Law of Medieval Papal Legation" (unpublished dissertation, Cornell University: 1980), 211, in a sermon of Arnold of Lisieux, PL 201.155: "Hic ordo est: unguentem praecedit in capite; a capite descendit in barbam, barbam quidem Aaron; a barba usque in oram vestimenti defluxit. A capite, scilicet Christo, in barbam scilicet praelatos ecclesiae, a praelatis in populum, in subjectos. In capite autem omnis perfectionis est plenitudo, omnis perfectio plenitudinis."

46. Schatz, "Papsttum und partikularkirchliche Gewalt," 84–85.

47. Ibid., 107–111.

contemporary canonists and theologians were not yet discussing ecclesiastical jurisdiction in such clear and unequivocal language. Arguments about the source of jurisdiction in the church come only later in the century. Second, this passage—the closest Innocent ever came to making a claim that all jurisdiction flows from the pope—is not free from logical ambiguity. If we consider the passage as a statement on jurisdiction, then Innocent's opening statement is difficult to reconcile with the second part. "The Lord," wrote Innocent, "called the other apostles to a share of responsibility." Thus Christ granted the apostles their jurisdictional authority directly. Later theorists who asserted that all jurisdiction is derived from the pope were always careful to show that Christ called only Peter to fullness of power. Afterwards, they argued, Peter bestowed or delegated authority to the other apostles.[48] Unless one maintains that Innocent made an implicit distinction between the power of jurisdiction and order—Christ granted only their priestly order to the apostles when he bestowed on them their "share of responsibility"—one must admit that the passage is not consistent if read as a discussion of ecclesiastical jurisdiction.

Still if the passage is not a model of clarity for jurisdictional questions, we should not blame Innocent. He was writing not about the origins of jurisdiction but about papal primacy, for the text is an unambiguous statement of the superiority of papal to episcopal authority. If Innocent had considered the question, I suspect that he would have written that the pope was the source of all jurisdiction within the church. As Christopher Cheney has observed so well, "If Innocent did not foresee the later exploitation of papal prerogatives and diplomatic manoeuvres of his successors, they acted none the less in line with his actions and his cast of mind."[49] Cheney had Innocent's deeds in mind when he wrote this, but his words could apply just as well to the pope's thoughts on papal authority.

Innocent developed a robust justification for papal primacy. He established papal prerogatives to oversee bishops on a firm theoretical foundation. Although, as we have seen, Innocent's thought was not completely accepted by later canonists and theologians, his vision of the papacy became dominant in the thirteenth-century church. No other pope was as important for edging papal monarchy toward absolutism.

---

48. For a number of examples, see Wilks, *Problem of Sovereignty*, 380–90.
49. Cheney, *Pope Innocent III and England*, 408.

The Canonists and "Plenitudo Potestatis"

The glosses of the canonists to *Quanto personam* bubbled with new ideas. Their response to Innocent's definitions of "plenitudo potestatis" was less animated and certainly less creative. There are two reasons for this. First, as noted, some of Innocent's most novel descriptions of "plenitudo potestatis" appear in letters not included in canonical collections. Second, in the letters that were placed in the collections, "plenitudo potestatis" occurs rather infrequently. Consequently the spirit of Innocent's thought was not fully incorporated into the commentaries of the canonists until the late thirteenth century. Hostiensis was primarily responsible for giving Innocent's thought proper legal garb. His definitions of "plenitudo potestatis" did not always adhere to the letter of Innocent's intentions, but they were certainly faithful to his spirit. In order to understand the breadth and the limits of papal power in the minds of the lawyers, we shall look at their thought before Hostiensis and then examine his doctrine of papal authority.

Historians have thoroughly explored the origins of "plenitudo potestatis" and its historical development.[50] Pope Leo I first used this terminology to describe the difference between the delegated authority of a legate and the authority of the pope. Later, Pope Gregory IV (833) contrasted the "fullness of power of the Roman church" with the "shared responsibility" of the bishops.[51] Subsequently the pope's authority was commonly defined by comparing his authority to that of the bishops. The canonists developed the classic definition of papal fullness of power during the twelfth century and, at the beginning of the thirteenth, Johannes Teutonicus wrote in his Ordinary Gloss to the Decretum:

The authority of the pope is without limits, that of other bishops is limited because they are called to a share of the responsibility [*pars sollicitudinis*] not to the fullness of power [*plenitudo potestatis*].[52]

In another gloss, he further defined the relationship of the pope and the bishops:

---

50. See particularly R. L. Benson, "Plenitudo potestatis: Evolution of a Formula from Gregory IV to Gratian," *Collectanea Stephan Kuttner,* SG 14 (Bologna: 1967), 4:195–217. Alfons M. Stickler, "La 'Sollicitudo omnium ecclesiarum' nella canonistica classica," *Communio* 13 (1972): 547–86 and Gaudemet, *Le gouvernement de l'église,* 117–30.

51. Benson, "Plenitudo potestatis," 200–203.

52. Johannes Teutonicus, D. 11 c. 2 v. *plena auctoritate:* "Papae auctoritas plena est, aliorum episcoporum semiplena est, quia ipsi sunt in partem sollicitudinis vocati non in plenitudinem potestatis, ut 2 q.6 Decreto et Qui se scit."

All bishops are called by the pope to a share of the responsibility, but not to the fullness of power.[53]

The juridical meanings of these definitions are not certain. The canonists settled on this terminology but did not delineate its meaning. It is a classic case of formula substituting for thought. Many implications of the formula, though, are beyond doubt. The canonists placed the pope at the head of the ecclesiastical hierarchy; he was the only bishop who could exercise jurisdiction throughout the church. All other bishops were limited to exercising their offices within the boundaries of their dioceses. The pope had jurisdiction over all *causae maiores* (major cases), such as the deposition of bishops.[54]

If read literally, the canonists' formulation of "plenitudo potestatis" might also be interpreted to mean that bishops derived all their jurisdiction from the pope. The canonists, however, shied away from drawing this conclusion.[55] We must ask, therefore, whether "plenitudo potestatis" was used by the canonists as a shorthand definition of the bishops' jurisdictional position within the church. Did the canonists understand "in partem sollicitudinis" to mean delegated authority, i.e., episcopal jurisdiction that was derived from the pope?

Certainly it can be said that the twelfth-century canonists never stated clearly that the bishops' administrative and judicial authority was either derived from or delegated by the pope. There are many references to papal

---

53. Johannes Teutonicus, D. 100 c. 10 v. *vices:* "quia omnes vocantur ab eo in partem sollicitudinis non in plenitudinem potestatis, ut 2 q.6 Decreto." Stickler, "Sollicitudo omnium ecclesiarum," 554–61, lists a large number of texts from the late twelfth and early thirteenth centuries.

54. Benson, "Plenitudo potestatis," 202, points out that the reservation of "maiores causae" dates back to at least the fifth century.

55. Modern historians are divided over the question of whether they interpret the formula "Plenitudo potestatis . . . pars sollicitudinis" to mean that episcopal jurisdiction is derived from the pope. Gabriel Le Bras, "Le droit romain au service de la domination pontificale," *Revue historique de droit français et étranger* 27 (1949): 377–98, stated that most canonists and theologians never admitted that episcopal power was merely delegated. Tierney, *Foundations,* 142–46, does not believe this formula meant that bishops had delegated powers. However, Benson, "Plenitudo potestatis," 217; Watt, *Theory of Papal Monarchy,* 76, 79–80; and Stickler, "Sollicitudo omnium ecclesiarum," 553–61, interpret the formula to mean that episcopal authority was delegated or ultimately derived from the pope. Ullmann, "Eugenius IV," 377–78 n. 66, makes the interesting point that the church has always sidestepped the issue in its official decrees on episcopal authority. For a summary of opinions and the importance of the issue for the secular-mendicant controversy, see John Marrone, "The Ecclesiology of the Parisian Secular Masters, 1250–1320" (unpublished dissertation, Cornell University: 1972). Gaudemet, *Le gouvernement de l'église,* 118–19.

"plenitudo potestatis" in the writings of the canonists which papalists could have interpreted as showing that all power of jurisdiction came from the pope,[56] but lawyers and theologians of the twelfth century were not inclined to follow the logic of the formula's argument. During the pontificate of Innocent III, some canonists began to formulate definitions of papal authority (some of which did not cite "plenitudo potestatis") that came very close to assertions that bishops derived their jurisdiction from the pope.

Alanus Anglicus, writing ca. 1206, described how the pope bestowed the sword on the emperor. He compared the bestowal of the sword on the pope to the granting of jurisdiction to bishops:

> Likewise, one may not object that Constantine granted Pope Silvester temporal jurisdiction as in D. 96 c. 30. [The emperor], therefore has his sword from the pope. The pope, nevertheless, does not give [his sword] to himself, but the electors do. So too, every bishop has his bishopric from the pope; but the pope does not grant it himself, rather the canonical election of the clergy [grants it].[57]

Although this passage has its share of ambiguity, Alanus seems to be arguing that the pope bestows the sword on the emperor at the imperial coronation and consecration. Earlier in the gloss, he pointed out that Huguccio believed the emperor had full imperial jurisdiction before his coronation and confirmation by the pope.[58] Alanus disagreed with Huguccio. The emperor does not have full jurisdiction before his confirmation by the pope. The pope, however, receives his sword at the time of his election.[59]

---

56. E.g., Bernold of Constance; see Benson, "Plenitudo potestatis," 212–13. Benson thinks that Bernold's concern was not with jurisdiction, but with judicial prerogatives. See, however, his discussion of Rufinus in *Bishop-Elect,* 85.

57. Alanus Anglicus, D. 96 c. 6 [Cum ad verum], 2nd. recension, printed by Alfons M. Stickler, "Alanus Anglicus als Verteidiger des monarchischen Papsttums," *Salesanium* 21 (1959): 362: "Similiter non obviat quod Constantinus iurisdictionem temporalem Silvestro concessit, ut dictum est ut lxiii. di. Ego Lodo. [c. 30]. Habet ergo gladium a papa. Papa tamen sibi non tribuit set eligentes. Set quilibet episcopus habet episcopatum a papa, set tamen papa non tribuit set canonica clericorum electio." See also Marrone, "Ecclesiology," 27.

58. Alanus Anglicus, loc. cit.: "Secundum eum [i.e. Huguccionem] habet gladium tantum a deo et non a papa quantum ad coronationem et confirmationem: antequam habet totam imperialem iurisdictionem."

59. It might be tempting here, because of the abrupt change in Alanus' argument, to read "sibi" in n. 57 as "ei"; the passage would then read: "The emperor has his sword from the pope; the pope nevertheless does not give it to him, the electors do." If this translation were correct, it would seem to destroy the logic of Alanus' argument. His point was just the opposite of Huguccio's: only after his coronation and confirmation by the pope does the emperor receive full imperial jurisdiction. If the electors granted the emperor the sword, he would have full jurisdiction. Therefore, it seems unlikely that Alanus would have written that the electors bestowed the sword upon (*ei*) the emperor.

The next step of Alanus' reasoning is not absolutely clear; he seems to have tacitly asked, "How can the cardinal electors be said to bestow the sword since Peter and his successors received it from Christ?" The question is implied by his next statement: although a bishop is created through a canonical election, every bishop still receives his bishopric from the pope. Alanus observed that even though election is the vehicle of selection in the church, jurisdiction is still granted by Christ or the pope—from above. In this respect the church differed from the secular state. The imperial electors did not bestow the sword; the pope did. In the church, the electoral body was the source of jurisdiction. However, we should not press the gloss too far for meaning it may not have. It is too cryptic and compressed to establish his position on the origins of episcopal authority with certainty.[60]

As noted, Alanus was one of the few canonists who broached the problem. Although canonists of the late twelfth and early thirteenth centuries cited Johannes Teutonicus' "omnes vocantur ab eo in partem sollicitudinis non in plenitudinem potestatis" many times—with small variations, they devoted few words to an analysis of the formula.

Two main points should be noted about the canonists' interpretation of "plenitudo potestatis." First, they eschewed Innocent's imagery, biblical exegesis, and metaphors. The pope's exegesis of John 1.42—if they knew it—did not attract them any more than it attracted theologians. They observed that the first pope, Peter, was equal to the first bishops, the apostles, in order and dignity of consecration, but Peter had the fullness of administration, which the other apostles did not.[61] The bishops were the successors of the other apostles and inherited the status of the apostles in the church.[62] In their glosses, the canonists contrasted the bishops' and the pope's jurisdiction: the pope's extended throughout the church, but the bishops' was limited to their dioceses. Second, during and immediately after Innocent's pontificate, "plenitudo potestatis" did not appear with great regularity in the works of the canonists. For example, Johannes Teutonicus mentioned the

---

60. Only by inference can we discern the canonists' thought about the jurisdictional relationship between the pope and bishops. See Johannes Teutonicus' gloss in which he argued that even though a metropolitan's right to consecrate a bishop may be held through the authority of the Apostolic See, the metropolitan has his own right to consecrate. Therefore, the bishop's authority is not derived from the pope; see Chapter 4, n. 77.

61. Johannes Teutonicus, D. 21 c. 2 v. *pari:* "Arg. quod omnis episcopus sit par apostolico quantum ad ordinem et rationem consecrationis. . . . Petrus tamen maior fuit aliis in adminstratione." Also his gloss to C. 24 q. 1 c. 18 v. *Petri pari.*

62. Johannes Teutonicus, C. 16 q. 1 c. 24 v. *apostolorum:* "Episcopi enim tenent locum ipsorum."

term a handful of times in all his works. A glance at the index of the new edition of Raymond of Pennafort's *Opera omnia* reveals that Raymond referred to papal "plenitudo potestatis" exactly six times.[63] The paucity of discussion in the works of these canonists makes it difficult for us to determine exactly what they meant when they cited the term in their glosses.

The anonymous author of the apparatus *Servus appellatur*[64] probably came closest to defining what the early thirteenth-century canonists intended when they said that the pope had plenitude of power within the church:

I believe that his is a special power: that if the pope should so order, any action can be taken in any church, since the church is one . . . and he is the pastor of the entire church [*in solidum*] others having been called to a share of the responsibility.[65]

The distribution of jurisdiction is not the topic of this gloss. Rather the canonist emphasized the pope's position in the hierarchy and in particular his supreme, overriding authority within the church. As judge and administrator, the pope could take cognizance of any problem in any diocese. The pope is pastor of the entire church. His "plenitudo potestatis" sets him apart from all other bishops. He is placed above all patriarchs, archbishops, and bishops.

Later in the thirteenth century, "plenitudo potestatis" began to pullulate in canonistic commentaries. No one, perhaps, gave the term a more-frequent or more-extended reading than did Hostiensis. Just as Huguccio surpassed his contemporaries in the twelfth century, Hostiensis dominated those of the thirteenth. He studied at Bologna, taught at Paris, and became bishop of Sisteron (1244), archbishop of Embrun (1250), and cardinal bishop of Ostia (1262). He served popes Innocent IV, Alexander IV, and Urban IV as a papal diplomat. He also represented King Henry III of England on several

---

63. For Johannes Teutonicus, see my unpublished dissertation (Cornell University: 1972). Raymond of Pennafort's writings have been indexed by Xaverio Ochoa and Aloisio Diez in their three volume edition of his works (Rome: 1975–78).

64. On this apparatus which Franz Gillmann attributed to Laurentius, see Knut W. Nörr, "Der Apparat des Laurentius zur Compilatio III." *Traditio* 17 (1961): 542–43.

65. Gloss to introductory letter of 3 Comp. v. *seruus*, Paris, B.N. 3932, fol. 103r [Bamberg, Staatsbibl. can. 19, fol. 116v]: "Istud tamen in eo speciale credo quod eo stipulante potest adquiri actio cuilibet ecclesie, cum una sit ecclesia, ut di. xxi. Quamuis, et ipse sit pastor in solidum, aliis in partem sollicitudinis uocatis." First printed by Franz Gillmann, *Des Laurentius Hispanus Apparat zur Compilatio III. auf der Staatlichen Bibliothek zu Bamberg* (Mainz: 1935), 78. Jacobus de Albenga wrote a similar gloss to 5 Comp. 3.4.5 (X 3.5.34) v. *friuolam*, Cordoba, Bibl. de Cabildo 10, fol. 326v [Admont 22, fol. 244r]: "Si legatus posset, multo fortius dominus papa qui habet plenitudinem potestatis, ut ii. q.vi. Decreto et supra de usu pal. c.ii. lib. iii. Omnes ecclesie pleno iure pertinentur ad papam, ut ix. q.iii. c.penult. et ult. jac."

missions. Hostiensis recognized the importance of the church's corporate structure, and while reforming the statutes of the bishopric of Grasse in 1244, he seems to have given the cathedral chapter a more important role in the administration of diocesan affairs. He finished his commentary on the Decretals of Gregory IX after renouncing his office because of illness in 1270. The canonist died in 1271.[66]

John Watt has collected seventy-one passages in which Hostiensis discussed "plenitudo potestatis."[67] Hostiensis' glosses contrast markedly with statements of Innocent III and the earlier canonists in that they do not describe papal authority in highly rhetorical and exaggerated language. Like the other canonists, Hostiensis was not attracted to Innocent III's biblical exegesis and metaphors. Further, he did not explore or develop a theory of jurisdiction in the church on the basis of "plenitudo potestatis." He never wrote that episcopal authority was delegated by the pope from his "plenitudo potestatis." What is quite remarkable about Hostiensis' glosses is the sharing of authority that he granted to the cardinals, another example of his reliance on corporate theory to describe legal relationships within the church.

Hostiensis did substitute precise definitions for the rhetoric of his predecessors. Laurentius Hispanus had written "[the pope] changes the nature of things by applying the essences of one thing to another . . . he can make iniquity from justice." Johannes Teutonicus added: "He makes something out of nothing."[68] Hostiensis summed up these papal powers by coining the term, "suppletio defectuum." As a part of his exercise of papal authority, the pope could correct a deficiency of fact or of law. This allowed him to remedy legal problems, errors, and procedural deficiencies.[69]

Hostiensis acknowledged his debt to Innocent III, whose letter was the source of the new term. Innocent had confirmed the election of Albert, the archbishop of Magdeburg, even though some of the electors had been excommunicates. Two canons of the cathedral chapter brought this irregularity to Innocent's attention. Innocent responded in his letter to the chapter and

---

66. On Hostiensis, see Charles Lefebvre, "Hostiensis," DDC 5:1211–27. Clarence Gallagher, *Canon Law and the Christian Community: The Role of Law in the Church According to the "Summa aurea" of Cardinal Hostiensis,* Analecta Gregoriana 208 (Rome: 1978). Gallagher provides a complete bibliography.

67. Watt, "Use of the Term 'Plenitudo potestatis' by Hostiensis," 162. In the paragraphs that follow, I am indebted to Watt's work.

68. See Chapter 1, nn. 14 and 37 for these texts and a discussion of them.

69. Hostiensis, X 1.36.1 v. *minus firmitatis, Commentaria* (Venice: 1581), 1: fol. 178v: "si forsan ibi posset notari in aliquo defectus facti vel iuris, nos supplemus totum ex certa scientia de plenitudine potestatis." Watt, "Use of the Term 'Plenitudo potestatis' by Hostiensis," 181, no. 37. See also no. 3, 9, 11, 26 in Watt's Appendix B.

clergy of Magdeburg that in spite of the irregularity, the election was still canonical. The pope had remedied any defect in the procedure from the fullness of his power (*supplentes de plenitudine potestatis, si quis in ea ex eo fuisset defectus*).[70]

With "suppletio defectuum" Hostiensis defined one element of the pope's fullness of power: the pope's authority to correct any judicial problem within the framework of the judicial system. In his later writings, he characterized "plenitudo potestatis" as the pope's right to transcend positive law and sometimes even natural or divine law. The pope exercised this transcendental authority when he gave dispensations for vows, particularly vows of marriage and religion, and for impediments to marriage and ecclesiastical promotion. The canonists described this attribute of the pope's "plenitudo potestatis" as being "supra ius," or "above the law."[71] Hostiensis listed a number of examples of this prerogative in his *Summa*.[72]

The pope could act "supra ius" in two different ways: he could abrogate positive law, or he could grant dispensations from the provisions of natural or divine law. For the second, Hostiensis introduced another distinction in his discussion of papal authority: that between the pope's ordinary power, "potestas ordinata," and his absolute power, "potestas absoluta." Again, the inspiration for Hostiensis' introduction of this dualism was Innocent's "divina auctoritas." Hostiensis not only drew out the implications of Innocent's thought, he also illustrated how the pope's divine authority could be used and what its limits were.

He illuminated the difference between these powers when he discussed nonconsummated marriages. Since a valid, consummated marriage rested on divine law, the pope, he thought, could only interpret it.[73] He could not legislate or render a judicial decision that would change or alter the validity of such a marriage. The pope might annul a consummated marriage because of an impediment, but he could not dissolve it simply because the parties wanted the marriage bond broken. If he did, he violated divine law.

A nonconsummated marriage was another matter. Commenting on a decretal in which Innocent III permitted a wife who had not yet consum-

---

70. Innocent III, IX 261, PL 215.1093–94, 4 Comp. 1.3.5 (X 1.6.39). Watt, "Use of the Term 'Plenitudo potestatis' by Hostiensis," 175.

71. See James Brundage, *Medieval Canon Law and the Crusader* (Madison-Milwaukee: 1969), 46–65; and Cheney, *Pope Innocent III and England*, 59–71.

72. Hostiensis, *Summa aurea* (Venice: 1586), cols. 319–22.

73. Hostiensis, X 3.32.7 v. *consummatum, Commentaria*, 2: fol. 118v: "Matrimonium vero consummatum sortitum effectum ex lege divina, et circa istud papa potest interpretari tantum."

mated her marriage to enter a monastery, Hostiensis wrote that Innocent rendered this decision from his ordinary power, since he did not dissolve the marriage, but "augmented the bond of love." The church could make statutes or do whatever it pleased in nonconsummated marriages.[74] Although his train of thought is not absolutely clear, Hostiensis seems to have allowed the pope to legislate in or dispense from nonconsummated marriages on the basis of his absolute power. The pope could permit a woman to enter a monastery after her marital vows with his ordinary power because he did not, in this case, dissolve the marriage. Most other actions the pope might take that touched a nonconsummated marriage would be justified by his absolute power. Hostiensis concluded that when the pope dissolved a nonconsummated marriage, he must always have cause.[75] He also cited the opinion of Mattheus Rubeus Orsinus, cardinal deacon of S. Maria in Porticu, who said that if one partner of a nonconsummated marriage wished to enter a monastery and the other was unwilling, the pope could dissolve the marriage and permit passage to the monastic life. The partner who remained outside of the monastery could even contract a second marriage.[76] "What were the origins of such great authority?" asked Hostiensis. His answer was the same as Innocent III's. He cited *Quanto personam* and two other decretals in which Innocent had established the pope's right to exercise the office of God on earth.[77]

---

74. Ibid.: "Papa circa non consummatum matrimonium hanc constitutionem facere etiam de potestate ordinata. Et est ratio: quia cum per tale matrimonium charitas, que consistit in spiritu inter Deum et iustam animam tantum representetur, supra de bigam. Debitum. Nihil absurdum sequitur, si talis possit religionem intrare, quia non dissolvitur, sed potius augetur per hoc vinculum charitatis. . . . Vnde et circa matrimonium non consummatum potest ecclesia interpretari et statuere quicquid placet, dum tamen iusta causa subsit.

75. Ibid: "Hac etiam ratione considerata, possent sponsi de praesenti ante carnis copulam authoritate papae adinvicem absolvere, sicut legitur in sponsalibus de futuro . . . et potest reddi ratio: quia ante carnis copulam utroque consentiente in dissensu contrarius actus congruus intervenire potest, arg. infra de reg. iur. Omnis res, licet altero invito hoc non posset. . . . Sed post carnis copulam hoc non posset fieri, quia nec actus contrarius congruus intervenire posset, arg. ff. de pact. Ab emptione. Hoc autem intelligo de potestate absoluta, non de potestate ordinata, nisi alia causa subesset; non enim fit quod hic statuitur sine causa." Cf. Watt, "Use of the Term 'Plenitudo potestatis' by Hostiensis," 184.

76. Hostiensis, loc. cit.: "Statuere potuit et hoc, quod coniunx ante carnis copulam etiam invito consorte posset religionem intrare, et alius in seculo remanens cum alia contrahere, impedimento hoc non obstante. Et hanc rationem reddidit mihi dominus Matthaeus sanctae Mariae in Porticu diaconus cardinalis." Matthaeus Rubeus Ursinus, cardinal deacon of S. Maria in Porticu (1262–1305), Conrad Eubel, *Hierarchia catholica medii aevi* (Regensburg: 1913), 1:51.

77. Hostiensis, loc. cit.: "Et si quaeras unde procedit tanta potestas ecclesiae, vide quod legi. et no. supra de translat. episcop. cap. i. respon. i. et cap. ii. et iii. [Quanto personam]."

Hostiensis refined Innocent III's conception of the divine foundation of papal authority to exercise certain prerogatives by creating "potestas ordinata" based on decretals and canons of the church, positive law, and "potestas absoluta" based on the pope's office of vicar of Christ. It is clear, however, from a number of Hostiensis' glosses that he did not think the pope's "potestas absoluta" could be exercised arbitrarily or "sine causa." No one could judge the pope, but God would exact his vengeance if the pope acted arbitrarily or irresponsibly.[78] In the gloss on nonconsummated marriages we have been discussing, he remarked:

When a marriage has not been consummated, we do not offend God. We can legislate concerning such marriages whatever we please from our "potestas absoluta." That is from our "plenitudo potestatis." This is true. But it is not proper that the reins be loosed too much in this case. It is not advisable.[79]

Hostiensis identified the pope's "potestas absoluta" with his "plenitudo potestatis." In context, the gloss argues that the pope's "potestas ordinata" represents the pope's human authority, "potestas absoluta" his divine.

While adopting Innocent III's view that the pope could exercise certain prerogatives because he had divine authority, Hostiensis carried this idea one step further. Innocent and the earlier canonists had not made a distinction between the pope's divine and ordinary authority. Hostiensis himself did not do so in his early writings; rather, the distinction seems to have been a late development of his thought. In his *Summa aurea* and the first two books of his Commentary on the Decretals of Gregory IX, he did not equate "plenitudo potestatis" and "potestas absoluta," and did not even mention "potestas absoluta." In the last three books of his Commentary, however, he embraced Innocent's argument that in certain cases the pope was empowered to act only because he had divine authority, and he called this extraordinary power "potestas absoluta."

His most extensive discussion of papal absolute power was in book three of his Commentary, in which he discussed the pope's authority to permit a monk to leave his monastery. The question he posed was whether the pope could grant a monk the right to own property or to marry. He

---

78. See Watt, "Use of the Term 'Plenitudo potestatis' by Hostiensis," no. 7, 25, 32, 48, pp. 178–84.

79. Hostiensis, loc. cit. [Vat. lat. 1446, fol. 114v]: "Vbi ergo deest coniunctio corporum nihil statuimus contra Deum. Et ideo circa tale matrimonium possumus statuere quicquid placet de potestate nostra absoluta, idest de plenitudine potestatis, quod et verum est. Sed non expedit quod in hoc casu nimis laxet habenas, nec et tutum est." [Also collated with Vat. lat. 2546, fol. ci. verso]. Also see his gloss to X 5.31.8 v. *ita*, discussed below.

concluded that the pope could grant such a dispensation if there was cause. If not, both the pope and the recipient of the dispensation sinned.[80]

Hostiensis illustrated his thought with several concrete cases. If the pope granted a dispensation to a monk in which he gave him permission to marry, and if there was no cause or necessity for the dispensation, could such a dispensation be valid? In his solution, Hostiensis established limits for the pope's "potestas absoluta." If the monk's wife thought the dispensation was valid, he wrote, then the marriage was licit. However, the monk sinned every time he asked his wife for the conjugal debt. Hostiensis seems to have assumed that the monk would have known he had received a dispensation without good reason. On the other hand, if the pope granted a dispensation to a monk to own property without cause, the dispensation itself was invalid. The distinction that Hostiensis made between the two cases was that the marriage was licit because, if not, the monk's wife, an innocent party in the affair, would have been injured. The second dispensation injured or prejudiced no one except the monk who had received it. The dispensation could, therefore, be invalidated.[81] Although these cases were certainly not drawn from life, Hostiensis illustrated two commonplaces of medieval political thought: reason must inform all legal actions and a judicial decision should not harm a third party. Princes and the pope were bound by the same rules.

An important practical question remained. How could one know whether a dispensation of the pope made without cause was valid or not? Hostiensis' answer drew on a distinction that the canonists had long made between positive law and the general state of the church.[82] As part of his explanation, he wrote:

---

80. Hostiensis, X 3.35.6 [Cum ad monasterium] v. *nec summus pontifex*, fol. 134r: ' nisi ex causa, quamvis enim papa dispensare possit, si tamen iusta causa dispensationis non subsit, peccat, et papa dispensans, necnon et ille cum quo dispensatur."

81. Ibid.: "Sed quid si dispenset papa cum monacho in casu, in quo dispensandum non esset, puta quod uxorem ducat, nec est necessitas, vel utilitas dispensandi? Respondeo si mulier quam ducit dispensationem factam credit bonam et licitam, tenet matrimonium et tenetur monachus reddere debitum, sed ipsum sine peccato exigere non potest. Si vero concederet papa alicui monacho quod haberet proprium et causa non subesset, omnino dispensatio nulla esset, nec ipsum excusaret. Ratio diversitatis haec est: quia ex dispensatione habendi proprium nemini praeiudicatur, nec alicui prodest nec obest nisi illi cum quo dispensatur. Vnde ibi nisi subsit utilitas, non valet dispensatio. Secus autem est in matrimonio ubi dispensatio prodest vel praeiudicat alii, scilicet coniugi."

82. See Gaines Post, "Copyists' Errors and the Problem of Papal Dispensations 'Contra statutum generale ecclesiae' or 'Contra statum generalem ecclesiae' According to the Decretists and Decretalists circa 1150–1234," SG 9 (Bologna: 1966), 359–405. J. Hackett, "State of the Church: A Concept of the Medieval Canonists," *The Jurist* 23 (1963): 259–90.

Some say, and perhaps with reason, that in those matters which are contrary to a tacit or expressed vow or contrary to the Gospels, a papal dispensation is not valid unless made with cause. The same can be understood if he dispenses from the general state [or statute] of the Church. This is not true in those dispensations from positive law. . . . In these matters, only the will of the dispenser is necessary.[83]

If the pope exercised his absolute power, "ex causa," "pro utilitate," or "pro necessitate," he did not sin. Rather, he acted on divine authority, the highest expression of his "plenitudo potestatis." If he acted without cause, he sinned, and under certain circumstances his act was invalid.

The pope's absolute power had another limit; he could not grant dispensations indiscriminately. The pope might legitimately act in a single case, but he could never make sweeping changes contrary to the state of the church: he could not decree that all monks could marry.[84] "The Apostolic See does not grant dispensations easily," Hostiensis wrote in another gloss, and he clearly meant that the pope should not grant frivolous dispensations.[85]

One last example further highlights Hostiensis' thought. When he discussed the pope's authority to grant dispensations from vows, he noted that the pope could permit a Saracen king of great power and eminence to marry a certain nun whom he desired if the king was prepared to convert to Christianity and bring his entire kingdom with him into the Christian fold.[86]

In solving this particular problem, Hostiensis faced several difficulties. A dispensation from the vow of chastity could be granted for only the most serious reasons. Hostiensis observed that there were some canonists who felt that the pope did not have this authority. They argued that no reason could

---

83. Hostiensis, X 3.35.6 v. *nec summus pontifex*, fol. 134r: "Dicunt etiam quidam, et forte non male, quod sicut in his quae sunt contra votum tacitum vel expressum, vel contra evangelium, non prodest papae dispensatio, nisi ex causa facta. Idem intelligendum est, si dispenset in his que sunt contra statutum ecclesiae generale, arg. xxiiii. q.i. Memor sum [c. 10] et c. Si ea destruerem [C. 25 q. 2 c. 4]. Hoc tamen non est verum in his dispensationibus quae fiunt tantum contra ius positivum. . . . In his enim dispensationibus sufficit sola voluntas dispensatoris etiam sine causa."

84. It was a common idea that the pope might act in a single case, but not in many; see Chapter 4, pp. 152–53.

85. Hostiensis, X 1.20.2 v. *tibi ex maxima*, fol. 121r: "Pro certo teneas quod cum nato de adulterino, vel incestuoso vel monchali coitu, nisi ad religionem transeat, sedes apostolica de facili non dispensat."

86. Hostiensis, X 3.34.1 v. *et Deo*, fol. 124v: 'Argum. ergo expressum, quod si aliquis Rex Saracenorum magnae potentiae cum toto regno suo paratus sit baptizari et converti ad dominum dummodo papa det sibi in uxorem talem sanctimonialem, quamvis velatam et Deo consecratam, quod dominus papa in hoc casu poterit dispensare."

be grave enough to break a vow of chastity. Such vows could be broken only if they could be converted into an "equal good," and these canonists thought nothing could be equal to the "good" of chastity in the eyes of God. The question was not new and had been debated in the schools since the twelfth century.[87]

In spite of earlier canonistic opinion, Hostiensis decided that the pope could give the nun to the king of the Saracens and create from their match a licit marriage. To those who argued that chastity was the highest possible state of perfection, he replied that it was more useful to the church of God, to the common good (*res publica*), and to God for a woman to lose her virginity in order to save ten, possibly a hundred thousand souls. The Lord himself became flesh to save thousands. Christ considered public, not private utility, and so should the nun. Quoting St. Ambrose, Hostiensis asked, "If the son of God paid tribute, who are you who dares not pay?"[88] He then asked more rhetorically:

What professor would be so presumptuous that he would try to take away the power—rather more to disparage papal fullness of power—of the vicar of Christ from giving both his own and another's soul under the pretext of piety? When they

---

87. Brundage, *Medieval Canon Law,* 44–50, and the older literature cited there. On the papal right of dispensation from natural law, see J. de Brys, *De dispensatione in iure canonico praesertim apud decretistas et decretalistas usque ad medium saeculum decimum quartum* (Bruges: 1925), 201–3, 221–26. Also Stephan Kuttner, "Pope Lucius III and the Bigamous Archbishop of Palermo," *Medieval Studies Presented to Aubrey Gwynn* (Dublin: 1961), 409–54, now reprinted in *The History of Ideas and Doctrines of Canon Law in the Middle Ages* (London: 1980). For the lawyers' views on natural law, see Rudolf Weigand, *Die Naturrechtslehre der Legisten und Dekretisten von Irnerius bis Accursius und von Gratian bis Johannes Teutonicus* (Munich: 1968); and Gabriel Le Bras, Charles Lefebvre, and J. Rambaud, *L'Age classique 1140–1378: Sources et théorie du droit.* Histoire du droit et des institutions de l'Eglise en Occident 7 (Paris: 1965), 352–557.

88. Hostiensis, X 3.34.1 v. *et Deo,* fol. 124v: "Sed nec obstat, quod dicunt, quod eque bonum, vel maius reperiri non potest, nam per exemplum praemissum, ubi non agitur de salute unius animae tantum, sed plurium, et per hoc quod hic dicitur minus bene dicere convincuntur: utilius siquidem est ecclesiae Dei, et reipublicae et Deo magis acceptum, quod virgo, quamvis Deo dedicata, salvet animam suam in matrimonio vivens caste, xxxi. di. Nicena [c. 12] et ad salvandum secum perducat forsan plusquam decem, vel centum milia animarum . . . quod evidenter dominus comprobavit quando incarnari voluit, et animam suam, quae nec peccaverat pro multis, immo pro omnibus peccatoribus dare, non suam privatam utilitatem in hoc considerans, sed publicam et communem. Si ergo dominus ob multorum salutem animam suam dedit, quis tu tantus qui ex hac causa animam tuam dare negas? Ad hoc pertinet quod dicit Ambr. 'Si filius Dei censum solvit quis tu tantus, qui putas non solvendum,' xi. q.i. Magnum [c. 28]."

are given with cause, the pope's dispensations and his actions are not those of man, but of God, as can be read and noted in the chapters under the title about the translation of bishops.[89]

Here Hostiensis did not call this authority of the pope "potestas absoluta," but it is undoubtedly what he meant. In such glosses, Hostiensis took Innocent III's conceit that the pope could act on divine authority and shaped a precise, juridical definition of when and under which circumstances the pope could exercise his absolute power.

Although Hostiensis granted great authority to the pope in the church, he circumscribed the pope's power by the unwritten constitution of the church and by a deep understanding of "medieval constitutionalism." He had a strong sense of the corporate structure of the church. The idea of the church as a body could be extended in two directions. Innocent III had used the metaphor to emphasize the authority of the head. Hostiensis emphasized the necessity and the desirability of the head and the body working together. His conception of the church as a corporate body centered on the pope and the cardinals—not on the pope and bishops. He described the cardinals as being part of the pope's "body" and made it plain in a number of glosses that the pope should always consult the college of cardinals in all important matters.[90] Even when the pope acted on his "potestas absoluta," he should proceed with the cardinals' participation:

But it is not customary for the pope to act without the counsel [*consilium*] of his brothers, i.e. the cardinals, in those cases specially reserved to the pope as in the

---

89. Ibid.: "Immo quis tam praesumptuous magister, qui non solum animam suam dandi, sed etiam alienam sub quodam pallio pietatis summo pontifici Christi vicario conatur subtrahere potestatem, quinimmo et detrahere plenitudinem potestatis, actus nempe et dispensationes summi pontificis ex causa facti non sunt hominis sed Dei, ut patet in eo quod leg. et not. supra de translat. episcop. cap. ii. et iii. [Quanto personam]."

90. Brian Tierney and John Watt have thoroughly explored Hostiensis' thought on the relationship of the college of cardinals and the pope. They differ about whether Hostiensis thought that the pope was obligated to legislate with the cardinals. See Watt, "The Constitutional Law of the College of Cardinals: Hostiensis to Johannes Andreae," *Mediaeval Studies* 23 (1971): 127–57; Tierney, "Hostiensis and Collegiality," *Proceedings of the Fourth International Congress of Medieval Canon Law*, ed. Stephan Kuttner, MIC, Series C, 5 (Città del Vaticano: 1976) 401–9; Watt, "Hostiensis on *Per venerabilem*: The Role of the College of Cardinals," *Authority and Power: Studies on Medieval Law and Government Presented to Walter Ullmann*, ed. Brian Tierney and Peter Linehan (Cambridge: 1980), 99–113. See also Giuseppe Alberigo, *Cardinalato e collegialità: Studi sull'ecclesiologia tra l'XI e il XIV secolo* (Firenze: 1969), 52–109.

foregoing verses. He cannot do anything in this matter [to unite two bishoprics or to make one bishop subject to another, the topic of the decretal upon which he was commenting] from his ordinary power, as in *Novit*. Rather he acts from his absolute power, as in *Proposuit*.[91]

The two references in this gloss help to explain the canonist's thought. In his gloss to *Novit*, Hostiensis wrote that a bishop and his chapter were one body; the bishop should never do anything important without the counsel (*consilium*) of his chapter.[92] The second reference to *Proposuit*, on which he based his assertion of "potestas absoluta," is not quite as clear. He made two points in his commentary to the decretal. First, the pope was above positive law, even though he should depart from it only rarely. Second, the pope may grant dispensations in many cases from "the Apostle, the Old Testament, a vow, or an oath." He could not grant a dispensation from the "status ecclesiae," and his dispensations could never injure the faith.[93] In the context of his thought, Hostiensis' meaning is fairly straightforward. However, his gloss is a bit muddled because he misplaced the reference to *Novit* slightly. It should have come after "verses." *Proposuit* then defines the type of authority the pope and the cardinals exercise together.

Hostiensis' "potestas absoluta" had a long and distinguished career in political thought. It was adopted by theologians and later by secular monarchs.[94] In the process of transmission, its meaning changed, but the constitutional elements that were so important in Hostiensis' glosses were never completely lost. In the sixteenth century when theorists wrote of "absolute

---

91. Hostiensis, X 5.31.8 v. *ita,* 2: fol. 72v: "Set nec papa haec, vel alios casus sibi specialiter reservatos, ut in praemissis versibus, consuevit expedire sine consilio fratrum suorum, idest cardinalium. Nec istud potest facere de potestate ordinaria, arg. supra de his quae fiunt a praelat. Novit [X 3.10.4] licet secus sit de absoluta, supra de concess. praeben. Proposuit [X 3.8.4]."

92. Hostiensis, X 3.10.4 v. *Novit,* fol. 45r: "Cum episcopus et capitulum unum corpus sint, inhonestum est, quod episcopus fratres despiciat et extraneorum consilio utatur. Ideo in institutionibus hoc fieri prohibetur." v. *caput:* "unde quia unum corpus estis, nec aliquid magnum debetis facere sine consilio." v. *sine consilio:* "Et idem forte dicendum, scilicet consensum canonicorum requirendum esse, ubicumque eorum interest."

93. Hostiensis, X 3.8.4 v. *supra ius* and v. *dispensare,* fol. 35r.

94. See Francis Oakley, "Jacobean Political Theology: The Absolute and Ordinary Powers of the King," *Journal of the History of Ideas* 29 (1968): 323–46; John Marrone, "The Absolute and the Ordained Powers of the Pope: An Unedited Text of Henry of Ghent," *Mediaeval Studies* 36 (1974): 7–27. According to my reading of Henry of Ghent's text, Henry has adopted Hostiensis' distinction for the papal exercise of "potestas absoluta": he can exercise absolute power without sin if he has acted "cum causa"; an act can be sinful, but licit, or an act may be sinful and not licit.

power," they were not insensitive to earlier limitations on the right of a monarch to violate the law with impunity.[95]

Absolute power had its first signs of life in the claims of Innocent III in *Quanto personam*. The political theorists of the sixteenth century adopted the concept and brought it to maturity. Hostiensis stood between the pope and the theorists and acted as midwife. He had great respect for the pope's conception of papal authority and found inspiration in Innocent's vision. Indeed, this is not the only example we have of his having given Innocent's thought precision.[96]

Although Hostiensis founded much of his thought on Innocent III's decretals, their views of papal monarchy differed in significant ways. Innocent exalted papal power, nurtured it, but never limited papal prerogatives or authority. He attempted to develop a coherent doctrine of papal monarchy through which the pope's unique position in the ecclesiastical hierarchy could be sustained and strengthened. On the other hand, Hostiensis not only emphasized the corporate structure of the church and the pope's obligation to govern with the consent of the cardinals, he also set limits on papal "potestas absoluta." When the pope exercised his ordinary power, he was bound by custom, positive law, and the unwritten constitution of the church. As for the pope's absolute power, Hostiensis always emphasized that this was an extraordinary, seldom-used power. Although the pope could exercise the office of God on earth, he must do so rarely and only with great care. Most important, Hostiensis did not simply equate "potestas absoluta" with arbitrary authority. "Potestas absoluta" could be used in matters touching the sacraments, but could never be used to justify the complete subjugation of lesser prelates to the pope.

By the end of the thirteenth century, papal monarchy had reached full maturity. Chroniclers, theologians, canonists, and poets described papal authority and papal titles in very similar ways. In large part, this was because Innocent III's views had become deeply entrenched in canonistic and theological thought. A vocabulary of power had been established. Aegidius de Fuscarariis, the first lay canonist to teach at Bologna, described (perhaps with a touch of irony in his words) how it felt to appear before the pope:

If your lips tremble and your face blanches, if you stutter and your body shakes, no one should be surprised. I who will speak rise in the presence of him who has the

---

95. Oakley, "Jacobean Political Theology," 335–46. For the use of "potestas absoluta" by medieval theologians beginning with Abelard, see ibid., 332–35.

96. For another striking example of Hostiensis' taking a basic idea of Innocent's and giving it a legal foundation, see Pennington, "Innocent III's Views," 55, 60.

power of loosing and binding—whom the temporal powers of the earth obey. There is no one who dares say to him: why do you do this?[97]

Aegidius' words would have certainly pleased Innocent III. They sum up a century's development of the rhetoric of papal monarchy.

97. Aegidius de Fuscarariis, *Ordo iudiciarius*, ed. Ludwig Wahrmund, Quellen zur Geschichte des römisch-kanonischen Prozesses im Mittelalter 3.1 (Innsbruck: 1916), 260: "Si livent labia, si pallet facies, si lingua balbutit et membra quaelibet contremescunt, nullus debet admiratione moveri, quia in illius praesentia locuturus assurgo, qui ligandi et solvendi obtinet potestatem, cui oboediunt imperia et regna terrarum, et nemo est, qui audeat dicere: cur ita facis."

CHAPTER THREE · EPISCOPAL TRANSLATIONS, RENUNCIATIONS, AND DEPOSITIONS: INNOCENT III, MASTER HUGUCCIO, AND HOSTIENSIS

Although the language with which the canonists described the authority of the pope had fully matured by the end of the thirteenth century, the polemicists of the fourteenth century continued to squabble over the breadth of papal authority with remarkable vigor and endurance. The issue of papal authority remained a central problem of political theory, and almost every fourteenth-century figure of any note wrote about papal authority at some time during his career.

In this and the next two chapters, we shall survey the extent to which the canonists permitted the pope to interfere in episcopal affairs. First, we shall examine the intellectual background that led to Innocent III's decretal *Quanto personam,* and then we shall outline Innocent's doctrine of the papal supervision of episcopal translations, depositions, and renunciations and the thirteenth-century canonists' reception of it.

The translation of bishops was a controversial issue in the early church. Conciliar statutes of the fourth and fifth centuries forbade the translation of bishops, and it is not clear whether there could be a dispensation from these rules. By the end of the fifth century, however, episcopal synods had begun to authorize translations. During the early Middle Ages, the archbishop and his suffragans often arranged for the translation, deposition, and abdication of bishops in a synod. This was especially true north of the Alps. In 394 the Council of Constantinople decreed that a provincial council was the appropriate judicial body to hear episcopal cases. Papal involvement in these matters came slowly. A first step was taken at the Council of Sardica in 343. The council permitted sentences of deposition to be appealed to the pope for final hearing. A few texts in early collections of canon law stated that bishops should never be judged without consulting the pope, but in practice, these canons were often ignored.[1]

By the twelfth century, the judgment of bishops had generally become a papal prerogative, but tensions between old and new practices remained. In 1157, Bishop Hilary of Chichester argued his bishopric's important case against Battle Abbey before the young king, Henry II. He stood before Henry and his barons disputing the right of the king to grant ecclesiastical exemptions by royal charter. This was a dangerous argument to make in the presence of a king who was sensitive to any infringement of royal prerogative. Hilary pointed out that since no one could judge a bishop save the pope, no one, not even the king, could grant ecclesiastical privileges. Henry was amused by the first part of Hilary's argument: "Very true, a bishop may not be deposed. But with a good push like this he could be ejected."[2] To the second part, he exploded in anger. Perhaps the king could not judge bishops, but he certainly could grant royal privileges to churches if he wished. His predecessors had bestowed many privileges on monasteries, and he would not concede that he no longer had this prerogative.

In the eleventh and twelfth centuries, papal involvement in episcopal translations was sporadic.[3] Archbishop Lanfranc of Canterbury held a council of English bishops in 1074. The council issued a canon by which three bishops were translated: Hermann from Sherbourne to Salisbury, Stigand from Selsey to Chichester, and Peter from Lichfield to Chester. This action

---

1. Jean Gaudemet, *L'église dans l'empire Romain (IVe–Ve siècles)*, Histoire du droit et des institutions de l'église en Occident 3 (Paris: 1958), 365–66. On the Council of Sardica in general and translations in the early church, see H. Hess, *The Canons of the Council of Sardica A.D. 343: A Landmark in the Early Development of Canon Law* (Oxford: 1958), 71–89. Cheney, *Pope Innocent III and England*, 71–79, discusses earlier customs of deposing and translating bishops.

2. *The Chronicle of Battle Abbey*, ed. and trans. Eleanor Searle (Oxford: 1980), 186–87: " 'Nullus episcopus, nulla persona ecclesiastica absque eius [i.e., papae] iudicio uel permissione a sede ecclesiastica deponi possit.' Ad hec rex protensis manibus, 'Verissimum est,' ait, 'episcopum non posse deponi, sed ita,' manibus pulsus protensis, 'poterit expelli.' "

3. Gaudemet, *L'église dans l'empire*, 356–63. L. Ober, "Die Translation der Bischöfe im Altertum," AKKR 88 (1908): 209–29, 441–65, 625–48; and 89 (1909): 3–33. Gaudemet, *Le gouvernement de l'église*, 107–12.

was taken "by the generosity of the king and the authority of the synod."[4] Nonetheless, local churches sought permission for translations more commonly in the eleventh and twelfth centuries than before.

Official papal decrees or pronouncements touching translations were rare. The issue was not a matter of great importance. Pope Gregory VII stated in the *Dictatus papae* that only the pope could depose a bishop, but he did not reserve the translation of bishops to papal authority; nor did he maintain that bishops who wished to abdicate their offices came under the special purview of the papacy.[5] As we saw in Chapter 1, Innocent III vigorously asserted the pope's prerogatives to approve and sanction episcopal translations, but he also moved just as energetically to prevent any bishop from renouncing his office or from being deposed without prior papal permission. In a letter to Bernard of Balbi, the bishop of Faenza, written in August 1198, Innocent forcefully described the pope's prerogatives:

Although it might seem that a pope might not dissolve a spiritual marriage—that is a marriage of a bishop and his church—nevertheless from customary usage, which is the best interpreter of law and the sacred canons, the pope has full power [*plena potestas*] in this matter and may dissolve a spiritual marriage through the abdication, deposition, and translation of a bishop. These powers are reserved to the Apostolic See. There should be no doubt about these matters, since the pope acts in these affairs through divine rather than human authority, for he is called not the vicar of man, but the vicar of the one true God. Although we are the successors of the prince of the apostles, we are not Peter's, or any apostle's, or any man's vicars, but we are the vicars of Jesus Christ. Therefore, one whom God, not man, has joined together spiritually, the vicar of man does not sunder, but the vicar of God; the vicar of God separates a bishop from his church, as when we have sometimes removed bishops from their sees through abdication, deposition, and translation. These three are justly

---

4. *The Letters of Lanfranc Archbishop of Canterbury*, ed. and trans. Helen Clover and Margaret Gibson (Oxford 1979), 76–77, also Gibson's introduction, 2–3. The text reads: "Concessum est regia munificentia et sinodali auctoritate." This decree would not, of course, preclude later papal approval. See also Margaret Gibson, *Lanfranc of Bec* (Oxford: 1978), 144.

5. *Dictatus papae* 3,13,25. *Das Register Gregors VII.*, ed. Erich Caspar, MGH Epistolae selectae (Berlin: 1920), 2.1: 201–8: "III. Quod ille solus possit deponere episcopos vel reconciliare.... XIII. Quod illi liceat de sede ad sedem necessitate cogente episcopos transmutare.... XXV. Quod absque synodali conventu possit episcopos deponere et reconciliare." See Caspar's notes to XIII, pp. 204–5. The *Dictatus* of Avranches, however, stated that papal permission was necessary: 12. "Non mutantur de sede ad aliam sedem episcopi sine illius iudicio." On the disputed authorship of the *Dictatus* of Avranches, see Hubert Mordek, "*Proprie auctoritates apostolice sedis:* Ein zweiter Dictatus papae Gregors VII.?" DA 28 (1972): 105–32, at 115 for text, and the response of Friedrich Kempf, "Ein zweiter Dictatus papae? Ein Beitrag zum Depositionsanspruch Gregors VII." *Archivum Historiae Pontificiae* 13 (1975): 119–39.

reserved, as we have shown, to the Roman pontiff, who retained for himself fullness of power, although he has called other bishops to a share of responsibility.[6]

With language reminiscent of *Quanto personam*, Innocent thus established the theoretical basis of papal prerogatives. He had come to the papal throne with a clear conception of the papal prerogatives he wished to accentuate. His vision of the papal office danced clearly before him, and litigants at the papal court soon learned that although Innocent might tolerate and forgive many things, he would not overlook any instance in which papal rights were ignored.[7] Typically, Innocent established his claims in this letter on the rights of the pope's office and the origins of that office, not on the grounds that bishops derived their jurisdiction from the pope. God, not man or historical precedent, was the source of papal rights. As the vicar of God, the pope could dissolve the bond between a bishop and his church by divine authority. Of course, if Innocent assumed episcopal authority was delegated, divine authority would not have been necessary. The pope could have acted in his own right.

The surviving decretals of Innocent's twelfth-century predecessors do not display the same forceful vision of papal monarchy. As historians have recognized for some time, Innocent was imaginative and innovative in creating a vocabulary of papal authority.[8] The importance of Innocent's thought becomes clear when one examines the works of the canonists who wrote in the last half of the twelfth century.

---

6. Innocent III, Register I, 472–74, no. 326. (PL 214.291): "Licet autem videri posset ex hiis, quod summus pontifex spirituale matrimonium—episcopi scilicet et ecclesie—separare non possit, cum tamen ex consuetudine, que est obtima legum interpres, et sacris canonibus habeatur, quod per cessionem, depositionem et translationem, que soli sunt sedi apostolice reservata, super hoc plenam habeat potestatem: sane intelligentibus id nullum dubitationis scrupulum generabit, cum non humana sed divina fiat auctoritate, quod in hac parte per summum pontificem adimpletur, qui non hominis puri, sed veri Dei vere vicarius appellatur. Nam quamvis simus apostolorum principis successores, non tamen eius aut alicuius apostoli vel hominis, sed ipsius sumus vicarii Jesu Christi. Unde quos Deus spirituali coniunctione ligavit, non homo, quia non vicarius hominis, sed Deus, quia Dei vicarius separat, cum episcopos a suis sedibus per eorum cessionem, depositionem et translationem aliquando removemus. Que tria ex hac, quam ostendimus, ratione merito sunt Romano tantum pontifici reservata; qui, licet alios episcopos vocaverit in partem sollicitudinis, sibi tamen retinuit plenitudinem potestatis."

7. Cheney's discussion of the case in which the monks of the cathedral chapter of Christ Church, Canterbury, opposed the attempt of Archbishop Baldwin to establish a collegiate church at Lambeth is particularly instructive (*Pope Innocent III and England*, 208–20).

8. Watt, *Theory of Papal Monarchy*, 85; Pennington, "Pope Innocent III's Views," 60–61.

Gratian stressed the supreme legislative authority of the pope, his primacy in all judicial matters, but said little in his *dicta* about the panoply of conflicting texts he included in his collection that touched upon the judgment of bishops.[9] Despite Gratian's failure to underline the pope's right to judge bishops in his Decretum, twelfth-century kings already acknowledged the pope's prerogatives in episcopal trials. Since the pope could not participate personally in the judgment of bishops, papal legates acted as the pope's representatives. Kings found this system convenient. When Frederick Barbarossa wished to rid himself of Henry, archbishop of Mainz, for example, he acted through two cardinals sent by Pope Eugenius III.[10] A number of Gratian's texts thus reflected practices of earlier centuries when the pope did not concern himself with every episcopal deposition or translation. At that time, these matters were left in the hands of the primate, archbishops, and bishops of a province acting together in episcopal synod.[11]

Gratian did not bring all his conflicting texts into accord, but he did explain why ecclesiastical judicial practice had sometimes deviated from canonical theory. He thought that a bishop should normally be judged with the pope's knowledge and permission, but he acknowledged that there were many cases in which bishops had been condemned without papal approbation. He explained these chapters of the Decretum as special cases that had been permitted in order to maintain peace in the church.[12]

The chapters that seemed to allow the judgment of bishops by archbishops, primates, and other prelates did not attract much attention from the canonists who immediately followed Gratian. Perhaps they were satisfied with Gratian's explanation. Stephen of Tournai noted that now only the pope could depose a bishop; but in earlier times perhaps it had been possible

---

9. On Gratian's ecclesiology, see Stanley Chodorow, *Christian Political Theory and Church Politics in the Mid-Twelfth Century*, 178–86.

10. Otto of Freising, *Gesta Friderici I. imperatoris*, ed. Georg Waitz and B. von Simson, 3rd ed., MGH, Scriptores rerum Germanicarum in usum scholarum 46 (Hannover-Leipzig: 1912), 2.8: 110–11.

11. The most important chapters in Gratian in which bishops judge bishops are: C. 2 q. 1 c. 5 (Primates); C. 2 q. 4 c. 3 (Nullam); C. 2 q. 6 c. 11 (Decreto); C. 2 q. 6 c. 36 (Si episcopus accusatus); C. 2 q. 7 c. 44 (Lator); C. 6 q. 3 c. 2 (Scitote); C. 6 q. 3 c. 3 (Denique); C. 6 q. 4 c. 1, c. 2, c. 4 (Si quis episcopus [all three]).

12. C. 3 q. 6 p.c. 9: "Aliquando inconsulto Romano pontifice plerique episcoporum dampnati inveniuntur, et alii in eorum subrogati locum, quorum dampnationem et subrogationem pro bono pacis ex dispensatione tollerasse legitur ecclesia."

for primates to depose bishops.[13] Several canonists repeated Stephen's conjecture that practice in the church had changed.[14] Although metropolitans and primates had once judged bishops, all canonists now agreed that this practice was uncanonical.[15]

Early lawyers did not discuss the texts dealing with the trials and judgment of bishops systematically or completely. Gratian had scattered them in several different parts of the Decretum where he treated, in the main, questions of judicial procedure. By the very design of the Decretum, Gratian placed primary emphasis upon procedure and evidence, without dwelling upon papal primacy. In this respect, he differed from the canonists who composed their collections during the tumultuous eleventh century when the primacy of the Roman church was a crucial question.[16] Gratian was also not greatly interested in the juridical relationships of the ecclesiastical hierarchy; he accepted papal monarchy as an established fact. Consequently, he did not begin the Decretum with a discussion of the papal office, nor did he define the judicial prerogatives of the pope with any precision. As Benson has written, Gratian's "treatment of office was subtle and lucid," but he "failed to create a systematic terminology and conceptual scheme explaining the nature of ecclesiastical jurisdiction."[17] Gratian left the task to his successors at Bologna.

---

13. Stephen of Tournai, *Die Summa Über das Decretum Gratiani*, ed. Johann F. von Schulte (Giessen: 1891), 159 to C. 2 q. 1 c. 5 v. *non ante sententiam:* "suspensionis. Nam depositionis sententiam non potest in episcopum metropolitanus proferre sine sententia Romani pontificis. Vel dicere forte poteris, quia primates possunt, metropolitani non possunt episcopum deponere, quod de neutris concedo sine sententia domini papae. Aut forte dices, quia antiquitus poterant, modo non possunt."

14. *The Summa Parisiensis on the Decretum Gratiani*, ed. Terence P. McLaughlin (Toronto: 1952), 101 to C. 2 q. 1 c. 5; Rufinus, *Die Summa decretorum des magister Rufinus*, ed. Heinrich Singer (Paderborn: 1902), 285 to C. 6 q. 4: "Verumtamen hoc totum hodie dicimus antiquatum, cum finis cause episcopalis semper ad sedem apostolicam sit referendus."

15. E.g., *Summa 'Elegantius in iure divino seu Coloniensis'*, ed. Gérard Fransen and Stephan Kuttner, MIC, Series A, 1.2 (New York–Città del Vaticano: 1969–1978), 167–68.

16. The Collection in 74 Titles began with the rubric "De primatu Romane ecclesie"; Anselm of Lucca's *Collectio canonum* also began with a title devoted to Roman primacy. Gratian did not follow the organization of his Gregorian predecessors, and this lack of focus on hierarchical order resulted, I think, in a lack of clarity in his thought on jurisdictional matters. See Chodorow, *Christian Political Theory,* 186. For a discussion of the importance of Gregorian canonical collections for crystallizing ideas of papal primacy, see Ullmann, *The Growth of Papal Government*, 262–309. Of course, we cannot expect Gratian to have answered questions that his contemporaries did not ask, but which we wish they had.

17. Benson, *Bishop-Elect*, 55.

Master Huguccio and Papal Prerogatives

The first of Gratian's successors to grapple with the conflicting texts touching upon the judgment of bishops and to mold these texts into a system of thought was Huguccio of Pisa.[18] By creating a coherent doctrine of papal prerogatives, he anticipated and prepared the way for Innocent III's forceful assertions of papal rights. Although the story that Innocent studied with Huguccio at Bologna is without firm evidence, their conceptions of the papal office were quite similar, in spite of some important differences.[19]

I have mentioned Huguccio earlier, but he is so important for the development of law in the twelfth century that it is necessary to say a few words here about the man and his work. Huguccio taught at Bologna in the late twelfth century. Some time before 1191, he stopped working on a commentary on Gratian's *Decretum*, leaving it unfinished.[20] His work was of extraordinary quality and length. His *Summa* is without a doubt the most sophisticated commentary produced by any twelfth-century lawyer. Canonists continued to read and cite his opinions for three centuries after his death. Remarkably, copies of his *Summa* were still being made in the fifteenth century.[21]

In a gloss to a chapter taken from Pseudo-Isidore, Huguccio composed a long list of papal prerogatives that defined papal fullness of power. The chapter, attributed to Pope Damasus, stated that no one should presume to

---

18. The most detailed biographical sketch of Huguccio is Corrado Leonardi, "La vita e l'opera di Uguccione da Pisa, decretista," SG 4 (Bologna: 1956) 45–120. A study of his ideas of papal primacy can be found in M. Ríos Fernández, "El primado del romano pontífice." Other studies include L. Prosdocimi, "La 'Summa Decretorum' di Uguccione da Pisa: Studi preliminari per una edizione critica," SG 3 (Bologna: 1955), 350–74; Alfons Stickler, "Uguccio de Pise," DDC 7 (Paris: 1965) 1355–1362 contains a bibliography of works on Huguccio to 1961. Guiseppe Cremascoli, "Uguccione da Pisa: Saggio bibliografico," *Aevum* 42 (1968): 123–68. The most recent study of Huguccio's thought is Titus Lenherr, "Der Begriff 'executio' in der Summa Decretorum des Huguccio," AKKR 150 (1981): 5–44, 361–420.

19. For the problems with the evidence that Innocent studied with Huguccio, see Pennington, "The Legal Education of Pope Innocent III," 70–77, and "Pope Innocent III's Views," 51–53.

20. I intend to write a short study of the sources for Huguccio's life. It is not absolutely certain, in my mind, that we can identify the canonist and the grammarian who was bishop of Ferrara as the same person.

21. Leonardi, "La uita Uguccione da Pisa," 89–98, lists forty-three manuscripts, twenty of which he dates to the fourteenth century. However, Florence, Biblioteca Laurenziana Fesul. 125 and 126 is from the fifteenth century. Cosimo de Medici ordered it to be copied and his command is preserved in the inscription to the manuscript.

usurp matters granted solely to the Apostolic See. To the words "matters granted to this see," Huguccio wrote:

These are numerous: the deposition of bishops . . . the abdication of bishops . . . the translation of bishops . . . the exemption of bishops from the power of another . . . the restitution of a bishop [to his see].[22]

Huguccio listed a number of other papal prerogatives that did not directly touch episcopal jurisdiction.[23] Later canonists continued to expand this list until, in the mid-thirteenth century, Hostiensis listed sixty matters in which papal authority must be brought to bear.[24]

Noting that some chapters in the Decretum permitted a synod of bishops to bring a wayward bishop to trial, Gratian and the early canonists resorted to historical explanations to unify their texts. A few earlier canonists had conjectured that ecclesiastical law had been different in the early Middle Ages. They were essentially correct. However, this explanation did not satisfy Huguccio.

Huguccio turned to another text taken from Pseudo-Isidore stating that the apostles and their successors had decided that no bishop could be judged without the authority of the Apostolic See. For Huguccio this decretal proved that the pope's prerogative to try bishops dated from apostolic times; thus all chapters of the Decretum that seemed to contradict the pope's sole right to hear episcopal cases would have to be interpreted through this decretal:

The solution of the previously stated contrary view is reproved here, namely that it was once permitted, but that it is not now licit. From this letter, however, one may gather that from the times of the apostles this was true, namely that primates and metropolitans could investigate the case of a bishop, receive testimony, examine the

---

22. D. 17 c. 3 (Huic sedi) v. *concessa*, Admont 7 fol. 19r–19v [Klosterneuburg 89, fol. 20r]: "Hec autem multa sunt: scilicet episcoporum depositio, ut iii. q.vi. Quamvis [c. 7]; episcoporum abrenunciatio, ut vi. q.iii. Denique [c. 3]; episcoporum mutatio, ut vii. q.i. Mutationes [c. 34]; episcoporum exemptio a potestate alterius, ut xvi. q.i. Frater noster [c. 52]; episcoporum restitutio, ut ii. q.vi. Ideo [c. 17]." On this gloss see Watt, *Theory of Papal Monarchy*, 84.

23. Loc. cit.: "Questio fidei, ut xxiiii. q.i. Quotiens [c. 12]; Dispensatio in consanguinitate uel affinitate, ut xxxv. q.viii. De gradibus [c. 1]. Difficultas negotii et iudicum dissensio, ut infra c. Multis [c. 5]. et di. xii. Preceptis [c. 2]. Restitutio hereticorum, cognitio enormium, ut xii. q.ii. De uiro [c. 17]. Absolutio sacrilegorum qui uiolentas manus mittunt in clericos, ut xvii. q.iii. Si quis suadente [c. 29]. Priuilegium appellandi ad ipsam a quocumque iudice omnibus premissis mediis, arg. ii. q.vi. Ad Romanam [c. 6], et auctoritas congregandi uniuersalia concilia, ut in hac di. aperte continetur."

24. Watt, "The Use of the Term 'Plenitudo potestatis' by Hostiensis," 166–67.

merits of the case; nevertheless they ought to reserve the definitive sentence at all times to the pope. And so bishops are never permitted to depose another bishop. It can be said, if someone wishes to defend falsehood, that as in early times and now, it was not then and is not now permitted, but in the intervening time, it was licit. This was because so many evil men prevented bishops from going to Rome. But if this were true, they had tried bishops with the permission of the Apostolic See.[25]

In the matter of papal prerogatives, historical explanations of conflicting practices were not apposite. Just as the Supreme Court today often shapes history to serve its ends, so too Huguccio adopted a single historical interpretation for every chapter of the Decretum discussing episcopal depositions. Those chapters that seemed to contradict his assumptions were valid only if it were tacitly understood that the bishops had a papal mandate authorizing them to judge a bishop.[26]

Another chapter taken from Pseudo-Isidore, a letter attributed to Pope Felix, stated quite clearly that primates—generally, but not always, understood at this time to mean either primates, metropolitans, or archbishops—could hear testimony and then carry out sentences of condemnation (*sententiam proferant damnationis*).[27] The original text of Pseudo-Isidore had an important clause which Gratian omitted, "supported by apostolic authority" (*apostolica freti auctoritate*). There was another chapter in Pseudo-Isidore attributed to Pope Zepherinus that repeated the wording of the Pseudo-Felix almost exactly and also included the crucial phrase.[28] Many of the early collections included the excerpt from Zepherinus, but not the section of

25. Huguccio to C. 3 q. 6 c. 7 (Quamvis) v. *ab apostolis*, Admont 7, fol. 179v–180r [Klosterneuburg 89, fol. 157r]: "Hic reprobatur illa solutio contrarietatis predicte, scilicet quod olim licuit, set nunc non licet; set ex ipsa littera colligitur quod a tempore apostolorum hoc obtinuit, scilicet quod primates et metropolitani possunt [causam *add.* K] episcopi discutere, attestationes recipere, merita cause examinare, set diffinitiuam sententiam semper pape debent reseruare, et sic numquam licuit eis deponere episcopos. Posset tamen dici siquis uellet defendere falsitatem quod primo non licuit, nec nunc licet, set medio tempore licuit propter persecutores quorum multitudine episcopi impediebantur ne possent ire Romam; set si hoc uerum fuit, de licentia apostolica fuit."

26. Ibid., v. *diffinire:* "idest diffinitiua sententia terminare ad depositionem, hic signantur multa contraria, ut supra ii. q.i. Primates [c. 5] contra et q.iiii. Nullam [c. 3] contra, et q.vi. Decreto [c. 11] contra, Si episcopus accusatus [c. 36] contra, et q.vii. Lator [c. 44] contra, et vi. q.iiii. c.i. et ii. et iiii. contra. In quibus omnibus uidetur innui quod episcopi et metropolitani possint deponere episcopos, set supra ii. q.i. Primates [c. 5] inuenies solutionem." See nn. 32 and 33 below.

27. C. 2 q. 1 c. 5., Hinschius, ed., *Decretales Pseudo-Isidorianae*, 198.

28. Ibid., 131. JK + 80. A significant difference between the two letters is that Zepherinus wrote that primates and patriarchs may judge bishops.

Felix.[29] Gratian may have taken his chapter attributed to Felix from Burchard of Worms, omitting the phrase when he placed the letter in the Decretum.[30] Gratian's purpose in this section of the Decretum was not to discuss the judgment of bishops, but to describe court procedure. The particular question he addressed was whether those guilty of manifest and notorious crimes were entitled to a trial or whether the perpetrators of notorious crimes could be convicted without the protection of normal legal procedure. He placed the letter in the Decretum because it stated that a bishop should either be self-confessed or be convicted by canonically examined witnesses before primates passed judgment on him. Consequently, Gratian probably did not omit the phrase purposely, for whether the primates acted on papal authority was not critical for his legal point. In the sixteenth century, the *correctores Romani*, without recognizing the letter as a forgery, correctly inserted the words into the decretal for the official edition of the Decretum issued by Pope Gregory XIII.

When Huguccio confronted this chapter in his *Summa*, he combined his historical analysis with a textual study of the letter. He might have quickly solved the problem if he had compared the text to that in Burchard of Worms' Decretum.[31] Instead, he attacked the sentence "They may not pronounce a judgment of condemnation (*non ante sententiam proferant damnationis*) before "they had heard witnesses or a confession of the defendant." Huguccio noted that bishops could render sentences of suspension or excommunication without papal permission. Thus the word "condemnation" (*damnationis*) must be a gloss that had corrupted the text. Consequently, those who would argue that this chapter allowed a synod of bishops to condemn a bishop were mistaken.[32] Even though he was wrong, it was an ingenious piece of textual criticism.

---

29. *Collectio canonum Remedio Curiensi episcopo perperam ascripta*, ed. Herwig John, MIC, Series B, 2 (Città del Vaticano: 1976), 40: 158; *Diversorum patrum sententie sive Collectio in LXXIV titulos digesta*, ed. John Gilchrist, MIC, Series B, 1 (Città del Vaticano: 1973), 84: 62; Anselm of Lucca, *Collectio canonum*, ed. Friedrich Thaner (Innsbruck: 1906–15; reprinted Aalen: 1965), 3.66: 148; Burchard of Worms, *Decretum* (PL 140.594), 1.154; Ivo of Chartres, *Decretum* (PL 161.398), 5.245; Ivo of Chartres, *Panormia* (PL 161.1211), 4.135. The transmission of the decretal is complex, and I have listed only a selection of collections.

30. Burchard, *Decretum* (PL 140.594), 1.157.

31. Leonardi, "La vita Uguccione da Pisa," 109, notes that Huguccio cited Burchard often.

32. Huguccio to C. 2 q. 1 c. 5 (Primates), v. *sententiam*, Admont 7, fol. 152r–152v [Klosterneuburg 89, fol. 134r]: "suspensionis, uel excommunicationis quam primas uel archiepiscopus potest sufferre in suum suffraganeum, ut di. xii. De his [c. 13] et di. xxxiiii. Quorum-

Huguccio then dealt with a slightly different interpretation of these texts. Some say, he wrote, that primates, but not metropolitans, could depose bishops. Others say that episcopal deposition was formerly permitted, but now it was possible only with papal approval. Huguccio thought that neither of these solutions was correct. A synod of bishops may examine a case, but it may not render judgment without papal approval. In every case where it seems that bishops are condemned or deposed, it should be understood that they are judged only because of a delegation of papal power or a special papal mandate.[33]

In his glosses to the other pertinent chapters of the Decretum, Huguccio developed the same arguments: the deposition of bishops was a special affair that required papal authority. Papal judgment of bishops was a prerogative that the pope could delegate, but which other bishops could never usurp.[34] This had been a papal prerogative and had been reserved to the pope's fullness of power since the time of the apostles.

EPISCOPAL TRANSLATIONS

Few chapters in the Decretum treated episcopal translations. In the last half of Causa 7, question 1, Gratian gathered together most of the texts

---

dam [c. 1] et xi. q.iii. Si quis episcopus in concilio [c. 7], et secundum hoc nullum hic assignatur contrarium. Vel 'sententiam dampnationis': Vnde quidam libri habent istum genitiuum, set glosa fuit. Et secundum hoc assignantur hic contraria quia hic innuitur quod primates possint condempnare episcopos, set xii. di. Preceptis [c. 2] contra, et iii. q.vi. Accusatus [c. 5] contra, Quamvis [c. 7] contra, Multum [c. 8] contra, Dudum [c. 9] contra."

33. Ibid.: "Ad hoc dicunt quidam quod primatibus licet deponere episcopos et non metropolitanis. Alii dicunt quod olim licuit, set nunc non licet condempnare episcopum sine conscientia pape. Set neutra istarum solutionum ualet, quia a tempore apostolorum hoc obtinuit quod causas depositionis episcoporum primates et metropolitani et episcopi possunt examinare set non diffinire sine licentia domini pape, ut iii. q.vi. Quamuis [c. 7]. Vbicumque ergo inuenitur quod tales condempnauerint episcopos uel quod possint eos deponere intelligendum est ex delegatione et speciali mandato domini pape ut hic et infra eodem q.iiii. Nullam [c. 3] et q.vii. Lator [c. 44]."

34. Huguccio to C. 2 q. 6 c. 36 (Si episcopus accusatus) v. *deiecerint*, Admont 7, fol. 165r [Klosterneuburg 89, fol. 145r]: "Credo hoc esse factum speciali auctoritate domini pape, alias non liceret, ut iii. q.vi. Quamuis [c. 7]. Ex delegatione ergo apostolici poterant episcopum deponere; uel dicatur hoc capitulum loqui de suspensione quam preter conscientiam pape potest inferre episcopo. Metropolitanus tamen per se nedum cum concilio, arg. xii. di. De his [c. 13] et x. q.iii. Quia cognouimus [c. 6] et di. xviiii. Placuit [D. 18 c. 10] Si quis metropolitanus [c. 13]."

touching the problem.[35] A key text in this section of the Decretum was yet another letter from Pseudo-Isidore, written by the putative Pope Anterius to all the bishops of Christendom.[36] The letter offers an interesting contrast to the decretal of the Pseudo-Felix on episcopal deposition. As the decretal appears in Gratian, Anterius wrote that episcopal translations must always be supported by the authority of the Apostolic See (*sacrosanctae Romanae sedis auctoritate et licentia*). The canonists from Huguccio to Hostiensis almost always cited this letter, *Mutationes,* when they wished to justify an allegation that papal fullness of power reserved the translation of bishops to the pope. The phrase, "with the authority of the holy Roman see," was however not in the original forgery nor in a number of later collections.[37] It made its first appearance in the eleventh century. The anonymous compiler of the Collection in Seventy-Four Titles interpolated two almost identical phrases at the beginning and end of the letter. He wished there to be no doubt by whose authority episcopal translations were sanctioned.[38] Anselm of Lucca, Ivo of Chartres' *Panormia,* Polycarpus, and finally, Gratian, placed the decretal as found in the Collection in Seventy-Four Titles in their collections.[39] The *correctores Romani* noticed that the two phrases were not in the original letter or in the letter as it appears in several major collections. Nevertheless, they kept the phrases in the Roman edition, where they enclosed them within brackets. The *correctores* adopted this fine touch to reconcile their fear of seeming to diminish papal prerogatives with their quest for historical and textual accuracy.[40]

---

35. Gratian touched upon the problem briefly in his dictum at C. 21 q. 2 p.c. 3.

36. Hinschius, ed., *Decretales Pseudo-Isidorianae,* 152–53, JK +90.

37. The chapter without the interpolation begins *De mutatione.* It is found in *Collectio canonum Remedio Curiensi,* 51: 164–65; Burchard, *Decretum* (PL 140.569), 1.77; Bonizo of Sutri, *Liber de vita Christiana,* ed. Ernst Perels, Texte zur Geschichte des römischen und kanonischen Rechts im Mittelalter 1 (Berlin: 1930), 3.66: 93; Ivo of Chartres, *Decretum* (PL 161.381), 5.183.

38. *Collectio in LXXIV Titulos,* 188: 117–18. Gilchrist, p. cxi, does not know of an earlier collection that incorporates the phrases. The Gregorian canonists were conscious of enhancing papal power and prerogatives. It may have been, Gilchrist conjectures, a gloss originally.

39. Anselm of Lucca, *Collectio canonum,* 6.90: 313–14; Ivo of Chartres, *Panormia* (PL 161.1145), 3.69. The *Panormia* has the second interpolation, but not the first. Polycarpus 1.10.3, see Uwe Horst, *Die Kanonessammlung Polycarpus des Gregor von S. Grisogono: Quellen und Tendenzen,* MGH, Hilfsmittel 5 (München: 1980), 109. Gratian, C. 7 q. 1 c. 34.

40. *Correctores Romani* to C. 7 q. 1 c. 34: "Haec verba non leguntur in epistola Anteri, neque in Panormia, neque apud Burch. et Ivonem. Sunt tamen apud Anselmum et in Polycar. et vetustis Gratiani exemplaribus. Idem quoque est de verbis illis prope finem capitis: 'non tamen

In his commentary to Gratian, Rufinus was the first canonist to analyze the different types of translation. He observed that since the question of episcopal and clerical translations had never been properly treated, he would now define three types of translation. A translation might move a person to a place, or a place to a person, or a place to a place.[41] Rufinus noted that transferring the bishop of Bologna to the archbishopric of Ravenna would constitute the translation of a person to a place. The dignity of the person changed, but not the state of the church. When a place was translated to a person, the status of the place was changed by the person. Thus, if monks were installed in a secular cathedral chapter, the monks would remain unchanged, but the chapter would henceforward be a monastic foundation. A place was transferred to a place when a dignity or institution was moved from one place to another.[42] Rufinus thought that an episcopal translation should always be made with the authority of the pope and should serve either the utility of the church or be required by necessity. A person should never, however, move to a position of lesser dignity.[43] He did not specify the role of the metropolitan and his suffragans in a translation, nor did Rufinus indicate at what point the pope should approve a translation. These questions had not yet arisen.

Some chapters of the Decretum seemed to justify translation of a bishop through the authority of an episcopal synod. A canon from the Council of Carthage sanctioned the transfer of a bishop from one see to another with the permission of a synod.[44] In one of his *dicta*, Gratian appeared to condone the translation of a bishop even on his own authority if the needs of the church (*causa utilitatis*) demanded the translation. He also wrote that a bishop who has transferred to another see remains the bishop of the first, but, if another bishop replaces him, the newly elected bishop holds the bishopric too.[45]

---

sine sacrosanctae Romae sedis auctoritate et licentia,' quae propter hanc causam virgulis sunt inclusa."

41. Rufinus to C. 7 q. 1 a.c. 1, v. *Ambitionis enim causa* (ed. Singer, p. 290): "Quoniam circa episcoporum et clericorum mutationem longa nunc et spatiosa vagatur deambulatione questio, ideo ad presentis rei documentum sciendum est quod locorum triplex invenitur in canonibus mutatio: aut enim mutantur persone per loca, aut loca per personas, aut loca per loca."

42. Ibid., 290–91.

43. Ibid., 291.

44. C. 7 q. 1 c. 37 (Episcopus de loco).

45. C. 7 q. 1 p.c. 42 (Qui vero): "Qui vero causa utilitatis transfertur nequaquam ad priorem redire cogitur. Est etiam alius casus in quo episcopus vivente episcopo substituitur. Cum enim aliquis relicta priori cathedra sua auctoritate ad aliam transierit, si alius ei substitutus

For Huguccio, the conciliar canon presented no difficulty. He noted that a synod could not transfer a bishop unless the pope had convened it.[46] Gratian's *dictum* raised the legal problem of whether two bishops could simultaneously claim a bishopric. Huguccio saw a further problem: could the archbishop ordain a new bishop when the first bishop abandoned his see? Huguccio rejected both notions and most of Gratian's *dictum:*

Here Gratian errs. If a bishop leaves his church and transfers to another with the intention of abandoning his church, because of ambition or fickleness, he ceases to be bishop of the first church when he is replaced by another bishop. Otherwise, a church could have two bishops, which cannot be. . . . Some say that the metropolitan can ordain a new bishop immediately, even without having consulted the pope, but I do not believe it. An episcopal abdication, condemnation, or any translation may not be made or received without the permission of the pope.[47]

Huguccio was not the first canonist to attribute all of these prerogatives to the pope. He brought to full circle ideas that extended back to the early church. The reformers of the eleventh century injected new life into these notions of papal authority through their collections of canon law. Pope Gregory VII probably summed up much of their thought in the *Dictatus papae.* But Huguccio was the first canonist of the twelfth century to bring all Gratian's conflicting texts concerning the pope's prerogative in the depo-

---

fuerit, licet ille prioris ecclesie episcopus esse non desierit, substitutus tamen episcopatum habebit."

46. Huguccio to C. 7 q. 1 c. 37 (Episcopus de loco) v. *sinodi,* Admont 7 fol. 204r [Klosterneuburg 89, fol. 178r]: "Ad hoc congregate de auctoritate pape quod aliter non liceret, ut supra eadem Mutationes [c. 34] et infra eadem Sicut alterius [c. 39]."

47. Huguccio to C. 7 q. 1 p.c. 42 (Qui vero) v. *non desierit esse episcopus prioris ecclesie,* Admont 7, fol. 204v [Klosterneuburg 89, fol. 178v]: "Hic non dicit verum Gratianus. Cum enim episcopus causa ambitionis uel leuitatis dimittit suam ecclesiam et transit ad aliam uel habet suam pro derelicta, et alius ibi substituitur, desinit esse episcopus illius ecclesie. Alias duo episcopi simul essent eiusdem ecclesie, quod esse non debet, ut supra e. In apibus [c. 41]. Item in sequenti capitulo [c. 42], episcopus qui prior ibi dicitur successor illius. Ergo iam primus mortuus est [*om.* A] illius ecclesie; ergo nullum ius habet in ea, nec aliquid cum ea commune, arg. supra eadem, Quam periculosum [c. 8] et xxi. q.ii. Si quis iam [c. 3]. Set quando desinit esse episcopus illius ecclesie? Dicunt quam cito accipit aliam uel habet suam pro derelicta; et secundum hoc etiam inconsulto papa metropolitanus potest statim ibi [uel A] ordinare alium episcopum, quod ego non credo. Cum episcopalis abrenuntiatio uel condempnatio uel qualiscumque mutatio non debeat recipi uel fieri sine licentia pape, arg. vi. q.iii. Denique [c. 3] et supra eadem Mutationes [c. 34], credo ergo [*om.* A] quod desinat esse episcopus illius ecclesie cum papa sententiauerat in eum uel cum habet ratam eius dimissionem et abrenuntiationem saltem interpretiuam." Gloss is printed partially in Ríos Fernández, "Huguccio," 8.85 n. 46.

sition, transfer, and abdication of bishops into congruence.[48] Huguccio was vague about one matter: how were episcopal translations to be made? He did not describe the canonical procedure and gave no indication at what point in the process papal approval should be sought. Nevertheless, he did establish a firm juridical foundation for Pope Innocent III's resolve to prevent any slight of papal prerogatives, and, at the same time, he eliminated any lingering claims that episcopal synods might have had jurisdiction in these matters. The rise of papal authority inevitably eroded the sense of episcopal collegiality that characterized the church of the early Middle Ages. Huguccio fully supported this trend; he was a monarchist, not an episcopalist.

Innocent III probably did not read and was not influenced by Huguccio's great *Summa* while he studied at Bologna or even later. Most of Huguccio's arguments do not appear in Innocent's decretals. Fundamentally, although the pope and lawyer sought the same ends, they arrived at them by different means. Huguccio stressed the historical origins of papal prerogatives, finding evidence in early papal decretals to support his conception of papal authority. His history was skewed by a reliance on many forged decretals; nevertheless, the common lawyer will quickly recognize his clever use of case law to support his position.

As we shall see, Innocent also made an important innovation in the procedure through which translations were granted. He distinguished between a postulation and an election. A bishop could not be elected to another see, he could only be postulated. If an election rather than a postulation took place, Innocent considered this an infringement of papal prerogatives. The election had to be quashed. Theoretically Innocent's vision did not depend upon legal or historical precedents. He explicitly rejected the idea that papal prerogatives rested on the precedents of Peter and the early popes. "We are," he said, "not Peter's, or any apostle's, or any man's vicars, but we are the vicars of Jesus Christ." When he approves an episcopal translation or deposition, the pope acts not as the vicar of man, but as the vicar of God.[49]

The pope's conception of papal authority was historical only in so far as Christ had established his vicar on earth at a certain moment in the grand development of God's plan. According to Innocent, Christ established a new

---

48. Although Rufinus defined different types of translations, he did not explain the conflicting texts in Gratian; see his commentary to C. 7 q. 1 (ed. Singer), 291–94. He did, however, at C. 7 q. 1 p.c. 19 v. *ambitionis enim causa,* develop a general theory of clerical translations.

49. For the text of this quotation, see n. 6 above.

dispensation, a new era, and a new ruler to guide the affairs of men—the pope. Innocent thus ignored the jumbled facts of history. He did not need earlier decretals to establish the truth of his position; canonistic case law was unimportant. In the end, there is the simple elegance of genius in Innocent's thought. Fundamentally, one should note, his vision was theological not legal.

Huguccio finished writing his *Summa* to the Decretum around 1191, at the time when canon law added a significant new body of material to its corpus. As important as his *Summa* was, his thought on episcopal translation and abdication did not immediately sweep the field. Bernard of Balbi (of Pavia) compiled a new, systematic collection of papal decretals, most of which dated from the second half of the twelfth century. Although Bernard's compilation was a supplement to Gratian, its structure was very different. Bernard divided his collection into five books and subdivided each book into titles, treating different aspects of ecclesiastical law under each.[50] He included a title in book one that collected a number of papal letters discussing the renunciation of an ecclesiastical office. For the abdication of bishops, the most important letter was Alexander III's decretal *Litteras*. Almost no decretals in *Compilatio prima* touched upon episcopal translations.[51] Bernard did put a canon in his collection from the Council of Sardica, *Non liceat,* that forbade a bishop to move from one bishopric to another. Although most early glosses to this canon specified that the bishop needed papal permission to transfer, one anonymous glossator noted that an episcopal translation must have the authority of a synod, but said nothing about the pope.[52]

An examination of episcopal translations in the twelfth century reveals that practice was no more uniform than theory. Until Innocent III's pontifi-

---

50. Gabriel Le Bras, "Bernard de Pavia," DDC 2 (Paris: 1937), 782–89. On the first systematic collections and *Compilatio prima,* see Stephan Kuttner, *Repertorium der Kanonistik (1140–1234): Prodromus corporis glossarum,* Studiie test: 71 (Città del Vaticano: 1937), 309–44. Gérard Fransen, "Les diverses formes de la Compilatio prima," *Scrinium Lovaniense: Mélanges historiques Étienne Van Cauwenberg* (Louvain: 1961), 235–53. Gabriel Le Bras, Charles Lefebvre, and J. Rambaud, *L'âge classique 1140–1378: Sources et théorie du droit,* Histoire du droit et des institutions de l'Eglise en Occident 7 (Paris: 1965), 224–30. Hans Erich Feine, *Kirchliche Rechtsgeschichte,* 1: *Die katholische Kirche,* 5th ed. (Köln-Wien: 1972), 276–86, with extensive bibliography.

51. There was a title on the general problem of clerics who transferred to the monastic life, *De regularibus et transeuntibus ad religionem* (1 Comp. 3.27).

52. Anonymous gloss (School of Petrus Brito) to 1 Comp. 3.4.1 (X 3.4.1) [Non liceat] v. *in hac re,* Brussels, Bibl. royale 1407–9, fol. 33r: "scilicet in transitu de ciuitate ad ciuitatem; unde prohibetur nisi auctoritate sinodi, vii. q.i. Episcopus de loco [c. 37]." For a description of similar anonymous commentaries to 1 Comp. see R. Weigand, *Traditio* 21 (1965): 489 n. 33.

cate, kings, prelates, and the popes themselves had not developed an under-standing of exactly what role the pope was to play in a translation. Two important translations of the mid-twelfth century illustrate the problems and ambiguities that arose from lacunae in the law: the translation of Wichmann, the bishop of Zeitz-Naumburg to the archbishopric of Magdeburg in 1152 and the translation of Gilbert Foliot from Hereford to London in 1163.

Wichmann was a vigorous, hardheaded ecclesiastic of noble family whose long career spanned almost the entire second half of the twelfth century. In 1148, while still a young man, he became bishop of Zeitz-Naumburg. He proved himself an able bishop, supporting the policies of Albrecht the Bear and working skillfully in German politics.[53] In 1152 the archbishopric of Magdeburg fell vacant. The chapter was divided between two candidates. One part of the chapter elected Gerhard, the provost; the others cast their votes for the dean, Hazzon. Unable to compromise, the two parties sought out Frederick Barbarossa in Saxony. Although Frederick tried to bring about a reconciliation, in the end he presented the chapter with his choice, Wichmann. Otto of Freising, our main source for these events, thought that Frederick's decisions were perfectly consonant with the electoral provisions of the Concordat of Worms.[54]

The bishops of Germany, including Otto of Freising, wrote to Pope Eugenius III informing him of the translation and asking him to approve it. At the same time, Provost Gerhard hurried to Rome where he complained bitterly about Frederick's decision. All concerned learned quickly of Eugenius' displeasure when they read the letter the pope sent to Germany. He did not focus on the issue of the disputed election, which was arguably within Frederick's domain, but rather on Wichmann's translation. He emphasized that a translation must be made only under the pressing need of utility and necessity, adding that translations demanded much greater agreement among the electors than normal elections.[55]

---

53. Willy Hoppe, "Erzbischof Wichmann von Magdeburg," *Geschichtsblätter für Stadt und Land Magdeburg* 43–44 (1908–09), 134–294; 38–47. Also printed in *Die Mark Brandenburg, Wettin und Magdeburg: Ausgewählte Aufsätze,* ed. Herbert Ludat (Köln-Graz: 1965), 1–152. Horst Fuhrmann, *Deutsche Geschichte im hohen Mittelalter* (Göttingen: 1978), 157–58; Geoffrey Barraclough, *The Origins of Modern Germany* (New York: 1963), 261–65; Peter Munz, *Frederick Barbarossa: A Study in Medieval Politics* (London: 1969), 56–58.

54. Otto of Freising, *Gesta Friderici* I. 2.6–8 (pp. 106–10).

55. Ibid., 109: "Cum enim translationes episcoporum sine manifestae utilitatis et necessitatis indicio divinae legis oraculum non permittat, cum etiam multo amplior quam in aliis electionibus cleri et populi eas debeat prevenire concordia, in facienda translatione de venerabili fratre nostro Guicmanno Cicensi episcopo nichil horum est, sed solus favor principis expectatus,

Eugenius may have had a copy of the Pseudo-Anterius letter *Mutationes* before him in the form in which it was found in Burchard of Worm's or Ivo of Chartres' *decreta*. This version of the letter stressed that episcopal translations should be made only because of the common good and necessity. The letter went on to say that the election and exhortation of the priests and people should precede a translation, a stipulation that justified Eugenius' stress on concord and unanimity in any translation. On the other hand, Eugenius may have been citing the decretal from Gratian, interpreting the two interpolated phrases "with apostolic authority" to mean that the pope's approval should be sought for a translation. In the twelfth century, papal approbation, consultation, or approval of a translation came after a formal election had been made. Eugenius may have understood the bishops' letters as fulfilling their obligation to seek apostolic approval.

Next, Eugenius sent two cardinals to Germany with authority to depose certain German bishops. They deposed one bishop and replaced another because of his age, but when they attempted to hear Wichmann's case, Frederick ordered the cardinals to leave his realm. Eugenius died shortly afterwards, and Pope Anastasius IV unsuccessfully attempted to settle Wichmann's translation by sending Gerard, cardinal deacon of S. Maria in Via Lata, to negotiate with Frederick. After the legate's fruitless visit and two years of unsuccessful negotiations, Frederick sent Wichmann and his party to Rome. Anastasius laid the pallium on the altar of St. Peter. If Wichmann thought he had been canonically elected, commanded the pope, he should take the pallium from the altar. Wichmann hesitated. Finally, two men in Wichmann's party took the pallium and gave it to him.[56] The new archbishop of Magdeburg became one of Frederick's most loyal supporters and remained bishop of Magdeburg until his death in 1192.

The translation of Gilbert Foliot to London was a more orderly affair. He had become bishop of Hereford in 1148, gaining a reputation as a keen administrator who was learned in law. When his cousin Richard of Belmeis, the bishop of London, died in May 1162, Gilbert was an obvious candidate

---

et, nec inspecta necessitate illius aecclesiae nec considerata utilitate personae, clero nolente, immo, ut dicitur, ex parte maxima reclamante, in Magdeburgensem eum dicitis aecclesiam supplantandum."

56. *Chronicon montis sereni,* to 1154, MGH Scriptores 23.149; see F. Winter, "Erzbischof Wichmann von Magdeburg," *Forschungen zur deutschen Geschichte* 13 (1873): 111–55 and Hoppe, "Erzbischof Wichmann," 3–7. Hoppe interprets Anastasius' refusal and delaying tactics as being the pope's defense against Frederick's pressure. The situation was very complex. Certainly Anastasius was concerned with much more than the issue of Wichmann's translation and election.

for the vacant see.[57] Upon Henry II's long-awaited return to England in January 1163, he met with the cathedral chapter of London on 6 March. The cathedral chapter unanimously postulated Gilbert. Thomas Becket approved their choice, and the king added his consent. Alexander III happened to be in Paris, and Henry, Thomas, and the historian, Ralph de Diceto, sent letters asking the pope to confirm their choice.[58] In Alexander's reply to Gilbert he gave his reasons for approving Gilbert's transfer:

> You should not hesitate to assume your burden that is known to come from the authority of divine dispensation. Since the strictures of the holy canons prohibit translations of persons from one church to another without evident and manifest cause, we grant this translation, having considered the reasons put forward by Henry, and also his wishes and desires.[59]

It is likely that every aspect of Gilbert's translation would have satisfied Innocent III. In Thomas Becket's letter, the selection of Gilbert is described as a "postulatio," for which, to use Becket's words, an "ordinatio apostolica" was obtained.[60] In contrast to the translation of Wichmann, the legal procedure was rigorous, and the king and the English clergy observed canonical rules. Pope Alexander's letter emphasized the same concerns as Eugenius'. Like Eugenius, he cited *Mutationes* indirectly, stressing that necessity and utility should be the basis of all translations. Both popes did not claim explicitly that the pope had an exclusive right to approve translations, although they presupposed that papal approval should be sought. Gilbert

---

57. Adrian Morey and C. N. L. Brooke, *Gilbert Foliot and his Letters* (Cambridge: 1965), 149–53.

58. The main sources for Gilbert's translation are Ralph de Diceto, *Ymagines historiarum*, ed. William Stubbs, RS 68 (London: 1876), 1.308–9, and letters of Gilbert and Thomas Becket and others, collected in *The Letters and Charters of Gilbert of Foliot*, ed. Z. N. Brooke, A. Morey, C. N. L. Brooke (Cambridge: 1967), 183–86, also printed in *Materials for the History of Thomas Becket*, ed. James C. Robertson, RS 67 (London: 1875–85), 5:27–30, 175–78. On Diceto, see Charles and Anne Duggan, "Ralph de Diceto, Henry II, and Becket," *Authority and Power: Studies on Medieval Law and Government Presented to Walter Ullmann* ed. Brian Tierney and Peter Linehan (Cambridge: 1980), 59–81.

59. *Letters and Charters of Gilbert Foliot*, 184 (JL 10837): "non dubites tamen onus assumere quod ex diuine dispensationis arbitrio noscitur prouenire. Cum enim translationes personarum de una ad aliam ecclesiam absque euidenti et manifesta causa fieri sacrorum canonum inhibeant sanctiones, nos certas necessitates et causas a principe nobis propositas, et ipsius principis uotum et desiderium attendentes, translationem ipsam concedimus."

60. Ibid., 185: "Magna itaque super hoc deliberatione habita, conuenerunt in hoc unanimis cleri postulatio, uoluntas domini regis et nostra, ordinatio quoque apostolica, et ob communem regni utilitatem et ecclesie necessitatem, ad ecclesie Londoniensis regimen transferri, et in ea curam et sollicitudinem pastoralem gerere debeatis."

Foliot's early years as bishop of London were stormy, rocked by the turbulence of Becket's dispute with Henry, but he weathered them to die in office in 1187.

Not all English translations conformed so exactly to the rules Innocent would lay down. In 1184, Baldwin, bishop of Worcester, was elected to Canterbury, and Walter, bishop of Lincoln, was chosen archbishop of Rouen. Both were elected; they were not postulated to Rome. Walter's election was not without dissension, for the cathedral chapter of Rouen was not of one mind. They chose arbitrators and the election was *per compromissum*. Henry II was in France, and he participated in the proceedings, bringing about a royally sponsored agreement.[61]

Ralph de Diceto and Gervase of Canterbury provide detailed information about Baldwin's translation.[62] Pope Lucius III wrote to the suffragans of Canterbury and the convent urging them to elect a new archbishop within two months. Councils were held at Reading, Windsor, and London. After long negotiations in which Henry II again took part, Baldwin was elected. The bishops wrote a letter to Lucius in which they announced Baldwin's election and asked for the pope's assent. They also requested a papal mandate ordering the monks of Canterbury to adhere to their decision.[63] Gilbert Foliot announced the election publicly.

Henry and Baldwin went to Canterbury together. Baldwin declared that he would not take possession of the see unless the monks consented to his election. Insisting that they were the electoral body with the sole legal right of election, the monks would not recognize the electoral rights of the bishops. They ignored the issue of Baldwin's translation, even though a number of chapters in Gratian stipulated that an episcopal synod should approve all translations. The monks refused to acknowledge that the bishops had any jurisdiction. It was a messy situation. Almost all the canonical rules for both elections and translations were ignored.[64] Finally, the monks elected Baldwin

---

61. Ralph de Diceto, *Ymagines*, 2.21: "sicque cum omnium pace qualiquali Walterus Lincolniensis episcopus electus est in archiepiscopum."

62. Ibid., 2.22–24, 36; Gervase of Canterbury, *The Chronicle of the Reigns of Stephen, Henry II., and Richard I.*, ed. William Stubbs, RS 73 (London: 1879), 1:313–25.

63. Ralph de Diceto, *Ymagines*, 2.24 (JL 15030): "Vestrae igitur paternitati humiliter supplicamus, quatinus, juxta desiderium nostrum et totius ecclesie Anglicanae, ipsius electionem confirmare velitis, ut in amministratione ad quam Domino disponente vocatus est, de manu misericordiae vestrae suscipiat plenitudinem potestatis."

64. Ibid., 2.24. Gervase of Canterbury, *Chronicle* 1:322–24: "Clarum quidem est quod electio episcoporum, quam in impetu suo fecerunt, quasi nulla est, quia praesumptuosa et penitus cassanda. Nos ergo in nomine Sanctae Trinitatis eligimus virum venerabilem dominum Baldewinum."

and wrote to Lucius asking him to confirm their choice. Lucius approved the election—without indicating any preference for an electoral body—and sent the pallium to Baldwin.[65]

These two rather straightforward, ordinary elections are probably typical of late-twelfth-century translations. Writing about the same time, Huguccio insisted that a council of bishops could arrange an election and translation only if it had been summoned by the pope. Those involved in actual translations, it seems, paid little attention to legal theory. However, even Huguccio did not draw a clear distinction, as Innocent III would do, between a postulation of a bishop who wished to move to another see and an election. The law governing translations was still nebulous.

These generalizations about twelfth-century translations must be tentative, for a study of episcopal translations remains to be written. Some facts are certain, however. Translations became more frequent in the twelfth century, although we do not have sufficient information in many cases to judge the procedures followed. The number of translations increased dramatically after 1150. Between 1100 and 1149, there were twenty-one in Spain, Italy, France, Germany, and England. In the next two decades, there were seventeen, and from 1170 to 1199, forty-seven. During the eighteen years of Innocent III's pontificate, thirty bishops left their sees for new posts. The rate remained fairly constant from the 1170s until the end of Innocent's pontificate—about fifteen every ten years.[66] Innocent's interest in establishing firm rules and exercising papal control over all translations probably stemmed from a desire to make the procedure regular and to clarify papal authority. He was not concerned, it seems, with abuses. He did not complain in his letters about bishops abandoning their sees and seeking more-attractive posts. Translations remained common during his pontificate.

Innocent wasted no time establishing rules for translations. The patri-

---

65. Ralph de Diceto, *Ymagines*, 2.36 (JL 15388): "Et electionem tuam quam, ex literis quas gestarunt et relatione propria canonicam esse cognovimus ac Deo et hominibus approbatam, habita deliberatione cum fratribus nostris . . . curavimus confirmare. Pallium preterea plenitudinem pontificalis officii fraternitati tuae concessimus."

66. These numbers are based on the information in P. B. Gams, *Series episcoporum ecclesiae catholicae* (Regensburg: 1873–86) and Conrad Eubel, *Hierarchia catholica medii aevi* (Monasterii: 1913). Gams was often inaccurate, and he overlooked a number of translations. My figures, even though based on his faulty information, are a rough guide to the number of translations in the twelfth and early thirteenth centuries. Richard Kay has compiled a list for the thirteenth and fourteenth centuries in *Dante's Swift and Strong: Essays on Inferno XV* (Lawrence, Kans.: 1978), 115. The number of translations continued to rise during the thirteenth century. There were an average of 25.5 translations in each decade between the pontificates of Innocent III and Boniface VIII.

arch of Antioch, Peter, had transferred Laurentius from Apamea to Tripoli and confirmed him. He justified his right to translate a bishop without papal approval by citing the example of his predecessor, who had moved another bishop a few years earlier. Innocent's reply in his decretal, *Cum ex illo,* was unequivocal. The pope had jurisdiction over all important cases, including depositions and translations of bishops. Christ had granted the Roman bishop this authority through a general privilege given to St. Peter and his successors. Nothing, he said, could be done in these matters without the consent of the pope.[67]

A few months later, Innocent addressed the issue again. The archbishop of Tours had presided over an episcopal synod that approved the move of William of Chemille from Avranches to Angers. Innocent wrote to the archbishop of Rouen and instructed him that William should be suspended from his office if the facts of the case were as he understood them. He justified his actions by inserting the text of the letters to the patriarch of Antioch and the bishop of Tripoli, "lest we seem to enact anything new in this matter."[68] Innocent must have anticipated possible objections to his claims. Somewhat surprisingly, he did not cite precedents from Gratian's Decretum or use Huguccio's arguments. The references to earlier canon law in the cited letters are vague and oblique. It is odd that Innocent should refer to letters written only a month earlier which did not contain more-detailed arguments than the letter he had just written. If Innocent wished to cite precedents, he could have inserted *Mutationes* from Gratian's Decretum. The decretal dated back to the early church, had long been part of the canonical tradition, and would have made his point: papal approval was necessary for all translations. By this time (April 1198), Innocent had determined the pope's prerogative to sanction translations. He had not yet established his other important clarification of procedure: the distinction between postulating a candidate to another see and electing him.

When the question of episcopal translations engaged Innocent's attention once more in August 1198, he had worked out a more elaborate description of papal prerogatives and had established a clear judicial procedure through which translations could be made. In a letter to Bernard of Balbi, bishop of Faenza and an eminent canonist, he no longer cited recent prece-

---

67. Innocent III, Register I, 77–78, no. 50 [3 Comp. 1.5.1 (X 1.7.1)].

68. Innocent III, Register I, 175–78, no. 117 [Rain. 5.2]: "Ne vero novum aliquid super hoc statuere videamur, quod contra venerabilem fratrem nostrum . . . patriarcham Antiochenum et Laurentium Tripolitanum dictum episcopum, in simili casu sedes statuit apostolica, presentibus litteris fideliter duximus exprimendum." Other letters treating this translation are Register I, no. 442, 443, 447, 530; Register II, no. 18.

dents, but presented a fully developed theory. The archbishops of Milan and Ravenna, with their suffragans, had informed Innocent that they had elected Bernard to the bishopric of Pavia. They asked for his approval of the translation.[69]

Innocent's response followed several different avenues of thought. He developed his description of the bishop's marriage to his church anticipated in several important respects by Huguccio.[70] Although the metaphor of marriage had been used since the early church to describe the relationship of a cleric and his church, Huguccio and Innocent made this idea central to their ecclesiology. Innocent also stressed that the pope had the authority to translate bishops because he was the vicar of God and acted on divine authority. He underlined the procedure that should always be followed. Ascribing negligence to the bishops—but not, implicitly, culpability—Innocent pointed out that one may not speak of an election in an episcopal translation, but only of a postulation.[71] Huguccio had insisted that a synod of bishops must have prior papal approval before making a translation, but this stipulation would have created many practical problems in synodal deliberations. Innocent's new procedural solution was practical as well as legally satisfying.

Innocent's definition of the old legal terms "utility" and "necessity" in Bernard's letter signaled an important change from traditional twelfth-century papal attitudes toward translations. Eugenius III and Alexander III had stressed that there must be a need for any translation. Since episcopal translations were becoming more frequent, it must have been growing difficult to argue that a translation was either necessary or useful in the traditional legal sense of those words. Innocent noted that he had consulted the cardinals in the curia and asked under what circumstances a translation could be considered necessary and useful. The conference was not, it seems, completely solemn. Bernard had spent some time at the curia, and Innocent's letter to him has the unmistakable tone of one old friend whimsically bantering with another. He argued that Bernard's translation fulfilled "evidens utilitas" because his knowledge would be transferred from a small city to a larger, from a less-populous diocese to a greater, and from a less-noble church to a greater. Therefore, Bernard would be able to pay out even greater interest

---

69. Innocent III, Register I, 472–74, no. 326.

70. Benson, *Bishop-Elect,* 121–28, 144–49. Schatz, "Papsttum und partikularkirchliche Gewalt," 108–9, notices the same development in Innocent's thought.

71. Innocent III, Register I, 473–74, no. 326. For the beginning of this letter see n. 5 above. It continues: "Licet, quod negligentie ipsorum ascribimus, ipsi te elegisse scripserint, quem eis eligere non licuit sed tantummodo postulare: quia, cum esses spiritualiter alligatus uxori, nisi facta prius solutione in te non poterat legitime consentiri."

for the money-talent given to him *(creditum tibi talentum sub usuris ferti-lioribus valeas erogare)*.[72] Innocent's subtle pun and humorous juxtaposition of the language of moneychangers led him to his more "subtle" definition of "urgens necessitas." Innocent noted that since the chapter and clergy had sent nuncios to Rome at great expense to obtain his permission for Bernard's translation, it would reflect poorly on him and the Roman church if they returned with their task unfinished.[73] So much for new definitions of "evidens utilitas."

Although unwarranted conclusions cannot be drawn from Innocent's irony and humor, ideas about episcopal translations had changed. Innocent and Bernard obviously knew the texts in Gratian that demanded serious reasons for making an episcopal translation. Innocent may have developed the theme of a bishop's marriage to his church more thoroughly than any earlier pope, but he did not draw the conclusions he might have from the metaphor. If he had followed his metaphor of a bishop's spiritual marriage to his see to its logical conclusion, he would have permitted episcopal translations for only the most serious reasons and under the most pressing circumstances. But Innocent's punning wit was not entirely frivolous. His primary concern centered on exercising and defending a papal prerogative, and he used the metaphor of a bishop's marriage solely to justify his claim that only the pope's divine authority could sanction a bishop's divorce from his see.

Innocent conceived of the church as a hierarchy, and during his pontificate he translated bishops frequently. A bishop might climb the ladder leading to high ecclesiastical office through a hierarchy of episcopal sees. In this sense Innocent's policies were harbingers of the changing character of episcopal office in the medieval church. In the late twelfth and early thirteenth centuries, advancement from one episcopal see to a more important one became a *cursus honorum*. A bishop left one church to wed another because he was a good pastor, not a bigamist. Moreover, bishops were no longer

---

72. Ibid., 474: "Visum est nobis et fratribus nostris non modicum utile, ut de minori civitate ad maiorem, de minus populosa diocesi ad populosiorem, de minus nobili ad nobiliorem ecclesiam transire debeas, ubi concessum tibi scientie et eloquentie donum ad profectum plurium exercere et creditum tibi talentum sub usuris fertilioribus valeas erogare." Innocent used the metaphor of usury from talent in a letter he sent to Emperor Henry VI before his pontificate; see Werner Maleczek, "Ein Brief des Kardinals Lothar von ss. Sergius und Bacchus (Innocenz III.) an Kaiser Heinrich VI." DA 38 (1982): 564–76.

73. Innocent III, Register I, 474: "Necessarium etiam subtiliter intuentibus videbatur, cum, si a sede apostolica nuntii, quos dicti capitulum et clerus Papienses ad nos destinaverant, vacui redivissent, preter personarum laborem et magnitudinem expensarum, quas frustra fecisse dolerent, dissentionis inconveniens ecclesie Papiensi forsitan proveniret, quod nobis et ecclesie Romane posset ab aliquibus imputari."

drawn almost exclusively from the local region. The church was becoming more national, or even international, and cathedral chapters did not object to an outsider—that is someone not native to the local diocese—governing them. A local bishop could marry his church for life. A more cosmopolitan prelate put, perhaps, less value on marital fidelity. Innocent may have given the rhetoric describing the marriage of a bishop and his church its final form, but paradoxically his policies belied his rhetoric.[74]

Innocent ended his letter to Bernard by appending a list of recent episcopal translations. He was not attempting to establish that only the pope could make translations as in his letter to the bishop of Rouen; rather he was demonstrating that bishops were often moved. Therefore, he could permit Bernard to move from Faenza to Pavia.[75]

By August 1198, Innocent's thoughts on translation had been fully developed. Of the early letters discussed above, only the patriarch of Antioch's letter found a permanent place in the canonical collections. The other letters included in the title treating episcopal translations in the Decretals of Gregory IX were written later: *Quanto personam* in September 1198, concerning Conrad of Querfurt's translation, and *Inter corporalia* to the dean and chapter of Angers in January 1199.[76] Although there were several other translations during his first year, Innocent introduced no new rules, but relied on his earlier precedents.[77]

---

74. Schatz, "Papsttum und partikularkirchliche Gewalt," 107, notes that Innocent's theory of spiritual marriage is a "Fremdkörper" in his thought and that he was not logically consistent. Generalizations about Innocent's motives behind episcopal appointments and translations are difficult to make. The same is true of the policies of his successors. Much more will have to be done before we may generalize safely about papal providees to bishoprics in the later Middle Ages; for now see the following suggestive studies which capture the complexities of the problem: Robert Brentano, "Localism and Longevity: The Example of the Chapter of Rieti in the Thirteenth and Fourteenth Centuries," and Charles McCurry, "*Utilia Metensia*: Local Benefices for the Papal *Curia*, 1212–c. 1370," both in *Law, Church, and Society: Essays in Honor of Stephan Kuttner*, ed. Kenneth Pennington and Robert Somerville (Philadelphia: 1977), 293–323.

75. Innocent III, Register I, 474, no. 326. He listed four episcopal translations and the translation of Hubertus Crivelli, archbishop of Milan to Rome in 1185, when he became Pope Urban III.

76. Innocent III, Register I, 765–69, no. 530 [3 Comp. 1.5.2 (X 1.7.2)] and 495–98, no. 335 [3 Comp. 1.5.3 (X 1.7.3)]; Conrad of Querfurt's translation and this letter are discussed in Chapter 1 above. Innocent's decretals and thought about episcopal translations have been examined recently by Kay, *Dante's Swift and Strong*, 122–54. My interpretation of these developments differs from Kay's in several respects; we agree, however, that Innocent redefined the basis of the pope's right to translate bishops.

77. Mauritius of Blason, from Nantes to Poitiers: Register I, 719–22, no. 490, 491, 492, 493. Nicholas of Hvar, from Hvar to Zara, ibid., 773–74, no. 535.

The large number of noncanonical translations during Innocent's first year indicates a lack of rules and commonly accepted canonical procedures. I have found no canonist, not even Huguccio, who stipulated that a postulation was the proper electoral procedure to follow. Although the canonists had long agreed that a candidate who failed to conform to the canonical rules of election should be postulated, this doctrine had never been applied to translations. The English clergy conformed to this procedure when they engineered Gilbert Foliot's translation to London, but this anticipation of later practice seems to have been rare in the twelfth century.

Bernard of Balbi's translation splendidly illustrates the unsettled state of procedure governing translations at the beginning of Innocent's pontificate. Bernard was a learned canonist, knowledgeable of curial procedures, and the author of a tract on elections. Nevertheless, in his own translation, he did not anticipate Innocent's objections. He could have easily avoided any difficulty with Rome by simply instructing the bishops to call his election a postulation. Bernard must have been rather annoyed to discover that his translation did not conform to canon law.

Innocent moved swiftly and effectively to clarify the law of translation, and his contribution to the theory of episcopal translations was lasting. His solution was characteristic of the man; it took practical difficulties into account and was a model of simplicity.

The rate of episcopal translations held constant during the thirteenth century, but the number of translations increased dramatically in the fourteenth century. Pope Boniface VIII transferred bishops frequently. In eight years he sanctioned seventy-two. Several Avignonese popes translated well over one hundred bishops during their pontificates.[78] A peripatetic bishop who traveled from one post to another must have felt much like a member of the modern diplomatic corps. However, there is no evidence, as far as I know, that contemporaries saw translations as an abuse.[79]

---

78. Kay, *Dante's Swift and Strong*, 115.

79. Kay maintains that Dante rejected papal claims to transfer bishops. I know of no publicist, theologian, or lawyer who questioned this papal prerogative. I think it would have been quite extraordinary if Dante had taken such an unusual position. Kay concludes that Dante placed Andrea dei Mozzi in the Inferno because the pope had translated him from Florence to Vicenza. He overlooks an objection to his thesis. If Dante wished to condemn translations, he would have been better served to use Mozzi's successor to the Florentine see, Franciscus Monaldeschi, who was a double offender. He had been translated from Melfi to Orvieto (1280) to Florence (1295). Eubel, *Hierarchia catholica*, 1:250, 334, 508.

RENUNCIATION OF THE EPISCOPAL OFFICE

The last *causa maior* over which Innocent claimed jurisdiction was episcopal renunciation. Bishops resigned their sees with some frequency in the twelfth century. Gams lists eighty-three bishops who resigned between 1100 and 1198.[80] Yet in spite of these numbers, renunciations were never taken as lightly as translations. During his pontificate, Innocent III refused to allow several bishops to resign.[81] His famous decretal letter to Riccus of Cagliari, *Nisi cum pridem*, was a eulogy of the episcopal office and an argument against episcopal resignations. Nevertheless, if we again rely on Gams, the number of episcopal resignations rose during his pontificate. Gams lists twenty-six bishops who resigned between 1198 and 1216. This is an average of fourteen per decade in contrast to ten per decade between 1150 and 1198.[82]

Gratian did not deal with episcopal resignations in his Decretum. Canonists thought that renunciation was a species of translation. Perhaps, Gratian thought so too. Even without explicit legal prohibitions, however, bishops did not abandon their office frivolously. In the eleventh century, Peter Damian sought to resign the cardinal bishopric of Ostia several times. He longed for the tranquility of his monastery at Fonte Avellana, but Pope Nicholas II refused to relieve him of his burden. Later, he wrote to his old friend, the pope-elect Gregory VII, asking that his abdication be accepted.[83] These let-

---

80. I have arrived at this figure from a survey of Spain, England, Germany, France, and Italy (including Sardinia and Corsica) in Gams, *Series episcoporum*, see n. 66 above. Gams lists 32 bishops who resigned before 1149, 51 after.

81. Cheney, *Pope Innocent III and England*, 78–79, discusses several English cases in which Innocent refused to allow bishops to abdicate. On clerical renunciation of office in general, see Franz Gillmann, "Die Resignation der Benefizien: Historisch-dogmatisch dargestellt," AKKR 80 (1900): 50–79, 346–78, 503–69, 665–708; and 81 (1901): 223–42, 433–60. Pier G. Caron, *La rinuncia all'ufficio ecclesiastico nella storia del diritto canonico dalla età apostolica alla riforma cattolica* (Milano: 1946). The renunciation of the pope has received particular attention. Martin Bertram, "Die Abdankung Papst Cölestins V. (1294) und die Kanonisten," ZRG Kan. Abt. 56 (1970): 1–101; and Horst Herrmann, "Fragen zu einem päpstlichen Amtsverzicht," ZRG Kan. Abt. 56 (1970): 102–23. See also Peter Herde, *Cölestin V. (1294): (Peter vom Morrone), der Engelpapst* Päpste und Papsttum 16 (Stuttgart: 1981).

82. According to the information in Gams, 10 bishops resigned between 1170 and 1179; 13 between 1180 and 1189; 11 between 1190 and 1198. Again these figures are only for the countries mentioned in n. 80. Caron, *La rinuncia*, 86–89, lists a number of examples of episcopal renunciation from the seventh to the twelfth century.

83. *Opuscula* 19 and 20, PL 145.423[425 male]–456. See J. Joseph Ryan, *Saint Peter Damiani and his Canonical Sources: A Preliminary Study in the Antecedents of the Gregorian Reform* (Toronto: 1956), 72–73; and Rudolf Hüls, *Kardinäle, Klerus und Kirchen Roms, 1049–1130* (Tübingen: 1977), 99–100.

ters reveal that Damian believed a bishop could abdicate for a good reason, such as a vocation for the monastic life, or out of necessity.[84] Like a veteran soldier retired from the rigors of the frontier, Damian wanted the quiet of the community.[85] He believed his strongest argument was precedent. In the past, many bishops driven by divine love had resigned their dignities to enter monasteries. He listed thirty bishops and told the stories of twenty-four. Not all of them had resigned to enter monasteries, but many had. Which pope, he asked, had ever prevented a bishop from resigning?[86] Generally prelates abdicated for two reasons: they wished to enter a monastery to spend their last days contemplating God, or they became ill. In the early Middle Ages, the contemplative life was the perfect state for a man who wished to worship and honor God. Damian's argument was likely in accord with the beliefs of many eleventh-century clerics.

Peter Damian sought papal permission to abdicate. He may have thought papal assent was necessary due to his elevated status as a cardinal bishop. If he had consulted books on canon law, he could have interpreted the canons and decretals on translation as being applicable to renunciation. But the legal question remained unexplored during most of the twelfth century. The earliest papal decretal touching the problem in the post-Gratian collections was a letter of Alexander III to the archbishop of Lund, *Litteras*.[87] Alexander counseled the bishop not to step down because he was useful to the church of Lund. The bishop knew, wrote Alexander, that the sacred canons bound him and he could not abdicate without papal permission.[88] In his *Summa* under the title "de renunciatione," Bernard of Balbi noted that papal per-

---

84. PL 145.424: "Hic mihi fortassis obiicitur, semel acceptum dimitti regimen non licere. Ad quod breviter dico quod sentio. . . . Neque tamen hoc dicimus, ut passim deseri episcopatum liceat, nisi videlicet id fieri necessitas, sive rationalis quaelibet causa deposcat." Damian's source for this idea is probably one of the chapters on translation discussed above, very likely *Mutationes*. On Damian's renunciation, see Caron, *La rinuncia*, 89–90.

85. PL 145.423[425 *male*]: "cedo iure episcopatus . . . et ut quiescendi municipium veterano et emerito militi permittatur, imploro."

86. PL 145.441: "triginta procul dubio, qui pro divino amore suis renuntiaverunt sedibus, episcopos invenimus. Dicat mihi perscrutator veterum, dicat historiarum, vel annalium quilibet indagator, tot sanctis patribus pastoralem custodiam deserentibus quis unquam apostolicae sedis pontifex obstitit? Quis eorum quemlibet vel per legationis apices reprehendit, vel per synodalem sententiam condemnavit?"

87. 1 Comp. 1.5.1 (X 1.9.1) [JL 14008]. Written to Eskil, archbishop of Lund, 1138–77. Cf. Caron, *La rinuncia*, 146–47, for Eskil's renunciation and other examples from the twelfth century.

88. 1 Comp. 1.5.1: "nosti ex sacrorum canonum institutione te vinciunt, ut liberum non habeas absque nostra permissione volatum."

mission was necessary for an episcopal renunciation and cited *Litteras.*[89]

At the end of the twelfth century, for reasons that are difficult to explain, the canonists began to ask for the first time whether a bishop could abdicate and enter a monastery without papal permission. Some thought he could. A chapter of Gratian's Decretum, *Duae sunt*, attributed to Pope Urban II, became the authority most often cited to justify a bishop's right to enter the monastic life without papal approval.[90] If this chapter reflects the thought of Urban, it is a text with radical implications for ecclesiastical discipline. Urban described two types of law, public and private. Private law, he said, was written in a man's heart by inspiration of the Holy Spirit. As St. Paul had said: "The law of God is written in their hearts."[91] If a man is infused by the holy spirit, he may enter a monastery despite any constraints of public law. Private law was worthier than public law.[92] *Duae sunt* focuses on the perennial tension in every organized religion or society: when, if ever, a matter of conscience may justify an individual's violation of positive law.

In the first recension of his gloss to *Duae sunt*, Alanus Anglicus (ca. 1192) asserted that if a bishop wished to enter a monastery, he must have papal permission.[93] In a second recension of his gloss, written sometime before 1206, he noted that other canonists thought *Duae sunt* justified the

---

89. Bernardus Papiensis [of Balbi], *Summa decretalium*, ed. E. A. T. Laspeyres (Regensburg: 1860), 9: "hinc excipitur resignatio episcopatus, quae sine Romani pontificis auctoritate fieri non debet, ut infra eodem c. 1" [*Litteras*].

90. The authenticity of this chapter has been questioned since the eighteenth century, see Stephan Kuttner, "A Forgotten Definition of Justice," *Mélanges Gérard Fransen*, SG 20 (Rome: 1976), 2:83 n. 44, reprinted in *The History of Ideas*. See Caron, *La rinuncia*, 94–95.

91. C. 19 q. 2 c. 2: "Lex vero privata est, que instinctu S. Spiritus in corde scribitur, sicut de quibusdam dicit Apostolus: 'Qui habent legem Dei scriptam in cordibus suis.' "

92. Ibid.: "Si quis horum in ecclesia sua sub episcopo populum retinet, et seculariter vivit, si afflatus Spiritu Sancto in aliquo monasterio vel regulari canonica salvare se voluerit, quia lege privata ducitur, nulla ratio exigit, ut a publica lege constringatur. Dignior est enim lex privata quam publica." The text is, as Kuttner remarks, strange. The decretal begins with "inquit" to describe Urban's thought. Either Urban is citing an unknown author, or the decretal is a report of what Urban said in a sermon or on some other occasion. Further, the text as we have it has joined together two different texts. The second begins at Friedberg's §1. The canon first appears in the *Polycarpus* (ca. 1110). On the other issues surrounding a "transitus" in C. 19 q. 2, see G. Melville, "Zur Abgrenzung zwischen Vita canonica et Vita monastica: Das Überstrittsproblem in kanonistischer Behandlung von Gratian bis Hostiensis," *Secundum regulam vivere: Festschrift für P. Norbert Backmund O. Praem.* ed. G. Melville (Windberg: 1978), 205–43. Melville does not note that "vel regulari canonica" is not in the original text of the chapter.

93. Alanus Anglicus to C. 19 q. 2 c. 2 (Duae sunt) v. *sub episcopo*, Seo de Urgel, Bibl. Capit. 113 (2009), fol. 124r: "Secus de episcopo qui sine licentia pape non potest migrare, arg. supra vi. q.iii. Denique, supra vii. q.i. Mutationes [c. 34], Suggestum [c. 46], Sciscitaris [c. 47], infra de renun. Litteras." On Alanus see Stickler, "Alanus Anglicus."

translation of a bishop to a monastery without papal approval.[94] He repeated his discussion of the problem when he glossed Alexander III's decretal
Litteras in *Compilatio prima:*

Hence it seems that a bishop cannot enter a monastery without papal permission . . .
just as a canon regular may not enter a foundation with a stricter rule unless he has
the permission of his prelate. . . . Others say that he may, as it is permitted in the
chapter *Duae sunt.* . . . The first solution is the better one.[95]

Ricardus Anglicus was one of those who believed that a bishop could
enter a monastery without papal permission. He wrote a caustic gloss to
Litteras in which he observed that some canonists thought simplemindedly
that papal permission was necessary. On the basis of the chapter *Duae sunt*
in Gratian, Ricardus argued that papal permission was not necessary. For
him, *Litteras* was intended as a "counsel," not a command.[96]

Ricardus seems to have held a minority position. I have found no other
canonist who supported his interpretation of *Duae sunt.* In a gloss quoted
by the *Glossa Palatina* and Alanus, Johannes Bassianus denied that *Duae
sunt* justified a bishop's renunciation of his office to enter a monastery

---

94. Alanus Anglicus, op. cit., Paris, Mazarine 1318, fol. 259r [Paris B.N. 15393, fol.
170v]: Alanus repeated, with fewer citations, the gloss in his first recension and added at the
end: "Quod tamen quidam negunt." *Summa Elegantius,* 1:155, notes the difference between
"migrare" and "transferre."

95. Alanus to 1 Comp. 1.5.2 (X 1.9.1) [Litteras] v. *nexibus preceptorum,* Zwettl 30, fol.
4v [Florence, Laur. S. Croce IV sin. 2, fol. 4v, v. *ligate sunt*]: "Huic uidetur quod episcopus non
possit transire ad religionem sine licencia pape, arg. precedens capitulum et arg. vii. q.i. Mutationes [c. 34], quod quidam concedunt. Similiter nec canonicus regularis ad districtiorem sine
licentia prelati sui, arg. xviiii q. iii. c.i. et ii. Alii dicunt quod licet, arg. xviiii. q.ii. Due [c. 2];
similiter canonici regulares, arg. infra de regular. transeunt. ad relig. c.i. [1 Comp. 3.27.1 (X
———)] Sane [1 Comp. 3.27.10 (X 3.31.10)]. et secundum eos hoc [capitulum *add.* F] loqui de
consilio capitulum. Vel noluit iste transire ad religionem sicut nec ille de quo loquitur precedens
capitulum. Similiter secundum eos illa capitula xviiii. q.iii. c.i. et ii. intelliguntur de transeuntibus causa leuitatis. Prior solutio melior."

96. Ricardus Anglicus to 1 Comp. 1.5.2 (X 1.9.1) [Litteras] v. *absque nostra permissione,*
Munich, Staatsbibl. 6352, fol. 4v [Modena, Bibl. Estense 968, fol. 4r, Vat. Pal. lat. 652, fol. 4r]:
"Arg. quod episcopus non possit ingredi monasterium sine licentia pape, ut vii. q.i. Mutationes
[c. 34], quod multi simpliciter faterentur. At ego credo quod possit, arg. xviiii. q.ii. Due [c. 2] i.
q.vii. Petrus potestatem [C. 2 q. 7 c. 40], infra de regular. Ad petitionem (1 Comp. 3.27.1
[X ———]). Huic capitulo respondeo quod consilium est et probo per uerba hic posita 'rogandum
et monendum' etc.; per uerbum 'quietis' et usque 'relaxari,' infra de regular. trans. ad relig.
Sane (1 Comp. 3.27.10 [X 3.31.10])." Ricardus also noted that translations were customary in
a short gloss to the canon from the Council of Sardica and cited *Duae sunt* as evidence. 1
Comp. 3.4.1 (X 3.4.1) v. *in hac re,* Munich 6352, fol. 32v: "Ecce presumi ex eo quod fieri
solet, simile infra xviiii. q.ii. Due, supra de appell. Peruenit."

without papal permission. He maintained that the "common good" of the church dictated that bishops should remain in their sees. A good bishop was harder to find than a good lesser prelate. Therefore, stricter regulations for episcopal abdication and translation were required.[97] Only lesser prelates could enter a monastery without the permission of their superiors.

Huguccio had seen the danger of the doctrine in *Duae sunt* for his contention that papal permission was always needed for episcopal abdication. Early in the thirteenth century, Johannes Teutonicus reported that Huguccio thought if a bishop was guided by the secret law of God, he could abdicate without papal permission.[98] But Johannes was mistaken; Huguccio's interpretation of the chapter completely eviscerated the text of any radical implications. First, he noted that the chapter could not have general application to all ranks of clergy. The wording eliminated bishops, monks, and canons regular.[99] He then pointed out that public law took precedence over private law in four different cases: a minor cannot enter a monastery

---

97. *Glossa Palatina* to C. 19 q. 2 c. 2 (Duae sunt) v. *sub episcopo*, Vat. Reg. 977, fol. 175v [Vat. Pal. lat. 658, fol. 63v]: "Attende quod hec constitutio locum habet in minoribus prelatis qui populum regunt. Secus autem in episcopis qui sine licentia romani pontificis migrare non possunt, ut vii. q.i. Suggestum [c. 46], Sciscitaris [c. 47], Quis dabit [p.c. 48 § 4] Alex. iii. Litteras tuas, quia plus in episcopatu quam in monasterio proficiunt, cum communis utilitas multorum sit preponenda priuate, ut vii. q.i. Scias frater [c. 35] et quia difficilius inuenitur bonus episcopus quam inferior prelatus, arg. xxiii. di. Quod episcopus. Maior districtio in eius mutatione requiritur, arg. vii. q.i. Sicut alterius [c. 39] Quemadmodum in episcopi promotione districtior obseruantia postulatur, ut lxi. di. Miramur [c. 5]. bar." Alanus repeated this gloss in his apparatus: Vat. Ross. lat. 595, fol. 175v, which is also signed "bar." On the author of the *Palatina*, see Alfons Stickler, "Il decretista Laurentius Hispanus," SG 9 (Bologna: 1966); 461–549.

98. Johannes Teutonicus to 3 Comp. 1.8.4 (X 1.9.10) v. *tamen cedes*, ed. Pennington, 93. Huguccio did write that a cleric could obey the pope or God if he left his church without the permission of his bishop. But Huguccio restricted his idea to the lower clergy. Huguccio to C. 9 q. 3 c. 21 [Per principalem], v. *in monachos*, Admont 7, fol. 215r [Klosterneuburg 89, fol. 187r]: "Quid si clericus iurasset quod numquam relinqueret ecclesiam sine consensu episcopi, et postea papa uocat eum, et episcopus contradicit? Obedire debet pape, nec facit contra iuramentum quia sine omni iuramento tenetur clericus non relinquere ecclesiam suam sine licentia episcopi, et tamen inuito episcopo licite obedit pape et spiritui sancto, arg. xviiii. q.ii. Due [c. 2]. Obedientia enim dei et pape semper est excepta a quolibet uinculo quo clericus tenetur suo [episcopo *add.* K]." Cf. Ríos Fernández, "El primado," 8:91.

99. Huguccio to C. 19 q. 2 c. 2 (Duae sunt), v. *sub episcopo*, Admont 7, fol. 300r–300v [Klosterneuburg 89, fol. 259v]: "Per hoc remouet episcopos qui sine licentia pape transire non possunt. Set quare dicit tantum de clericis qui regunt ecclesias? Nonne et aliis licet [*om.* A] sic transire? Sic, set gratia exempli de talibus fecit mentionem." Ibid., v. *seculariter:* "Per hoc remouet monachos [et canonicos *add.* K] regulares qui sine consensu sui abbatis uel prioris transire non possunt, ut infra eadem q.iii. Statuimus [c. 3] et xx. q.iiii. Monacho [c. 2], Monachum [c. 3]."

against the will of his father; a married person cannot join a monastery against the will of the spouse; monks and canons regular must obey their superiors; and a bishop cannot leave his bishopric without papal permission.[100] Huguccio cleverly observed, however, that even in these four cases one might argue that Urban's private law could be preserved. A person who violates public law in these cases is not infused with a good, but rather with a malign spirit inspired by God's enemies.[101] Huguccio domesticated the text completely.

Since Innocent III became involved in a series of cases in which he established, without any equivocation, the absolute right of the pope to approve episcopal abdications, translations, and depositions, those canonists who wrote after 1198 could no longer hold that there might be exceptions.[102] In the first recension of his gloss to *Compilatio prima*, written in the early years of Innocent's pontificate, Tancred precluded any possibility of episcopal abdication without papal permission by referring to a decretal of Innocent III, *Nisi cum pridem*.[103]

---

100. Ibid., v. *dignior:* "Idest dignum in uita eterna constituens, uel 'dignior,' idest eficatior ad soluendum quam illa ad ligandum. In iiii. casibus tamen lex publica preiudicat legi priuate: scilicet ratione etatis ut si impubes intret monasterium reuocatur a patre uel tutore infra annum et diem [dicta A] ut xx. q.ii. Puella [c. 2]. Ratione uinculi [intelligi A] matrimonialis [matrimonialiter A] ut si alter coniugum altero inuito uelit intrare monasterium, non potest, et si intrauerit reuocatur, ut xxxiii. q.v. Si dicat [c. 1] et xxvii. q.ii. Agathosa [c. 21] Si quis coniugatus [c. 22]. Ratione obedientie et subiectionis ut in canonico regulari uel monacho, ut infra eadem, q.iii. c.i. et ii. et iii. et xx. [x. A] q.iiii. Monacho [c. 2], Monachum [c. 3]. Ratione dignitatis et communis utilitatis, ut in episcopo qui sine licentia pape episcopatum deserere non potest, ut vii. q.i. Mutationes [c. 34] et § Cum autem [p.c. 48 § 3] et in extra. Litteras [Litteris A] [1 Comp. 1.5.2 (X 1.9.1)]." Innocent III later used *Duae sunt* to justify canons regular who translated without permission, 3 Comp. 3.24.4 (X 3.31.18), see also Melville, "Zur Abgrenzung," 228–29.

101. Ibid.: "Set si [*om.* A] subtiliter uelis inspicere, in nullo tali casu publica lex preiudicat legi priuate, cum in talibus lex priuata non sit, et ea non ducatur. Non enim bono set maligno spiritu ducitur si puer inuito patre, uel monachus siue canonicus regularis inuito abbate uel priore uel uxor inuito marito siue econtrario, uel episcopus inuito papa intret uel uelit intrare monasterium. De puero tamen si est capax doli, non est explorati iuris, quod inuito patre uel tutore non possit intrare monasterium, sicut in xx. causa dicitur."

102. See Chapter 1 and in this chapter Innocent's letter to the bishop of Faenza quoted in n. 6.

103. Tancred to 1 Comp. 1.5.2 (X 1.9.1) [Litteras] v. *absque nostra permissione*, Admont 22, fol. 4v[1st rec.] (Cordoba Bibl. de Cabildo 10, fol. 9r[2nd rec], Bamberg, Staatsbibl. can. 19, fol. 4v[1st. rec.]): "Nota quod licet canonicus regularis uel quiuis monachus possit ad artiorem transire religionem inuito prelato suo, ex quo licentiam petiit transeundi. Episcopus tamen sine licentia domini pape transire non potest, ut hic extra. iii. eodem titulo Nisi cum pridem (3 Comp. 1.8.1 [X 1.9.10]) et hoc totum continetur infra de regul. et trans. Ad religionem licet quibusdam (3 Comp. 3.24.4 [X 3.31.18]). t." Also his gloss to 1 Comp. 3.4.1 (X 3.4.1) [Non liceat] v. *transire*, Admont 22, fol. 34r: "Sine licentia domini pape, nec etiam electo confirmato, ut infra de translat. episc. Inter corporalia, lib. iii. t."

This decretal was virtually a treatise on episcopal abdication. Written in 1206, it was addressed to Riccus, the bishop of Cagliari. Riccus wished to abdicate and petitioned Innocent for permission. From Innocent's answer, we can surmise that Riccus gave a series of reasons justifying his request. Innocent covered so many different possibilities in his letter, however, that we cannot know exactly why Riccus wished to abdicate, and the pope ruefully acknowledged that even he did not know Riccus' reasons.[104] Yet judging from Innocent's answer, the bishop may have wanted to enter a monastery, for he seems to have written, citing Urban's *Duae sunt*, that he could abdicate if he were infused with the Holy Spirit. Innocent summarized the bishop's arguments:

But you say that the spirit inspires when he wishes, and you do not know whence he may come or to whom he may go (John 3.8); there is no one who can know completely the paths of the spirit. Indeed, those who are guided by the Spirit of God are not bound by the law, because where the Spirit of God is, there is liberty (2 Cor. 3.17). Therefore, if permission to abdicate was not given to you by man, nevertheless you may abdicate because God has given you the right.[105]

Innocent's description of the bishop's allegations amounts to a paraphrase of *Duae sunt*.

The pope responded to these arguments in general terms. He did not address the problem of public and private law, but simply stated that whoever abdicated without permission acted against the Holy Spirit, not with it. He also echoed Huguccio's more "subtle" objection that the bishop was infused with a malignant spirit if he transferred without papal permission. How, asked Innocent, can you know that your inspiration is heavenly?[106] The end of the matter was that Riccus did not step down, but remained bishop of Cagliari until 1217.[107]

Innocent did not allow bishops to throw off their burdens of office

---

104. 3 Comp. 1.8.1 (X 1.9.10) [1206]: "Quia igitur diversas tibi causas super hac causa distinximus, et propter quam earum cedere desideres ignoramus. . . ."

105. Ibid.: "Sed dices, quod 'spiritus ubi vult, spirat, et nescis, unde veniat, aut quo vadat,' et ideo non est qui possit vias illius spiritus perscrutari; qui vero spiritu dei aguntur, non sunt sub lege, quoniam ubi spiritus dei ibi libertas. Quare si cedendi tibi licentia data ab homine non fuerit, nihilominus tamen cedes, quia data est tibi cedendi a deo."

106. Ibid.: "Certe desipis, sic si sapis. Nam quomodo spiritu dei agitur qui contra spiritum dei agit? Si enim vera sunt quae premisimus, immo quia indubitanter sunt vera, procul dubio contra spiritum dei agit, qui aliquid horum contra veritatem attentat, quoniam ipse est spiritus veritatis. Porro si dicas quod forsitan alia est causa latens propter quam cedendi voluntas tibi coelitus inspiratur, et nos siquidem respondemus: tu quomodo scis, quod talis inspiratio sit coelestis?"

107. See Innocent III, Register I, 477–80, no. 329. Eubel, *Hierarchia catholica*, 1:156.

easily. He insisted that the active life, the care of one's flock, the bond of a bishop to his church, were far more important than a prelate's personal wishes. Bishops should shoulder their responsibilities. The desire or even the inspiration of retreating to a life of solitude, prayer, and personal piety did not sway him. He returned several times to the same theme in *Nisi cum pridem*. The active life, represented by Martha, was not to be scorned. The life that Martha chose was both more useful and more fruitful than the contemplative, or monastic, life represented by Mary. Thus, he concluded, the pope would more readily permit a monk to become a prelate, than a prelate a monk.[108]

In his commentary to the decretal, Henricus de Segusio added "therefore the public good ought to be preferred to private." This notion had been prevalent in western thought since Greco-Roman times.[109] Although St. Thomas Aquinas praised the *vita contemplativa*, which Petrarch and others would later eulogize in a different context,[110] Innocent III emphasized both sides of the formula that described authority within the church: *Plenitudo potestatis et pars sollicitudinis*. The pope and bishops exercised power, but they were also responsible for the care of their respective flocks. With authority came responsibility.[111]

There had been, since the eleventh century, a growing appreciation of

---

108. 3 Comp. 1.8.1 (X 1.9.10): "Nec putes quod ideo Martha malam partem elegerit, quae circa plurima satagebat, quia Maria optimam partem elegit, quae non auferetur ab ea; quoniam, licet illa sit magis secura, ista tamen est magis fructifera, et licet illa sit magis suavis, haec tamen magis est utilis, cum in foecunditate sobolis lippitudo Liae Rachelis pulchritudini sit praelata; quamvis simul in unum et contemplativus esse valeas et activus legislatoris exemplo, qui nunc ascendebat in montem, ut ibi gloriam Domini cum maiori cerneret libertate, nunc vero descendebat in castra, ut cum utilitate maiori necessitatibus populi provideret. Quapropter facilius indulgetur, ut ascendat monachus ad praesulatum, quam praesul ad monachatum descendat." Innocent had already made a similar argument at loc. cit. Friedberg n. 76.

109. Henricus de Segusio to X 1.9.10 v. *utilis*, *Commentaria* (Venice: 1581), 1: fol. 93v: "Et sic est preferenda, quia communis utilitas prefertur privatae." The classical and medieval background of the "common good" is discussed in the following articles: Thomas Honsell, "Gemeinwohl und öffentliches Interesse im klassischen römischen Recht," ZRG Rom. Abt. 95 (1978): 93–137; Jean Gaudemet, "Utilitas publica," *Revue historique de droit français et étranger* 29 (1951): 465–99; Michael Hoeflich, "The Concept of Utilitas Populi in Early Ecclesiastical Law and Government," ZRG Kan. Abt. 67 (1981): 37–74.

110. Thomas Aquinas, *Summa theologiae*, 2:2 q.180 art. 1. The tension between the two "vitae" became increasingly sharp as the early medieval ideal lost its appeal in the later Middle Ages. See Hans Baron, *The Crisis of the Early Italian Renaissance* (Princeton: 1966), chap. five and six.

111. Stickler, "Sollicitudo omnium ecclesiarum," emphasizes this aspect of canonistic thought with a large number of texts.

the virtues inherent in the active life.[112] In the thirteenth century, however, new religious movements, especially the Franciscans and Dominicans, presented alternatives to the older monastic ideals, and their commitment to preaching and devotion exacerbated the tension between the lives of Martha and Mary. The new orders did not think of the ecclesiastical hierarchy as a road to salvation; they attracted some of the best men of the age. At the same time, the church needed prelates of courage and piety. The followers of St. Francis who became bishops—particularly those whose souls and minds were most inflamed by his gentle spirit—must have often reflected upon the difficulty of reconciling the life in the valley with that on the mountain. Still many Franciscans did become bishops in the thirteenth century; each must have had his own story.[113]

The Franciscan chronicler, Salimbene de Adam, tells the story of one such bishop, Rainaldo of Arezzo.[114] A Franciscan lector at Rieti, he had so impressed the canons of the cathedral by his piety that they elected him bishop. The burdens of pastoral care did not weary Rainaldo as much as the accusations of ambition and vainglory thrown at him by his fellow Franciscans. Salimbene knew Rainaldo well and was present when an old Franciscan, who had been bishop of Turin, reproached him for having accepted the episcopal staff and mitre. The Franciscans, said the old man, were the order of perfection. He who remained a Franciscan until his death was without doubt saved. Rainaldo was struck dumb, for he knew the old bishop spoke the truth. What answer was there to this argument? Salimbene recited Innocent III's decretal *Nisi cum pridem* to Rainaldo and the old bishop, outlining their duties and obligations. Although he probably did not remember the decretal in the detail with which he transcribed it into his chronicle, Salimbene chose the key sections of the decretal in which Innocent had praised the life of Martha. He also pointedly quoted Innocent's words at the beginning of the decretal; there were only four reasons for episcopal renunciation: saving one's soul and a need for solitude were not among them.

---

112. I. S. Robinson, "Gregory VII and the Soldiers of Christ," *History* 58 (1973): 169–92, discusses a Gregorian ideal that emphasized the importance of the active life for laymen. Typically, Gregory described the active life by using images and vocabulary from the military life. For other early authors who praised and valued the *vita contemplativa*, see Melville, "Vita canonica," 212–13.

113. W. R. Thomson, *Friars in the Cathedral: The First Franciscan Bishops, 1226–1261* (Toronto: 1975) discusses Franciscans who became bishops. Also see John B. Freed, *The Friars and German Society in the Thirteenth Century* (Cambridge, Mass.: 1977); and Robert Brentano, *Two Churches: England and Italy in the Thirteenth Century* (Princeton: 1968), chap. 3.

114. Brentano, *Two Churches*, 184–89, tells Rainaldo's story based on Salimbene, *Cronica* (Bari: 1942), 467–77. See Thomson, *Friars in the Cathedral*, 225–28.

Innocent's decretal was one of the few authorities, perhaps the only one, Salimbene could have cited to defend the active life and the virtue of high ecclesiastical office. If Innocent brought a clear conception of papal prerogatives to the throne of St. Peter, he also brought an understanding of the duties that the Roman bishop and his episcopal brothers shared. The same fire did not burn within Innocent's successors, nor did they have the same sense of purpose.

Rainaldo eventually traveled to Genoa and then to Perugia, hoping that Pope Innocent IV would accept his resignation. A faint echo of Urban's *lex privata* can be heard in Salimbene's account. After the cardinals had implored Rainaldo not to resign, they said, "What if an angel has spoken to him or if God has said such things to him?" What Rainaldo thought the cardinals meant is not clear. But he was not to be thwarted. He even told Innocent that nothing of his episcopal ordination would remain after his resignation, no matter what the pope might say. In the end, Innocent relented in the face of Rainaldo's intransigence.

Rainaldo might have been a man of any age. Like most who feel their convictions deeply, he carried his own portable universe with him. In it, he was always at the center. When his beliefs conflicted with law and theology, he could sweep doubt away with equanimity. All legal systems concede that law can never apply in all cases without exception, and the abyss Rainaldo created between moral righteousness and the fallibility of human law can never be bridged completely. It is deep and eternal. In the end, even popes can never be certain whether the voice of one soul proclaims a higher truth than that of the law.

HOSTIENSIS ON EPISCOPAL TRANSLATIONS AND RENUNCIATIONS

Later canonists accepted without reservation Innocent III's decretals establishing formal procedures and rules for episcopal translations and renunciations. Of the thirteenth-century canonists, Hostiensis incorporated the spirit and theory of Innocent's thought most completely into his commentaries. Although his glosses to *Quanto personam* and Innocent's other decretals are less rhetorical than those of his predecessors, his comments on them reveal a keen interest in understanding the theoretical basis of Innocent's ecclesiology.

Hostiensis grasped the implications of Innocent's thought as well as possible objections to it. Innocent had shifted the emphasis in discussions about the origins of papal monarchy. The pope was no longer simply the heir of St. Peter—the vicar of Peter—he was the direct heir to Christ. He derived his authority directly from Christ and not from any human intermediary. When Hostiensis glossed Innocent's words in *Quanto personam*, "the pope exercises the office of the true God on earth," he wrote that the consistory of God and the pope ought to be considered the same because the pope took God's place on earth. Whatever the pope does has binding force if he does not err ("clave non errante").[115]

In his examination of *Quanto personam*, Hostiensis noted a serious philosophical and theological paradox in Innocent's thought. If Christ had retained the authority to translate prelates for himself, on what account did he grant it to St. Peter and his successors? And Hostiensis pointed to the central problem of terminology in Innocent's thought, although he formulated the problem obscurely: "If you are man, as what are you [when you call yourself] Michael, that is what are you as God?"[116] Hostiensis' question was addressed to the pope. His reference to Michael underlines a critical tension in Innocent's claims. When he asked, "What are you [when you call yourself] Michael?" he was alluding to the story of the archangel Michael and Lucifer. Lucifer said that he would soar above the clouds and rival God (Isaiah 14.14), and Michael had asked in astonishment, "Just as God?" ["Quis sicut Deus?"] This story justified Michael's name. Isidore of Seville wrote that Michael meant "qui sicut Deus," and that the archangel bore this name because he did the work of God on earth.[117] Innocent had asserted that the pope represented God on earth, but Hostiensis delicately and, perhaps ironically, asked which archangel symbolized the pope, Michael or Lucifer? Was the pope's claim like Lucifer's?

Hostiensis' answer was not as interesting as the question. He simply paraphrased Innocent's words in *Quanto personam*: "What we do, God does." Perhaps Hostiensis only wished to underline a weakness of Innocent's thought in the decretal. Although he avoided exploring the basis of Innocent's ideology in this decretal, he did examine the pope's divine authority in his commentary to two other decretals of Innocent, *Cum ex illo* and *Inter*

---

115. Hostiensis, X 1.7.3 v. *vicem*, *Commentaria*, vol. 1, fol. 84r: "Ergo consistorium Dei et papae unum et idem est censendum, extra d.n. de app. Romana, responso i. lib. vi. quia et locum Dei tenet . . . et in ligando et in solvendo ratum est quicquid facit, clave tamen non errante."

116. Ibid., v. *Non enim:* "Secunda pars in qua respondet tacitae obiectioni. Diceret enim aliquis ex quo dominus hanc potestatem sibi retinuit, quare dicis, quod ipsam concessit beato Petro, et suis successoribus? Et tu cum homo sis, ut quid sis Michael, idest quis ut Deus?"

117. Isidore of Seville, *Etymologiarum*, 7.5.12. Huguccio also tells the story in his *Agiographia*, 169.

corporalia.[118] We have already discussed these decretals and their place in Innocent's thought. Both contain much of the same imagery and rhetoric as *Quanto personam.*

In both *Quanto personam* and *Inter corporalia,* Innocent quoted Matthew 19.6, "What God has joined, man shall not separate," in order to justify the pope's right to annul a marriage of a bishop to his church. Hostiensis carefully explained what these words of Matthew meant in the context of episcopal translations:

You may explain the words of Matthew in the following fashion: "whom God has joined," whom God would have joined unless a canonical constitution forbade it, or whom he joined not prohibited by a canonical constitution, which the pope is also understood to do, provided it is not contrary to the faith.[119]

Hostiensis brought Innocent's ideas carefully down to earth. According to him, the pope may only preside over a spiritual marriage of a bishop and his church that conforms to positive ecclesiastical law and the faith. He continued:

"Man": that is an inferior to the pope. "Shall not separate": he may not presume to create any constitution, interpretation, or gloss through which they may be separated or not joined.[120]

The "man" in Matthew, wrote Hostiensis, was not all men, just all men other than the pope. The pope was still man: he had been granted a special privilege to act for God on earth. No one other than the pope may enact legislation or produce an opinion through which a bishop could be separated from his church. Hostiensis made it clear in another gloss that he had his professorial colleagues in mind when he wrote this gloss. Let them not write on behalf of divorce, he warned, and against marriage.[121]

---

118. X 1.7.1 and X 1.7.2.

119. Hostiensis, X 1.7.2 v. *divina, Commentaria,* vol. 1, fol. 82v: "Per illa verba superiora, 'quos Deus coniunxit, homo non separet,' quam sic potes exponere. 'Quos Deus coniunxit,' idest quos Deus coniungeret, nisi constitutio canonica prohiberet, vel quos coniunxit non prohibente constitutione canonica, quam et ipse, dummodo contra fidem non fit, facere intelligitur" [Vat. lat. 1444, fol. 64v].

120. Ibid.: " 'Homo': scilicet inferior papa. 'Non separet': idest non praesumat constitutionem vel interpretationem vel glossam facere, per quam separentur, vel coniungi non possunt."

121. Ibid., X 2.20.47 v. *dimittere copulatos,* fol. 103v: "et est istud contra magistros qui consueverunt glosare contra matrimonia et pro divortiis iudicare." Also loc. cit. v. *singulos gradus:* "cecus est ergo qui per glosam capitaneam conatur textum maxime tot fulcitum iuribus contra rationem et in periculo animarum subvertere et hanc destruere formam scriptam quam omnino servari oportet."

In his gloss to Innocent's decretal, *Cum ex illo*, Hostiensis presented his own justification for the pope's prerogative to oversee bishops. He may have avoided discussing this issue in *Quanto personam* because he did not find Innocent's argument that the pope exercised the office of God on earth congenial or compelling. *Cum ex illo* began:

The important cases belong to the Apostolic See from that general privilege, which Our Lord granted to St. Peter and through him to the Roman church. . . .[122]

Hostiensis glossed the words "general privilege," and there he established his interpretation of the pope's prerogative:

"General": between and over all Catholics; hence this constitution binds everyone. "Privilege": through the words of Matthew 16, "You are Peter," etc. to the words, "I shall give you the keys to heaven and earth." Through this privilege, He placed the Roman church above all other churches and gave Peter the power to loose and bind. . . . From this privilege, the pope has the authority to establish canons, through which all important cases are referred to him, according to Pope Innocent IV. And through these words that Christ spoke in Matthew 16, "whatever you have bound," etc. and those in John 21, "Feed my sheep."[123]

Hostiensis justified papal primacy in traditional terms. He linked Matthew 16.18–19 to John 21.17, a linkage that he borrowed from another of Innocent's famous discussions of papal authority, the decretal *Solitae*. Although in his later work Hostiensis distinguished between the pope's ordinary and absolute power to exercise jurisdiction within the church, his explanation of papal prerogative to regulate translations of bishops was matter-of-fact and prosaic.

If Innocent III had written a treatise on episcopal abdication in his decretal *Nisi cum pridem*, Hostiensis more than equaled the pope in his commentary to the decretal which occupies thirteen columns in the printed

---

122. X 1.7.1: "Cum ex illo generali privilegio, quod beato Petro et per eum ecclesiae Romanae Dominus noster indulsit . . . maiores causae . . . ad summum apostolicae sedis antistitem de iure pertineant."

123. Hostiensis, X 1.7.1 v. *generali* and v. *privilegio*, *Commentaria*, vol. 1, fol. 81v: "*generali*: inter et super omnes catholicos; unde et constitutio ista omnes astringit . . . *privilegio*: per illa verba Mat. xvi. 'Tu es Petrus,' etc. usque ibi, 'et tibi dabo claves regni celorum,' quo privilegio Romanam ecclesiam cunctis aliis ecclesiis praetulit et ei ligandi, atque solvendi potestatem contulit . . . ex illo privilegio potestatem habet condendi canones per quos ad papam causae maiores ecclesiae referuntur secundum d.n. Vel per illa verba quando Christus dixit Matt. xvi. 'Quodcumque ligaveris,' etc. . . . et illud Ioan. vl. [sic] 'Pasce oves meas,' infra de maior. et obed. Solite [X 1.33.6]."

edition. He was personally interested in the legal theory of renunciation because he had renounced his cardinal-bishopric due to illness during the conclave at Viterbo in June 1270. He noted in his commentary that some *periti* doubted the validity of his renunciation since there was no pope to sanction it. The legal problems surrounding his renunciation foreshadowed those of Pope Celestine V two decades later.[124]

Hostiensis defended the right of a cardinal to abdicate for serious reasons during a papal vacancy, but he did not sanction an episcopal renunciation without papal approval under any circumstances. In the key section of *Nisi cum pridem* in which Innocent III rejected the arguments of *Duae sunt,* Hostiensis denied the "liberty" of those who thought they had been infused by divine inspiration. He agreed with Innocent that Satan could pose as an angel of good and deceive the credulous. Further, he wrote, even if by divine miracle a man was granted a revelation from God, the pope should still judge whether it was a true miracle. That was the pope's prerogative. No one, concluded Hostiensis, should presume to desert his prelacy without the pope's permission. This rule must be inviolably observed.[125]

By the end of the thirteenth century, the pope's prerogative to sanction episcopal translations, depositions, and renunciations had been established. Although there may have been discrepancies between theory and practice, as in the case of Rainaldo of Arezzo, the pope's jurisdiction over bishops was not questioned. Innocent's vision of papal authority, which he had formulated so eloquently in the first years of his pontificate, had triumphed. The next threat to papal jurisdiction over bishops would come from secular monarchs, not from within the church. When King Philip the Fair tried Bernard of Saisset, the bishop of Pamiers, in royal courts, Boniface VIII understood that Philip had attacked a basic principle of papal monarchy.

CHAPTER FOUR ‹ THE PROVISION OF BENEFICES: PAPAL AND EPISCOPAL RIGHTS

Pope Boniface VIII sent the following stern letter, *Ausculta fili,* to King Philip the Fair of France in December 1301:

It is quite clear and a matter of established law that the Roman pontiff has supreme and effective power over ecclesiastical dignities, offices, and benefices, canonries and prebends whether they become vacant at the Roman Curia or elsewhere and that the bestowal of churches or dignities, offices, benefices and canonries does not and cannot belong to you, nor can anyone acquire any right in them from your bestowal except by the authority and consent, tacit or expressed, of the apostolic see.[1]

Since the pope claimed prerogatives in far weightier matters than that of provisions, Boniface's assertions in *Ausculta fili* were not radically new. The canonists and publicists had evolved theories of papal monarchy that could support these claims and much more. By 1301, the pope could demand recognition of his "plenitudo potestatis," of his supreme jurisdiction within the church, and of his right to subject all lesser prelates to his authority by drawing from a mature doctrine of papal monarchy.

Nevertheless, in spite of the rhetorical grandeur that enveloped papal monarchy, there was frequently a discrepancy between theory and practice. For example, theory granted the pope absolute authority over bishops, yet

---

1. Po. 25097, December 1301, in *Les registres de Boniface VIII,* ed. G. Digard, M. Faucon, and A. Thomas (Paris: 1921), 3: 328–32, trans. by B. Tierney in *The Crisis of Church and State, 1050–1300* (Englewood Cliffs, N.J.: 1964), 184. On the events surrounding the decretal, see Joseph Strayer, *The Reign of Philip the Fair* (Princeton: 1980), 267–75.

Boniface issued *Ausculta fili* because Philip had tried the bishop of Pamiers in a royal court, condemned him, and sentenced him to prison. The pope's will was often frustrated in lesser matters too. In studying the church of Rieti in the thirteenth century, particularly its relationship to Rome, Robert Brentano has found that the chapter of Rieti resisted papal provisions of benefices and offices with notable success. The church of Rieti won, he has written, a victory over the papacy for "localism and particularism." He concluded that the canons of Rieti were "tenaciously local in their attachments. Those local churches which were at all like Rieti (and at least there was Narni) offered a restricting social, external reality which mirrored 'the argument in favor of limited monarchy which we find in the writings of almost all the thirteenth-century canonists.' "[2] In this chapter we shall see how far canonistic theory supported the Reatine canons when they circumvented papal intervention, and to what extent the canonists limited papal authority to exercise jurisdiction over prebends in local dioceses.

In the later Middle Ages, papal provisions became a symbol of papal greed and corruption. Geoffrey Barraclough has described the origins of the system. In the beginning, the aims of the popes were modest. Only as the papacy became more powerful did they begin to make more frequent and onerous provisions. As papal monarchy grew, so did papal provisions.[3] The development of papal bureaucracy was responsible for the large number of requests for benefices in the thirteenth and fourteenth centuries. Clerics who labored in the curia or the households of the cardinals needed support which neither the pope nor the cardinals could give them; benefices from all over Christendom provided them with stipends.

In the middle of the twelfth century, the theoretical foundations for provisions had not yet been formulated. We find no trace of them in Gratian's Decretum. By the middle of the thirteenth century, papal registers were filled with papal mandates ordering bishops throughout western Europe to provide for papally favored clerics. And prebends and benefices were not the only provisions included in papal claims. Papal appointments of bishops became more frequent and eventually supplanted local elections.[4]

A Trinity College manuscript in Cambridge contains sixteen letters spanning the pontificates of three popes which illuminate a twelfth-century episode in the history of papal provisions. They tell a humorous story of

2. Brentano, "Localism and Longevity," 307–8.
3. *Papal Provisions: Aspects of Church History, Constitutional, Legal and Administrative in the Later Middle Ages* (Oxford: 1935; reprinted Westport, Conn.: 1971), 1–18.
4. K. Ganzer, *Papsttum und Bistumsbesetzungen*, 9–91.

Herveus of Meaux and supply interesting details about one cleric's quest for a stipend. Although Herveus' prebend is the tale's primary subject, the main characters are Pope Alexander III and Bishop Simon of Meaux (1177–94). Alexander cajoled, threatened, and pleaded with Simon to provide Herveus with an adequate benefice. Herveus had been, before he came to Rome, a canon of Meaux and now was a cleric in the household of Bernered, cardinal bishop of Palestrina. He had been given the income of one-half a prebend from Meaux, a practice that Pope Hadrian IV had condemned years before.[5] In spite of Hadrian's decretal, the bishop and chapter at Meaux continued the practice of bestowing half-benefices. Herveus now labored in Rome, supported by a prebend that was woefully inadequate.

Alexander's first two letters on Herveus' behalf were simple mandates to the bishop of Meaux and his cathedral chapter to give Herveus either the next vacant half-benefice or a whole one.[6] The legal issue was not simply a request that Herveus receive adequate support; since ecclesiastical benefices were not to be divided, the church of Meaux was transgressing canon law. The practice should stop.

A bishop's responsibility toward his clerics was defined only gradually during the twelfth century. Bishops sometimes ordained clerics but did not give them benefices. A canon of the Third Lateran Council prohibited this practice and ordered that any priest or deacon ordained in a diocese must be given a stipend *(conveniens stipendium)* unless the cleric had other means of support.[7] Later, Pope Innocent III extended this rule to subdeacons.[8]

Herveus carried Alexander's letters to Meaux but was not well received. As part of his response to Alexander—or Herveus—Bishop Simon pointed out that Alexander's mandate contradicted one of the Third Lateran canons, probably the canon that forbade reserving benefices of living clerics.[9] The pope's reply was sharp. Any action contrary to his mandate was null and void. The Lateran constitution did not apply because his mandate predated the council. If Simon did not obey, William of Champagne, archbishop of

---

5. I have discussed the Trinity manuscript, R.9.17, in "*Epistolae Alexandrinae:* A Collection of Pope Alexander III's Letters," to appear in a volume commemorating Alexander III by the Accademia senese degli Intronati. The letters are printed, but not in proper order, in *Epistolae pontificum Romanorum ineditae,* ed. S. Löwenfeld (Leipzig: 1885) and are discussed by Walther Holtzmann, "Die Register Papst Alexanders III. in den Händen der Kanonisten," QF 30 (1940): 69–80.

6. Löwenfeld, *Epistolae,* no. 311–12, 181–82.

7. COD, 214, c. 5.

8. Cheney, *Pope Innocent III and England,* 82, who cites Heckel's important articles.

9. COD, 215, c. 8. Alexander's response is too vague for us to be certain which of the Lateran decrees Simon cited.

Reims and papal legate, would carry out Alexander's orders.[10] At the same time, Alexander complained to the cathedral chapter that some in Meaux had misinterpreted his letters, and he ordered the chapter to induce Simon to carry out papal commands.[11]

Simon steadfastly ignored Alexander's mandates. A half-prebend of Constantius, the subchanter at Meaux, became vacant at the end of 1179 or the beginning of 1180. The bishop gave it to a boy who was the son of a nobleman. Herveus had been ignominiously passed over in favor of a seemingly unworthy candidate. Not just papal authority, but canon law as well seemed to be securely on Herveus' side. Alexander ordered Matthew, the bishop of Troyes, to quash the provision and admonish Simon to grant Herveus the prebend on apostolic authority.[12]

Alexander's next letter in the *Epistolae* was a plea and an admonition. He began his letter to Simon with a sketch of Simon's past virtue:

From what was said about you when you held a lower office, it seemed believable that if you would rise to a higher office, you would be an example of virtue to others and at that very last examination, you could anticipate glory.[13]

Alexander conjectured that Simon's early display of virtue had been pretense. Now he was proving obstinate and troublesome *(durus et gravis)*. He refused to give a prebend to Herveus in spite of Alexander's frequent mandates. Instead, he had given what was rightfully Herveus' to a young boy. This grant, wrote Alexander, was invalid, and Simon should not delay making Herveus' prebend complete.

Yet Bishop Simon was a hard man, and Alexander was far from Meaux. Alexander sent him a querulous letter reproaching him for his disobedience. "How shameful that someone who holds the office of bishop should glory in his recalcitrance." Alexander had even heard, probably from Herveus, that

---

10. Löwenfeld, *Epistolae*, no. 313, 182–83: "Nolumus enim quod constitutio, quam in concilio fecimus, impediat, quod a nobis ante concilium fuisse dinoscitur inchoatum." Although Löwenfeld dated the first letters to 1179, they bear the date "Kal. Julii." Since Alexander said he sent them before the council (March 1179), they must have been written in 1178.

11. Ibid., no. 314, 183–84: "Quidam, quod de misericordia facimus, violentiam interpretantur . . . mandamus, quatenus predictum episcopum diligentibus monitis ad id efficiendum inducatis."

12. Ibid., no. 319, 186–87.

13. Ibid., 320, 187–88: "Ex his, que de te in minori officio dicebantur, credibile videbatur, quod si ad maiora conscenderes, taliter te haberes, ut et aliis prestares virtutis exemplum et in extremo examine posses gloriam expectare."

Simon boasted he had never given a benefice to anyone who carried letters from the Apostolic See.[14]

Alexander insisted on Herveus' installation because he had only a half-benefice and because he was much more worthy than the nobleman's son. He did not argue for the acceptance of his own candidate; experience had taught him better. Rather he argued from firm legal ground. In contemporary law, it was generally agreed that an ecclesiastical benefice should not be divided and should be sufficient for a cleric to support himself comfortably.[15] These were Alexander's strongest arguments.

When Matthew of Troyes carried out his mandate, Bishop Simon closed his trap. Unknown to Alexander, Philip, the new king of France, had intervened to procure Constantius' benefice for the young boy. Bishop Simon must have informed Philip that Matthew of Troyes intended to injure royal prerogative, and Philip reacted predictably. Alexander and Herveus had been badly outmaneuvered.[16] Alexander was forced to write a plaintive letter to William of Champagne asking him to intervene with King Philip and to tell him of Bishop Simon's treachery. He should not bear ill will toward Matthew or Herveus. "They were not worthy of Caesar's anger."[17]

Matthew of Troyes had, nonetheless, integrated Constantius' half-benefice with Herveus'. Although Simon may have hoped that royal anger would remove Herveus from Meaux permanently, Alexander pressed on. He wrote to Matthew thanking him for his service, but he worried that the dean of Meaux, Michael, might not have installed Herveus through procurators. He admonished Michael and the cathedral chapter, prohibiting them from diminishing Herveus' new half-prebend in any way.[18]

Alexander III died in September 1181. Herveus may never have been granted his full rights at Meaux. The last mention we have of the case is in a letter of Lucius III to Dean Michael and the chapter of Meaux. The dean and, perhaps, Bishop Simon may have continued to create difficulties for Herveus. Lucius noted sadly that Herveus, in spite of his integrated prebend, had nowhere to rest his head and could not perform his duties at Meaux.

---

14. Ibid., no. 323, 190–91: "Illud autem molestius reputamus quod—unde verecundari deberes pariter et dolere—diceris gloriari iactans te nullum beneficium ad litteras apostolicas cuiquam tradidisse."

15. At the Council of Tours in 1163, Alexander had forbidden the division of benefices, see Robert Somerville, *Alexander III and the Council of Tours* (Berkeley-Los Angeles-London: 1977), 49.

16. Löwenfeld, *Epistolae*, no. 327, 194.

17. Ibid., no. 328, 195.

18. Ibid., no. 329, 196; no. 331, 197–98.

Lucius ordered the dean and chapter to provide a place for him. If they complied with his request, he promised that their petitions in Rome would be more speedily heard.[19]

The rules governing the provision of benefices did not coalesce into a neat body of principles until early in the thirteenth century. The twelfth-century papacy had not considered the right to bestow a benefice as part of its prerogative. Indeed the local ordinary's right of provision was never attacked frontally by any papal decretal in either the twelfth or thirteenth century. Even Clement IV's famous decretal of 1265, *Licet ecclesiarum,* marked no significant change in the law.[20] Clement mandated that all benefices of clerics who died in Rome should fall within the purview of the pope. In this case, the pope had an absolute right of provision. Clement was not inaugurating a new practice, but codifying a long-standing custom, and the canonists did not view *Licet ecclesiarum* as an innovation. Earlier when the pope requested or, in some cases, commanded a bishop to give a certain cleric a benefice, his action was the exception rather than the rule. The pope might bestow a benefice as part of a dispute in judicial proceedings, but even Innocent III never claimed the right to grant benefices at will as part of his "plenitudo potestatis." It is true that during Innocent's pontificate, petitioners came to Rome from all over Europe seeking papal mandates for benefices. However, these mandates did not give their bearers a "right" to a benefice. Most of them were requests not commands.

The petitioners fall into two classes. Clerics, like Herveus, who became members of the curia or part of a cardinal's household would ask for benefices, often relying on the generosity of their old bishops. Early canonists stipulated that a canon should be native to the land, although residence was not required. Other petitioners were members of the curia, often Italians, who received mandates for benefices in France, Germany, or England. Local churches had good reason for granting their requests. As litigation in the church became more complicated and frequent, a friend of the curia was a valued commodity, whether he was a former cleric of the diocese or an

---

19. Ibid., no. 349, 208–209. The text as printed in Löwenfeld contains several errors. I print it from the Trinity manuscript, fol. 123r: "Cum enim ad instantiam sancte memorie A. pape predecessoris nostri eius fuerit beneficium integratum, uerecundum nobis et molestum existit, quod sicut accepimus nondum habet, ubi caput reclinet et ecclesie impendat debitum famulatum. Inde est, quod uniuersitatem uestram per apostolica scripta rogamus attentius et mandamus, quatenus eidem Herueo domum ... hilariter assignetis." The next word of the letter should be "sollicite."

20. Barraclough, *Papal Provisions,* 153–59.

unknown Italian who had been "adopted" into the local church. The more important the curialist, the more valuable the connection.[21]

The decretals governing provisions become interesting when they discuss papal commands to give a benefice to a particular papal candidate. Alexander III's language to Bishop Simon was forceful if ineffectual:

And if you presume [to disobey our mandate], you should know that your presumption will be severely punished, and, by apostolic authority, we will invalidate your action and quash it completely [*irritum penitus decernimus et inane*].[22]

However, before ca. 1180 the decretists never, so far as I can tell, discussed the problem of papal provisions in detail. Alexander himself dealt with the issue in one of the first decretals to enter a number of collections, *Cum teneamur*. The letter was addressed to the bishop of London, who had asked the pope whether a cleric should be given a prebend in his church if he already had a suitable stipend. Alexander's answer was steeped in common sense. He wrote that the pope could never know all the facts of this or any other case. If a petitioner already had a suitable benefice, the papal mandate should not be fulfilled. However, if the cleric's benefice was mentioned in a mandate or if the prebend could be granted without scandal, then the papal request should be granted.[23] Alexander assumed that two circumstances invalidated a papal command: a willful suppression of fact or a lack of knowledge about the petitioner's worthiness.[24]

On the basis of Alexander's decretal, the canonists developed a theory that all papal provisions were subject to tacit conditions. Alanus wrote that a papal command of provision did not have to be obeyed if a reason could be given for disobedience.[25] He also thought Alexander's decretal presup-

---

21. Cheney, *Pope Innocent III and England*, 82–96. Jane Sayers has examined the number of Italians in thirteenth-century English secular cathedral chapters in "Centre and Locality: Aspects of Papal Administration in England in the Later Thirteenth Century," *Authority and Power: Studies on Medieval Law and Government Presented to Walter Ullmann*, ed. B. Tierney and P. Linehan (Cambridge: 1980), 115–26.

22. JL 13484, Löwenfeld, no. 313, 183: "Quod si presumpseris, presumptionem tuam noveris durius puniendam et nos factum tuum auctoritate apostolica irritum penitus decernimus et inane."

23. 1 Comp. 3.5.8 (X 3.5.6).

24. Stanley Chodorow discusses dishonest petitioners at the curia in "Dishonest Litigation in the Church Courts, 1140–98," *Law, Church, and Society: Essays in Honor of Stephan Kuttner*, ed. K. Pennington and R. Somerville (Philadelphia: 1977), 187–206.

25. Alanus Anglicus to 1 Comp. 3.5.8 (X 3.5.6) [Cum teneamur], v. *sustinebimus*, Karlsruhe, Aug. XL, fol. 22r [Florence, Laur. Santa Croce IV sin. 2, fol. 31v]: "Argumentum quod mandatum superioris non oportet adimplere ubi ratio non adimplendi reddi potest, ut supra de rescript. Si quando."

posed that if the petitioner's benefice was not adequate, it did not have to be mentioned. "This would be just," he wrote, "but I know that this rule is not observed in the papal curia."[26] The popes and the canonists envisioned a system in which a papal mandate could be ignored for a number of reasons.

In a letter to the bishop of Monza, Innocent III expanded Alexander's brief discussion of how papal letters were to be interpreted. The bishop had complained to Innocent that one of his canons had received a papal letter of provision to a benefice in Gorgonzola. The canon already had a suitable prebend in Monza. Innocent noted that the bishop "could understand how the canon's mandate had been obtained." In fact, there was nothing in the letter, he insisted, to offend the bishop's sensibilities. The petitioner was not described as a canon of Monza, no mention was made of his benefice, and the key clause was added: "if he would be worthy to receive an ecclesiastical benefice." Innocent presupposed Alexander's conditions and made them even more explicit.[27] A few years later, when Vincentius Hispanus glossed Innocent's decretal, he formulated a series of conditions that were to be tacitly understood in every papal mandate:

Note that many conditions are understood in papal mandates of provision: that he is a cleric . . . that he wishes to reside in the church named in the mandate . . . that he is a native of the land . . . that he is worthy . . . that the church is capable of supporting him . . . that the petitioner does not have a suitable benefice . . . that the church receiving the mandate might have a valid excuse for not granting it. . . . Hence the verse: *clericus indigena dignus pauper residensque.*[28]

Later canonists included Vincentius' gloss in their apparatus with very little

---

26. Ibid. v. *commode:* "Ergo si non possit commode inde sustenari, non oportet exinde fieri mentionem. Hoc iustum esset; scio tamen quod secus in curia pape obseruatur."

27. 3 Comp. 1.2.7 (X 1.3.17).

28. Vincentius Hispanus to 3 Comp. 1.2.7 (X 1.3.17), v. *nec Modecensis canonicus,* St. Gall 697, fol. 7r [Leipzig Univ. 983, fol. 93v]: "Nota cum inpetratur ad beneficium optinendum multe subintelliguntur condiciones: Si est clericus, ut hic et supra de transact. c.ult. lib. i. Si uult residere in ecclesia cui scribitur, infra de instit. Tua nobis et supra de cleric. non resid. In ecclesia, Relatum, lib. i. [1 Comp. 3.4.4 (X 3.4.4)] Si est de terra illa, lxxi. Hortamur et C. de episc. et cleric. In ecclesiis, et si est dignus ut hic, et supra de elect. Causam, lib. i. Si ecclesia sufficere potest, supra de instit. In congregandis, lib. ii. Si alias non habet beneficium competens ut hic et supra de prebend. Cum teneamur, lib. i. et generaliter si iustam excusationem habet ecclesia cui scribitur, supra de rescript. Si quando, lib. i. Et nota quod si papa scribit pro aliquo beneficiando non scribit pro beneficio nisi ut intitulato, non ut commendato, nisi hoc exprimat nominatim. Arg. vii. q.i. Pastoralis et xvi. q.i. Et temporis et xxi. q.i. Relatio. Hic ergo no. uersum: clericus indigena dignus pauper residensque." Tancred repeated the gloss in his apparatus, Vat. lat. 1377, fol. 150v, with a few omissions and additions.

change. Johannes Teutonicus injected a sense of class consciousness into the discussion: what might be suitable for one cleric might not be for another. If a petitioner was blessed with nobility, dignity, or knowledge, a benefice suitable for a poor or less-gifted cleric would not be acceptable or fitting. Such a petitioner could be given a second benefice.[29]

Even when a petitioner was worthy, papal mandates were often ignored. Bishop Simon's sturdy defense of his rights of provision was repeated again and again in the thirteenth century. The popes were hesitant to claim the authority of papal provision on the basis of their "plenitudo potestatis." In *Licet ecclesiarum* (1265), Pope Clement IV maintained that the provision of all ecclesiastical dignities fell under papal authority. He did not, however, claim that this prerogative was part of papal fullness of power:

It is known that the full disposition of churches, prebends, dignities, and other benefices pertains to the Roman pontiff. He may bestow not only those that are vacant, but also those which are to be vacant in the future.[30]

Thirteenth-century popes and canonists did not expand the doctrine of *Licet ecclesiarum*. Consequently, the decretal did not destroy local rights to bestow all ecclesiastical offices, from bishop to subdeacon. Not until the fourteenth century did Pope Urban V (1363) establish the pope's right to appoint all patriarchs, archbishops, and bishops.[31] Only then was the doctrine of *Licet ecclesiarum* followed to its logical conclusion.

Although there are not many precedents for Clement's decretal in earlier papal letters, the canonists had already formulated similar ideas early in the thirteenth century. The first instance I have found dates from ca. 1210–13. When Johannes Galensis glossed Innocent III's *Quia diversitatem*, he noted, "whether the archbishop has been negligent or vigilant, the pope may bestow a prebend."[32] Almost all the later canonists, as well as the Ordinary Gloss

---

29. Johannes Teutonicus to 3 Comp. 1.2.7 (X 1.3.17) v. *sufficientem*, ed. Pennington, 16.

30. Po. 19326, VI 3.4.2: "Licet ecclesiarum, personatuum, dignitatum, aliorumque beneficiorum ecclesiasticorum plenaria dispositio ad Romanum noscatur pontificem pertinere ita, quod non solum ipsa, cum vacant, potest de iure conferre, verum etiam ius in ipsis tribuere vacaturis."

31. Barraclough, *Papal Provisions*, 153–59. Ganzer, *Papsttum und Bistumsbesetzungen*, 75–76, 89–91. J. Robert Wright, *The Church and the English Crown, 1305–1334: A Study Based on the Register of Archbishop Walter Reynolds* (Toronto: 1980), 5–30.

32. Johannes Galensis to 3 Comp. 3.8.2 (X 3.8.5), v. *propter eius*, Munich, Staatsbibl. 3879, fol. 214r [Zwettl 30, unfoliated]: "circa alia non circa donationem. Vel uerior littera est 'preter', quia siue sit negligens siue uigilans, papa potest prebendas dare, xi. q.ult. Per principalem. Arg. supra eodem titulo c.i. Arg. supra de foro compet. c.ult. ar." Both manuscripts sign the gloss "ar."

to the Decretals of Gregory IX, repeated the substance of this gloss.[33]

The allegation Johannes cited to support his claim gives us an insight into the state of the legal question at the time he wrote. Gratian did not discuss papal provisions anywhere in his Decretum. However, Johannes justified his argument with a letter of Nicholas I to the emperor in which the pope established his right to call any diocesan cleric to Rome.[34] Galensis expanded the decretal's importance. On the basis of Nicholas' letter, he argued that the pope could call a cleric to Rome and bestow a prebend in any bishopric. There was little in the writings of the earlier canonists that prepared the way for Galensis' extension of the letter's meaning. When he glossed this chapter, Huguccio had asked if a bishop or an abbot could forbid a cleric or monk to obey a papal command to come to Rome. "No," said Huguccio, "a cleric or a monk must always obey the pope and God."[35] Both Alanus Anglicus and the author of the *Glossa Palatina* thought the pope should consult a cleric's prelate before calling him to Rome. If the prelate refused to consent to the cleric's transfer, the pope could act in spite of the superior's opposition.[36] Johannes Teutonicus used Nicholas' letter to prove that the pope could take a benefice from any cleric.[37] After Johannes Galensis, the canonists regularly cited this chapter to support the argument that the pope could take away and bestow benefices.

The canonists thought a key paragraph in *Quia diversitatem* also supported papal provisions. The decretal and the paragraph merit a close study.

---

33. The later canonists did not copy Johannes' but rather Laurentius' gloss. Laurentius gave the gloss its "received" form. Laurentius to 3 Comp. 3.8.2 (X 3.8.5) v. *et negligentiam poterat*, Karlsruhe, Aug. XL, fol. 181v [Admont 55, fol. 171r]: "Quia papa dare potest prebendas siue archiepiscopus sit negligens siue uigilans, arg. ix. q.iii. Per principalem, et ita hic arg. quod bona clerici dampnati deuoluenda sint in fiscum ecclesie. Si haberes talem litteram 'qui propter' etc. que [K = qui, *om.* A] falsa est, nec stare potest propter id quod premisit, 'non tamen ad capitulum' etc."

34. C. 9 q. 3 c. 21 [Per principalem].

35. For the text, see Chapter 3, n. 98.

36. Alanus Anglicus, 2nd rec. to C. 9 q. 3 c. 21 v. *ad nos conuocare*, Vat. Ross. lat. 595, fol. 132v: "Prius tamen consulto prelato eorum; set siue consentiat siue non, poterit eum uocare." The *Glossa Palatina* repeated the gloss, Vat. Pal. lat. 658, fol. 44r.

37. Johannes Teutonicus to C. 9 q. 3 c. 21 v. *ad nos conuocare*, Admont 35, fol. 145v [Munich, Staatsbibl. 14024, fol. 93v]: "Sicut papa priuat aliquem clerico suo. Eadem ratione, potest imperator aliquem priuare suo seruo, C. pro quibus causis serui pro premio libertatem accipere 1.i. [Cod. 7.13.1] Item aliqui potest rem suam auferre, et ut C. quadrien. prescript. Bene [Cod. 7.37.3] et papam similiter beneficium, xix. di. In memoriam, in extra. iii. de offic. deleg. Dilectus et extra. iii. de concess. prebend. non uac. Quoniam, et episcopum deponere. Set numquid omnes? Non, quia sic uniuersalem ecclesiam turbaret." Bartholomaeus Brixiensis edited this gloss to include opinions that were contrary to Johannes'.

It will allow us to see how the canonists edited and interpreted decretals and how their editing sometimes altered the decretal's original intent.[38] In this case, we can trace the process in some detail.

Innocent III sent *Quia diversitatem* to Peter of Capua, the cardinal deacon of S. Maria in Via Lata, ordering Peter to instruct all those who had been beneficed during the suspension of Geoffrey, archbishop of York, to resign their holdings. Only those clerics who had received their offices by special apostolic mandate or under the rules of canon eight of the Third Lateran Council should be exempt from the pope's mandate.[39] If a bishop had been negligent and had not exercised his right to make a provision within six months, then the right devolved to the cathedral chapter. Innocent explained how this six-month period was to be calculated if the bishop had been suspended, and condemned the collation of benefices by the king during the bishop's suspension.[40] The most important section of the letter reads:

And if they do not submit to your warnings, you should compel them by excommunication and removal from their benefices, without any possibility of appeal, notwithstanding any confirmation of their holdings they may have received from the Apostolic See in the standard form *[sub forma communi]*. The only exception shall be those who have received their prebends through a special mandate of the Apostolic See or from the chapter at York on the basis of the authority granted them by the Lateran council. Nevertheless, the time of six months stipulated by the Lateran Council shall not include the time of suspension. The Lateran canon was intended to correct prelates who were negligent or dilatory. Even if the archbishop had wished, any collations he made would not have been valid. Also, although the archbishop was suspended through his own fault, the granting of benefices did not devolve to the chapter at York through the guilt of the archbishop. But during the time in which the archbishop is suspended, the granting of benefices pertains to him who could bestow prebends even without his *(praeter eius)* negligence.[41]

---

38. For a discussion of the editorial practices of the canonists when they compiled canonical collections, see my essay "The Making of a Decretal Collection," 67–92.

39. Innocent referred to Lateran III canon 8 which was found in 1 Comp. 3.8.2 (X 3.8.2).

40. Po. 678, April 1199. Innocent III, Register II, 105–8, no. 57(60); See also Christopher R. and Mary G. Cheney, *The Letters of Pope Innocent III (1198–1216) Concerning England and Wales* (Oxford: 1967), 20, no. 111 and related letters. For the decretal's background, see Cheney, *Pope Innocent III and England*, 92–94.

41. Po. 678, April 1199. Innocent III, Register II, 107: "Quodsi monitis tuis acquiescere forte noluerint, eos ad id per excommunicationis sententiam et subtractionem aliorum beneficiorum suorum—non obstante confirmatione a sede apostolica obtenta sub forma communi, que confirmat beneficia et prebendas, sicut iuste ac pacifice possidentur—appellatione remota compellas; nisi forsan aliqui prebendas ipsas vel ex speciali mandato apostolice sedis vel auctoritate Lateranensis concilii ab Eboracensi capitulo sunt adepti; sic tamen, ut tempus suspen-

The key sentence is the last. Whom did Innocent have in mind when he wrote the granting of benefices pertains to him *(ad illum)* who can bestow a benefice while the archbishop is suspended? The canonists assumed that benefices were given by either the bishop, the bishop and chapter, or the chapter alone. If the bishop was suspended, the chapter might retain the right of provision if the chapter alone had the right to provide a certain prebend, or if, before the bishop had been suspended, a prebend had remained vacant for the six canonical months. Also "ad illum" might refer to an ecclesiastical superior: archbishop, primate, or pope. It is not exactly clear to whom Innocent referred.

Quia diversitatem was included in most of the early decretal collections. The first discussion of the problem was by a certain P., whose glosses are found in a manuscript that contains a collection of Innocent's decretals compiled in 1208 by Bernardus Compostellanus antiquus. The glossator observed that Innocent was correct when he said a suspended prelate who immediately sought absolution did not lose his right of provision. If, nevertheless, the prelate had been negligent, then certainly the chapter received the right.[42] When he glossed the words "even without his negligence," he noted that another reading was "on account of his negligence." If this reading was adopted for the text of the decretal, he said, then "ad illum" referred to the cathedral chapter.[43] The text of *Quia diversitatem* would then read:

But during the time in which the archbishop is suspended, the granting of benefices pertains to him who could bestow prebends on account of his negligence.

---

sionis in sex mensibus nullatenus computetur: cum illa Lateranensis concilii constitutio contra negligentes tantum et desides fuerit promulgata et tunc, si voluerit, non tamen valuerit archiepiscopus ipse in conferendis prebendis uti propria potestate, a qua etsi fuerit sua culpa suspensus, non tamen ad ipsum capitulum ex illa culpa prebendarum erat donatio devoluta, sed ad illum tempore suspensionis ipsius prebendarum donatio pertinebat, qui preter eius negligentiam et desidiam poterat prebendas donare."

42. Glossator P. to *Collectio Romana* 3.10.3 v. *ex illa culpa*, Modena, Bibl. Estense 968, fol. 184v: "Hoc uerum esse intelligas de illo qui non fuit negligens inpetenda absolutio; nam si fuisset negligens bene deuolueretur talis potestas ad capitulum, arg. c. di. Quoniam [c. 1], supra de rescript. Si autem. p." On Bernardus Compostellanus, see Stephan Kuttner, "Bernardus Compostellanus antiquus: A Study in the Glossators of the Canon Law," *Traditio* 1 (1943): 277–340. Also Pennington, "Making of a Decretal Collection," 69–70.

43. Glossator P., loc. cit.: "Alia 'propter,' et tunc expone 'ad illum' scilicet capitulum." There is no justification in the textual tradition for P.'s conjecture. In most of the decretal collections containing *Quia diversitatem*, the reading is "praeter eius": Rainer of Pomposa 8.1, Gilbertus 1. 7.1. But Oxford, Bodleian Tanner 8, p. 591, cited by the Cheneys, reads "propter eius," as does the text of the decretal found in British Library, Harl. 3834, fol. 277v *(Collectio Romana)*.

Because of this change of wording, the glossator argued that the cathedral chapter could bestow prebends while the bishop was suspended and when he was negligent. The pope, however, could intervene with a "special mandate of the Apostolic See."

P. may have been Petrus Beneventanus, the compiler of Innocent III's official collection of decretals, *Compilatio tertia*, finished ca. 1209/10.[44] Petrus included the decretal in his collection and made the change of wording suggested by P.[45] He probably made the change because he realized the decretal, as presently worded, suggested that only the pope (or possibly the archbishop) could bestow benefices when a bishop had been suspended. Although I have found no evidence in the glossators, this opinion may have been current in the schools.

As soon as *Compilatio tertia* appeared, the canonists disputed Petrus' editing of the decretal. The earliest, sparse set of glosses to the collection in a Florentine manuscript alerted readers that "ad illum" referred to the pope.[46] All the lawyers from Johannes Galensis on considered "praeter" the better reading.[47] Laurentius Hispanus put it forcefully:

If you have the words "qui propter" etc. [in your text], it is incorrect. "Qui propter" must be wrong because Innocent wrote just before this passage "the granting of benefices did not devolve to the chapter."[48]

Only Johannes Teutonicus hesitated to endorse the pope's prerogative. He conceded that if the word was indeed "praeter," then only the pope could take away the canons' rights of election. A legate, he added, could not.[49]

---

44. The Modena manuscript contains a number of glosses signed "P." which are not part of the "mixed" apparatus of Tancred, Laurentius, and Vincentius provided for many decretals. However, sometimes the P. has a suprascript "i"—e.g., the gloss printed in n. 42—and this abbreviation would seem to preclude a reading of Petrus. There is no other canonist between 1208–10 who would fit the abbreviation. Antonio García y García, "La Canonística Ibérica (1150–1250) en la investigación reciente," BMCL 11 (1981): 54–55, has suggested that these glosses might be attributed to Cardinal Pelagius Albanensis.

45. 3 Comp. 3.8.2 (X 3.8.5). I have checked a large number of manuscripts, and although some are corrected to "preter," most read "propter." Without P.'s gloss to the decretal in the Modena manuscript in n. 43, one might assume that the change of wording could have been a scribal error. The abbreviations for "preter" and "propter" are quite close.

46. Anonymous gloss to 3 Comp. 3.8.2 (X 3.8.5) v. *ad illum*, Florence, Bibl. naz. conventi soppressi da ordinare: Vallombrosa 36 (325), unfoliated: "ad papam" [interlinear gloss].

47. See n. 32 above for text.

48. Laurentius Hispanus to 3 Comp. 3.8.2 (X 3.8.5) printed in n. 33 above.

49. Johannes Teutonicus to 3 Comp. 3.8.2 (X 3.8.5) v. *propter eius*, Admont 22, fol. 199r: "Si habes in littera 'preter,' tunc patet quod papa solus potest auferre canonicis libertatem

However, Johannes undercut the force of his argument, and ended his gloss ambiguously by reminding his readers of the rule of Roman law that a rescript of the prince should not take away the "liberty" of election. Raymond of Pennafort put an end to this troublesome passage by changing "propter" to "praeter" in his edition of the Decretals of Gregory IX. The thirteenth-century canonists who glossed *Quia diversitatem* after 1234 agreed that the pope had the exclusive right to bestow benefices while a bishop was suspended. When he took up the issue in his commentary to the *Gregoriana*, Pope Innocent IV was the first to connect this papal right explicitly with papal "plenitudo potestatis."[50] This was an important step. Papal fullness of power had now become a justification for intervention in relatively unimportant diocesan affairs. Earlier canonists cited the pope's "plenitudo potestatis" to support their belief that the pope could act in matters of extraordinary importance. Innocent IV made "plenitudo potestatis" a much more pervasive assertion of papal monarchical rights.

Hostiensis brought academic and pastoral experience together when he glossed *Quia diversitatem*. Writing about the structure of the church, he described papal monarchy in far more concise terms than had been possible in the early thirteenth century. For him, papal fullness of power permeated every crack and crevice of the ecclesiastical polity. His ideas are tempered, however, by common sense (he was keenly aware of practical problems that arise in the quotidian administration of a diocese) and by a stronger sense of ecclesiastical collegiality than one finds, for example, in the decretals and sermons of Innocent III. Hostiensis' commentary on *Quia diversitatem* illustrates both of these points.

Following Innocent IV, Hostiensis wrote that the pope bestowed benefices in a suspended bishop's diocese from "plenitudo potestatis."[51] The pope was supreme in the church. He could indiscriminately confer benefices because all clerics are directly subject to him. Further, the pope is above the

---

eligendi, nam ipse rem alterius potest dare eo inuito, ut ix. q.iii. Per principalem. C. de quadri. prescript. Bene. Non ergo legatus ista potest, ut dixi supra de offic. leg. Dilectus, lib. eodem. Lex tamen dicit quod per rescriptum principis non possit auferri libertas eligendi, ut C. de duobus reis. l.ii. jo." Restricting the authority of papal legates was an important part of Johannes' ecclesiology, see Kenneth Pennington, "Johannes Teutonicus and Papal Legates," *Archivum Historiae Pontificiae* 23 (1983).

50. Innocent IV to X 3.8.5 v. *ad illum*, *Commentaria* (Frankfurt a/M: 1570), fol. 373r: "scilicet papam, et hoc ex plenitudine potestatis."

51. Hostiensis to X 3.8.5 v. *sed ad illum*, *Commentaria* (Venice: 1581), 2: fol. 36r: "scilicet papam ex plenitudine potestatis."

law.[52] Hostiensis also indicated when the cathedral chapter could bestow a benefice if a bishop had been suspended from his office. If the right of collation pertained only to the bishop, or if the prelate, together with the chapter, collated a benefice, then the chapter could not act. However, if the bishop participated in an election of a cleric to a new prebend as only one member of the chapter, of if the chapter alone had the right of collation, then the chapter could proceed without the bishop.[53]

Papal mandates of provision could create difficulties for bishops and cathedral chapters. Bishop Simon of Meaux had ignored papal mandates with impunity. In the thirteenth century, such arrogant disregard of papal decrees was not as easy. Bishops could still forestall an appointment with clever manipulation of legal technicalities and frequently found the legal system a handy vehicle for thwarting the pope's will. While commenting upon a decretal of Innocent III, the canonists asked whether an election that flouted a papal mandate of provisions could be valid. The decretal was *Inter caetera.*

Innocent had played some role in the early history of this case, and he reopened it because a certain Master P. made a desperate appeal to Rome.[54] The facts were these. During Celestine III's pontificate, a canon from Laon had renounced his benefice with the understanding that it would be given to a certain Canon H. Nevertheless, the bishop and chapter of Laon ignored the pact and granted the benefice to Master P. Canon H. appealed to Rome. The case was heard, wrote Innocent, with great hardship and expense for Master P., so that he was driven to the point of death itself. What was worse, judgment was given to Canon H. After Innocent became pope, Master P. did not ask for a reversal of the decision, but for mercy (*misericordia*).[55] Innocent ordered the bishop and chapter of Laon to elect Master P. to the next vacant

---

52. Ibid., v. *donate:* "Nota ergo quod dominus papa potest indistincte conferre beneficia, ix. q.iii. Cuncta et c. Per principalem, et est ratio quia quilibet subest ei immediate, ut ibi patet, et ii. q.vi. Ad Romanam et c. Qui se scit, et nota supra de offic. archpres. c.iii. § Confessione, et quia de iure potest supra ius."

53. Ibid., fol. 35v, v. *computetur:* "Nam si tamquam praelatus, una cum capitulo eligeret, tunc suspenso episcopo non posset capitulum eligere, nec econuerso." Hostiensis followed Innocent IV. He, however, made a distinction between the bishop electing with the chapter or electing as part of the chapter.

54. 3 Comp. 3.5.3 (X 3.5.17), Innocent III, Register I, 151–53, no. 103: "P. de Castaneto seriem negotii sui nobis exposuit, paterna super eum moti fuimus pietate. Cuius factum, cum ex certitudine rei, quam nos dum olim minori fungeremur officio tractaueramus. . . ."

55. Master P. had no legal grounds for an appeal and asked Innocent for mercy. The procedure is similar to letters of grace or letters of justice in English law.

benefice. "It is fitting," noted Innocent, "that the bishop should grant Magister P. a prebend *de iure,* since he had once granted him one fraudulently. *Inter caetera* was, then, not a court decision, but an administrative decree.

When glossing this decretal, the canonists asked whether a cathedral chapter could elect and provide for a new canon after having received a papal mandate instructing them to provide for another. Laurentius Hispanus thought that any election was invalid if it contravened a papal mandate of provision. He used analogies from Roman law to support his contention. He observed, however, that Innocent had not acted on this principle in a recent decretal, *Dilectus filius Gaulfridus,* that had not yet entered any of the decretal collections.[56]

Later, Johannes Teutonicus asked whether a collation made contrary to a papal mandate could have any validity. He outlined both sides of the question. On the one hand, there were decretals that would justify the validity of such collations—particularly Innocent's decision in *Dilectus filius Gaulfridus,* in which Innocent had ordered the bishop of Vercelli to carry out a papal mandate of provision. He instructed the bishop that if the canons of Novara had flaunted a papal mandate, he should order the canons to provide for both their own and the papal candidate.[57] On the other hand, the collation could simply be considered invalid for it had been made against the "living law," the pope.[58] Johannes' solution betrays an interesting view

---

56. Laurentius Hispanus to 3 Comp. 3.5.3 (X 3.5.17) v. *omnino frustrato,* Admont 55, fol. 168r [Karlsruhe, Aug. XL, fol. 179r]: "Ex quo enim resignauit W. ut daretur H., et non fuit ei data set magistro P., non uidetur resignata sicut nec ammittit possessionem qui sub quadam condictione eam cedit, ff. de acquir. pos. Si me in uacuam [Dig. 41.2.34]. Immo ex quo papa precepit alicui prebendam assignari et episcopus alii confert, non ualet collatio. Arg. infra de concess. prebend. c.i. quia eo ipso quod precepit eam dari isti, prohibuit dari cuilibet alii, ut ff. de condic. et demon. Cum ita legatum [Dig. 35.1.63] 'que enim Titio nupere prohibetur.' Sicut eo ipso quod iudicatur res mea per consequens iudicatur esse non tuam, ff. de procurat. Pomponius § ii. in fine [Dig. 3.3.40.2]. Non enim uidetur dolo carere si iam mota hereditatis controuersio soluat sine cautionibus legata, ff. ad leg. Falcid. Dolo carere [Dig. 35.2.41]. Licet contrarium fecerit Innocentius quia non cassauit institutionem factam post eius mandatum susceptum [suscetum MS] de quadam prebenda cuidam conferenda in Nouariensi ecclesia, set precepit ut ei receptio in canonicum prouideant donec uacetur prebenda quia plus ex hoc puniebantur, ut extra Innoc. Dilectus filius Gaulfredus; idem uidetur dicendum et si papa mandet ut post non ualeat collatio, arg. ff. de leg. i. Et hoc modo [Dig. 30.115]." K omits the section "cuidam—uacetur."

57. Johannes included the decretal in his own collection compiled in 1216: 4 Comp. 3.3.4 (X 3.5.27).

58. Johannes Teutonicus to 3 Comp. 3.5.3 (X 3.5.17) v. *in mandatis,* Admont 22, fol. 196v: "Set quid dices si papa mandat alicui dari prebendam aliquam, et canonici eam conferant alteri, numquid ualet collatio? Videtur quod sic, infra de hiis que fiunt a maiori parte capit. Ex

of ecclesiastical jurisdictional rights. He concluded that the election was valid, although the electors should be punished for ignoring a papal mandate. The election, he said, was canonical for the elected, but not for the canons. He compared the wayward canons to a sinning priest. A priest who is in mortal sin can bestow valid sacraments even though he himself sins. Borrowing another analogy from Roman law, he noted that although a donation may be defective, nevertheless it is still valid.[59]

In *Inter caetera,* Innocent III, however, had explicitly commanded that any collation contrary to his mandate was invalid and useless (*irritum et inane*), a phrase that became standard in letters of provision. Later canonists could not accept Johannes' opinion. Tancred interpreted his gloss in the narrowest sense. Johannes is right, he wrote, only if the pope simply ordered the canons to give a cleric a prebend. If the pope specifically forbade and nullified another collation, then Johannes was wrong.[60]

By the end of Innocent III's pontificate, the legal right of the pope to bestow benefices in any church had been established. Bishops and cathedral chapters might still show independence and recalcitrance, but the legal rules were firmly in place. Even so, some canonists still resisted the idea that a papal mandate, no matter how strongly worded, could be valid if the bishop

---

ore et infra de concess. preb. non uac. Cum nostris, et expresse dicitur extra. de conces. preb. et eccles. non uac. Dilectus, lib. iiii. quia nec sententia iudicis ad hoc sufficeret, ut ff. de pign. act. Non est mirum, supra de re iud. Cum aliquibus, in fine; item nec pactum, C. de condic. ob causam, Ea lege, nec obstat mandatum precedens, ut supra de in integ. rest. c.i. in fine; item quia licet persone sint obligate non tamen res siue prebenda de qua mandatum est receptum, ut ff. de poll. l.ii. ff. de contrahend. empt. l.ult. in fine. Arg. contra infra de donat. Per tuas, infra de concess. prebend. non uac. c.i. Item eo ipso quod papa iussit isti dari, prohibuit aliis dari, ff. de condic. et demon. Cum ita. Item talis electio facta est contra legem animatam, scilicet contra papam, ergo nulla est, ut x. di. Vides."

59. Ibid.: "Ego credo talem electionem tenere, licet ipsi puniendi sint per illam decretalem, Dilectus. Si queras an talis electio sit canonica, dico quod non est canonica quantum ad eligentes, set est canonica quantum ad electum. Sicut sacerdos in mortali existens illicite confert sacramenta aliis, ipsi tamen licite recipiunt. Donatio enim potest esse uitiosa et tamen tenet donum, ut infra de iure patron. Pastoralis et C. de rei uindict. Quotiens, uel dic quod licet peccent recedendo a mandato pape, non tamen peccant eligendo alium, sic xxvii. q.i. Nuptiarum."

60. Tancred to 3 Comp. 3.5.3 (X 3.5.17) v. *in mandatis,* Vat. lat. 1377, fol. 222r: "Verum est si papa mandasset solummodo illam prebendam alicui dari, ut posuit in questione, set si mandauit alicui dari et siquid inde presumptum fuerit, decernit irritum et inane, sicut in hac decretali continetur, in eo casu non ualet donatio, et irrita est sicut plane sonat hec littera, et quod non ualeat est arg. ff. de leg. i. Hoc modo . . . et quod dicitur extra. iiii. de concess. prebend. et eccles. Dilectus, scilicet quia non cassauit papa electionem factam post eius mandatum ideo fecit ut plus puniantur illi canonici Nouarienses prouidendo utrique. t."

thought it was unjust. And what was unjust could be narrowly defined as one particular case, or it could be a perennial abuse. Brian Tierney has shown that Bishop Grosseteste could marshall powerful arguments to defend his view that the never-ending stream of papal provisions in his day was an abuse of authority.[61] Grosseteste's letter of protest was a cry for justice. He pleaded that the pope should not provide benefices unless necessity dictated. Generally, his arguments for papal restraint can be fitted into contemporary canonistic thought. However, the specific argument with which he refused to obey Innocent IV's mandate of provision probably would not have convinced any canonist on legal grounds.

Hostiensis was the only thirteenth-century canonist I know who squarely faced the question of when a bishop could refuse to obey an unambiguous papal mandate of provision. Like Grosseteste, Hostiensis had a vigorous sense of justice. The church was more than the sum of its law and the rights of its monarch. The pope should conform his will to the public good; these words were more than just a distant echo of Roman law. As we have seen in Chapter 1, the canonists made this maxim an important part of their constitutional thought. Hostiensis posed a question concerning the pope's right to collate benefices that was, he says, regularly debated in the schools as a *quaestio dominicalis*.[62] Could the pope knowingly (*ex certa scientia*) order a bishop to bestow a benefice on an unworthy cleric? It is a ticklish question, but Hostiensis answered it succinctly. First, he suggested, one should assume that the mandate was fraudulent. If, however, it was valid and one was sure the pope acted knowingly, then the mandate could not be contravened, except possibly when the unworthiness of the cleric was so great and so manifest that the bishop could not grant a benefice to him in good conscience. Then even a papal mandate could be disobeyed.[63]

---

61. Brian Tierney, "Grosseteste and the Theory of Papal Sovereignty," 1–17; see also Barraclough, *Papal Provisions*, 120–52; Feine, *Kirchliche Rechtsgeschichte*, 205–12. Grosseteste's impassioned letter is printed in his *Epistolae*, ed. Henry R. Luard, RS 25 (London: 1861), 432–37, no. 128. See Leonard E. Boyle, "Robert Grosseteste and Pastoral Care," *Medieval and Renaissance Studies: Proceedings of the Southeastern Institute of Medieval and Renaissance Studies* (Summer 1976), ed. Dale B. J. Randall, Medieval and Renaissance Series 8 (Durham: 1979), 3–51. Boyle prints the text of the letter on pp. 40–44.

62. The canonists referred to those points of law that were commonly treated in the schools as a *quaestio dominicalis*. These questions were disputed as extraordinary lectures on Sunday. For a similar problem, see Johannes Teutonicus to 3 Comp. 1.6.5 v. *ante susceptionem*, ed. Pennington, p. 54.

63. Hostiensis to X 1.3.17 v. *impetratae, Commentaria*, 1: fol. 17r: "q.d. tali veritate tacita, qua expressa nullatenus litteras habuisset, et sic non valebant, ut infra eodem Super litteris. Quid si dominus papa ex certa scientia pro indigno scribat? Arg. est hic a contrario

Obedience to unjust papal commands and exactions was an ever-present issue in the church of the later Middle Ages. Although the canonists wrote glosses in which they exalted papal power, they also tempered papal authority by applying other principles through which papal commands might be judged. Hostiensis was far from being a critic of papal monarchy. His conception of Rome's authority was as elevated as that of any canonist of the thirteenth century. His thought was based on the supposition that even the pope must act according to high principles of justice. His justification for allowing a bishop to resist a papal command fits into a larger pattern of thought in which he developed a series of guide lines by which a cleric might judge when the commands of a superior, even those of a pope, might be disobeyed. He penned his gloss to a decretal of Pope Lucius III in which the issue of clerical obedience to his prelate was discussed:

Thus it is asked, when should the command of a superior be obeyed; if the superior were unworthy by the judgment of the apostolic see, that is, if he is a heretic, schismatic, rebellious, or excommunicated, then a subject ought never obey him. . . . If he were not unworthy, then the subject should always obey the commands of ecclesiastical censure. . . . Commands that a prelate issues should pertain to his office. If not, a command can be disobeyed with impunity. . . . If a prelate would command something that pertains to his office and his command is fitting, then a subject who does not obey must suffer a penalty. . . . If it is certain that the command is evil and unjust, then it should not be obeyed under any circumstances. . . . If there is doubt whether a command is fitting, a subject should obey if he can bend his conscience to his prelate's . . . and if he does not obey, unless he shows probable cause, he should be punished. If the subject cannot bring his conscience into conformity with his prelate's, then he should follow his conscience and not obey . . . even if his conscience is wrong.[64]

---

sensu, quod exceptio non potest opponi. Sed contra ff. de confir. tu. Vtilitatem; Quaestio dominicalis est. Tu dic quod prima fronte praesumitur rescriptum subreptitium, infra de aetat. et qual. Eam te. Sed si constat de certa scientia nihil opponetur, ut in dicta lege 'Vtilitatem,' infra de offic. del. Ex parte ii. xvii. q.iiii. § Qui autem, nisi forsan tanta, et tam patens esset indignitas, quod is, cui scribitur, salva conscientia obedire non posset, ut patet in eo, quod no. infra de temp. ord. Ad aures § i." Johannes Andreae thought that the pope could be disobeyed only if he commanded something that was heretical or that would disturb the "status ecclesiae," to X 5.39.44 v. *mortale, Commentaria* (Venice: 1581), 4: fol. 145rb.

64. Hostiensis to X 1.11.5 v. *debitam praepositis obedientiam, Commentaria,* 1: fol. 99v: "Cum queritur, utrum superioris imperio sit parendum: si superior indignus sit gratia sedis apostolicae, puta quia est haereticus vel schismaticus, vel rebellis, et excommunicatus, tunc non debet ei subditus in aliquo obedire. . . . Si vero indignus non est, tunc semper eidem quoad censuram ecclesiasticam est parendum. . . . Quo autem ad precepta, si praecepit id, quod ad

When this gloss is read together with the one quoted above on papal mandates of provision, it becomes clear that Hostiensis' "prelate" implicitly included the pope, for Hostiensis referred to this gloss when he discussed disobedience to a papal mandate. Although the canonists could easily write "who can resist the pope," they also refused to accept any theory of absolute obedience to an unjust monarch. They preferred to avoid questioning papal authority and prerogatives, but when necessary, they did not hesitate to explore the limits of the pope's "plenitudo potestatis."

Papal involvement in ecclesiastical provisions was not limited to the granting of benefices. Pluralism was a long-standing problem that continued to plague the church throughout the Middle Ages, and in response to recurring abuses, the papacy vigorously moved against pluralists in the late twelfth century. At the Third Lateran Council of 1179, Pope Alexander III decreed that a cleric was not normally permitted to have more than one benefice.[65] The Third Lateran canon renewed older conciliar decrees that prohibited pluralism. The most famous of these earlier canons was *Sanctorum* which Pope Urban II had issued at the Council of Piacenza in 1095, shortly before the first crusade.[66]

Although the canonists generally admitted that the *ius commune* of the church prohibited one cleric from holding two benefices,[67] by the end of the

officium suum non pertinet, impune non parebitur. . . . Sin autem praecipit hoc quod ad officium suum spectat et certum sit quod bonum est, qui non obedierit poenam luet. . . . Quod si certum sit, malum et iniustum esse quod praecipitur, nullatenus est parendum. . . . Verum si dubitetur de praecepto utrum licitum sit, debet subditus (si unquam potest praelati sui conscientiae suam conscientiam informare) in dubio obedire . . . quod si non fecerit, nisi ostendat causam probabilem, merito puniretur. Porro si non potest suam conscientiam prelati imperio conformare, sequatur conscientiam nec obediat . . . etiam si conscientia erronea sit."

65. Third Lateran c. 14 [1 Comp. 3.5.6 (X 3.5.5)]. See Ludwig Buisson, *Potestas und Caritas: Die päpstliche Gewalt im Spätmittelalter* (Köln-Graz: 1958), 93–95. On the collation of benefices in the later period see, G. Mollat, *La collation des bénéfices ecclésiastiques à l'époque des papes d'Avignon (1305–1378)* (Paris: 1921). An earlier version of the following paragraphs appeared as "The Canonists and Pluralism in the Thirteenth Century," *Speculum* 51 (1976): 35–48.

66. Gratian included the canon in his Decretum at D. 70 c. 2.

67. Tancred to 1 Comp. 3.5.6 (X 3.5.5) v. *aut plures ecclesias,* Admont 22, fol. 34v [1st rec.] [Lyon, Univ. 6, fol. 30v]: "Non potest quis de iure communi plures ecclesias uel prebendas habere quoad titulum uel prelationis uel canonicatus uel ordinationis, arg. hic et di. lxx. Sanctorum et xiii. q.i. c.i. lxxx. di. [Sanctorum—di. *om.* A] Episcopi. vii. q.i. In apibus, xxi. q.i. c.i. ii. et xvi. q.i. Presbyteros, x. q.iii. Vnio, nisi in casibus specialibus ut tamen aliquid dicamus ad excusandas excusationes in peccatis. Dicamus clericum plures posse habere prebendas, set unius tantum ecclesie erit clericus et canonicus intitulatus. In alia habebit ut beneficium quod etiam potest habere laicus, quia potest causa pietatis uel necessitatis uel obsequii prestiti uel prestandi ei concedi. . . . Alii dicunt predictis canonibus derogatum per contrariam consuetudinem papa

twelfth century, they conceded that a cleric could hold two benefices if he had a dispensation from the pope or his ecclesiastical superior (in most cases, the bishop), if poverty or lack of income afflicted a single church, or if one benefice were dependent on another.[68] The canonists knew that many bishops and their chapters customarily granted several benefices to a cleric. Alanus Anglicus, following Huguccio, thought that since the practice was so widespread, it constituted a general custom of the church and thus abrogated *Sanctorum*.[69] The *Glossa Palatina*, however, did not find this argument convincing. Recent papal decretals demonstrated that the general prohibitions against pluralism, especially the canons of the Third Lateran Council, were being enforced in the courts.[70]

As part of the reform legislation at the Fourth Lateran Council of 1215, Pope Innocent III promulgated *De multa*, which forbade any cleric from

---

sciente hoc. . . . Si enim esset peccatum, papa prohiberet. . . . Set dicendum est quod papa hanc consuetudinem expresse reprobat, infra eodem titulo, Cum non ignores, lib. ii. infra eodem titulo, Cum iam dudum, lib. iii. et ideo de iure communi plures habere non potest; secus ex dispensatione, lxx. di. Sanctorum. t."

68. When commenting on *Cum non ignores*, Tancred wrote, 2 Comp. 3.4.1 (X 3.5.15) v. *Cum non ignores*, Admont 22, fol. 104r: "Regulariter; casuale est enim quod plures possint habere ecclesias: dispensationis superioris, ut lxx. di. Sanctorum, propter paupertatem ecclesiarum, ut x. q.iii. Vnio et lxx. di. Sanctorum, propter raritatem clericorum, ut xxi. q.i. c.i. propter concessionem summi pontificis, xxi. q.i. Relatio; licet de iure communi unam intitulatam et aliam commendatam, xxi. q.i. Qui plures (*add*. alias Qui duas), cum una pendet ex altera, supra de etate et qual. Eam te, lib. i."

69. Alanus, 1st rec. to D. 70 c. 2 (Sanctorum) v. *in duabus*, Seo de Urgel 113 (2009), fol. 41r: "ff. de colleg. l.i. sicut enim una ecclesia duos habere prelatos simul non debet, ut infra vii. q.i. Sicut, ita nullus in duabus simul intitulandus est, ut infra xvi. q.vii. Per laicos, xxi. q.i. c.i. ii. Secundum hoc de iuris rigore; uel forte abrogatum est generali consuetudine ecclesie." For Huguccio's opinion see n. 76 below.

70. *Glossa Palatina* to D. 70 c. 2 v. *sine titulo*, Vat. Pal. lat. 658, fol. 18r–18v [Vat. Reg. lat. 977, fol. 51v, Salzburg, St. Peter's Archabbey a.xii.9, fol. 46v]: "Titulatur in duabus; H. dicit hoc capitulum hodie abrogatum per consuetudinem quam papa scit et tollerat, arg. iii. di. § Hec [p.c. 6], ff. de legibus, De quibus [Dig. 1.3.32]. Set confundit eum extra. de prebend. Cum iam dudum, extra. titulo eodem, Cum non ignores. M. dixit quod duas ecclesias intitulatas in eadem diocesi potest quis habere ex dispensatione episcopi, arg. de con. di.i. Omnes [c. 3 or c. 62] et hic. Vel de iure si tenues sunt, extra. de etate, Eam te [1 Comp. 1.8.5 (X 1.14.4 and 3.38.22)]. Set duas prebendas non potest in diuersis episcopalibus ecclesiis, quia de talibus loquitur hic, et xxi. q.i. Clericus [c. 1]. Set ex dispensatione archiepiscopi bene et episcopi in illa prouincia, sicut ex dispensatione pape, arg. lxv. Mos [c. 6]. Et cum ita habuit aliquis duas prebendas intitulatas in hac seruiet per medietatem anni et in illa per aliam, extra. de prebend. Relatum [1 Comp. 3.5.7 (X——)]. H. [B. Salzburg] uero dixit quod ecclesias duas intitulatas habere potest ex dispensatione episcopi, set canonicus prebendarius in duabus esse non potest, siue in eodem episcopatu siue in diuersis, nisi ex dispensatione pape."

possessing two benefices, whether the care of souls was attached to them or not. In certain cases though, especially for clerics who were *sublimes* or *literati,* the Apostolic See could dispense from this general rule.[71] It is likely that *De multa* represented a reform measure rather than an attempt to centralize the granting of dispensations. Innocent's concerns were probably with injudicious or indiscreet episcopal dispensations, not with the question of who had the right of dispensation. Nonetheless, whatever Innocent's intentions, the question was now posed: did *De multa* take the right of dispensation away from bishops?

The canonists first tried to fit *De multa* into current canonistic doctrine about pluralism. Vincentius Hispanus argued that "simple benefices" or income were not included in *De multa.*[72] He introduced the distinction that if a benefice with the care of souls (e.g., a parish church) was attached to any ecclesiastical office, a cleric could keep both the benefice and the office. Sometimes, he went on, such a benefice is given to an archdeacon, as in the case of the priory of St. Firmin in Montpellier. The pope could hardly have had such "dual benefices" in mind because laws should be interpreted according to local customs (*iura interpretanda sunt secundum prouincias*).[73] A canon may receive as many prebends as he can obtain, but he must be subject to only one bishop.[74] If a bishop wished to grant several churches to a learned man—a reason Innocent gave for holding several benefices—then

---

71. Fourth Lateran c. 29, 4 Comp. 3.2.4 (X 3.5.28): "Circa sublimes tamen et litteratas personas, que maioribus sunt beneficiis honorande, cum ratio postulauerit, per sedem apostolicam poterit dispensari." ed. García y García, 73–74.

72. Vincentius Hispanus to 4th Lat. c. 29, v. *poterit dispensari,* ed. García y García, 327: "Et ita in hoc casu non alius dispensare potest, quia sibi retinuit, extra. iii. de sentent. excom. Nuper, tamen ex littera illa 'maioribus' colligitur quod in minoribus dignitatibus et beneficiis paruis possunt episcopi dispensare. vin."

73. Ibid., v. *habens curam animarum annexam,* ed. García, 324–25: "ordinariam uel quasi. Si enim simplex beneficium uel redditus aliquos assignat michi episcopus et concedit in eis ius ligandi et soluendi, non intelligo constitutionem istam de tali, xviii. q.ii. Eleutherii mater, nisi dicas quod quicumque habet potestatem ligandi et soluendi, habet curam animarum. Et intelligo hoc de beneficio quod non est annexum alicui officio ut ei deseruiat. Sunt enim quedam parochie diuites assignate uestiariis monachorum uel canonicorum et non conferuntur alicui perpetuo; et quandoque committuntur archidiaconis, ut prioratus Sancti Firmini in Monte Pesullano. Non credo papam intellexisse de talibus, licet habeant curam, quia sunt annexe alicui officio, ut dixi, et iura interpretanda sunt secundum prouincias, di. lxxvi. Vtinam. Et quod hic dicitur quod 'habeat curam animarum,' hoc uerum est."

74. Ibid., ed. García y García, 325: "Secus in prebendis, de quibus dico quod potest quis habere plures, set unius episcopi erit clericus, et ita intelligitur di. lxx. Sanctorum, et derogatum est illi per contrariam consuetudinem, uel dic ut ibi. De simplicibus redditibus nulla dubitatio. uin."

his appointment could be postulated to the pope with the condition, "if it will please the pope."[75] Vincentius admitted the validity of *De multa,* but restricted its application in practice to major benefices with the care of souls and to pluralists' holding benefices in two bishoprics. Bishops could grant dispensations in other cases.

Huguccio had provided Vincentius with most of his ideas. The Pisan had distinguished between minor prebends—which could be given to a cleric with an episcopal dispensation—and major prebends—which could not. Further, he had also argued that a prebend could be granted to a cleric in another bishopric conditionally, with the stipulation: "if it will please the bishop."[76]

Vincentius' contemporary, Johannes Teutonicus, took an even more striking "episcopalist" approach. For Johannes, *De multa* raised the problem of whence bishops derived their powers of dispensation. He wrote a long, rambling gloss to *De multa,* in which he explored the relationship of papal and episcopal jurisdiction and the source of episcopal authority.

Johannes would not concede that *De multa* took away the bishops' authority to grant dispensations. Since Innocent, he thought, would always be careful not to infringe upon episcopal rights, he could not have intended that *De multa* should deprive bishops of their rights of dispensation. Johannes began his commentary on *De multa* at the point where Innocent III had stated that the Apostolic See could grant dispensations for plural benefices:

per sedem apostolicam: Do you understand by reason of this phrase that the power of dispensing in plural benefices is precluded from bishops, when they have this power from an ancient canon, *Sanctorum?* For just as the pope has authority over bishoprics, the bishops have authority over their churches. . . . It should not be be-

---

75. Ibid., v. *Circa sublimes et litteratas personas,* ed. García, 326: "Vel conferat isti litterato qui alia habet beneficia sub condicione 'si placuerit pape,' et substituat ei alium si pape non placuerit."

76. Huguccio to C. 21 q. 1 a.c. 1 v. *In duabus,* Admont 7, fol. 304r–304v [Klosterneuburg 89, fol. 263r–263v]: "Puta de speciali priuilegio pape potest quis preesse duobus episcopatibus, ut infra c. Relatio [c. 5]. Item de speciali priuilegio et prouisione episcopi potest quis preesse duabus ecclesiis minoribus, ut di. lxx. Sanctorum [c. 2]. . . . Dici potest derogatum esse canonibus clericos plures prebendas habere prohibentibus consuetudine sedi apostolice cognita, nec ab eo reprobata, immo ipso facto quandoque comprobata. Vel potest dici quod condictionaliter [*sic*] intelligitur talis prohibitio: quasi non debet quis in pluribus ecclesiis habere prebendas, scilicet sine uoluntate sui episcopi, nisi episcopo suo placuerit. Sicut et prohibitio de clericis non ordinandis ab alio episcopo facta est sub condictione [*sic*], scilicet sine consensu sui episcopi, nisi primus episcopus consensum adhibuerit." See n. 70 above for the *Palatina*'s report of Huguccio's opinion.

lieved that the pope would want to diminish the rights of other bishops. . . . And if the power of every bishop would not be preserved, surely the ecclesiastical order will be disrupted. . . . Whatever the pope does, it is always understood that he does it without prejudice to others. . . . It would not be thought that the Roman prince wishes to subvert the observance of law with one word. . . . And it matters not what is said here "through the apostolic see," because all dispensations which are made are granted through the see. I find many similar modes of expression. A metropolitan, for example, can consecrate a bishop by virtue of his own right, but, nevertheless, the canon says that he does this through the authority of the apostolic see.[77]

The gloss is a counterpoint to descriptions of papal authority so common in the canonists' commentaries. The pope must always conform his will to the law and to the constitution of the church. Johannes made two additional points. First, the bishops receive the right to grant dispensations to pluralists from a conciliar canon. Consequently, they are not dependent on the pope for the exercise of this prerogative. Second, the pope would not wish to diminish or infringe upon episcopal jurisdictional rights. Johannes cited the Roman law maxim *nec inde debet nasci iniuriarum occasio, unde iura prodierunt,* a favorite tag of the lawyers when they wished to argue that the monarch should live according to the law.

He compared the relationship of the pope to his bishops with that of the bishops to their subjects. The bishops have the same authority over subject churches as the pope has over bishoprics. The pope could override the jurisdiction of a bishop, but Johannes thought he would need a good reason for doing so. With a telling analogy, he noted that just because a bishop might be said to perform an act through the authority of the Apostolic See, this did not mean that a bishop could not act in his own right. The

---

77. Johannes Teutonicus to 4th Lat. c. 29, 4 Comp. 3.2.4 (X 3.5.28) v. *per sedem apostolicam poterit dispensari,* ed. García y García, 218: "Numquid ratione huius uerbi intelligis episcopis esse preclusam potestatem dispensandi circa pluralitatem stipendiorum, cum a canone antiquo hanc habeant potestatem, ut lxx. di. Sanctorum? Et sicut papa habet potestatem circa episcopatus, sic episcopi circa ecclesias, ut extra. ii. de exces. prelat. Sicut unire. Nec credendum est papam aliorum episcoporum uelle iura diminuere, ut xcix. di. Ecce et c. Nullus. Et si cuilibet episcopo sua potestas non seruatur, quid aliud est quam quod ecclesiasticus ordo confunditur, ut xi. q.i. Peruenit, in fine? Et quicquid papa facit semper intelligitur sine aliorum preiudicio facere, ut ix. q.iii. Nunc uero, C. de emancip. Nec auus. Nec inde nasci debet iniuriarum occasio unde iura prodierunt, ut extra. iii. de accus. Qualiter. Nec credendum est quod Romanus pontifex uno uerbo uelit totam iuris obseruantiam subuertere, ut C. de inoffic. testam. Si quando. Nec obstat quod hic dicitur, 'per sedem apostolicam' quia omnis dispensatio que fit per ipsam fit. Similes enim modos loquendi sepius inuenio. Nam metropolitanus suo iure potest consecrare episcopos, et tamen canon dicit auctoritate sedis apostolice ipsum facere, ut lxiiii. di. Ordinationes. Simile est extra. i. de offic. arch. c.ult."

metropolitan did not receive his authority to consecrate a suffragan bishop from the Roman see.

Johannes' allegation that the bishops exercised the right of dispensation from an ancient canon is a puzzle. The canonists always conceded that the pope could abrogate a disciplinary canon of any council. This was an undisputed part of papal legislative authority.[78] If the pope could abrogate any conciliar canon, why not in this particular case? The paradox is resolved by examining other glosses in which Johannes discussed ecclesiastical power and jurisdiction.

In a gloss to the Decretum, Johannes wrote that the Roman church derived a part of its authority from church councils. His exact words were "councils bestow primacy upon the Roman church, which is true secondarily; Christ himself principally bestowed primacy."[79] By connecting the origins of a part of ecclesiastical jurisdiction to councils, Johannes added a historical dimension to the development of the church's constitution. It was a common doctrine of Christian belief that the church was founded by God in the person of Jesus Christ. The headship of the church was given to St. Peter when Christ said to him: "You are Peter and upon this rock I shall build my church" (Matthew 16.18). If one wished to develop a coherent episcopal ecclesiology, one could insist that although Christ did select Peter to be the governor of the church, he also gave the other apostles an independent status within the ecclesiastical hierarchy. The apostles were the archetypes for the bishops and received their authority directly from Christ.[80] But Christ did not establish church councils, and Johannes' assertion that the pope received his primacy "secondarily" from councils is a novelty that remained embedded in his Ordinary Gloss to the Decretum.

Earlier, Huguccio had written that the pope had derived his primacy "secondarily" from councils:

It is said that the Roman church had its primacy from the Lord and not from councils, but I say that the church held its primacy principally from the Lord and

---

78. The canonists often stated that the pope could not change the canons of the first four general councils in matters of faith; see Le Bras, Lefebvre, and Rambaud, *L'âge classique*, 385–405.

79. Johannes Teutonicus to C. 3 q. 6 c. 9 v. *voluerunt:* "Sic ergo concilia dederunt primatum Romane ecclesiae quod verum est secundario, sed ipse Christus principaliter, ut 21 dist. Quamvis, 17 dist. § Hinc etiam et 9 q. 3 Aliorum."

80. For a discussion of the New Testament foundations of the papal office, called the Petrine Theory, see above Chapter 2; Tierney, *Foundations*, 23–46; and more generally, G. Schwaiger, "Der päpstliche Primat in der Geschichte der Kirche," *Zeitschrift für Kirchengeschichte* 82 (1971): 1–15.

through his authority, and secondarily from the councils by submitting himself voluntarily [*per uoluntariam concessionem*] to them.[81]

Unlike Johannes in his abbreviated gloss, Huguccio was not conceding one jot of papal authority. The papacy was divinely ordained and was superior to any general council. The pope had submitted himself to councils voluntarily in the past when the councils enhanced papal power, or, as the *correctores Romani* explained in a gloss to Johannes' text in the sixteenth century, when the councils declared which prerogatives Christ had given to the pope.[82] Huguccio had returned to a favorite idea of the canonists for which they found support in Justinian's *Codex,* in the law *Digna vox* (Cod. 1.14.4). Although the prince is not bound by the law, it is proper for him to submit to it. This doctrine could result in two quite different conclusions. One, put forward by Huguccio, did not admit that any papal authority might be lost by the pope's submission to the law. Heresy was the only crime for which the pope could be tried. The other, articulated by Johannes Teutonicus, granted that in certain cases the pope must submit to the strictures of the law.[83] For the most part, however, the canonists agreed that when the prince submitted his will to the law, such a submission did not compromise his *principatus.*

Although he was more circumspect in another gloss, Johannes almost certainly abbreviated Huguccio's gloss intentionally in order to magnify the role of the council within the church.[84] The idea that a conciliar canon could bestow jurisdiction was an integral part of Johannes' ecclesiology. The Roman church as well as the bishops received authority from the great councils of the past. Consequently, if the pope rescinded a canon on which a part of episcopal authority rested, he would infringe upon episcopal rights and

---

81. Huguccio to D. 17 p.c. 6 v. *iussione domini,* Admont 7, fol. 20r [Vat. lat. 2280, fol. 15r]: "Dicitur quod ecclesia Romana habuit primatum a domino et non a conciliis, set dico quod a domino principaliter et per auctoritatem habuit, a conciliis uero secundario et per uoluntariam concessionem se illis [illi A] submittendo."

82. The *correctores Romani* noted that "Concilia proprie non dederunt primatum Romane ecclesie sed explicarunt datum a domino," in an addition to Johannes' gloss to D. 17 p.c. 6.

83. The pertinent texts of Johannes are cited in Chapter 1 above.

84. Johannes Teutonicus to D. 17 p.c. 6 v. *iussione,* Admont 35, fol. 22r: "Habet ergo Romana ecclesia auctoritatem a conciliis [a domino A], set imperator a populo, ut xciii. Legimus. Contrarium huic signatur xxi. di. Quamvis et xxii. di. Omnes, ubi dicitur quod Romana ecclesia habuit primatum a domino, et non a conciliis." Also his gloss to C. 3 q. 6 c. 9 v. *voluerunt* (see n. 79). Bartholomaeus Brixiensis added: "Sed dic principaliter habuit a Domino, secundario a conciliis."

disturb the state of the church. Of course, this the pope could not do.[85]

Johannes used this argument in one other case. In his apparatus to *Compilatio tertia*, he wrote that a metropolitan can grant a dispensation to a bishop who has been elected from a minor order, because he has this right from a conciliar canon. Therefore, the metropolitan's authority to grant this dispensation should not be taken away.[86]

The rest of Johannes's gloss to *De multa* took up issues raised by earlier canonists. He thought that *De multa* referred to dispensations for benefices held in two different bishoprics. In this case, only the pope could dispense. Otherwise, the impossible situation would arise that a cleric would have two lords.[87] However, Johannes emphasized that if the two benefices were held in the same bishopric, then the local bishop could make the dispensation. The bishops were only forbidden to make indiscreet or rash dispensations, not those that were useful or necessary.[88]

In an unusual aside, Johannes mentioned a conversation he must have had with Innocent III at the papal curia. Supported by a suggestion of Huguccio, Vincentius Hispanus had argued that a cleric could be granted a second benefice if the grantor included the phrase, "si papae placuerit."[89] Johannes relished Innocent's scorn for Huguccio's and Vincentius' logic:

"Eligo istum si pape placuerit", non magis quam si diceretur, "Cognosco uxorem istius si uiro placuerit". [To say "I elect him if it will please the pope" is no different from saying, "I can lie with a man's wife if it will please him."][90]

---

85. Tierney, *Foundations*, 49–59.

86. Johannes Teutonicus to 3 Comp. 1.6.5 (X 1.6.20) v. *indulgentiam*, ed. Pennington, 51: "Vnde episcopus quantum ad omnia potest legitimare preterquam in episcopatu. In quibus autem episcopus possit uel non possit dispensare notaui l. di. Miror et i. q.vii. § Nisi. Item et dico quod metropolitanus adhuc dispensare potest cum episcopo in ordine minori, cum illud a canone habuit, ut lx. di. c.ult. nec sit ei ablata dispensatio." For his views on when a bishop could dispense, see C. 1 q. 7 p.c. 5 v. *ut plerisque*. The common opinion of the canonists was that a bishop could dispense in any matter which the pope had not reserved to himself. Jacobus de Albenga to 5 Comp. 3.27.1 (X 3.50.10), v. *sedis apostolice*, Cordoba, Bibl. de Cabildo 10, fol. 333r: "Non ergo inferior episcopus poterit in hoc casu dispensare, cum specialiter sibi dominus papa hanc dispensationem reseruauerit, et est simile supra de prebend. De multa, lib. iiii. Alias autem posset inferior episcopus dispensare nisi papa specialiter hanc sibi potestatem reseruasset, ut supra de sent. excomm. Nuper, lib. iii. jac."

87. Johannes Teutonicus to 4th Lat. c. 29, ed. García y García, 219–20. Pennington, "Canonists and Pluralism," 41.

88. Ibid., 42.

89. See nn. 72 to 76 above for Huguccio's and Vincentius' opinions.

90. Johannes Teutonicus to 4th Lat. c. 29, ed. García y García, 220, following, however, the reading of Johannes' words in some of the manuscripts and in 4 Comp.

Johannes' anecdote is another illustration of Innocent's acerbic sense of humor noted so often by contemporaries.[91] Beneath the humor, however, was Innocent's clear opposition to compromise measures or legal subterfuges that could have circumvented the intent of *De multa*. The canonists often used "si papae placuerit" in their discussions of vows and oaths—all vows and oaths, they thought, implicitly contained this exception[92]—but Innocent did not want to extend this concept to dispensations.

Johannes remained obdurate, however, in spite of Innocent's opposition. He continued to insist that a bishop could dispense from the prohibition that a cleric could not hold two benefices, especially if the bishopric were poor or rural.[93] He discussed the problem in two long glosses to Gratian's Decretum, using the same arguments to defend episcopal rights that he had used in his gloss to *De multa* and coming to the same conclusions.[94]

Johannes' opinions did not carry the field. Other canonists and even scribes who copied his Ordinary Gloss quarreled with him.[95] Tancred, the leading canonist in Bologna after Johannes, had no doubts that the canon had taken away all episcopal rights of dispensation for benefices having the care of souls. As soon as a cleric accepted a second benefice, he lost the first.[96] Following Vincentius, Tancred added that if it had been customary to

---

91. Tillmann, *Papst Innocenz III.*, 236–37; Cheney, *Pope Innocent III and England*, 3–10; Pennington, "Pope Innocent III's Views on Church and State," 52–53.

92. Johannes Teutonicus to 3 Comp. 1.2.9 (X 1.3.19) v. *intelligatur*, ed. Pennington, 18. Innocent accepted the idea for vows, see 3 Comp. 2.15.5 (X 2.24.19) [Venientes]. See Ullmann, *Medieval Papalism*, 66–73.

93. Johannes Teutonicus to C. 21 q. 1 a.c. 1 v. *in duabus:* "De iure communi, nullus potest habere plures ecclesias, nisi in sex casibus. . . . Et si episcopus dispensat cum aliquo, ut 70 dist. Sanctorum, et ubi est paucitas hominum, scilicet extra civitatem." 3 Comp. 3.8.3 (X 3.8.6) v. *iusta causa*, Admont 22, fol. 199v: "Ecce uerbum, nota dignum quod propter iustam et necessariam causam possit episcopus uel alius habere plures dignitates, inconsulto etiam papa, et esset iusta causa forte paupertas episcopatus."

94. Johannes Teutonicus to C. 21 q. 2 c. 3 v. *translatus* and D. 70 c. 2. v. *in duabus*.

95. In Munich, Staatsbibl. 14024, fol. 43v, the scribe who copied Johannes' gloss to D. 70 c. 2. v. *in duabus,* inserted in the middle of the gloss, after Johannes wrote "Dico quod non": "Tu dicas sic per constitutionem Honorii extra. de relig. dom. c.ult. et ab hoc loco, in antea, uacat glosa." In the same manuscript, on fol. 128v, the scribe added a "uacat" to Johannes' gloss to C. 21 q. 2 c. 3 v. *translatus*. The decretal to which the scribe referred is *Exspectavimus*, discussed below. De relig. dom. is the title after de statu monachorum in which *Exspectavimus* was placed.

96. Tancred to 2 Comp. 3.4.1 (X 3.5.15) v. *uelis concedere*, Admont 22, fol. 104r: "Hodie uero qui habet dignitatem uel ecclesiam cui sit animarum cura annexa, si secundam

receive benefices in two different dioceses, the pope could approve such customs after the fact.[97] He made a further distinction in his view by observing that a cleric who received a prebend without the care of souls in another diocese would not lose his first prebend *ipso facto* if the bishop had customarily made such grants. The pope, however, must have known of and tolerated the custom.[98] We know from a number of thirteenth-century sources that popes and English bishops gave *de facto* if not *de iure* assent to Tancred's opinion.[99]

The reactions of other canonists to these fine distinctions were sometimes sharp. According to Damasus Ungarus, Johannes, Vincentius, and possibly Tancred were "impudent."[100] No one, he wrote, should normally hold several dignities or churches. Those canonists who say a cleric can possess two benefices are wrong. When a cleric accepts the second, he loses

---

recipit, ipso iure uacat prima, ut infra de prebend. De multa, lib. iiii. Si uero prebendas uel alia ecclesiastica beneficia que curam animarum non habeant priuandus est, ut infra de prebend. Cum iam dudum, lib. iii."

97. Tancred to 1 Comp. 3.5.6 (X 3.5.5) v. *aut plures ecclesias,* Bamberg, Staatsbibl. can. 19, fol. 32r [Cordoba, Bibl. de Cabildo 10, fol. 40v]: "Vnde dico derogatum esse illi canoni, lxx. di. Sanctorum, per contrariam consuetudinem quam dominus papa scit et tollerat immo scribendo et concedendo approbat, sicut nuper fecit pro domino R. canonico Mutinensi pro canonica Placentina, dans sibi litteras suas. t." See text of first recension in n. 67 above. Tancred's text is difficult to reconstruct because some manuscripts of the second recension have the same text as the first and because those manuscripts that have the text in this note do not have a clear textual tradition.

98. Tancred to 3 Comp. 3.5.4 (X 3.5.18) v. *dignitatem,* Vat. lat. 1377, fol. 222r [Vat. lat. 2509, fol. 213r]: "Secundum antiqua iura et tempora huius constitutionis qui habebat unam dignitatem et aliam recipiebat, non erat ipso iure priuatus prima, set priuandus et spoliandus, ut supra de prebend. Relatum et c. Referente, lib. i. licet sit arg. contra xxi. q.ii. Si quis iam translatus. Hodie uero qui habet dignitatem cui sit cura animarum adnexa, si recipit similem dignitatem, ipso iure uacat prima, ut in constitutione domini Innocentii, De multa. Set quid si habens prebendam recipiat aliam prebendam sine animarum cura, numquid uacat ipso iure prima? Non. Numquid potest utramque retinere? Videtur quod non ut hic et supra eodem titulo, Quia in tantum, lib. i. supra lxx. di. Sanctorum. Ego credo per contrariam consuetudinem illis iuribus derogatum quam papa scit et tollerat, nec prohibuit consilium in constitutione, De multa, de prebendis, sed tantum de dignitatibus. t."

99. M. Gibbs and J. Lang, *Bishops and Reform, 1215–1272: With Special Reference to the Lateran Council of 1215* (London: 1934), 16–17, 172–73. See J. W. Gray, "Canon Law in England: Some Reflections on the Stubbs-Maitland Controversy," *Studies in Church History* (London: 1966), 3:48–68. Gray argues that the English did not want to accept *De multa* as a piece of legislation. Rather, as with the canonists, it was a question of interpreting the canon's intent.

100. On Damasus and his Hungarian origins, see Kuttner, *Repertorium,* 394–95.

his first automatically.[101] A benefice held with a canonical title cannot be held with another except, he conceded, in a few cases.[102] Goffredus da Trani inserted Johannes' entire gloss into his apparatus without any comment. However, he undoubtedly rejected Johannes' position.[103] He argued eloquently in his *Summa* that *De multa* must be interpreted as forbidding all types of pluralism. Tancred and the other doctors, he said, were not sympathetic to the poor and favored the rich.[104] Only the pope could give dispensations to pluralists. This, he said, was the current opinion of the Roman curia.[105]

In 1226 Pope Honorius III commissioned Tancred to compile a collection of his decretals from the papal registers. Honorius had issued a decretal clarifying the problem of dispensations for pluralists, *Exspectavimus hactenus exspectantes.*[106] Tancred, however, did not include it in his collec-

---

101. Damasus to 4th Lat. c. 29, v. *diuersas dignitates*, ed. García y García, 432–33: "Diligenter nota contra quosdam proteruos quod quis plures dignitates non potest habere, nec plures dignitates nec plures ecclesias. Dicunt autem quidam quod plures potest quis habere prebendas, quod falsum est, immo per receptionem secunde prebende amittitur titulus prime prebende, ut supra de concess. preb. uel eccles. non uac. Litteras, lib. iii. Et hoc est quod subicitur hic de personatibus curam animarum non habentibus."

102. Ibid.: "Ergo teneas generaliter quod nullum beneficium habitum cum canonico titulo habito, nisi in casibus notatis, supra de etate et qualit. Eam te. lib. i. d."

103. Goffredus inserted Johannes' gloss at X 3.5.28 v. *per sedem apostolicam*, Paris, B.N. lat. 15402, fol. 94r and Vienna, N.B. lat. 2197, fol. 83r–83v. He clearly rejected the substance of Johannes' gloss at X 3.8.9 v. *firmauit*, Paris, B.N. lat. 15402, fol. 97r: "Quod non licuit etiam dispensando, ut uidetur innuere lxx. di. Sacrorum, nisi iusta et necessaria, arg. supra eodem titulo, Cum nostris, in fine. Hodie uero hoc non liceret sine dispensatione sedis apostolice, ut supra de prebend. De multa, in fine. g."

104. Goffredus da Trani, *Summa super titulis decretalium* (Lyon: 1519; reprinted Aalen: 1968), fol. 127v: "Sed queritur an recepta secunda prebenda prima vacet ipso iure, et videtur quod sic, ut infra de concess. preb. Litteras. Vnde quod statutum est in beneficiis curam animarum habentibus, ut infra eodem c. De multa, et in personatibus de quibus idem iudicium est habendum, ut supra de elect. Dudum, etiam si curam animarum non habeant, ut in decretali, De multa, in fine. . . . Et intelligo hoc cum secunda prebenda recipitur ut titulus non ut simplex beneficium vel ut stipendium. Tancredus tamen et quidam alii doctores non compatientes pauperibus, sed divitibus blandientes, dixerunt hoc locum habere tantum in beneficiis curam animarum habentibus et in personatibus quibus loquitur hec decretalis, De multa, non autem in prebendis."

105. Ibid., fol. 128r: "Sed queritur an alius a papa dispensare possit in pluralitate beneficiorum et scripsit jo. quod sic in eadem diocesi. . . . Verius esse puto quod sive in eodem episcopatu sive in diversis nullus dispensare potest nisi papa, et sic curia tenet."

106. Pressutti 2268; Po. 6163, 6166. The decretal is printed in full by J. A. Riegger, *Compilatio quinta epistolarum decretalium* (Vienna: 1761) Appendix 3 (unpaginated). Tancred included the last part of the decretal in 5 Comp. 3.24.1 (X 3.41.10). Cf. Stephan Kuttner, "Zur Entstehungsgeschichte der Summa de casibus poenitentiae des hl. Raymond von Penyfort,"

tion.[107] He had marked the letter when he searched the registers for decretals, but he left the section on dispensations out of his final draft of *Compilatio quinta*.[108] He may have omitted *Exspectavimus* because he thought *De multa* adequately covered the problem or, more likely, because he thought *Exspectavimus* was too crude and did not contain the nuances he favored. Nevertheless, later canonists added *Exspectavimus* either to the body of *Compilatio quinta* or as an appendix to the collection.[109] Canonists cited the decretal to prove that only the pope could grant a dispensation to pluralists.[110]

Time did not make Johannes' defense of episcopal rights of dispensation more palatable. Bartholomaeus Brixiensis, who revised Johannes' Ordinary Gloss to the Decretum, wrote that Johannes' gloss to *Sanctorum* had no force. Following Tancred, he believed that bishops could grant dispensations for clerics to hold two or more simple benefices without the care of souls.[111] Most canonists in the 1230s and 1240s agreed with Bartholomaeus.[112] In the middle years of the thirteenth century, canonistic opinion

---

ZRG Kan. Abt. 39 (1953): 431 and "The Barcelona Edition of St. Raymond's First Treatise on Canon Law," *Seminar* 8 (1950): 65.

107. The section of *Exspectavimus* which treats dispensations reads: "Exspectavimus hactenus exspectantes *et infra.* Nec permittas quempiam habere plures personatus seu parochiales ecclesias post concilium generale, quibus cura sit animarum annexa, nisi forte super hoc habeat indulgentiam sedis apostolicae specialem." This text is from Riegger.

108. On the genesis of 5 Comp. and the markings in the Registers of Honorius III, see Leonard E. Boyle, "The Compilatio quinta and the Registers of Honorius III," BMCL 8 (1978): 9–19.

109. The text of *Exspectavimus* printed in n. 107 was added to 5 Comp. after 3.20.4 in London, B.L. Royal 11 C.vii, fol. 265r, Tours, Bibl. mun. 565, fol. 31r, Vienna, N.B. lat. 2077, fol. 24v, Paris, B.N. lat. 3933, fol. 136r, Paris, B.N. n.a.l. 2127, fol. 219r, Graz Univ. 374, fol. 395v. The text of the entire decretal was an appendix to 4 Comp. in Cordoba, Bibl. de Cabildo 10, fol. 304v and Bamberg, Staatsbibl. can. 19, fol. 255r–255v and to the Fourth Lateran Constitutions in Vienna 2183, fol. 107v. In Montecassino, Bibl. dell'Abbazia 468, listed in García y García, *Constitutiones Concilii quarti Lateranensis*, 130, the decretal was placed between c. 54 and c. 55 of the 4th Lateran Constitutions. Father Boyle argues *Exspectavimus* was part of Tancred's compilation, "Compilatio quinta," 14–16. For reasons given in my "The French Recension of Compilatio tertia," BMCL 5 (1975): 68–69, I do not think that *Exspectavimus* or the other *extravagantes* were part of Honorius' collection that was sent to Bologna.

110. E.g., Raymond de Pennafort as noted by Kuttner, "Zur Entstehungsgeschichte," 431; Zoen Tencararius, apparatus to 5 Comp. 3.4.3 (X 3.5.33) v. *inconcusse,* Tours, Bibl. mun. 565, fol. 24v and the unknown canonist in n. 95 above.

111. Bartholomaeus Brixiensis to D. 70 c. 2 v. *in duabus:* "Haec glossa nihil ualet, quia papa tantum dispensat circa plures ecclesias habentes curam animarum et plures dignitates, ut expresse dicit decretum De multa. Sed circa plura beneficia simplicia non uidetur episcopo dispensare prohibitum."

112. For the opinions of Jacobus de Albenga, Bernardus Parmensis, and Innocent IV, see Pennington, "Canonists and Pluralism," 44–45.

shifted back toward Johannes. Pierre de Sampsone (d. 1260) thought that bishops could grant dispensations for pluralists, but he gave a rationale that did not touch the delicate question of papal and episcopal rights:

I solve the problem thus, and I believe this solution is true. When a cleric receives a dispensation for holding several benefices, the dispensation either provides for a person or for churches. If for churches, examples of these dispensations might be that they are placed in the middle of perverse nations and cannot be defended except by a powerful cleric. Or perhaps the paucity of clerics is so great in the land that no one can be found who is learned except one. Or the churches are among heretics. Bishops may grant dispensations to such persons, because the *ratio* of the canon *Sanctorum* remains. If a bishop intends to provide for a person, he cannot dispense.[113]

Using a distinction between a benefit to the church and a benefit to an individual, Pierre avoided the problem of where the right of dispensation originated. Later, Bernard de Montmirat (Abbas Antiquus [d. 1296]) followed the opinion of his teacher.[114]

Hostiensis finally accepted Johannes' opinion. As we have already seen, Hostiensis was sensitive to the rights of bishops and never condoned the pope's right to act wrongly or arbitrarily. In his gloss to *De multa,* he noted that Tancred and Bernardus Parmensis were opposed to Johannes Teutonicus' theory of episcopal dispensation, as was the present-day Roman curia. Nevertheless, he said, right and natural reason justified Johannes. He then repeated the key sections of Johannes' commentary.[115]

Hostiensis agreed with Johannes that a bishop could grant a dispensation to pluralists, but he carried Johannes' argument to its logical conclusion. Johannes had implied that since the bishops had received their right of dispensation from a conciliar canon, even the pope could not take this right away. However, he had argued that Innocent III had not intended to take episcopal rights of dispensation away. Therefore Johannes did not dispute the pope's right to abrogate *Sanctorum,* the canon upon which Johannes'

---

113. Pierre de Sampsone to X 3.5.28 v. *dispensare,* Vienna, Nationalbibl. 2113, fol. 53v–54r: "Sed eam soluo sic, et uerum credo quia cum dispensatur cum aliquo ut possit habere plures ecclesias aut prouideretur ecclesiis aut persone. Si ecclesiis, puta quia sunt posite in medio nationis peruerse, et non possunt defensari nisi per aliquem potentem clericum, uel forte est tanta raritas clericorum quod in tota terra non inuenitur nisi unus qui sit persona literata, et ecclesie forte sunt inter hereticos, tunc potest episcopus cum talibus dispensare quia sic remanet ratio illius capituli lxx. di. Sanctorum et xxi. q.i. c.i. in fine. Si uero intendat prouidere persone, tunc non potest episcopus cum eo dispensare, etiam si nobilis sit et litterata persona ut hic."

114. Bernard de Montmirat, *In libris decretalium aurei commentarii uidelicet Abbatis antiqui, Bernardi Compostellani, Guidonis papae, Ioannis a Capistrano* (Venice: 1588) to X 3.5.28 v. *personatus,* fol. 96v. See Pennington, "Canonists and Pluralism," 45–46, for text.

115. Ibid., 46.

argument had been based. By the time Hostiensis wrote, the canonists conceded that Innocent had intended to abolish episcopal dispensations. Hostiensis attacked the problem frontally. He said that the pope could not annul the episcopal right in *Sanctorum:*

Therefore, if evident utility and, above all, urgent necessity of the church require a dispensation to be granted in such cases, what constitution could take episcopal dispensation away? For if any constitution would say this expressly, it would be irrational, burdensome to churches, and ought to be rejected. . . . Nor, indeed, is the constitution of man stronger than the constitution of God. . . . But I see that an oath, whose author is God, ought not to be preserved in such a case. . . . Even less then, ought a human constitution be preserved if it would say this. . . . And whenever necessity or evident utility demand a dispensation from the truth of law I understand that the opinion of Johannes is right.[116]

Earlier, Hostiensis had founded his opposition to a papal mandate for an unworthy candidate on the basis of an individual's conscience; here he used a common concept of the medieval lawyers, the *ratio* of urgent necessity, to defend episcopal rights of dispensation. The canonists believed that fundamental rules governed the legal system. *Necessitas non legem habet,* necessity knows no law, was one such rule. Hostiensis concluded that even the pope must conform to these principles. His position was not unusual among the canonists; they often circumvented papal authority by an appeal to principle. The canonists thought that principles or maxims formed an inviolable foundation of every legal system.[117]

Almost all the canonists after Hostiensis rejected the right of episcopal dispensations for pluralists.[118] It is not clear from their glosses, however, that

---

116. Hostiensis to X 3.5.28 v. *sed per sedem apostolicam,* vol. 2, fol. 24v: "Igitur si evidens utilitas, et maxime urgens necessitas ecclesiae requirit dispensationem fieri in talibus, quae constitutio poterit auferre dispensationem episcopis in hoc casu? Nam et si hoc diceret expresse constitutio aliqua, esset irrationabilis, et ecclesiis onerosa, et sic abijcienda. . . . Nec enim fortius est vinculum constitutionis hominis quam Dei. . . . Sed video quod iuramentum, cuius Deus author est in tali casu servandum non est. . . . Multominus ergo constitutio humana, et si hoc diceret, servanda esset. . . . Et in tali casu ubicumque necessitas vel evidens utilitas ecclesiae hoc exposcit, intelligo de veritate iuris esse vera in opinione Ioannis."

117. For several other examples, see Kenneth Pennington, "Pro peccatis patrum puniri: A Moral and Legal Problem of the Inquisition," *Church History* 47 (1978): 137–54.

118. E.g., Guillielmus Durantis, Antonius de Butrio, Zabarella. Jesselin de Cassagnes, Extrav. Johannis XXII 3.1 v. *dispensative,* thought a bishop could dispense. As far as I can tell, his opinion was unusual among the later canonists. On Jesselin and his works, see the important article by Jacqueline Tarrant, "The Life and Works of Jesselin de Cassagnes," BMCL 9 (1979): 37–64.

they were aware of the ecclesiological implications of the problem.[119] Nevertheless, in the second half of the thirteenth century, Hostiensis was even more adamant than Johannes Teutonicus that the bishops had jurisdictional rights within the church that not even the pope could legislate away.

The provision of benefices was not a simple, straightforward matter in the thirteenth century. A bishop who wished to obstruct the will of the pope might make a number of legal objections to a provision. A papal providee's undisputed legal right to a benefice might be difficult to prove. It was even more difficult to put the papal candidate in possession of the benefice. A letter of provision, no matter how strongly worded, was not a guarantee that a provision would actually take place. The complexities and difficulties are well illustrated by a decretal of Innocent IV, *Quia cunctis,* probably issued sometime between 1248 and 1250.[120] The canonists knew much more about the case than we can gather from the letter as it exists in both Innocent's *Novella* and Boniface VIII's *Sext.* Hostiensis wrote a long summary of the decretal for his apparatus to the *Novella.*

Innocent, said Hostiensis, always favored the nobility. He had given Draco of Bourbon a letter of provision to the first vacant prebend in Chartres. The letter contained the crucial phrase "irritum et inane," which invalidated any other contrary provision. A certain prior was appointed as the executor of the mandate. He went immediately to Chartres and read the pope's mandate to the cathedral chapter. There was an episcopal vacancy at the time. Matthew of Champs, who would become the next bishop in April 1247, was still a subdeacon of the cathedral chapter. Along with the other canons, he listened to the pope's mandate. The letter stipulated that Draco need not accept the first vacant benefice, but only the first benefice that was acceptable to him. He had first choice of each newly vacant prebend. After Matthew's election and consecration, the *praepositura* of Normandy became vacant when the provost died abroad. Draco's prior heard of the vacancy and offered it to him. Draco accepted the benefice. At the same time, some-

---

119. Nor have historians. Buisson, who devotes a number of pages to *De multa,* concludes that the decretal's importance lies in the later canonists' rejection of Innocent IV's claim that the pope could dispense "sine causa." Buisson asserts that the canonists adapted the Thomistic-Aristotelian concept that the pope must act reasonably and with equity. As we have seen, the canonists believed this long before the arrival of Aristotle and Thomas. See Le Bras, Lefebvre, and Rambaud, *L'âge classique,* 352–84, esp. 352–66.

120. VI 3.7.1. Po. 15124. The decretal is not found in the registers of Innocent because most of those years are lost. See Stephan Kuttner, "Die Konstitutionen des ersten allegemeinen Konzils von Lyon," *Studia et documenta historiae et iuris* 6 (1940): 70–131, reprinted in *Medieval Councils, Decretals and Collections of Canon Law: Selected Essays* (London: 1980).

one else—either Guglielmo Fieschi, cardinal deacon of St. Eustachio, or Bishop Matthew—bestowed the *praepositura* on Andrea Fieschi, the brother of the cardinal and nephew of the pope. The letter as it exists in the *Novella* or the *Sext* fails to mention the cardinal legate's involvement. Hostiensis must thus have had personal knowledge of the decretal's background.[121]

In terms of the law, the solution should have been straightforward. Draco had a papal mandate. It had been properly publicized. The necessary inhibitory clauses had been included in the letter. After reviewing the allegations on both sides, Innocent's decision was brief: Andrea was given possession; silence was imposed on Draco. Innocent wrote a long commentary to the decretal after it had been placed in his *Novella*. Although his gloss is wordy and a little confused, he concluded that Draco's prior should have issued a stay to Bishop Matthew before he had granted the benefice. Without a stay, the ordinary still had the right to make a presentation.[122]

In glossing the decretal Hostiensis was even more prolix than Innocent. He concluded that the case had been decided on dubious grounds:

I do not know if I would have rendered a decision for the pope's nephew after having reviewed the facts, for flesh and blood should not influence a judge's decision. Innocent did not want to be a hypocrite as was the scholar who wished to be thought wise by rendering judgments against his own so that he would be considered the wisest man of all.[123]

The lack of clear reasoning in *Quia cunctis* obviously disturbed Hostiensis.

There is no evidence that Andrea ever got possession of the benefice in spite of papal preferment. Although his name appears several times in the later years of Innocent's registers, he is never called a canon or provost of Chartres.[124] The only titles to appear in the registers are papal "capellanus"

---

121. Hostiensis to *Novella Innocentii quarti* [= VI 3.7.1], "Quia cunctis," 2: fol. 22v. Hostiensis provides details about the case that are not in the decretal as it is edited for the *Novella* or for the *Sext*. Some of the details are not corroborated in other sources. Guglielmo must have been a legate in northern France at the beginning of Matthew's episcopacy. In fact, in May, August, and October of 1247, Guglielmo was not in Lyons with Innocent IV, see Agostino Paravicini Bagliani, *Cardinali di curia e "familiae" cardinalizie dal 1227 al 1254* (Padua: 1972), 426. Paravicini does not note that Andrea was the brother of Guglielmo, ibid., 329–40. F. Bernini, "Innocenzo IV et il suo parentado," *Nuova rivista storica* 24 (1940): 178–99, lists a brother of Guglielmo named Giacomo, but not Andrea.

122. Innocent IV, *Commentaria* fol. 379r–382r.

123. Hostiensis, 2: fol. 24r: "Nescio si omnibus predictis consideratis pro nepote proprio iudicassem, nam et caro et sanguis debent retrahere . . . sed dominus noster [Innocentius] noluit apparere hypocrita sicut scholaris qui de novo pro sapiente venerat, et contra suos, quamvis iustitiam foverent dabat sententias ut hominibus iustissimus appareret."

124. Berger no. 6252, 7948, 8278.

and precentor of the cathedral chapter of Salisbury.[125] Draco is mentioned as the provost of "Oeya" and as sacristan at Chartres, but not as provost of Normandy.[126] This is not unusual. Unless there is corroborative evidence from local archives, it is often very difficult to discover whether a particular papal mandate of provision was ever obeyed.

Many examples show that a particular papal mandate was not carried out as the pope wished. The spirit of Bishop Simon of Meaux lived on, but in subtler and more sophisticated guises. Bishops were well aware of the limitations of provisions. They knew that the pope had great difficulty imposing his will on distant subjects, and they were quick to exploit the legal loopholes of the system. The disputes over conflicting claims could last for years.[127]

In 1231 Pope Gregory IX wrote to the bishop of Chichester about a provision to Master Alatrino, a papal "capellanus" and subdeacon. Alatrino was an important figure in the curia. Dating back to the early years of Innocent III's pontificate, he had served three popes. He had been entrusted with important diplomatic missions by Honorius III and Gregory IX.[128] Gregory had granted Alatrino the office of treasurer in Chichester after the death of Pandulf, the former officeholder. The bishop of Chichester, however, had granted the office to William of Neville before the papal mandate arrived. Legally, in this case, the bishop was on sound ground. Since the papal mandate had not arrived before he had selected and installed William, he was under no obligation to follow it. He asked Gregory to confirm William's appointment and noted, in passing, that the office of treasurer was attached to a sacerdotal office with the care of souls. The office of treasurer, therefore, demanded residence in Chichester. The bishop was prepared to object if Gregory had any intentions of pressing for Alatrino's appointment.

---

125. Ibid., no. 6224, 6329, 6843.

126. A privilege of Pope Alexander III of Sept. 1173 lists the dignities of Chartres, mentioning the *praepositura* of Normandy, PL 200.913–14.

127. Two perceptive essays illustrating this point are Brentano, "Localism and Longevity" and McCurry, "*Utilia Metensia*," both in *Law, Church and Society: Essays in Honor of Stephan Kuttner*, ed. K. Pennington and R. Somerville (Philadelphia: 1977), 293–323. For the success of provisions in the fourteenth century, see Wright, *The Church and the English Crown;* for the thirteenth, Sayers, "Centre and Locality," 122–124.

128. On his career, see Reinhold Elze, "Die päpstliche Kapelle im 12. und 13. Jahrhundert," ZRG Kan. Abt. 36 (1950): 179. Raoul Manselli, "Federico II ed Alatrino, diplomatico pontificio del secolo XIII," *Studi Romani* 6 (1958): 649–58. Kenneth Pennington, "Cum causamque: A Decretal of Pope Innocent III," BMCL 7 (1977): 101.

Gregory proposed a compromise. If the bishop would grant an equivalent benefice to Alatrino in the future and in the meantime give him an annual pension from the income of the treasurer's prebend, Gregory would confirm William's appointment.[129] Alatrino probably never saw his pension or his benefice. In 1238 Gregory sent a mandate to Otto, cardinal deacon of St. Nicholas in Carcere, ordering him to put Alatrino in possession of the benefice. From his letter, we gain a clear idea of how a papal mandate could be frustrated by clever subterfuges. William of Neville had never sent Alatrino a pension, and even though the benefice of cantor had become vacant, the bishop had not given it to Alatrino; instead he had granted him the church at Kirkford (Kuckefeld). Unfortunately, Gregory noted, the prior and convent of Lewes were the patrons of Kirkford. The bishop had an obligation to provide for Alatrino in his own church, not another's. Meanwhile, Alatrino and William's procurators had reached an agreement in Rome over the income from the treasury. Gregory lamented that the agreement was never put into effect because the chapter at Chichester had rejected it.[130]

Alatrino probably died shortly after this letter was written, since it is the last source that mentions him. He was undoubtedly an old man in 1238. In his long career, he had seen the pope's will frustrated many times, but the story related above cannot be categorized as either typical or atypical, for the movements of nonresident canons in cathedral chapters have been too little studied. What we know of their numbers and importance in the thirteenth and fourteenth centuries indicates that generalizations about them covering long spans of time and wide geographical areas are difficult.[131] Alatrino had had problems earlier in his career. Pope Honorius III granted a benefice to him in Aachen. There is a hint that he never received it.[132] In 1219 Honorius also granted him a provision of a *praepositura* at Coblenz, a provision that resulted in a protracted dispute. As in Alatrino's provision to

---

129. Auvray no. 575.

130. Auvray no. 4336.

131. Besides the studies cited in n. 127 above, see Kathleen Edwards, *The English Secular Cathedrals in the Middle Ages: A Constitutional Study with Special Reference to the Fourteenth Century*, 2nd ed. (New York: 1967), 83–96 and Wright, *The Church and the English Crown*, 119–67.

132. Po. 5685, Feb. 1218, Pressutti 1055. Pressutti 2929, Dec. 24, 1220, names a certain Otto as provost of Aachen. Of course, there could have been more than one provost in the diocese.

Chichester, a pension was eventually promised to Alatrino as a compromise.[133] Later, the holder of the *praepositura* (which had changed hands) and the cathedral chapter promised that Alatrino would receive a pension of ten marks of gold on the first Sunday of Lent.[134] The chapter would elect no future provost who did not vow to honor Alatrino's pension.[135] Again, Alatrino never saw his ten marks. By 1225, Honorius had lost his patience and ordered the archbishop of Trier to excommunicate the canons and place the church under interdict.[136] Because of the deteriorating relationship between Frederick II and Honorius III, and later, Gregory IX, Alatrino undoubtedly had little hope of pressing his claims in imperial lands. Sometime before 1236, because of his involvement in papal-imperial politics, he was stripped of his prebends in the empire.[137]

Bishops and chapters had learned that they might circumvent papal provisions by exploiting two factors. One was the distance of their diocese to Rome. The other was the resources of the providee. Alatrino pursued his benefices in Coblenz and Chichester for almost twelve years. His litigation and effort undoubtedly cost him time and money. Yet Alatrino had a great advantage over other clerics: he lived in Rome. In the end, the average cleric could carry his case only as far as his limited resources allowed. Cheney rightly observed that local cathedral chapters often had good reasons for wishing to give curial or royal officials prebends.[138] However, when they wished to resist, they could use the canon law effectively, for local resistance to provisions prevented popes from exercising their "plenitudo potestatis" without hindrance.

The canonists did not discuss the provision of benefices or the granting of dispensations for pluralists entirely in jurisdictional terms. The theme that recurs in their thought is the duty of the pope to respect the rights of bishops and chapters. They conceded that the pope might do almost anything in

---

133. Po. 6096, Pressutti 2135 and 2136, dated 1219; Pressutti 3322, dated 1221; Po. 6686, Pressutti 3471, dated 1221.

134. Pressutti 4252, dated 1223.

135. Ibid., Vat. Reg. 12, fol. 29r–29v: "Rursus tam ipse G. quam totum capitulum sub religione iurisiurandi ad hoc se personaliter obligabunt, promittentes sub huiusmodi iuramento quod in posterum neminem recipient uel eligent in prepositum uel canonicum nisi ad seruandum quod a nobis prouisum est."

136. Pressutti 5690.

137. Auvray 2482, dated 1236: "Quod Alatrinus subdiaconus et capellanus suis est beneficiis spoliatus."

138. Cheney, *Pope Innocent III and England*, 82–96, esp. 89–90.

singular cases. He might depose a bishop, bestow a prebend, or grant a dispensation anywhere in Christendom. They balked, however, at granting the pope power to ignore the rights and jurisdiction of bishops. Episcopal rights might occasionally be overlooked, but never eliminated.

CHAPTER FIVE ‹ PAPAL PRIVILEGES: PAPAL EXEMPTIONS FROM EPISCOPAL GOVERNMENT

The popes began granting privileges of exemption to religious institutions relatively late in the history of the church. The earliest monastic privileges were not, properly speaking, exemptions, but rather, to use Dom David Knowles' phrase, "charters of rights." During the turbulent early Middle Ages, monasteries sought guarantees of their liberties, as well as protection from secular dangers, and in their search they turned to both secular and ecclesiastical rulers. A typical monastery of the twelfth century often had a variety of documents from secular rulers and the papacy with which they claimed much. Knowles has written:

Exemption from episcopal control was not directly envisaged by grantor or recipient; the immunity was of a feudal, not of an ecclesiastical kind; the original canonical position of the bishops in England was tending in the ninth century to dissolve . . . and these royal charters aimed at keeping the monasteries free from all material aggression, from whatever quarter it might come.[1]

The earliest papal privileges of exemption—to be distinguished from privileges granting personal honors or protection—appeared in the eleventh century. In England, kings also granted privileges to ecclesiastical institutions. For example, by the time of Edward the Confessor some monasteries had

---

1. David Knowles, *The Monastic Order in England: A History of Its Development from the Times of St. Dunstan to the Fourth Lateran Council (940–1216)*, 2nd ed. (Cambridge: 1963), 577.

obtained royal privileges which granted them immunity from both royal and episcopal jurisdiction.[2]

On the Continent, the papal privilege of exemption given to Cluny in the early eleventh century marked the first step in a long process through which the terms of exemptions were defined.[3] Some monasteries were taken under the protection of St. Peter; others were given "liberty." While the terminology was vague, the juridical meaning of the terminology was equally indefinite.[4]

During the twelfth century, the popes and the canonists gradually made the meaning of papal privileges more precise. Although Gratian did not treat the problem of exemption from episcopal jurisdiction in his Decretum, several chapters touch related topics. For example, Causa 25 was devoted to papal privileges. Gratian's purpose in this Causa was to describe a privilege as an act of legislation. He gathered canons together proving that the papacy could grant privileges that contravened ecclesiastical law. He noted secondarily that later privileges always abrogated earlier ones.[5]

The matter of episcopal exemptions became of pressing importance in the 1160s and 1170s. In the decretal *Recepimus*, Pope Alexander III developed criteria for determining the status of a monastery from the wording of its privileges. Monasteries under papal protection regularly paid a tax to Rome. Some had privileges that freed them from the jurisdiction of the local bishop—they were called "commended" monasteries; others did not—and were called "protected." Alexander defined a commended monastery as one which paid tax for its liberty and fell only under the jurisdiction of St. Peter. A "protected" monastery paid an annual tax to the Apostolic See but was

2. Ibid., 578–79.

3. Gaston Letonnelier, *L'abbaye exempte de Cluny et le saint-siège: Etude sur le développement de l'exemption clunisienne des origines jusqu'à la fin du XIIIe siècle* (Paris-Ligugé: 1923), esp. 81–124.

4. Jacques Hourlier, *L'âge classique (1140–1378): Les religieux*, Histoire du Droit et des Institutions de l'église en Occident 10 (Paris: 1971), 442–44. The literature on privileges of exemption is listed in Knowles and Hourlier. Of the older literature, the most important is Georg Schreiber, *Kurie und Kloster im 12. Jahrhundert*, 2 vols. (Stuttgart: 1910); Léo Muller, "La notion canonique d'abbaye nullius," *Revue de droit canonique* 6 (1956): 115–44; David Knowles, "The Growth of Monastic Exemption," *Downside Review* 50 (1932): 201–31, 396–436. On exempt bishoprics, see Demetrio Mansilla, "Obispados exentos de la iglesia española," *Hispania sacra* 32 (1980): 287–321. On privileges in general, see D. Lindner, *Die Lehre vom Privileg nach Gratian und den Glossatoren des Corpus iuris canonici* (Regensburg: 1917); and Alphonse Van Hove, *De privilegiis [et] de dispensationibus* (Rome: 1935).

5. Chodorow, *Christian Political Theory*, 141–48.

not exempted from episcopal jurisdiction.[6] In order to distinguish an exempt from a nonexempt monastery, Alexander's privileges introduced the phrase "nullo mediante" into the sentence that described the monastery's status: "Qui nullo mediante ad jurisdictionem beati Petri et nostram specialiter pertinere noscuntur" (who especially pertain to our jurisdiction and that of St. Peter and who are under no one else).[7] With Alexander's pontificate, privileges became more specific in describing the rights and liberties of a monastery. If a monastery was exempt from episcopal taxes, obligations, or judgment, these liberties were carefully detailed.[8] The Latin word "exemptio" and its verbal form "eximere" began to appear in papal privileges of the second half of the twelfth century.[9]

Episcopal jurisdiction over monasteries could include a wide range of rights, and in the twelfth century monasteries were rarely completely exempted. A bishop could not—unless the abbot was remiss in his duties—discipline the monks. On the other hand, an abbot or monastery might be obligated to attend diocesan synods, pay taxes to the bishop, endure episcopal visitations, render oaths of obedience to the bishop, and carry out several other duties of lesser importance.[10]

During the second half of the twelfth century, bishops attempted to regain old prerogatives or to assert rights anew. Their new militancy resulted in part from the growth of canon law and in part from an increased understanding of the church as a juridical entity. Bishops also were faced with religious orders which aggressively claimed customary rights and resisted episcopal demands of obedience. Monasteries viewed reassertions of epis-

---

6. 1 Comp. 5.28.10 (X 5.33.8) [Recepimus]: "Inspicienda sunt ergo ipsarum ecclesiarum privilegia, et ipsorum tenor est diligentius attendendus, ut si fuerit deprehensum, quod ecclesia quae censum solvit specialiter B. Petri iuris exsistat et ad indicium perceptae libertatis census annuus conferatur, non immerito poterit speciali praerogativa gaudere. Si vero ad indicium perceptae protectionis census persolvitur, non ex hoc iuri dioecesani episcopi aliquid videtur esse subtractum."

7. JL 12734: Knowles, *Monastic Order*, 584, n. 2.

8. For various types of privileges, see *Papsturkunden in Frankreich, 7: Nördliche Ile-de-France und Vermandois*, ed. Dietrich Lohrmann (Göttingen: 1976): exemption from episcopal synods, p. 366, no. 98 and pp. 583–85, no. 279; right to conduct divine services during an interdict, pp. 472–73, no. 187 and pp. 483–85, no. 198; exemption from episcopal judgment, pp. 553–54, no. 250 and pp. 626–27, no. 318.

9. Ibid., 583–85, no. 279; 625–26, no. 317. Also *Acta pontificum Romanorum inedita*, ed. Julius von Pflugk-Harttung, 3 vols. (Stuttgart: 1881–86; reprinted Graz: 1958), 1:251, no. 271; 2:121, no. 157; 3:228, no. 226. Also the letters cited by Schreiber, *Kurie und Kloster* 1:28, n. 1.

10. Knowles, "Monastic Exemption," 205–8 and *Monastic Order*, 585–86. Hourlier, *L'âge classique*, 457–64.

copal rights that had fallen into desuetude as being infringements of custom
and, often, contrary to royal privileges with which they were endowed.[11]

The dispute between Bishop Hilary of Chichester and Abbot Walter of
St. Martin at Battle clearly illustrates these points.[12] Hilary was a learned
and illustrious figure who had already earned a reputation at the Roman
curia. After becoming bishop, he examined thoroughly all the rights and
possessions (*iura et dignitates*) of the diocese and decided that the abbot of
Battle should attend diocesan synods, pay episcopal taxes, provide expenses
for episcopal visitations, and render an oath of obedience.[13] Walter resisted.
He claimed that William the Conqueror had built the abbey after his great
victory at Hastings and had freed the new foundation from all "subjection,
oppression, and domination of bishops as in Christ Church, Canterbury."
He produced charters of William, William Rufus, and Henry I to prove his
claims.[14] The case was first heard before King Stephen, shortly before his
death, and afterwards by King Henry II. Hilary had the support of Archbishop Theobald, who had the ear of the new king. But the abbot was not
without resources. His brother was Richard de Lucy, the chief justiciar of
England and a powerful figure at the royal court.

According to principles of canon law, a secular ruler could not grant an
exemption from episcopal authority. Thus Hilary's case seemed impregnable,
and at first he was successful. With the help of Theobald, Hilary persuaded
Henry not to attach his seal to a confirmation of Battle's privileges. He also
obtained a letter from Pope Hadrian IV ordering Abbot Walter to obey his
bishop.[15]

In the end, however, canon law and canonical principles were of no use

---

11. Knowles, "Monastic Exemption," 208–18, discusses the illuminating cases of Bury
and St. Albans from the eleventh and early twelfth centuries. The Bury case began in the late
eleventh century.

12. Knowles has written about the Battle case in "Monastic Exemption," 218–25. The
chronicle of Battle Abbey has been newly translated and edited by Eleanor Searle (Oxford:
1980) and provides colorful details of the case (pp. 147–211).

13. *Chronicle of Battle Abbey,* 149.

14. Ibid. and p. 179. See also Eleanor Searle, *Lordship and Community: Battle Abbey
and Its Banlieu, 1066–1538* (Toronto: 1974), 30–35 and "Battle Abbey and Exemption: The
Forged Charters," *English Historical Review* 83 (1968): 449–80, as well as the intriguing
account in W. L. Warren, *Henry II* (Berkeley-Los Angeles: 1973), 428–32. Warren under-
estimates, I think, Hilary's willingness to lie in the face of royal anger. Consequently, his
conjecture that Hilary was lukewarm in his prosecution of the case is not convincing, nor, I
believe, supported by the evidence. Hilary was weak-kneed, not lukewarm. See also Raymonde
Foreville, *L'Eglise et la royauté en Angleterre sous Henri II Plantagenet (1154–1189)* (Paris:
1943), 91–92. Avrom Saltman, *Theobald of Canterbury* (London: 1956), 156–58.

15. *Chronicle of Battle Abbey,* 164–65, JL 10002.

in the kingdom of a tough-minded sovereign. The final confrontation between Hilary and Walter took place on 28 May 1157 before the king and his chancellor, Thomas Becket, together with Theobald, Walter's brother Richard, and many barons. The abbot's case depended upon recently forged charters that he presented to the court.[16] No one questioned the charters, and they were pronounced valid. Bishop Hilary made a vigorous defense of his rights. He argued the same point that Pope Gelasius had in his letter to Emperor Anastasius, which had become an important document for the protection of ecclesiastical liberties, particularly since the Investiture Controversy:

Hear all and understand! Jesus Christ our lord established two dignities and two powers for the governance of this world: one is spiritual, the other material. . . . It is impossible for any layman, indeed even for a king, to give ecclesiastical rights and liberties to churches. Ecclesiastical authority shows that those rights and liberties bestowed on churches by laymen cannot be valid under Roman law except with the permission and confirmation of the holy father.[17]

It was a common axiom of canon law that only secular law confirmed by the pope could be cited or held valid in ecclesiastical courts. Nevertheless, Henry II refused to acknowledge that William I's charter might not be valid; this idea was, he bellowed, an argument detrimental to his crown and royal prerogative.[18] The poor bishop was crushed by Henry's anger. He did not appeal to Rome. Instead, he capitulated and promised to respect the abbey's privileges.

In the thirteenth century when the monks of Battle Abbey again became involved in a dispute with the bishop over their exemption, they did not press their claims supported by royal charters.[19] Such claims would not have stood up in court. Already in the twelfth century most monasteries had petitioned the papacy for privileges confirming their claims of exemption.[20] Battle Abbey's reliance on royal charters was exceptional. Although no papal decretal in any twelfth-century canonical collection states that secular rulers could not grant ecclesiastical exemptions, Alexander III did enunciate the principle

---

16. Searle, "Battle Abbey and Exemption," 454–59.

17. D. 96 c. 10 [Duo sunt]. *Chronicle of Battle Abbey*, 185–86.

18. Ibid., 187.

19. Searle, *Lordship and Community*, 95–98.

20. Of the seven English cases of exemption that Knowles discusses, including Battle, the other six all had twelfth-century papal privileges in their muniments ("Monastic Exemption," 424–30).

during the course of a lawsuit in 1171.[21] The separation of church and state was, in this matter, a commonly accepted principle, even though, in the case of Battle, neither Henry II nor Thomas Becket adhered to it.

The primary concern of the church in the last quarter of the twelfth century was to define papal exemptions in more sophisticated and precise terms. In his decretal *Recepimus*, Alexander III had distinguished between the wording of a papal privilege that granted an exemption and one that bestowed protection. The papacy struggled with whether an exemption should be limited or whether it could be interpreted in the broadest possible terms. Did an exemption free a monastery from episcopal jurisdiction in all cases? Were monastic possessions also included in an exemption? Were exempt monks immune from episcopal jurisdiction no matter what their crime?

These questions are significant for canonistic constitutional thought. The canonists conceived of the church as comprising a multitude of rights, some of which overlapped. These rights or liberties were established by custom and tradition and could be violated for only serious reasons. Two commonplace axioms of the canonists illustrate the tension between ecclesiastical liberty and papal legislative power. One stated that the privileges of the prince are gifts, and that the gifts of a prince should be given the widest possible interpretation.[22] The other held that whatever the prince did should be done without prejudice to another.[23] Privileges of exemption juxtapose these two conflicting principles, for a papal privilege must, by its nature, injure the rights of someone. The development of exemption in papal legislation and in the commentaries of the canonists from the 1170s on highlights a sensitivity to the juridical rights and liberties of persons and corporations. The canonists' theories of exemption reveal much about their conception of the relationship of papal and episcopal jurisdiction.

---

21. *Acta pontificum Romanorum inedita*, 3:228–29, no. 226: "Sane, cum super hiis fuisset hinc inde diutius litigatum, privilegiis principum quantum ad libertatis donationem et monasterii exemptionem, quia nec illi nec alii laici huiusmodi possunt ecclesiis libertatem donare. . . ." Alexander also declared the bulls of popes Zacharias and Leo IX to be forged, giving grammatical and diplomatic reasons for his decision. Alexander issued other decretals dealing with forgeries. So did his successors. Pope Innocent III's famous decretals were the last step in a long development. See Chodorow, "Dishonest Litigation," 191–97; Peter Herde, "Römisches und kanonisches Recht bei der Verfolgung des Fälschungsdelikts im Mittelalter," *Traditio* 21 (1965): 291–362.

22. Damasus to 4th Lat. c. 57 v. *predictorum locorum coniunctim*, ed. García y García, 453: "priuilegia sunt principis beneficia, et beneficia principis latissime sunt interpretanda."

23. The gloss of Johannes Teutonicus to 4th Lat. c. 29, cited above in Chapter 4, n. 77 is a trenchant statement of this principle. Also his gloss to De cons. D. 1 c. 6 v. *dispendio*: "nota principis privilegium nulli debet praeiudicare."

Huguccio of Pisa was one of the first decretists to explore the issues raised by exemptions. In his gloss to a letter of Pope Gregory the Great in Gratian's Decretum, *Frater noster,* which reported the case of Hadrian, bishop of Thebes, he discussed the unusual exemption of a bishop from his archbishop.[24] According to Gregory's letter, his predecessor had exempted Hadrian from the jurisdiction of his archbishop, Lanseus, and his primate, John. Nevertheless, the two bishops had brought Hadrian to court and convicted him. Although the facts of the case were far from clear, Huguccio thought he understood the dispute and gave a lucid description of the problem. The primate had rendered a judgment against Hadrian in a criminal case and had deposed him. Lanseus had condemned him in a civil matter. Gregory ordered John to restore anything Hadrian had lost and forbade Lanseus to exercise any jurisdiction over him. If Lanseus thought he had any jurisdiction over Hadrian, he should bring the question to the attention of Gregory's representative.[25]

Huguccio also examined the legal implications of papal exemptions. First, he noted that if the archbishop had any rights over Hadrian, he did not lose them even though he had infringed upon his suffragan's liberties. Distinguishing between the office a person held and the person himself, he wrote: "In ecclesiastical matters, a crime of a person cannot injure the church."[26] Then he asked the key question that exemptions raised. Can the

---

24. C. 16 q. 1 c. 52 [Frater noster].

25. Huguccio to C. 16 q. 1 c. 52 v. *Frater,* Admont 7, fol. 276v [Vat lat. 2280, fol. 215v, Klosterneuburg 89, fol. 239v]: "Casus planus est. Johannes erat primas; Lanseus archiepiscopus erat sub illo. Adrianus erat simplex episcopus sub Lanseo, et eo mediante sub Johanne. Contingit quod apostolicus predecessor Gregorii predictum Adrianum cum eius ecclesia ex toto exemit a iurisdictione Lansei et Johannis, postquam exemptionem Johannes condempnauit eum in causa criminali [ciuili A] et deposuit. Lanseus condempnauit eum in causa ciuili, unde scribit Lanseo et inuehitur in utrumque illorum et precepit ut Adrianus ex toto ut restituatur contra Iohannis sententiam. Lanseo precipit ut decetero nullam iurisdictionem exerceat in illum uel eius ecclesiam, et sine dilatione restituat ei res quas ei abstulit. Facta restitutione, si credit se habere aliquod ius in illis rebus contendat ordine iuris coram suo responsali."

26. Ibid., v. *uentiletur,* Admont 7, fol. 277r [Vat. lat. 2280, fol. 215v]: "Set nonne ille si quod ius habebat in illis debuit amittere et eo ipso cadere [eadem A] a iure suo quia contra ius et sua auctoritate eas inuasit? Sic uidetur arg. infra eadem q.vi. Placuit et C. unde iu. Si quis in tantam. Set dico illud habere locum in rebus priuatorum, set non in rebus ecclesiasticis. Non enim delictum [debitum A] persone redundat in dampnum ecclesie, ut infra eadem q.vi. Si episcopum; siue ergo ipse spoliator tolleretur in administratione illius ecclesie siue alius loco eius ponatur, agere poterit pro eisdem rebus de [rebus ecclesie *add.* A] iure ecclesie." For the decretists' conceptions of office, see Benson, *Bishop-Elect,* 64–71, 90–95; Tierney, *Foundations,* 55–67, 78–79; Gaudemet, *Le gouvernement,* 115–30. Martinien van de Kerckhove, "La notion de juridiction chez les décrétistes et les premiers décrétalistes (1140–1250)," *Etudes*

pope take rights away from a prelate or church and give them to another? Huguccio was convinced that *Frater noster* proved the pope could. He could take away a prebend or a church from any cleric, just as Pope Alexander III had stripped Archbishop Conrad of Mainz of his dignity. The pope must act, however, with cause; otherwise, he sins.[27] Huguccio quickly added that even if the pope did sin, nothing could be done. The pope had fullness of power. Judgment of papal actions must be left to God.[28]

Huguccio did not believe that the power of the pope was absolute, even though he gave the pope very broad authority to grant an exemption to a monastery or to depose a cleric. He felt that a papal privilege should be given the broadest possible interpretation; thus he maintained that John did not have even the slightest claim of jurisdiction over Hadrian because of Hadrian's privilege.[29] He conceded that a pope should act with cause, but papal authority was not encumbered or limited by this obligation.

Nevertheless, papal legislation had already begun to limit the scope of papal privileges. At the Third Lateran Council of 1179, Alexander III issued a canon, *Cum et plantare,* that restricted a latitudinarian interpretation of an exemption. Alexander explained that bishops had complained about the Templars and the Hospitalers, as well as other monks with papal privileges, who challenged episcopal authority and caused scandal in the church. Alexander thus set firm limits on the rights of exempted monasteries. They should not receive tithes from laymen without the permission of the bishop. They should not admit excommunicated persons to their religious services. Unless they possessed the church "pleno iure,"[30] exempt monks could not install or dismiss priests in the church in which they had patronage without episcopal permission.

---

franciscaines 49 (1937): 420–55. Also Pierre Gillet, *La personnalité juridique en droit ecclésiastique spécialement chez les décrétistes et décrétalistes et dans le Code de droit canonique* (Malines: 1927), 150–68.

27. Huguccio, loc. cit.: "Ex hoc capitulo aperte [experte A] probatur quod papa potest unam ecclesiam alii substrahere, similiter potest clericum et monachum eximere a potestate sui prelati, ut viiii. q.iii. Per principalem [c. 21]. Cuilibet clerico etiam potest subtrahere ecclesiam et prebendam suam ex iusta causa ut fecit Conrado archiepiscopo, idest Maguntino, Alexander iii. Set et si hoc facit sine causa peccat."

28. Ibid.: "Set non est qui ei resistere ualeat cum plenitudinem habeat potestatis, ut ii. q.vi. Decreto [c. 11], Qui se scit [c. 14], nam qui eum iudicat, Dominus est, viiii. q.iii. Aliorum."

29. Ibid., v. *aliquid iurisdictionis,* Admont 7, fol. 276v: "etiam minimum. Et est arg. quod beneficium pape latissime interpretandum est sicut et principis, arg. xii. q.ii. Qui manumittitur et ff. de constit. princ. Beneficium." The *Glossa Palatina* repeated Huguccio in its gloss to C. 16 q. 1 c. 52 v. *omnem ante,* Vat. Pal. lat. 658, fol. 57v [Vat. Reg. lat. 977, fol. 162v].

30. Third Lat. c. 9, COD, 215–16, 1 Comp. 5.28.3 (X 5.33.3).

Alexander's decree touched on many issues. The rights of patronage and the issue of monastic possessions would give rise to much litigation in the next thirty years. It was sometimes very difficult to disentangle the complicated rights of exempt institutions. Perhaps the most vexing problem the canonists and the papacy faced was whether a monastic exemption should also apply to parish churches in which the monks had the right of patronage. If papal privileges were always given a very broad interpretation, a privileged monastery might encroach relentlessly on the rights of the diocesan bishop. Another issue that generated much discussion was whether a diocesan bishop could correct or judge an exempt cleric under any circumstances. Innocent III was the first pope to deal with this question, and the complexity of the problem intrigued the later canonists. We shall now consider the juridical development of each of these problems.

EXEMPT MONASTERIES AND THEIR POSSESSIONS

In the early church, monks were not priests and, consequently, did not exercise a pastoral office. Later, it became common for a monk to be ordained, and, with ordination, they often cared for their flocks in parish churches outside the walls of their monasteries. During the twelfth century, many of these monastic priests claimed exemptions from the diocesan bishop and also asserted their rights to collect tithes and gifts from the churches committed to them. Bishops opposed this usurpation of rights and some even called for a suppression of all exemptions.[31]

When Gratian confronted the issue of monastic priests, he devoted an entire Causa to the question. He began his examination with the basic question: could monks exercise public ecclesiastical offices? He continued by asking who should appoint monks to churches, whether episcopal rights over parishes could be obtained through prescription, and other ancillary questions.[32]

Although Gratian included a number of canons that forbade monks to exercise public ecclesiastical offices such as public preaching, funeral services and masses,[33] he concluded that monks could exercise such duties if they

---

31. Muller, "Notion canonique," 128–29. Hourlier, *L'âge classique*, 457–78. Gaudemet, *Le gouvernement*, 285–92.

32. C. 16 dictum Gratiani ante q. 1.

33. C. 16 q. 1 c. 1–12.

had the permission of their abbot and the bishop.[34] Later canonists never questioned Gratian's conclusions. When the Franciscans and Dominicans came into conflict with local bishops in the thirteenth century, the issue was not whether they could preach but whether they had to have episcopal permission to preach.

Gratian treated monastic churches with much less detail. He cited only three authorities. The first was an apocryphal letter attributed to Pope John that permitted monks to invest priests in their churches.[35] The other two chapters were conciliar canons of Urban II, and they both emphasized that monks who held parish churches should be invested with the consent of their diocesan bishops and should be subject to them.[36] Gratian reconciled the discordant texts in his dictum at the end of the question:

> Thus Pope Urban prohibits the investiture of parish churches by monks, although Pope John permits it. But John's decretal should be understood as treating those chapels that bishops concede to monks with full rights [*omni iure suo*]. The chapter of Urban deals with those chapels which abbots build on their estates, in villages, or in their fortifications.[37]

The early decretists accepted Gratian's distinction. Rufinus added that a monastery that had a privilege exempting all its chapels, no matter how many it possessed, was entirely immune from diocesan law. Such monasteries had the right to invest their churches without episcopal participation.[38]

Gratian and the early decretists overlooked one crucial problem in their analysis. Could a bishop alienate all his and his successors' rights by granting

---

34. C. 16 q. 1 c. 13–42. Hourlier, *Les religieux*, 472–74.

35. C. 16 q. 2 c. 1.

36. C. 16 q. 2 c. 6–7. References to c. 6, *Sane* appear in papal privileges of the twelfth century given to bishops and monasteries. To monasteries the canon guaranteed that the abbot should consent to the installation of a priest. To bishops it confirmed the necessity of obtaining his consent as well. See *Acta pontificum Romanorum inedita*, 1: 241, no. 327; 3: 394, no. 466.

37. C. 16 q. 2 p. c. 7: "Ecce Urbanus Papa prohibet investituras parrochialium ecclesiarum per monachos fieri, quas Iohannes Papa eis concessit. Sed illud Iohannis Papae intelligendum est de illis capellis, que cum omni iure suo ab episcopis monachis conceduntur. Istud autem Urbani intelligendum est de illis quas abbates in propriis prediis edificant in villis vel in castellis suis."

38. Rufinus, *Summa decretorum*, to C. 16 q. 2, p. 357: "Excipiuntur capelle eorum monasteriorum, que tanto privilegio decorata sunt, ut omnes, quotquot capellas habent, a lege diocesiana libere et immunes maneant; talium namque monasteriorum capelle per ipsos tantum monachos instituentur."

a monastery a complete exemption? Gratian assumed that a bishop could. However, later canonists began to understand that the inalienability of diocesan rights was a constitutional limitation on the authority of the bishop. A bishop could not grant a monastery in his diocese an exemption from episcopal rights and jurisdiction without the consent of the pope.[39]

Huguccio explored the subject in all its ramifications.[40] Realizing that Gratian's question was not properly framed, he described the ways that monastic chapels could be founded. A layman or a bishop could bestow a chapel on the monastery, or the monastery could build one on its lands. If a layman gave the chapel to the monastery, the monks could exercise only the right of patronage. Laymen cannot grant greater rights to a monastery, observed Huguccio, than they themselves have.[41]

If a bishop established the church, the rights of the bishop depended on the type of grant. The bishop might reserve spiritual rights, temporal rights, or jurisdiction to himself. If the bishop granted spiritual and temporal rights to the monastery, he might still reserve the rights he had over the other clergy in his diocese: ordination, judgment, the bestowal of sacramental chrism,

---

39. Peter Riesenberg discusses inalienability in canon law in *Inalienability of Sovereignty in Medieval Political Thought* (New York: 1956), 48–80. Also Marcel David, *La souveraineté et les limites du pouvoir monarchique du IXe au XVe siècle* (Paris: 1954) and Ernst Kantorowicz, "Inalienability: A Note on Canonical Practice and the English Coronation Oath in the Thirteenth Century," *Speculum* 29 (1954): 488–502.

40. Muller, "Notion canonique," 130, n. 63 prints part of Huguccio's gloss. He does not discuss the complexities of Huguccio's distinctions.

41. Huguccio to C. 16 q. 2 a.c. 1 v. *De capellis*, Admont 7, fol. 279r–279v [Vat. lat. 2280, fol. 217v, Klosterneuburg 89, fol. 241v]: "Hic intitulatur secunda questio, scilicet an in capellis monachis ex donatione episcoporum concessis presbyteri sint instituendi per monachos an per episcopos? Quod ut melius pateat notandum quod capelle monachorum aut proueniunt ad eos ex donatione laicorum aut ex donatione episcoporum, aut ex propria fundatione, scilicet quod fundarunt eas in solo suo; si ex donatione laicorum tantum ius patronatus consecuntur monachi, ut in extra. Cum seculum [1 Comp. 3.33.16 (X 3.38.13)]. Nec distingo in hoc casu, licet jo. distinxit, an ante consecrationem uel post laici sic dent ecclesiam monachis. Non enim plus possunt in monachos conferre quam ipsi habent. Set nichil habent ibi nisi ius patronatus, ut in extra. Relatum [1 Comp. 3.33.14] Quamuis simus [1 Comp. 3.33.10 (X 3.38.9)], nam in rebus ecclesiasticis laici nil iuris habent ex quo collate sunt in ecclesiam, ut x. q.i. Nouerint [c. 6]. Ergo siue ante consecrationem siue post laici dent ecclesiam monachis pro concessione laicorum nil in rebus ecclesie poterunt sibi uendicare; solum ergo ius patronatus ibi habebunt, et solam electionem [presumpt. A] presbiterorum, sicut et laici habebant siue monasterium sit priuilegiatum siue non, ut in extra. Cum seculum." See also Peter Landau's fine study on the rights of monastic patronage, *Ius Patronatus: Studien zur Entwicklung des Patronats im Dekretalenrecht und der Kanonistik des 12. und 13. Jahrhunderts* (Köln-Wien: 1975), 186–94.

and obedience. These prerogatives would remain untouched. Such a chapel belonged to the monastery "pleno iure," and the monks installed the priest. The bishop, however, could judge or suspend the priest without consulting the abbot. The abbot had to be consulted only in the case of deposition or removal from office. If one understands Gratian's interpretation of Pope John's letter in this sense, wrote Huguccio, then the Master's definition of "pleno iure" was correct.[42]

The bishop's grant could bestow temporal rights, but not spiritual. If the bishop abdicated his temporal rights, argued Huguccio, the abbot and bishop would install the priest jointly. The priest had to answer to the bishop in spiritual matters: the care of souls, tithes, first fruits, offerings, and the sacraments. To the abbot the priest had to give an accounting for temporals: the possessions and income of the church. The canons of Urban II and the Third Lateran canon, *Cum et plantare,* discussed chapels of this type, which are said to belong to the monastery "non pleno iure."[43]

Huguccio introduced an important distinction between a monastery that possessed a papal privilege and one that did not. The bishop granted in a privilege only what he had the authority to grant. If the bishop bestowed a chapel on a privileged monastery whose exemptions extended to present and

---

42. Huguccio, loc. cit.: "Item si ex donatione episcoporum reffert an donatio sit facta aliquo expresso uel excepto an simpliciter, scilicet nullo expresso uel excepto. In primo casu si episcopus expressit aliquid in quo uolebat ecclesiam dare monachis, intelligtur omnia illa sibi retinuisse, uerbi gratia, 'do uobis illam ecclesiam.' Quoad temporalia si nichil expressit, set excepit aliquid quod sibi uolebat retinere, omnia alia intelligitur concessisse, uerbi gratia, 'do uobis illam ecclesiam excepta inuestitura spiritualium uel excepto annuo censu' et huiusmodi. In primo casu ergo respiciendum est quid actum sit uel dictum a principio. Si enim dedit episcopus quoad temporalia et quoad spiritualia, set iurisdictionem in clericos sibi reseruauit ordinariam quam habet in omnes clericos sui episcopatus, nisi sint exempti, scilicet ut ordinet eos et iudicet si peccauerint et sacramenta ecclesiastica ab eo recipiant et debitam reuerentiam sibi exibeant in sinodo et in cathedratico et huiusmodi, tunc monasterium instituet ibi presbiterum et quoad spiritualia et quoad temporalia, irrequisito episcopo, et talis capella intelligitur pertinere ad monasterium pleno iure et in hoc casu episcopus presbiterum illum poterit suspendere et excommunicare et ciuiliter iudicare sine abbate, set non potest illum deponere uel ab ecclesia remouere sine abbate, et in hoc casu Gratianus intelligit sequens capitulum, Visis."

43. Ibid.: "Si uero dedit illam ecclesiam [*om.* A] quoad temporalia et non quoad spiritualia, tunc abbas et episcopus communiter instituent ibi presbiterum; abbas uero ad temporalia, episcopus ad spiritualia, et talis institutus respondebit episcopo de spiritualibus, scilicet de cura animarum, decimis, primitiis, et oblationibus, et officio et sacramentis ecclesiasticis, et abbati respondebit de temporalibus, scilicet de possessionibus et redditibus ecclesie temporalibus in quo casu loquuntur duo sequentia capitula, scilicet, Sane, Statuendum, ut in concilio Romano, Cum et plantare, et talis capella dicitur spectare ad monasterium non pleno iure."

future possessions, the abbot then had full power over the priest and could exercise every episcopal right except that of deposition. The abbot obtained his authority from his papal privilege, not from the episcopal grant. The bishop, said Huguccio, could never grant the right to judge such priests, nor could he exempt a monastic priest totally. Such authority belongs only to the pope.[44] He added that if it were not possible to know under what conditions the bishop made his grant to the monastery, then the chapel would have the same juridical status as any other chapel the monastery possessed.[45]

Finally, if the monks constructed a chapel on their own estates, its status depended on the privileges of the monastery. If privileged, the bishop had no jurisdiction. If not privileged, or only partially privileged, the abbot and the bishop installed the priest together. The abbot had jurisdiction over temporal matters, the bishop over spiritual ones.[46]

---

44. Ibid.: "Si uero episcopus simpliciter dedit, scilicet nullo expresso uel excepto, intelligitur omne ius suum quod ibi habebat et dare poterat monasterio dedisse et quoad temporalia et quoad spiritualia. Set refert an dederit monasterio priuilegiato cum suis capellis habitis uel habendis aut <non>; si dederit monasterio sic priuilegiato, idem habebit priuilegium abbas in illa ecclesia data quam in aliis suis quia instituet ibi presbiterum quoad spiritualia et quoad temporalia et destituet eum si peccauerit. Set non deponet eum quia ibi exiguntur vi. episcopi. Ille institutus recipit ordinationem et ecclesiastica sacramenta undecumque uoluerit abbas in tali ecclesia. Habet abbas tantam potestatem non ex donatione episcopi, set ex priuilegio apostolici, nam ex donatione episcopi non posset hoc totum consequi. Si uero dedit monasterio non priuilegiato capellis suis saltem habendis, tunc abbas in illa ecclesia omne ius episcopi habebit quod in alium episcopus potest transferre. Habebit ergo institutionem quoad temporalia et quoad spiritualia, retenta tamen ab episcopo ordinaria iurisdictione quam habet in omnes clericos sui episcopatus nisi sint exempti, scilicet ut ordinet eos, iudicet de excessibus eorum, prestet eis sacramenta ecclesiastica: talia nullus episcopus potest in alium transferre. Vnde dico quod nullus episcopus potest monasterio aliquam ecclesiam concedere sic pleno iure. Hoc enim esset illam ecclesiam ex toto eximere dictione sui iuris episcopatus quod soli pape competit, ut viiii. q.iii. Conquestus [c. 8] Nunc uero [c. 20] Per principalem [c. 21] et supra eadem q.i. Frater [c. 52]."

45. Ibid.: "Et in hoc casu Gratianus intelligit sequens capitulum 'Visis' quod si non constat quid actum sit a principio, scilicet an donatio sit facta simpliciter an aliquo expresso uel excepto, intelligitur tunc episcopus sic dedisse ecclesiam sicut monasterium habet suas alias capellas. Si ergo illud monasterium est priuilegiatum predicto modo, idem priuilegium habebit in illa ecclesia quod habet in aliis in suo solo fundatis, non ex donatione tantum episcopi, set ex priuilegio apostolici. Si uero non sic est priuilegiatum uel nullo modo, idem iuris habebit in illa quod in aliis in suo solo fundatis."

46. Ibid.: "Si uero ratione fundationis monachi habent capellas, scilicet quia fundauerunt eas in suo solo, tunc distingit aut priuilegiatum est monasterium cum suis capellis habitis et habendis aut non. Si sic est priuilegiatum episcopus nichil habebit in illa capella quoad temporalia uel spiritualia uel aliquam ordinariam iurisdictionem. Si uero nullo modo est priuilegiatum uel non sic, abbas et episcopus communiter instituent ibi presbiterum, abbas quoad temporalia,

The patronage and income of monastic chapels were important issues over which monasteries and bishops frequently became entangled in thickets of litigation. Huguccio's analysis did not cover all possible legal questions. Exempt monasteries could lose and gain rights through prescription. In an English case, Pope Alexander III decided that if an exempt chapel had paid tithes for thirty years, then the monks would have to pay tithes, even though they may earlier have been exempt. They lost their right through prescription.[47] Later, Innocent III changed the time of prescription in ecclesiastical matters to forty years. There is some evidence, however, that a forty-year prescription was in use before Innocent's legislation.[48] The canonists thought that monasteries could gain liberties from their diocesan bishops through prescription, even winning those rights that pertained to the bishop's ordinary jurisdiction. Conversely, if a bishop exercised uninterrupted jurisdiction over an exempt monastery for forty years, he acquired a permanent right by prescription.[49]

Jurisdiction over chapels could be obtained through prescription or from a monastery's privileges. In his commentary, Huguccio assumed that a monastery's privileges might include present and future possessions. Later popes and canonists generally interpreted the provisions of privileges strictly, not broadly. If a chapel of a monastery was exempt, the monastery's privilege must name the monastery's exempt possessions specifically. Otherwise they were not included under the umbrella of exemption. Further, future possessions were not granted the same exemptions as a matter of practice.[50]

Two decretals of Pope Innocent III established the limits of monastic exemption. The first reported Innocent's decision in a case between the bishop of Coimbra (Portugal), Peter Soeiro, and the nearby monastery of Santa Cruz. Over a number of years the monastery had been given at least eleven chapels by the king of Portugal and other laymen. The monks had

---

episcopus quoad spiritualia, ut infra eadem q. Sane, Statuendum, et in concilio Romano, Cum et plantare."

47. 1 Comp. 5.28.9 (X 5.33.6) [Si in terra].

48. 3 Comp. 5.16.5 (X 5.33.15) [Accedentibus]. For an example of a forty-year prescription predating Innocent's letter see n. 53 below.

49. Johannes Teutonicus to 3 Comp. 2.17.2 (X 2.26.12) v. *impendatis*, ed. Pennington, 296–97, to 3 Comp. 2.17.5 (X 2.26.15) v. *ius episcopale*, 302–3, to 3 Comp. 2.17.6 (X 2.22.16) v. *nullam penitus*, 305.

50. There were exceptions. Innocent III's privilege to the Templars in March 1200, granted them an exemption for present and future possessions. See Cheney and Cheney, eds., *Letters of Pope Innocent III* 32, no. 197, printed on pp. 210–11: "Cum omnibus suis ecclesiis, oratoriis, et obedientiis, possessionibus et bonis suis que in presentiarum legittime habere dinoscitur aut in futurum concessione pontificum, liberalitate regum vel principum, oblatione fidelium. . . ."

taken possession of the chapels without the assent of the bishop. They had received, with the help of the king, an episcopal privilege of liberty from Peter's predecessor, Michael Paës (1158–76), who had been a canon of Santa Cruz before he became bishop.[51] Although Peter Soeiro claimed that this privilege had been extorted from Michael, it is likely that Michael needed little inducement to grant the privilege to his old house.

The bishop's privilege was a remarkable document, no matter how it had been obtained. With the consent of his chapter, he bestowed a privilege of absolute liberty. The monastery and its possessions—present and future— were to be free from all burdens and all episcopal jurisdiction. "The bishop should not have any authority, even the slightest, to command, prohibit, or ordain, unless he should be asked, so that the canons may always have the perfect liberty of their predecessors."[52] Michael Paës' immediate successor, Bermudo (1177–82), attempted to regain his episcopal rights, but without much success.[53] Michael's privilege was later confirmed by popes Urban III and Celestine III.[54]

At the beginning of Innocent III's pontificate, Peter Soeiro vigorously pursued his episcopal rights.[55] He obtained a mandate for judges delegate to investigate the legality of Michael's privilege and, in a separate action, he contested the exemptions that the monks claimed for newly built churches.[56]

In 1203 Innocent decided the case. He declared that the bishop's privi-

---

51. The facts of the case can be gathered from Innocent's final decision, PL 215.114–24, 3 Comp. 5.16.4 (X 5.33.14) [Cum olim], dated 1203.

52. Bishop Michael Paës issued the privilege in March 1162. It is printed in *Portugaliae monumenta historica, Scriptores* 1 (Lisbon: 1856): 72–73 and was later included in Innocent's letter of instruction at the beginning of the litigation, see Innocent III, Register I, 487–90, no. 332: "Nec habeat ibi episcopus quamlibet potestatem imperandi vel prohibendi vel aliquam ordinationem, quamvis levissimam, faciendi, nisi fuerit rogatus, quatinus canonici semper maneant im maiorum suorum perfecta libertate."

53. *Papsturkunden in Portugal,* ed. Carl Erdmann (Berlin: 1927), 246–47, no. 73: "predictum priorem et fratres attentius moneatis, ut eidem episcopo de ecclesiis quas infra eius episcopatum habere noscuntur, episcopalia iura persoluant, nisi autentico scripto sedis apostolice uel ipsius episcopi seu predecessorum suorum aut quadragenaria prescriptione temporis se possint ab eius impetitione tueri." Also 256–58, no. 83 and 84.

54. Ibid. 325–28, no. 111 [Urban III]; 350, no. 129 [Celestine III]. According to the letter of 1203, PL 215.119, Alexander III also approved the bishop's privilege.

55. Innocent III, Register I, 319–20, no. 224; two other letters illustrate Peter's determination: Innocent III, Register II, 355–59, no. 187 (196); 400–401, no. 205 (214).

56. Ibid. 320–21, no. 225: "quod in illis tantum villis quas de novo edificant, episcopalia iura valeant obtinere."

lege was invalid, even though it had been confirmed by earlier popes. He offered two reasons. The first was that a bishop could not legally grant a privilege that would enormously injure episcopal rights.[57] Although Innocent did not explain his underlying assumptions, he probably believed that the prerogatives of the bishop should not be alienated injudiciously, for such alienations would eventually undermine the constitutional position of the bishop in his diocese.[58] Innocent's second reason rested on the episcopal privilege itself. He found that the copy of the privilege had erasures and that the subscriptions were all in one hand. These two facts seemed to support the bishop's allegation that the canons of the cathedral chapter had not been consulted or had been coerced into consenting to it.[59]

Innocent also decided that Santa Cruz was an exempt monastery, subject to the pope "nullo mediante." He based this part of his decision on papal privileges in which Santa Cruz and its possessions were exempted from episcopal jurisdiction.[60] It is significant that although Innocent could have adopted a broad interpretation of Santa Cruz' privileges, he did not. He recognized earlier papal but not episcopal privileges. Bishop Michael's privilege had been confirmed, but Innocent refused to validate it, even though he had a legal right to do so. Although Huguccio and the canonists thought that the pope could grant a full and total exemption from episcopal authority, Innocent elected to limit the monastery's privileges.[61]

In a similar, but less-complicated case, Innocent also interpreted another monastery's privileges narrowly. The case was famous and became an

---

57. 3 Comp. 5.16.4 (X 5.33.14), PL 215.117: "infirmantes sua sententia libertatem quam dictus M. Colubriensis episcopus in enorme detrimentum Colubriensis ecclesiae contulerat monasterio S. Crucis, canonicorum assensu per praeconem episcopi et portarium regis extorto."

58. For the importance of canon law for concepts of inalienability, see James Ross Sweeney, "The Problem of Inalienability in Innocent III's Correspondence with Hungary: A Contribution to the Study of the Historical Genesis of Intellecto," *Mediaeval Studies* 37 (1975): 235–51 and "The Decretal Intellecto and the Hungarian Golden Bull of 1222," *Album Elemér Màlyusz* (Brussels: 1976), 91–96. Also see Post, *Studies in Medieval Legal Thought*, 415–33.

59. 3 Comp. 5.16.4 (X 5.33.14), PL 215.121–22: "quia nobis constitit evidenter extortum fuisse in episcopi concessione canonicorum assensum, et concessionis paginam in aliquot lineis habuisse rasuras, et subscriptiones singulas fuisse singulis subscribentium manibus adnotatas; scriptum autem quod nobis exhibitum fuerat, nec rasuram praetendere, nec variis manibus et subscriptionibus variatum, sed a primo ad ultimum eadem potius manu conscriptum, libertatem ab ipso episcopo concessam, irritam decernimus et inanem."

60. Pope Urban III's privilege is printed in *Papsturkunden in Portugal*, 325–28, no. 111.

61. For Huguccio's text, see n. 44 above.

important part of the canon law of exemption. Mauger, the bishop of Worcester, claimed jurisdiction over the monastery of Evesham and over certain churches adjacent to the monastery, called of the "Vale." A monk of the monastery, Thomas of Marlborough, participated in the long dispute at Rome and wrote a lengthy description of the case.[62] The monks had an impressive set of privileges. Although the early papal privileges were undoubtedly forged, Innocent examined them carefully in the curia and declared they were genuine. He confirmed Evesham's full exemption from episcopal jurisdiction.[63]

From a legal point of view, Evesham's exemption was a straightforward matter. Either the monastery had genuine papal privileges granting it an exemption, or it did not. Innocent decided it did. The question whether the churches of the Vale were also exempt was more complex. The monastery could have gained an exemption for its churches through its privileges or through prescription. Marlborough put forward two arguments at the papal curia. First, since Evesham was exempt, its possessions should be exempt. Second, Pope Constantine's privilege granted liberty to "that place," which phrase, he said, should be understood as the monastery and its possessions. To support his interpretation, Marlborough echoed the Roman rule of law: "The gifts of the emperor should be interpreted broadly."[64] His six-month sojourn in Bologna had taught him some law and a few appropriate maxims.

Marlborough gave an extended explanation of his contention. The monastery, he said, had long exercised episcopal rights in the chapels. Further, the chapels were so close to the monastery that they must have been included in Pope Constantine's original exemption.[65] When Innocent turned to the proctor of the bishop and asked for a reply to Marlborough, the lawyer cleverly responded with yet another maxim that was calculated to please the pope: "I should not argue about a papal privilege. He who makes

---

62. *Chronicon abbatiae de Evesham*, 102–29.

63. 3 Comp. 5.16.6 (X 5.33.17), dated 1206. The case of exemption has been thoroughly discussed by Knowles, *Monastic Order*, 331–45, and "Monastic Exemption," 396–401.

64. *Chronicon abbatiae de Evesham*, 138: "Matrix ecclesia, videlicet Eveshamensis quae est caput, est exempta, ergo et capellae vallis quae sunt membra. . . . In privilegio Constantini papae continetur, 'Ipsum ergo locum quem regia potestas regiae libertati donavit et nos auctoritate Dei et sanctorum apostolorum et nostra donamus.' Locus iste non tantum monasterium sed etiam omnes possessiones ecclesiae nostrae complectitur, ut beneficium imperatoris amplissime et benignissime interpretetur." The maxim to which Thomas referred is taken from Dig. 1.4.3. Innocent III used the maxim in his decretals: 3 Comp. 1.2.6 (X 5.40.16) and 3 Comp. 3.18.3 (X 3.24.6).

65. *Chronicon abbatiae de Evesham*, 186–88.

law has the right to interpret his law."[66]

Innocent was not persuaded by Marlborough's arguments. He refused to interpret a privilege broadly. He instructed new judges delegate that they should examine Evesham's royal privileges and determine whether the churches of the Vale had been part of the monastery's possessions. If not, then they should investigate whether the abbey had established an exemption for the churches through prescription.[67]

In another decretal, *Cum capella*, issued shortly after the decision of the Evesham case, Innocent informed the bishop of Langres that canons who hold parish churches and have privileges of exemptions are exempt only in the churches for which they have exemptions. If they hold parish churches without privileges of exemption, they owe their bishop obedience.[68] Again, he limited the extension of privileges.

Innocent did not, however, develop a clear doctrine. He advised the archbishop of Lund that if the bishop's predecessor had exempted the monks of All Souls from paying tithes unconditionally, then the monks were exempted from tithes not only on the lands they possessed, but also on lands they might acquire in the future.[69] On the strength of this decretal, *Quia circa*, the canonists raised the issue of interpreting exemptions. Innocent had interpreted the archbishop's privilege broadly and interrupted his pontificate's rather general pattern of legislative restraint. Would the doctrine of *Quia circa* establish a precedent for future papal decisions?

At first the canonists were reluctant to reach a conclusion. In his discussion of Innocent's letter and in his Ordinary Gloss to the Decretum, Johannes Teutonicus pointed to the legal difficulties but did not offer an unambiguous solution.[70] Vincentius Hispanus tried to solve the problem by

---

66. Ibid., 189: "Pater sancte, ego nonquam in vita mea amplius super privilegiis summi pontificis disputabo, sed vos cuius est condere pro voluntate vestra interpretamini ea [cf. Cod. 1.14.12 and Dig. 46.5.9]." The medieval lawyers formulated the principle as "Eius enim est interpretari, cuius est condere." Innocent III quoted the maxim at 3 Comp. 5.21.4 (X 5.39.31).

67. *Chronicon abbatiae de Evesham*, 191–93.

68. 3 Comp. 5.16.6 (X 5.33.16), dated 1206.

69. 4 Comp. 5.12.5 (X 5.33.22) [Quia circa], PL 215.914–16, dated 1213.

70. Johannes Teutonicus to 4 Comp. 5.12.5 (X 5.33.22) v. *sed futuri*, ed. Antonio Agustín [see text in n. 78 below] and to C. 16 q. 1 c. 52 v. *aliquid iurisdictionis*, Admont 35, fol. 182v [Vat. lat. 1367, fol. 159v]: "Arg. ex eo quod quis eximitur semper uidetur exemptus uniuersaliter et etiam cum suis ecclesiis, in authen. ut eccles. ro. in prin., quia beneficia principum large, etc. ff. de const. prin. Beneficium. extra. iii. de rescript. Olim. Arg. contra extra. iii. de relig. dom. Constitutus, in fine et Cum capella."

distinguishing between chapels that were dependent on exempt churches and those that were not. The first were exempt. He did not, however, define a dependent chapel.[71]

The question intrigued the canonists, and they analyzed the problem with ingenious arguments from Roman law. In the late 1230s, Bartholo-maeus Brixiensis explored the issues in his *Quaestiones*. If an abbot, he asked, had received a papal privilege granting an exemption to a monastery and its chapels, could the chapels which the monastery acquired subse-quently also be exempt?[72]

He presented the arguments for a liberal interpretation of the monas-tery's exemption in the first part of the *Quaestio,* claiming that the gifts of the prince should be broadly interpreted and justifying his position with the maxim of Roman law.[73] He also cited several examples from Roman law in which agreements or contracts covered future rights or possessions in addi-tion to those stipulated at the time of the agreement. His most interesting example was taken from the Digest and was based on an urban servitude "ne luminibus officiatur." A text of Pomponius stated that if the servitude protecting sunlight was attached to property, it covered future as well as

---

71. Vincentius Hispanus to X 5.33.16 [Cum capella], v. *in quantum,* Paris, B.N. 3967, fol. 196v–197r [Paris B.N. 3968, fol. 164r]: "Quod tollitur ex forma ipsius, supra eodem Porro et c. Recipimus. Et per hanc decretalem soluitur questio de abbate qui acquisiuit priuilegium a domino papa quod monasterium suum cum omnibus suis capellis esset exemptum ab omnibus episcopis per omnia; procedente uero tempore, acquisiuit capellas quas contendis eodem pri-uilegio retinere, episcopo loci contradicente. Et distinguendum est in hac questione per decre-talem istam utrum acquirat nouas capellas prioribus accessorias an que principaliter se habeant ab illis omnino segregate. In priori casu participiant priuilegio, in secundo casu non . . . uinc. Et plura arg. de hac materia pro et contra inuenies, xvi. q.i. Frater noster [c. 52], xii. q.ii. Cognouimus [c. 29]. Item ex hac decretali patet quod exemptus potest iudicari ab episcopo ratione rei non exempte, sic supra de maior. et obed. Per tuas [3 Comp. 1.21.3 (X 1.33.7)], ut dixi supra eodem, Tuarum. jo. Et arg. supra de foro compet. Postulasti. uinc." The first section of Vincentius' gloss "Quod tollitur . . . stipulamur. uinc." is quoted by Johannes Teutonicus and Tancred in their commentaries to *Compilatio tertia,* but I have not found it among Vincentius' glosses to 3 Comp.

72. Bartholomaeus Brixiensis, *Quaestiones,* no. 58 printed in *Tractatus universi iuris* (Lyon: 1549) vol. 17, fol. 44r: "Abbas quidam impetravit privilegium a papa quod monasterium suum esset exemptum cum omnibus capellis suis, postea acquisivit alias capel-las quas ex eodem privilegio ostendit munitas. Episcopus soci contradicit. Queritur quid iuris."

73. Ibid.: "Quod sint exempte probatur: Quia beneficium principis largissime est inter-pretandum, ut ff. de constit. prin. Beneficium et extra. de donat. Cum dilecti, in fine [3 Comp. 3.18.3 (X 3.24.6)]."

existing light.[74] In addition to the Roman law texts, Bartholomaeus also cited Innocent III's decretal on future tithes, *Quia circa*. He thought that Innocent's text could also justify the extension of a privilege to future possessions.[75]

In the next section of the *Quaestio*, Bartholomaeus developed arguments against granting the exemptions of a monastery to all new churches and possessions by citing different texts of Roman law. If someone sold a lake and ten feet of shoreline around the lake, future increases in the lake's size would not mean that an additional ten feet of shoreline would be added. Likewise a pact between heirs could cover only those possessions existing at the time of the agreement. Such a pact could not cover future possessions unknown at the time. If, for example, a testator established a bequest of silver dishes in his will, any silver obtained after he made the will would not be considered part of the bequest.[76]

Bartholomaeus did not commit himself to a definitive answer. In his solution to the *Quaestio* he wrote:

Tancred answered my question about this matter by saying that a privilege did not extend to future chapels, only to those held at the time of the privilege. Johannes [Teutonicus] believed the same in his commentary to *Cum capella:* unless the new

---

74. Ibid.: "Item si ita cautum sit ne luminibus officiatur, non solum de presentibus luminibus, sed etiam de futuris intelligitur, ut ff. de servit. urb. pred. Si servitus imposita [Dig. 8.2.23], nam et rei que nondum est servitus acquiri potest, ut in predicta lege in fine, et ff. de servit. rust. pred. Labeo [Dig. 8.3.10]." The lawyers were very inventive in their use of Roman law, and they shaped many of their ideas with Roman doctrines. Much work remains to be done along the lines begun by E. F. Vodola in "Fides et culpa: The Use of Roman Law in Ecclesiastical Ideology," *Authority and Power: Studies on Medieval Law and Government Presented to Walter Ullmann*, ed. Brian Tierney and Peter Linehan (Cambridge: 1980), 83–97 and in "Legal Precision in the Decretist Period: A Note on the Development of Glosses on 'De consecratione' with Reference to the Meaning of 'Cautio sufficiens,'" BMCL 6 (1976): 55–63.

75. Bartholomaeus Brixiensis, loc. cit.: "Item casus iste videtur expressus; nam si quis impetravit privilegium super decimis recipiendis, illud privilegium extenditur non solum ad possessiones acquisitas sed ad acquirandas, ut extra. de privileg. Quia circa; ergo istud privilegium extendetur ad futuras capellas."

76. Ibid.: "Item si vendidi lacum et circa lacum x. pedes, illi decem pedes intelliguntur qui erant circa lacum tempore venditionis. Vnde si lacus excreuerit non habebit emptor alios x. pedes, ff. eodem titulo Rutilia, Polla. . . . Item si pactum de rebus hereditariis fiat inter co-heredes, non intelligitur fieri nisi de rebus que tunc temporis apparebant, ut ff. de pact. Tres fratres, sic et privilegium concedi intelligitur capellis quas tunc monasterium presentialiter possidebat. Item legavit aliquis argentum viatorium, non videtur legatum nisi illud quod erat viatorium tempore testamenti, ut ff. de auro. et arg. le. Medico, in principio [Dig. 34.2.40]."

chapels were dependent on the old they were not exempt. Some say privileges should extend to future chapels and cite *Quia circa* to justify their allegation.[77]

Although Tancred may have told Bartholomaeus personally of his opinion, he never wrote about the matter so decisively. At least I have found no gloss of Tancred in which he expressed this view. Nor was Johannes Teutonicus' opinion so unambiguous. Nevertheless, from his gloss to *Quia circa*, one may conclude that he leaned in the direction of interpreting privileges restrictively.[78]

Giles Constable has studied the history of monastic tithes and traced the development of papal decretal legislation touching them.[79] He noted that in the early twelfth century many monasteries, especially Cistercian foundations, were given exemptions from paying tithes on the produce of their lands. By the mid-twelfth century, a series of questions had arisen concerning monastic exemptions that parallel the problems we have been considering. First and foremost was whether an exempt monastic house had to pay tithes on lands newly brought under cultivation or newly acquired. Pope Hadrian IV (1154–59) enacted legislation restricting monastic freedom from tithes on these "noval" lands.[80]

Although later popes, particularly Alexander III, revised some of Hadrian's measures, Constable has collected enough contemporary evidence to illustrate the issues surrounding tithes that concerned clerics of the twelfth century. John of Salisbury, for example, wrote in the *Policraticus*:

Hence it is that the blessed Hadrian when he saw these privileges being thus turned into a means of avarice, not wishing to revoke them altogether, yet restricted their

---

77. Ibid.: "Solutio. T. mihi respondit quod privilegium non extenditur ad capellas habendas, set ad habitas tantum. Idem credit Jo. super decre. de privileg. Cum capella [appella *male*], nisi forte capelle postea acquisite essent prioribus accessorie. Quidam tamen contrarium dixerunt per predictam decretalem, Quia circa."

78. Johannes Teutonicus to 4 Comp. 5.12.5 (X 5.33.22), v. *sed futuri*, ed. Agustín: "Arg. quod in privilegiis verbum generale ad futura extenditur, ut 12 q.2 Cognovimus, supra de decimis, Ex parte, lib. 3, C. que res pig. oblig. poss. l.ult. ff. de servit. urban. praed. Si servitus. Arg. contra supra de censibus, Quando, lib. 2, supra de decim. Tuam, lib. eodem et supra eodem, Cum capella . . . sed hic ideo contra dantem fit interpretatio, ne excogitata fraude obvient liberalitati suae . . . secus si certa ponuntur, in eo casu non extenditur ad alia. . . . Sed ubi generale nomen ponitur, semper extenditur ad omnia appellata. . . . Si autem eque potest retorqueri ad ius commune, sicut ad privilegium; potius interpretandum secundum ius commune . . . sic enim est interpretatio facienda, ut nemini sit onerosa." This last clause is, I think, Johannes' opinion.

79. Giles Constable, *Monastic Tithes from Their Origins to the Twelfth Century* (Cambridge: 1964). For the following paragraphs I am indebted to pp. 270–309 of Constable's study.

80. Ibid., 279.

scope by the limitation that what such men may withhold from the fruits of their labor should be interpreted solely with reference to lands newly brought under cultivation. For thus they will be able to enjoy their privileges without serious infringement of the rights of others.[81]

Constable observed that "the change in papal policy also increased the pressure from local authorities on the privileged monks either to pay tithes or to give adequate compensation for the tithes from which they were technically free."[82] He described Pope Alexander's revision of Hadrian's policy as an atempt "to preserve the rights of all churches, including of course the privileged monasteries, and to maintain as far as possible all existing agreements."[83]

Preserving existing rights of all churches is a key concept in understanding the constitutional thought of the canonists in the twelfth and thirteenth centuries. They conceived of the church as possessing a bewildering variety of rights. The origins of these rights lay in grants, customary usage, privilege, or canonical practice. Although the rights of the clergy and of institutions often came into conflict, canonists believed that the ecclesiastical liberties of each should be preserved whenever possible.

Constant restraint was an important element of canonistic thought. The pope could take episcopal rights away, but he should do so only with cause and good reason. When deluded by self-interest, even contemporaries did not clearly understand these deep-seated ideals.

When the monks of Evesham advised their abbot, Roger Norreys, to have their exemptions confirmed at the Roman curia, they argued that "the Roman Church was most favorably inclined to cases of liberty."[84] They were sure that Rome would support papal privileges of any monastery against the depredations of an aggressive bishop. Indeed, the Roman church and the pope did defend Roman prerogatives vigorously. Nothing angered young Pope Innocent more than judges or litigants who ignored or failed to observe the rule that all litigation ceased upon an appeal to Rome.[85] Nevertheless,

81. Ibid., 286–87. *Policraticus*, ed. C. C. J. Webb (Oxford: 1909), 2: 197–98, book 7, c. 21. The translation is from John Dickinson, *The Statesman's Book of John of Salisbury* (New York 1927), 318–19.

82. Constable, *Monastic Tithes*, 289.

83. Ibid., 302.

84. *Chronicon abbatiae de Evesham*, 113–14: "causa nostra, quae libertatis est, inter omnes causas magis favorabilis est, et maxime apud ecclesiam Romanam, cui volumus, sicut debemus, nullo mediante, subjeci; quae etiam diligit exemptiones."

85. Cheney, *Pope Innocent III*, 113.

from what evidence we have, Innocent III did not favor a broad interpretation of papal privileges; nor did he grant many new exemptions during his pontificate. In England, as Cheney has pointed out, "Innocent III made no grant of exemption *de novo* to an English monastery."[86] In his handling of grants of exemption, he preserved the exemptions of those houses that could prove them. He was not anxious to take episcopal prerogatives or rights away.

Constable's sketch of monastic tithes shows a parallel evolution in the legislation of popes Hadrian IV and Alexander III. Similarly, in the Fourth Lateran decrees treating tithes, Innocent limited the privileges of the Cistercians. They must, in the future, pay tithes on all newly acquired lands that had previously paid tithes.[87] Once again, papal legislation protected existing liberties and rights.

When he treated exemptions in his Commentary, Hostiensis developed sophisticated legal justifications for the constitutional thought of the canonists. He wrote that all privileges should be interpreted strictly. The reason for this is, he argued, that privileges are always granted in prejudice of an ordinary's authority and jurisdiction. Those who are privileged often abuse their status and perpetrate many offenses.[88] Therefore, papal privileges, in particular, should be strictly interpreted. If the pope inflicted a great injury with his privilege, it should be limited. A bishops' privilege, like that of the archbishop of Lund, could be broadly interpreted. The difference arises, argued Hostiensis, because the pope grants a more general privilege than a bishop, and the prince should not injure anyone's rights.[89]

Hostiensis applied these principles to the problem of newly acquired monastic possessions. He posed the question of whether future chapels could

---

86. Ibid., 196. See Cheney's comments on pp. 186–87 as well.

87. Constable, *Monastic Tithes,* 306. 4th Lat. c. 53, 54, 55.

88. Hostiensis to X 5.33.16 v. *privilegio quod nullus archiepiscopus, Commentaria,* 5: fol. 84vb: "Sic ergo circa exemptiones stricte interpretantur et est ratio: quia fiunt in ordinariorum potestatis et iurisdictionis praeiudicium qui valde favorabiles sunt, ut patet, xi. q.i. Pervenit [c. 39] et q.iii. Qui resistit [c. 97] et in eo quod legitur supra de appell. Vt debitus. Et quia privilegiati consueverunt abuti privilegiis, supra eodem, Tuarum §i. in principio, et occasione ipsorum multas insolentias committere." Hostiensis' allegations give even more force to his thought. *Pervenit* is a letter of Pope Gregory the Great in which he wrote that if the jurisdiction of each bishop is not preserved, ecclesiastical order will be violated.

89. Ibid., to 5.33.22 v. *una et eadem substantia,* fol. 86rb: "Si papa concedat privilegium et infligat enorme gravamen, restringitur, supra de decim. Suggestum. Si vero episcopus, dilatatur ut hic. Ratio est quia papa dat privilegium generalius quam episcopus, et princeps non consuevit praeiudicare, C. de eman. Nec avus [Cod. 8.48(49).4] Sed episcopus potest iuri suo renuntiare et ideo imputet sibi si non excepit, ut hic dicitur."

be exempt on account of a monastery's privileges and reexamined Vincentius' gloss on the subject. Unlike his predecessors, however, he had little difficulty deciding the issue. "I believe that those who say that an exemption should never be extended to future possessions are correct," he concluded. To justify his position, he repeated: privileges should always be interpreted strictly.[90]

BISHOPS AND EXEMPT CLERICS

A privileged monastery had an exemption of place. The members of the monastery were protected from episcopal jurisdiction as well. During the twelfth century, the canonists did not explore the possibility that a monk who was exempt in his monastery might, under certain circumstances, commit crimes for which he could be summoned to an episcopal court. In the causae in which Gratian treated questions of jurisdiction, he included several chapters which dictated that a crime should be tried where it had been committed. He also cited a number of chapters stipulating that litigants should always be tried in their own courts. They should not petition for their case to be heard by a judge who was not their local ordinary.[91] Nevertheless, Gratian's texts did not prod the canonists to investigate the question of exempt clerics. The canonists probably reasoned that if a privilege granted a monastery and its monks an exemption, the monks were simply exempt.

Papal legislation after Gratian opened the question of personal exemptions. At the Council of Verona (1184), Pope Lucius III decreed that when dealing with heretics, bishops could judge clerics whose privileges exempted them from diocesan jurisdiction. This canon, *Ad abolendam,* granted full jurisdiction to bishops over heretics who possessed papal privileges.[92] Still heresy was a special crime, whose horror led the church to establish a

---

90. Ibid., to 5.33.16 v. *in quantum,* fol. 84vb: "Solutio. Si capellae acquisitae de novo sint antiquis accessorie, tunc eodem privilegio gaudent; si vero sunt omnino separatae, non gaudent . . . secundum quosdam. Alii indistincte dicunt quod hec exemptio numquam extenditur ad futura, arg. supra de rescript. c. finali et c. Eam te, quod puto verius, arg. ff. de au. et ar. le. Si ita est legatum. Et est ratio ut nota supra eodem, responso i. [Reference to gloss quoted in n. 88]."

91. C. 1 q. 3–4; C. 3 q. 6.

92. 1 Comp. 5.6.11 (X 5.7.9): "Si quis vero fuerint, qui a lege dioecesanae iurisdictionis exempti, soli subiaceant sedis apostolicae potestati, nihilominus in his, quae superius sunt contra hereticos instituta, archiepiscoporum vel episcoporum subeant iudicium, et eis in hac parte, tamquam a sede apostolica delegatis, non obstantibus libertatis suae privilegiis observentur."

number of unpleasant and unique penalties and procedures.[93] *Ad abolendam* was thus a specific exception to the general rule, and the canonists were not inclined to use it as a precedent to expand the cases in which exempt clerics might be judged.

The matter was, however, taken up in a larger context. Monks who belonged to religious orders possessing privileges of general exemption disturbed the tranquillity of local bishops. The litigiousness and the depredations of the Cistercians, the Hospitalers, and the Templars were notorious. At the beginning of his pontificate, Pope Innocent III sent a letter, *Tuarum*, to Archbishop Absalon of Lund in which he permitted the archbishop to punish the Hospitalers of St. John for crimes they committed in his jurisdiction. The Hospitalers held papal privileges, but, wrote Innocent, those who abuse their privileges should lose them.[94]

Innocent was raising a sticky issue. Papal privileges granted rights to their bearers that could be taken away only by the pope. Alexander III had decreed that heretics lost their privileges, and the canonists found this to be a reasonable rule. Heresy was, indeed, an exceptional case. Now Innocent was broadening the number of cases in which bishops might ignore papal privileges without defining the limits of episcopal authority to do so. The canonists saw the problem and began to explore the circumstances under which a bishop might act. Although they had hesitated to extend *Ad abolendam*, they used *Tuarum* to argue that bishops might exercise jurisdiction over privileged clerics in a wide variety of cases.

Shortly after *Tuarum* was written, the author of the *Glossa Palatina* asked if the bishop of Bologna could excommunicate a Roman cleric or a Templar for a crime. He concluded that if the crime were notorious and the offender contumacious, he could. If not, the bishop did not have jurisdiction. A bishop did not have authority *(prelatio)* over privileged clerics unless they committed a crime *(ratione delicti)*.[95] *Ratione delicti,* however, was a very broad concept that could include almost any kind of offense.

---

93. Pennington, "Pro peccatis patrum puniri," 137–54.

94. Innocent III, Register I, 673–74, no. 450: "Verum, quia privilegium meretur ammittere, qui permissa sibi abutitur libertate." L. De-Mauri, *Regulae iuris,* 11th ed. (Milan: 1976), 187, notes that this rule is a *regula iuris communis.* It was not a rule of Roman law. Innocent III quoted the maxim from the Decretum, C. 11 q. 3 c. 6 or D. 74 c. 7. See the comments of the *correctores Romani* for the origins of the maxim.

95. *Glossa Palatina* to C. 6 q. 3 c. 4 [Placuit] v. *alter episcopus eum excommunicauerit,* Vat. Pal. lat. 658, fol. 40r–v [Vat. Reg. lat. 977, fol. 116r]: "Set numquid enim est Romanum uel Templarium, ratione delicti potest Bononensis episcopus excommunicare? Videtur quod sic, in authen. de mandat. princip. Quod si delinquentes inueneris, ubi dicitur ne permittas priuile-

The context in which the canonists most often discussed this issue was the right of a bishop to judge a cleric from another diocese. Both Alanus and Ricardus Anglicus thought that a bishop could punish a cleric who committed a crime in his jurisdiction, even if the cleric was privileged.[96] Before Innocent III's decretal *Tuarum,* the canonists had been dependent on two *authentica* of Justinian to justify the loss of privileges through abuse.[97] Although an argument from Roman law carried weight in the minds of the canonists, it did not have the same force as a papal decretal.

The anonymous canonist who composed the apparatus *Servus appella-tur* presented the most detailed early discussion of the problem. He compared the status of an exempt cleric to the legal status of a slave. A slave is not half free and half unfree, but a privileged cleric can be subjected to an ordinary's jurisdiction in some circumstances and not in others. An example would be a Templar or a Hospitaler who had been granted the care of a church that was not exempt. In matters touching the church, the Templar was not exempt, but was under the bishop's jurisdiction.[98]

---

giis aliquibus uti [Pal.: in] nocentes, [Authen. 3.4.4 and 3.4.5 (Nov. 17)]. Arg. etiam extra. in<noc.> de priuileg. Tuarum. Arg. contra expressum eodem titulo c. penult. et uidetur expressum C. ubi de curiali uel cohort. l.ii.[Cod. 3.23]. Arg. ff. de offic. proconsul. Si in aliquam §ii. [Dig. 1.16.7.2], ubi dicitur quod proconsul non potest intromittere se de causis fiscalibus. Dic eos puniendos ubi crimen notorium est, nec emendare uoluerint. Alias non, quid enim iam ualeant eorum priuilegia? Cum nulla prelatio sit nisi ratione delicti, ut xxii. di. De Constantin-opolitano *[sic]*." Salzburg, St. Peter's Archabbey a.xii.9, fol. 97v also collated. On the authorship of the *Palatina,* see Stickler, "Il decretista." It is surprising that the canonists did not connect *ratione delicti* to Innocent III's *ratione peccati* in Novit (3 Comp. 2.1.3).

96. Ricardus Anglicus to 1 Comp. 5.28.8 (X——) [Sane], v. *ecclesias suas interdicere,* Munich Staatsbibl. 6352, fol. 76r [Bamberg Staatsbibl. can. 20, fol. 51v]: "Quid autem si in parrochia alicuius eorum delinquant, nonne ratione delicti cohercendi sunt? Respon. Quia in prouincia quis delinquid, ibi iuri subiaceat, omni cessante priuilegio, ut C. ubi de crimine agi oportet et vi. q.iii. Placuit. Vbi ergo locum hoc habet priuilegium? Respon. circa causas infamie, ut ii. q.v. Presbyter. Item ne pro delicto principis eorum ecclesie interdicantur, ut supra de spon. Non est uobis [1 Comp. 4.1.13 (X 4.1.11)]." Also collated with Salzburg, St. Peter's Archabbey a.ix.18, fol. 111r. Alanus Anglicus to loc. cit. v. *ut ipsos,* Karlsruhe Aug. XL, fol. 77v [Halle Ye 52, part III, fol. 85v]: "tamquam parrochianos. Verum tamen si in episcopatibus eorum deli-querint, <si> sit manifestum, a locorum episcopis possunt excommunicari, ut vi. q.iii. Placuit, et etiam secundum leges, non obstante priuilegio, ad iudicium trahi, ut authen. de mandat. §princip. Non permittas [Nov. 17.5]. A."

97. Alanus Anglicus [2nd rec.] to C. 6 q. 3 c. 4 v. *depredationis,* Paris, Mazarine: 1318, fol. 166r [Paris, B.N. lat. 15393, fol. 117r]: "Idem esset de quocumque alio crimine in alterius parochia commisso, arg. iii. q.vi. c.i. ff. de offic. presid. l.ii. C. ubi de crimine l.i. [Cod. 3.15] authen. contra Qua in prouincia [post Cod. 3.15.2 = Nov. 69.1], uel contractu."

98. *Servus appellatur* to 3 Comp. 5.16.6 (X 5.33.16) v. *a te tenent,* Bamberg, Staatsbibl. can. 19, fol. 215r: "Set aliud est in seruitute ut ibi quia non potest esse seruus pro parte et pro parte liber. Set in iurisdictione potest quandoque eam exercere in certis casibus, in aliis non, ut

The canonist went on to expand the scope of the question. He asked whether a bishop could excommunicate a Templar or a Hospitaler whose orders held privileges granting their members general exemptions. He cited the opinion of a certain B. who held that either the notoriety of the crime or, according to Roman law, simply the crime itself *(ratione delicti)* placed the wrongdoer under episcopal jurisdiction.[99] Further, just as a Roman citizen might be excommunicated in the provinces, so too a privileged cleric might lose his exempt status. B.'s opinions are strikingly similar to those given in the *Glossa Palatina*.

The author of *Servus appellatur*, however, was not satisfied. On the basis of a letter of Pope Gregory the Great, the canonist argued that a privileged cleric could not lose his exemption so easily.[100] When an exempt cleric transgressed, he wrote, the pope, not the bishop, had jurisdiction. He conceded that there were cases in which a bishop could have jurisdiction. The crime of heresy was one example. He noted, however, that even in the case of heresy, the bishop's jurisdiction could be said to have been delegated by the pope. A judge, he concluded, could not judge an exempt cleric for a crime or a breach of contract unless the law stipulates that he may.[101]

The solution proposed by the author of *Servus appellatur* was too

---

no. supra de offic. iud. ord. Duo et c. Pastoralis, resp. i. Item idem credo in Templario uel Hospitalario, si per eum regatur ecclesia que non sit exempta."

99. Ibid.: "Set esto quod Templarius et Hospitalarius in mea diocesi peccat, numquid ratione delicti possum eum excommunicare? Est expressum C. ubi de crimin. agi oport. authen. Qua in prouincia, nam ibi dicit omni priuilegio cassare, quod concedebat B. ratione delicti, arg. vi. q.iii. c.ult. extra. de rapt. c.i. authen. ut nulli iud. § Si uero coll. ix. Alii dicunt hoc esse uerum in crimine notorio, alias secus, per ea vi. q.iii. Placuit. Arg. extra. de appellat. Cum sit Romana, in fine. Et B. dicebat idem in quolibet priuilegiato, quod in ciue Romano; nam sicut ciuis Romanus posset excommunicari ratione delicti commissi in prouincia ita et quilibet priuilegiatus secundum eum."

100. Gregory's letter "Frater noster," C. 16 q. 1 c. 52, is discussed in this chapter, nn. 24–25.

101. *Servus appellatur* to 3 Comp. 5.16.6 (as in n. 98): "Set contra eos facit xvi. q.i. Frater noster. Set potest dici quod ipse non delinquerat in eorum iurisdictione; unde si in episcopatu suo deliquid, cum iam exemptus esset, ad papam spectabat de causa cognoscere. Item contradicit extra. de heretic. c.ult. ubi dicitur quod etiam in causa hereseos non auctoritate sua, set tanquam delegati possunt procedere contra personas priuilegiatas. Set posset dici quod ideo ibi dicit papa tanquam legati ut specialius uideantur habere quasi iurisdictionem sicut delegatur causa iudici ordinario suo. Alias uel potest dici quod non possit iudex ratione delicti uel contractus de eis iudicare nisi in illo casu ubi inuenitur expressum, arg. xxv. di. Qualis. ff. de offic. eius cui man. l.i. C. de procur. Maritus, et facit ad hoc iam dictum capitulum, Frater noster, licet contrarium dicere in ciue Romano, nam maioris auctoritate est exemptio hominis quam legis."

restrictive for most other canonists who were not attracted to such a broad interpretation of privileges. Tancred thought that a cleric's privilege should be read, and, if it contained no provision granting exemption from prosecution, the bishop could summon the cleric to court, provided his crime was notorious.[102] If a crime were secret, then the cleric would be exempt from episcopal jurisdiction. Only the pope could exercise jurisdiction over secret crimes.[103] Tancred apparently found the following opinion (attributed to Vincentius in his Apparatus) persuasive: "The pope knows that the Templars are always in someone else's province, and he knows that they commit wrongs. Nevertheless, he maintains that they should not be punished."[104]

Tancred introduced another consideration. Classical Roman law distinguished among various social positions of those who held imperial privileges. "Curiales" could be punished wherever they sinned, unless they were in military service or held imperial privileges. A "clarissimus" could be tried where he committed his crime, even if he held an imperial privilege. "Illustres" could be brought to court only by a judge whom the emperor had delegated.[105] Although these classes do not conform to the ranks of medieval

---

102. Tancred to 2 Comp. 1.6.2 (X 1.10.2) [Sicut nobis] v. *predictos excessus*, Cordoba, Bibl. del Cabildo 10, fol. 97r [Vat. lat. 1377, fol. 103v]: "Ergo si exempti sunt, eorum excessus episcopus punire non poterit, arg. xvi. q.i. Frater noster, alias inutile esset eorum priuilegium, quod latissime interpretandum est, ut infra de rescript. Olim, lib. iii. infra de donat. Cum dilecti, lib. iii. Set contra: Perdiderunt priuilegium per delictum, xi. q.iii. Priuilegium, et ubi quis deliquid puniendus est, omni priuilegio cessante, ut dicit lex, C. de crim. agi oport. authen. Qua in prouincia." This letter, *Sicut nobis,* was attributed to Pope Clement III in the decretal collections; see Innocent III, Register II, 12–13, no. 5.

103. Tancred, loc. cit.: "Respon. Circa hoc ita est tenendum quod primo exemptionis priuilegium inspici debet, et secundum quod ibi expresse continetur seruandum est; nec ad res nec ad personas extendi debet nisi quatinus continetur in eo. . . . Et si ibi non continetur expresse prohibitum pro notorio delicto ab eo episcopo in cuius diocesi deliquerint puniendi sunt. . . . Si uero eorum excessus est occultus sine speciali licentia domini pape non debet se intromittere. t."

104. Tancred [Vincentius] to 1 Comp. 5.28.3 (X 5.33.3) [Cum et plantare] v. *robor auctoritatis episcopalis eneruant*, Cordoba Bibl. del Cabildo 10, fol. 88r [Graz, Univer. 138, fol. 74r]: "Alii dicunt quod nullo modo potest eos aliquis punire, nam papa istud reseruauit sibi quod sic probatur: nonne papa scit quod templarii in aliena prouincia semper sunt, utique et scit quod delinquunt, et tamen dicit quod non puniantur, ut infra eodem, Sane." This gloss is in Vincentius' apparatus to 1 Comp. It is, however, buried in the margin of Leipzig Univ. 983, fol. 56v and cannot be read from the microfilm. Vincentius did not include the gloss in his gloss to the *Gregoriana*.

105. Ibid.: "et quasi aliqui dicuntur curiales punientur ubi inuenientur nisi sint in armata militia. Illi enim conuenientur sub magistro militum. Vel nisi habeant priuilegium imperiale . . .

society, the rules follow faithfully those found in the *Corpus iuris civilis* of Justinian.

Tancred's contemporary, Johannes Teutonicus, sketched canonistic opinions on both sides of the question.[106] He noted that some canonists believed a privileged cleric could be tried for a notorious but not a secret crime.[107] This distinction, he thought, was unsatisfactory. He decided that a better distinction could be drawn between "matters" *(res)* that were exempt and "matters" that were not:

You may more reasonably say that if the holder of a privilege commits a crime in a nonexempt matter—as in a contract or an evil act, such as killing a person or committing adultery—the local bishop can punish such a crime because it touched nonexempt matters, even though the person who committed the crime was exempt. But if he commits a crime in an exempt matter—by exercising his office badly or by alienating the goods of his church—then he may be punished only by the pope. Therefore, where the act of an exempted person prejudices someone else, the bishop may punish him; otherwise not.[108]

---

et quia si clarissimus delinquid conuenitur ubi delinquid cessante priuilegio. . . . Set illustres non nisi sub iudicibus specialiter deputatis a principe, C. eodem, l.iii. vinc. Quid super hoc tenendum sit quere infra de suppl. neg. prelat. c.i. lib. ii. t." See Giles Constable's discussion of twelfth-century descriptions of social classes in "The Substructure of Medieval Society According to the Dictatores of the Twelfth Century," *Law, Church, and Society: Essays in Honor of Stephan Kuttner,* ed. K. Pennington and R. Somerville (Philadelphia: 1977), 253–67.

106. Johannes Teutonicus to C. 6 q. 3 c. 4 [Placuit] v. *parochianum,* Admont 35, fol. 135r [Vat. lat. 1367, fol. 110v, Bamberg Staatsbibl. can. 13, fol. 97v]: "Set numquid episcopus potest punire exemptos qui delinquent in sua diocesi? Videtur quod sic per capitulum istud supra iii. q.vi. c.i. et extra. i. de heret. Ad abolendam, in fine, ubi dicitur quod nullum priuilegium iuuat, et extra. iii. de priuileg. Tuarum, in fine. Item negligentiam talium potest supplere, ut extra. ii. de capell. monach. De minori [2 Comp. 3.23.2 (X——)], extra. i. de priuileg. Cum et plantare, et excessus eorum punire, et extra. ii. de priuil. Patentibus. Item quia ratione delicti perditur priuilegium, xi. q.iii. Priuilegium. Item quia reatus omnem honorem excludit, C. ubi senat. l.i. Item qua in prouincia quis delinquid, illic iuri subiaceat: nullo se excusaturus priuilegio, ut C. ubi de crimine agi oport. <authen.> Qua in prouincia. Nec enim pretextu priuilegii concessi flagitorum crescet auctoritas, ut C. de priuil. schol. l.ii. lib. xii. Ad idem est in authen. de mandat. princ. § Quod si delinquentes, inueneris, ubi dicitur 'non permittas nocentes uti aliquibus priuilegiis.' § Econtra probatur quod non possint puniri, ut extra. i. de priuil. Sane, et extra. iii. eodem, Cum capella et xvi. q.i. Frater noster, et expresse dicitur extra. ii. de supplen. negl. prelat. Sicut. Si enim tales possent puniri sicut alii, inutile esset priuilegia ipsorum. Item proconsul non potest se intromittere de causis fiscalibus, ff. de offic. procon. Si in aliquam *(sic)* § i."

107. Ibid.: "Solutio. Quidam dicunt quod pro occulto delicto a solo Romano pontifice possunt puniri, set pro notorio possunt puniri ab episcopo loci per id quod est extra. iii. de priuileg. Tuarum."

108. Ibid.: "Melius dicas quod si priuilegiatus delinquid circa rem non exemptam, ut in contractu uel in maleficio, occidendo hominem uel adulterando cum aliqua, tale delictum potest punire episcopus loci, quia etsi persona exempta sit, tamen res in qua delinquitur non est

Johannes' distinction was much more elegant than earlier attempts of the canonists to define the limits of papal privileges. Using a vague and indefinable standard, a judge often had difficulty deciding whether the notoriety of any particular crime was sufficient to bring the case under his jurisdiction. Johannes divided all cases into those that were covered by privilege and those that were not. Consequently, a bishop could, according to Johannes, excommunicate a privileged cleric for an offense that was quite minor, such as living in taverns.[109]

The canonists were reluctant to choose one single interpretation of papal privileges. Vincentius Hispanus and Tancred included Johannes' gloss as well as their own in their apparatus, but the question remained open.[110] Of the next generation, Goffredus da Trani supported Johannes' interpretation.[111]

Sometime between 1250 and 1253, Hostiensis analyzed the status of exempt clerics in his *Summa aurea*. He reviewed earlier opinions and examined the legal difficulties. Not completely satisfied with Johannes Teutonicus' solution of *res exemptae* and *res non exemptae*, he turned to Tancred's distinction of secret and notorious crimes. He also adopted Teutonicus' distinction between an act that injured a second party and one that did not.[112] Hostiensis argued that, first, privileges must be examined to deter-

---

exempta. Si uero delinquid circa rem exemptam, puta male gerendo se in officio suo uel alienando res ecclesie sue, in his a solo papa punitur. Vbi ergo factum exempti preiudicium affert non exemptis bene punit episcopus loci, secus si non affert. Et hec distinctio probatur, extra. iii. de priuileg. Cum capella et extra. ii. de feriis, Significantibus [2 Comp. 2.5.1 (X——)]." Johannes repeated this gloss almost word for word at 3 Comp. 5.16.1 (X 5.33.11) v. *post interdictum*, Admont 22, fol. 263v.

109. Johannes Teutonicus to 4th Lat. c. 62 v. *nec in tabernis aut aliis locis incongruis hospitentur*, ed. García y García, 266: "Tunc enim ratione delicti possunt a diocesano episcopo excommunicari, licet sint exempti, ut extra. iii. de priuil. Tuarum."

110. Vincentius Hispanus and Tancred quoted Johannes' gloss to Tuarum v. *post interdictum* (n. 108). Vincentius to X 5.33.16 v. *in quantum*, Paris, B.N. lat. 3967, fol. 196v–197r. Tancred to 3 Comp. 5.16.1 (X 5.33.11) v. *post interdictum*, Vat. lat. 1377, fol. 271r.

111. Goffredus da Trani to X 5.33.16 [Cum capella] v. *priuilegii*, Paris, B.N. lat. 15402, fol. 171r. Also v. *parochiales ecclesias:* "Item ex hac decretali sumitur illa distinctio quod si priuilegiatus delinquat in re cuius priuilegium habeat, exemptus est a iurisdictione ordinarii et propter ea puniri non potest ab eo nisi notorie delinquat, et supra eodem titulo, Patentibus et c. Tua. Si autem delinquat in re uel circa rem non priuilegiatam exemptio locum habet non, quia priuilegium illud sit reale non personale ut hic. G."

112. Hostiensis, *Summa aurea* (Venice: 1586) col. 1709–10: "Solutio. Dic quod aut exempti delinquant notorie aut occulte. Si exemptus notorie delinquit, puniri potest per ordinarium, ut infra eodem Patentibus et c. Tuarum, et sic intelligi debent iura inducta, supra eodem

mine whether an exempt cleric could be judged. If a privilege stated expressly that he could be judged only by the Apostolic See, then, no matter what his crime, a bishop could not summon him to court.[113] If a privilege contained no clause of absolute exemption, then, noted Hostiensis, it must be decided whether the act injured another party. If the act did not injure another party and was a *res exempta,* then the act was not actionable and could not be punished. If, however, a cleric committed a crime openly and notoriously in a *res exempta* and if he also injured another party, then the bishop could exercise jurisdiction in the matter.[114]

Although Hostiensis accepted Teutonicus' distinction between *res exemptae* and *res non exemptae,* he did not believe that all acts that touched *res exemptae* were immune from prosecution. Hostiensis did not expressly say so, but it must be assumed that he, like Johannes Teutonicus, thought that a cleric could be punished for acts in *res non exemptae.*

Pope Innocent IV decided the question definitively. He had not treated the problem in any depth in his commentary on the Decretals of Gregory IX. However, in the constitution *Volentes,* which he issued between January 1250 and February 1251, Innocent rendered all previous discussions nugatory. He included *Volentes* in the third recension of his *Novellae.* Later, it was placed in the Sext of Boniface VIII.[115]

---

sub § respon. i. et vers. sequenti usque ad uersic. 'Contrarium probo.' Et patet ibidem in uersic. 'Quid plura' si uero occulte delinquat, tunc non potest puniri, nisi a papa, et sic possunt intelligi iura inducta, supra eodem sub § uersic. In contrarium; sed certe per eadem iura inducta, que loquuntur nedum in occultis, sed etiam in notoriis, hec solutio reprobatur Ioannis distinctionem."

113. Ibid., col. 1710: "Sed ne videar tantorum doctorum sententias uno verbo tollere velle, sic distinguo: quando quaeritur utrum exemptus delinquens [*add.* ed. 1570] puniri debeat, refert utrum in privilegio hoc expressim contineatur quod quantumcumque delinquat, a nemine citra sedem Apostolicam iudicetur, uel puniatur, uel alia quaecunque verba similia, idem expressius innuentia, et tunc standum est priuilegio sicut sonat infra eodem, Porro."

114. Ibid.: "Sed et hoc potest subdistingui, quia et si hoc in priuilegio specialiter non caueatur, sed simpliciter eximitur, puta quia dicitur in priuilegio quod censum praestat ad iudicium perceptae libertatis, infra Recepimus, in casu autem isto delinquit in rem uel circa rem priuilegiatam non praeiudicando alii aut preiudicando. Item aut notorie aut occulte. Si exemptus delinquat circa priuilegiatam rem sine praeiudicio priuato alterius, referendum est papae, et sic loquitur de statu mon. Ea que § Haec eadem. Et sic priuilegiatus manet in percepta libertate, ut innuunt uerba priuilegii, et secundum hoc etiam potest intelligi, supra de sup. negl. prelat. c. secundo, quia si ecclesiae illae exemptae sunt, ergo committitur delictum in re priuilegiata, nec episcopo cui non subsunt ecclesiae potest aliquid praeiudicium generari. Sin autem alii praeiudicat, et palam siue notorie delinquat, corrigi potest, quod male faciet per censuram ecclesiasticam, ut infra eodem, Patentibus et c. Tuarum."

115. Kuttner, "Konstitutionen des ersten allgemeinen Konzils von Lyon," 70–131. On the various recensions of Innocent's *Novellae,* see P. J. Kessler, "Untersuchungen über die Novellengesetzgebung Papst Innocenz IV." ZRG Kan. Abt. 31 (1942): 142–320; 32 (1943): 300–383; 33 (1944): 56–128.

Volentes has all the attributes of a general constitution, which the pope issued *proprio motu*. Unlike most papal decretals that respond to specific requests for instruction, *Volentes* was promulgated to solve a problem of interpretation which had not been resolved in the schools. No one had asked the pope to render a decision, as there is no trace of a recipient in any of the sources.[116] The style of the letter betrays, I think, something of the pope's background. The rhetorical question inserted in the main body of the letter is typical of canonistic commentaries, but unusual in papal decretals. Since Innocent resolved the problem in language that echoes the style of the can-onistic commentaries, the decretal confirms the pope's intellectual training. Unlike most professors, however, Innocent could end the debate in the schools by "inviolable decree" *(declaratione irrefragabili):*

We define by inviolable decree that however much exempt clerics enjoy their right, nevertheless by reason of delict, or contract, or case, for which they are summoned, they may be convened before ordinary judges of that place, and these judges may, in this matter, exercise jurisdiction over them. Do exempt clerics lose, by this, their right? By no means. The ordinary may not summon exempt clerics if the delict is committed in an exempt place or if a contract is entered or a case is litigated where they are not domiciled. If they transgress, or make a contract, or *res ipsa consistat,* in another place, they can be summoned [to that place] on account of these matters. The diocesan bishop may not transfer the case on pretext of place of residence (if clerics are summoned to where they transgressed for these reasons) or have any power of enjoining that exempt clerics answer a summons from another place.[117]

Innocent's solution evolved from at least one previous decretal.[118] The pope incorporated earlier notions of the canonists, especially Johannes Teu-tonicus' distinction between *res exemptae et non exemptae*. He made the concept of place crucial in determining who had jurisdiction in a particular case. Earlier canonists had considered only the diocese as a territorial unit.

---

116. The inscription, "in concilio generali Lugdunensi" in the *Editio Romana* is incorrect.

117. VI 5.7.1: "Declaratione irrefragabili diffinimus, quod quantumcumque sic exempti gaudeant libertate, nihilominus tamen ratione delicti sive contractus aut rei, de qua contra ipsos agitur, rite possunt coram locorum ordinariis conveniri, et illi quoad hoc suam in ipsos iurisdic-tionem, prout ius exigit, exercere. Numquid ergo carent omnino in his commodo libertatis? Non utique quia nec coram ordinariis ipsis, dummodo sit in loco exempto commissum delic-tum, vel contractus initus aut res litigiosa, nec ubi domicilium habent, si alibi delinquant, vel contrahant, aut res ipsa consistat, conveniri possunt aliquatenus super istis: nec domiciliorum praetextu locorum dioecesani (si ubi deliquerunt vel contraxerunt aut res ipsa consistit, illi conveniantur) remittendi eos illuc, vel ipsis, ut illic responeant, iniungendi habeant aliquam potestatem."

118. Kuttner, *Medieval Councils,* "Retractationes," 12, notes that a decretal of Innocent IV, *In generali,* 14 May, 1245 (Po. 11633), was an antecedent to *Volentes.*

If a privileged cleric committed a crime inside his own diocese, he was exempt from episcopal jurisdiction, provided he transgressed in *res exemptae*. In a transgression of *res non exemptae*, Innocent considerably narrowed the place of exemption to the monastery itself. Unlike Hostiensis, Innocent did not permit the summoning of a cleric who transgressed in *res exemptae* to his local ordinary if his crime was notorious. He limited the ordinary in two other circumstances. Normally, if a diocesan cleric committed a crime in another diocese, the cleric's bishop could petition that the case be returned to his jurisdiction. A bishop lost this right if the cleric was exempt. He also could not enjoin an exempt cleric to answer a summons from another bishop.

Later canonists were persuaded by Innocent's solution. In his commentary to the Decretals of Gregory IX, Hostiensis modestly wrote that Innocent's solution was congruent with the solution found in his *Summa*.[119] Bernardus Parmensis and Bernardus Compostellanus Junior also concurred with Innocent's solution.[120] Compostellanus added that Innocent's vague designation of "locus exemptus" in which a cleric was immune should include the cemetery, houses, and lands of the monastery.[121] Bernardus' definition of an exempt place was generally accepted by later canonists.

Innocent IV interpreted papal privileges strictly. He did not grant extensive rights of immunity to their bearers and followed the line of development already established by earlier canonists. During the first half of the thirteenth century, the lawyers had fostered and developed a doctrine of "limited" privileges. When given a choice between "the gifts of the prince should be given the widest possible interpretation" and "whatever the prince did should be done without prejudice to another," the canonists almost always chose the latter.

THE CANONISTS' DOCTRINE OF PRIVILEGE AND THE SECULAR-MENDICANT CONTROVERSY

By the middle of the thirteenth century, the canonists had evolved a sophisticated doctrine of privilege. At the same time, the church was shaken

---

119. Hostiensis to *Volentes*, VI 5.7.1, v. *declaratione*, in *Commentaria* (Venice: 1581), fol. 30r: "Nec mireris de prolixitate posita ibi [i.e., in his *Summa aurea*] quia totum illud notavimus antequam esset istud ius promulgatum, unde et in fine diximus et comprobantur haec in authen. domini nostri, extra. eodem, Volentes, et cum iura nova opiniones quas sequimur pro magna parte comprobent."

120. Bernardus Parmensis to X 5.33.11 v. *privileglii beneficio;* Bernardus Compostellanus Junior to *Volentes*, v. *coram locorum ordinariis*, Syracuse Univ. MS 1, fol. 10v.

121. Ibid., v. *exempto:* "Per hoc quod dicit 'loco exempto' debet intelligi tam de monasterio exempto quam cimiterio et domibus monasterii et artis [sic] que sunt iuxta ecclesiam, arg. illorum decretorum, xvi. q.i. Necessaria."

by the secular and mendicant theologians' vociferous dispute over the nature of papal privileges given to the Franciscan and Dominican orders. As a result of this controversy, a generation of theologians examined the constitution of the church and its theoretical foundations. Formerly, theologians had never given much attention to problems of authority and jurisdiction within the church. After the thirteenth century, they could not ignore them; constitutional questions became an important part of their discipline.

At first glance, the role of the canonists in this dispute was minor. They wrote no *consilia* discussing the issues, and they did not participate in the polemics of the theologians. They did, however, have opinions about the legal problems of the dispute. Bernardus Parmensis noted in his Ordinary Gloss that even if they had papal privileges, the Dominicans and Franciscans must have permission of the local priest to hear confessions.[122] Hostiensis agreed with Bernardus. The canonists' discussion of the friars' privileges can be understood only in the context of the canonists' theory covering papal grants, and there is no doubt that they created a doctrine of privilege that supported the position of the secular theologians.

Hostiensis investigated the question in his Commentary to the Fourth Lateran canon, *Omnis utriusque sexus,* which stipulated that all Christians must confess their sins to their parish priest at least once a year.[123] He asked whether a confession made to someone other than the parish priest was valid. He concluded:

I do not think that a general privilege, no matter how broad, given to a penitent or to a confessor, stating that one may confess his sins once a year without the permission of his parish priest, can prejudice the statute that one must make a confession to his parish priest once a year. Rather, the permission of the parish priest is still necessary, unless it is specifically permitted that the parish priest's permission is not necessary.[124]

If any general privilege conferred the power to ignore the rights of parish priests, then ecclesiastical order and discipline would be destroyed. There-

---

122. Bernardus Parmensis to X 5.38.12 v. *alieno sacerdoti.* See the text of Bernardus' gloss in the Introduction, n. 10 above.

123. 4th Lat. c. 21, X 5.38.12.

124. Hostiensis to X 5.38.12 v. *a proprio sacerdote, Commentaria,* 2: fol. 102v: "Sed nec putamus quod quantumcunque ex generali licentia confitenti uel sacerdoti data confiteatur quod praeter parochialis proprii sacerdotis licentiam, saltem quantum ad confessionem sibi semel in anno faciendam huic statuto praeiudicari debeat, immo adhuc requirenda est licentia sacerdotis parochialis, nisi hoc exprimatur: quod istud liceat sine sua licentia."

fore, he maintained, as he had in his discussion of monastic exemptions, that privileges should be interpreted strictly.[125] For Hostiensis, the church's constitution consisted of a collection of rights and duties, some established by Christ, others created by custom. Here, as earlier, he arrived at his conclusions through a sensitive weighing of various rights and liberties in the church.

Hostiensis' mature doctrine of privilege offers an interesting contrast to the ecclesiology of the mendicant theologians. The theologians focused on the jurisdictional relationships within the church, creating a doctrine that bestowed authority and jurisdiction upon the pope. They asserted that bishops and all lesser prelates in the church derived their powers of jurisdiction from the pope. In their own terms, these were powerful arguments.

In 1304 a moderate Dominican theologian, John of Paris, wrote a *Quaestio disputata* in which he discussed the pope's right to grant friars a general privilege of hearing confessions. Although John was not a lawyer, he knew the legal arguments that could be used against the friars' privileges and cited all of Hostiensis' objections to a broad interpretation of the friars' privileges. He referred specifically to Hostiensis' Commentary on *Omnis utriusque sexus* as representative of canonistic thought.[126]

John responded to Hostiensis' arguments by examining the source of ecclesiastical jurisdiction. If the pope granted jurisdiction to all prelates and clerics in the hierarchy, any arguments based on the "rights" of these clerics must fail. The pope could give, and the pope could take away. All jurisdiction is held from Christ; therefore, he concluded, having received his authority from Christ, Peter granted jurisdiction to all other clerics and prelates within the church.[127] Although he knew a respectable amount of canon law, John

---

125. Ibid.: "Secunda, quia si sentiamus contrarium tali praetextu, poterunt omnes sibi subtrahi, quod non debet velle superior, sicut nec vellet, quod idem sibi fieret, arg. supra de offic. ord. Cum ab ecclesiarum, cum suis concordantiis. Ex hoc contingeret confundi ordinem ecclesiasticum, et disciplinam ecclesiasticam vilipendi, contra id quod legitur xi. q.i. Peruenit, supra de priuil. Vt priuilegia § i. ver. penult. § Illud, ver. penult. Est ergo interpretatio talis licentiae restringenda." Hostiensis' doctrine of monastic exemptions, to which he refers in this gloss, is discussed in nn. 88–90 above.

126. John of Paris, *De confessionibus audiendis*, 31–34.

127. Ibid., 47: "Ex quibus patet, quod iure diuino habet Romanus pontifex superioritatem super omnes; immo totam iurisdictionem habet a Christo et omnis iurisdictio a Petro ad ceteros est deriuata." John described the origins of papal jurisdictional authority in more traditional terms in his *De potestate regia et papali*. He compared the pope's authority over the church to a bishop's right of governance over his diocese and recognized the inherent rights of inferior prelates. See Tierney, *Foundations*, 163–67.

of Paris undoubtedly did not fully appreciate the two issues that shaped Hostiensis' thought: the inviolability of individual rights within the church and the canonists' doctrine of privilege. This is understandable. No one but a doctor of laws could have understood the subtle and nuanced thought that comprised the canonists' doctrine of privilege. John and his colleagues preferred a theory of jurisdiction to explain the constitutional structure of the church. It was simpler; it was easy to defend; and most important, it gave the mendicants a much stronger legal position.

The secular-mendicant controversy has an important place in the evolution of the thought defining papal authority. As the theologians explored the meaning of sovereignty and authority, they altered the conceptual framework of monarchical power. Shifting the discussion of the church's constitution from inviolable rights to jurisdiction, they cleared the way for a theory of absolute monarchy, a theory that eventually became the foundation of papal monarchy in the modern church. It was an important turning point in the history of political thought.

CONCLUSION

Papal monarchy was one of the great creations of the Middle Ages. The pope was the first European monarch for whom a sophisticated theory of kingship was developed, and the canonists of the twelfth and thirteenth centuries were primarily responsible for shaping the theoretical structure upon which papal monarchy rested. The theory they created, however, was not a logical, coherent system. Nor, once it had been formed, was it static. Rather, the theory of monarchy we find in the writings of the canonists is as likely to perplex us with its contradictions as to enlighten us with its intricacies.

I wrote this book to illustrate the variety of canonistic political and constitutional thought defining the relationship of the pope and bishops. During this period, as we have seen, the canon lawyers attributed extra-ordinary powers to the pope and, at the same time, limited him in surprising ways. On the one hand, they placed the pope firmly at the apex of Christian society. He derived his authority from Christ and exercised absolute authority within the church. No one but God could judge him in most matters, and no one could question his judgments, except in matters of faith. On the other hand, the canonists stopped short of granting the pope unbridled authority. He was bound by the state of the church, the *status ecclesiae* (the unwritten constitution of the medieval church), and by the frailty of his humanity. He was one man with two offices; he was the representative of God on earth and the servant of God's people, *servus servorum Dei*.

Innocent III underlined the pope's two natures by emphasizing his divine authority. Although Innocent did not submerge the pope's humanity—on the contrary he stressed the nobility of worldly tasks in *Nisi cum pridem*—he transformed papal monarchy into a work of divine art. He strengthened its structure, painted a more intricate and subtle portrait of it, and cleaned and restored old images to reveal the eternal truth of its iconography. His most significant contributions to papal monarchy were his brilliant and sweeping letters that unequivocally established papal authority over bishops. Yet Innocent, too, had a sensitivity to episcopal rights, which he demon-strated most clearly in his doctrine of privilege.

Among the canonists, Huguccio was the most like Innocent in spirit. He, like the other canonists, leavened his description of papal majesty with the reminder that the pope's obligation to render justice and to exercise his office for the public good was more weighty than that of other rulers. But Huguccio's enthusiasm for the benefits of a strong central authority shines through much of his work. Except in the case of heresy, Huguccio was very reluctant to limit papal prerogatives or authority in any way. In the thirteenth century, Hostiensis was much more sensitive to possible abuses of power than Huguccio had been in the late twelfth. This contrast may not be due to any real difference between the two lawyers. Rather it may simply reflect a mild reaction of the times against the rapid and tangible success of papal institutions under the vigorous and effective leadership of popes Innocent III, Gregory IX, and Innocent IV.

The canonists never completely lost touch with the deeply rooted sensibilities of the age in which they lived. Medieval political thought has several characteristic features that recur in almost all medieval discussions of kingship. It limited the monarch's right to exercise his authority arbitrarily, and it protected the rights of subjects. The canonists of the late twelfth and early thirteenth centuries included these common medieval concerns in their writings. They were not out of step with the thought of their contemporaries. What sets them apart from other writers who discussed government and monarchy, such as, for example, the man who wrote Bracton's *De legibus*, is the emphasis they placed on the pope's sovereignty within the church. As we saw in the first three chapters, they wrote their most detailed descriptions of papal authority when they examined the relationship of the pope to his bishops. In the early thirteenth century, Pope Innocent III and the canonists established the pope's universal jurisdiction and sovereignty over the bishops and the church. Had one read only the first three chapters of this book, one could have justifiably concluded that the phrase "canonistic constitutional thought" was inappropriate and misleading and that the canonists never limited papal authority in any meaningful way.

There are, in actuality, two distinct and, to a certain extent, incompatible sides to canonistic thought. Although much of the language of the lawyers was, upon careful scrutiny, exaggerated and florid descriptions of prerogatives common to all monarchs, constitutional or absolute, the canonists did not emphasize the constitutional elements of their ecclesiology, and the cumulative effect of their work was to place the pope and his office above ordinary rulers. It is certainly true and worth repeating that the language of the canonists describing papal prerogatives led inexorably to the less-nuanced and more-literal interpretations of those same phrases by later writers. The twelfth- and thirteenth-century canonists did not preach a theory of absolute monarchy, but they prepared the way.

The primary limitation that the canonists placed on the pope was a profound respect for the collective rights of other members of the ecclesiastical hierarchy. After building a formidable theory of papal monarchy, the canonists did not conclude that the pope's supreme sovereignty reduced the bishops to officers whose authority was simply delegated by the pope or derived from him. The bishops had rights that the pope should safeguard. Christ had established the "status ecclesiae" in which the bishops occupied an important place, and even the pope could not destroy it.

Papal sovereignty over the church clashed with episcopal rights most publicly during the secular-mendicant controversy. The mendicants rested their constitutional theory on the pope's supreme jurisdiction over the church and on their contention that the pope granted all jurisdiction and authority to inferior prelates. The seculars, as Brian Tierney has written, "did deny most emphatically that the pope was the source of their own jurisdiction; they maintained rather that papal headship was defined by divinely established fundamental law of the church, which also attributed autonomous authority to each bishop in his own diocese."[1]

The canonists understood these issues before they became matters of great concern and dispute. They did not, however, frame their discussions of jurisdiction and papal authority in the same terms that would become common during the secular-mendicant controversy. If we wish to understand the canonists' constitutional thought, and in particular their views of episcopal authority, we must examine it at those points in their discussions where papal and episcopal authority directly meet, such as papal provisions, dispensations for pluralists, privileges of exemption, translations, renunciations, and depositions. After considering each of these topics, we can ask whether the canonists who wrote before the secular-mendicant controversy supported the seculars or the mendicants with their constitutional theories.

As with all interesting questions, there is no simple answer. The canonists were not of one mind on any issue. Johannes Teutonicus and Hostiensis articulated most clearly an "episcopalist" ecclesiology in their writings, but it would be anachronistic to call them episcopalists. They were not consciously defending episcopal prerogatives and rights. Johannes argued that a part of episcopal jurisdiction was derived from councils and other sources. He defended episcopal jurisdictional rights to grant dispensations to pluralists and had decidedly eccentric views on the rights of papal legates.

---

1. Tierney, *Religion, Law, and the Growth of Constitutional Thought*, 61–62.

He limited the authority of legates to interfere in diocesan affairs, to grant prebends, to take away the right of election, and to hear the complaints of diocesan clerics before they had been presented in episcopal court.[2]

Of any twelfth- or thirteenth-century canonist, Hostiensis developed the most elaborate ecclesiology recognizing episcopal rights. He employed a variety of arguments to justify his position. Like Teutonicus, he conceived of the bishops as occupying an independent status within the church; they were subject to the pope, but in extreme cases, they could resist papal authority. His most singular claim, never before put forward by any canonist, was that a bishop could refuse to obey a direct papal mandate made *ex certa scientia* if it violated his conscience.

Bishop Robert Grosseteste had made the same claim when he wrote his passionate and famous letter in which he refused to grant a prebend to Innocent IV's nephew. Grosseteste's letter was an act of righteous anger. He was not a lawyer and did not know that a sophisticated legal argument could be made to support his stand. The convictions of Hostiensis and Grosseteste arose from a view of the church in which even papal authority could not obliterate the rights and duties of local bishops and prelates.[3]

These ideas and patterns of thought lived on after the thirteenth century. William of Ockham trenchantly described secular and ecclesiastical government as being a collection of rights and "liberties." In a stirring passage on papal fullness of power, Ockham limited the pope's right to take away the rights of laymen and clergy:

They say "save their rights and liberties" to note that the pope cannot take away the rights and liberties of emperors, kings, and others, clerics and laymen, if they are unwilling to sacrifice their rights and are without guilt or blame, unless it is a case of necessity or the common good.[4]

Ockham had not forged a novel doctrine in the heat of fourteenth-century polemics; rather he summarized a century of canonistic thought on papal authority. There is not a word in the above passage to which Johannes Teutonicus or Hostiensis would have objected.

Until the thirteenth century, there had been widespread agreement, un-

---

2. K. Pennington, "Johannes Teutonicus and Papal Legates." See p. 128 n. 49.

3. Tierney, "Grosseteste and the Theory of Papal Sovereignty," 1–6. Boyle, "Robert Grosseteste," 30–31. Boyle argues that Grosseteste did not oppose the provision itself but the "non obstante" clauses. I would put equal emphasis on another of Grosseteste's concerns: the prebend would have deprived those under his care "de lacte et lana ovium Christi."

4. William of Ockham, *Opera politica*, ed. H. S. Offler 2nd. ed. (Manchester: 1974), 1: 35, from the tract "Octo quaestiones de potestate papae."

conscious agreement for the most part, about the proper structuring of the church and the rights that inhered to each status within it. The thought of the thirteenth-century canonists is permeated with these ideas. Their notions about how the church should be governed continually reflect constitutional assumptions that conceived of the church as a body in which the rights of all members of the hierarchy, even those outside the clerical ranks, were protected and respected. The most pervasive example of this is the evolution of corporate theory in canon law. Corporate theory lies at the base of conciliar thought and most other western theories of government founded on the rights of the community. Although some lawyers developed a corporate theory in which all jurisdictional rights were centered in the head of the corporation, the beginnings of corporate theory arose from a view of ecclesiastical governing bodies in which the wishes of the *maior pars* were tempered by the rights of the *minor pars*. Monasteries, cathedral chapters, the college of cardinals, the church itself, all could be and were described as corporations whose members exercised autonomous rights and held precious liberties.[5]

The most famous constitutional maxim of the medieval period, *quod omnes tangit ab omnibus approbari debet,* is yet another expression of these same principles.[6] When the lawyers cited *quod omnes tangit* to justify the calling of church councils and to describe the proper electoral theory in a cathedral chapter, it was always with the clear understanding that the rights and liberties of all members of a group must be considered and protected. This was a consensus upon which almost all medieval political theory rested.

This generally accepted consensus was severely tested during the secular-mendicant controversy. Some of the polemicists who supported the mendicants rejected a church constitution in which the bishops had rights not derived from the pope. Instead they constructed a church in which all relationships were determined by a theory of jurisdiction. The bishops derived their jurisdiction from the pope; therefore the bishops were like papal legates—officers of the pope who could not claim an independent jurisdictional status within the church.

The canonists had built their theory of ecclesiastical government on a series of interrelated beliefs. Once these beliefs were challenged, they had to fashion theories describing the origins of episcopal rights and jurisdiction.

---

5. For a discussion of medieval corporate theory, see Michaud-Quantin, *Universitas.*

6. The concept of inherent rights to which *quod omnes tangit* gave expression was central to medieval thought, see Yves-M. Congar, "Quod omnes tangit ab omnibus tractari et approbari debet," *Revue historique de droit française et étranger* 35 (1958): 210–59.

The episcopalists emphasized that the bishops were the heirs of the apostles and that the authority of the apostles was independent of St. Peter's. By the end of the thirteenth century, the structure of the church was discussed in terms that were different from those employed at the beginning of the century. These debates asked questions that we think of as being essential to any systematic theory of government: from where does a monarch derive his authority and how is jurisdiction distributed in a kingdom?

Pope Innocent III's contribution to these matters was significant. He intuitively grasped the constitutional position of the bishops and realized the necessity of constructing arguments for papal monarchy independent of human authority and historical precedents. Thus he emphasized the pope's right to act on divine authority and his power to exercise God's office on earth. He transformed the pope from the "vicar of Peter" into the "vicar of Christ."

The step was an important one, and it was a harbinger of future solutions to constitutional problems. Monarchs of the late Middle Ages and early modern Europe cited juridical concepts like "the common good" and "necessity"—these ideas would be combined into a single phrase, "reason of state"—to justify their rights to enact "unconstitutional" measures, such as levying taxes without the consent of the realm.[7] They also adopted many terms from the canonists' arsenal, such as "plenitudo potestatis," to describe secular kingship. But like Innocent, they returned to the old idea of divinely established authority. John Neville Figgis described this development with his typical eloquence:

the civil sword is God's ordinance no less than the ecclesiastical; or in "terms of art" the power of the prince comes immediately from God, not mediately through Pope or Kirk.[8]

Divine right kingship could be called Innocent III's divine authority in secular garb.

---

7. On reason of state, see Post, *Studies in Medieval Legal Thought,* 301–9.

8. John Neville Figgis, *Political Thought from Gerson to Grotius: 1414–1625* (New York: 1960), 82.

BIBLIOGRAPHY

PRIMARY WORKS

MANUSCRIPTS CITED

Admont Stiftsbibliothek
    MS 7
        Huguccio. *Summa.*
    MS 22
        Tancred. *Apparatus to 1 Comp.* 1st rec. (with 2nd rec. added in later hand).
        Tancred. *Apparatus to 2 Comp.* 1st rec. (with 2nd rec. added in later hand).
        Johannes Teutonicus. *Apparatus to 3 Comp.*
        Jacobus de Albenga. *Apparatus to 5 Comp.*
    MS 35
        Johannes Teutonicus. *Glossa Ordinaria to Decretum.*
    MS 55
        Ricardus Anglicus. *Apparatus to 1 Comp.*
        Laurentius Hispanus. *Apparatus to 3 Comp.*
Alba Iulia, Bibl. Batthyaneum
    MS II.5
        Tancred. *Apparatus to 1 Comp.* 2nd rec.
        Johannes Teutonicus. *Apparatus to 3 Comp.*
Bamberg, Staatsbibliothek
    MS Can. 13
        Johannes Teutonicus. *Glossa ordinaria to Decretum.*
    MS Can. 19
        Tancred. *Apparatus to 1 Comp.* 1st rec.
        Apparatus "Servus appellatur" to 3 Comp.
    MS Can. 20
        Ricardus Anglicus. *Apparatus to 1 Comp.*
Brussels, Bibliothèque Royale
    MS 1407–9
        Apparatus to 1 Comp.
Cambridge, Trinity College
    MS R.9.17
        Epistolae Alexandrinae.
Cordoba, Biblioteca del Cabildo
    MS 10
        Tancred. *Apparatus to 1 Comp.* 2nd rec.

Tancred. *Apparatus to 2 Comp.* 2nd rec.
Jacobus de Albenga. *Apparatus to 5 Comp.*
Florence, Biblioteca Laurenziana
   MS Fesul. 125–26
      Huguccio. *Summa.*
   MS S. Croce IV sin. 2
      Alanus Anglicus. *Apparatus to 1 Comp.*
Florence, Biblioteca nazionale
   MS Conventi soppressi da ordinare: Vallombrosa 36 (325)
      Compilatio tertia, una cum glossis.
Graz, Universitätsbibliothek
   MS 138
      Tancred. *Apparatus to 1 Comp.*
Halle, Universitätsbibliothek
   MS Ye 52
      Alanus Anglicus. *Apparatus to 1 Comp.*
Karlsruhe, Landesbibliothek
   MS Aug. XL
      Alanus Anglicus. *Apparatus to 1 Comp.*
      Laurentius Hispanus. *Apparatus to 3 Comp.*
Klosterneuburg, Stiftsbibliothek
   MS 89
      Huguccio. *Summa.*
Leipzig, Universitätsbibliothek
   MS 983
      Vincentius Hispanus. *Apparatus to 3 Comp.*
London, British Library
   MS Royal 11 C.vii
      Jacobus de Albenga. *Apparatus to 5 Comp.*
   MS Harley 3834
      Bernardus Compostellanus antiquus. *Collectio Romana.*
Lyon, Bibliothèque de l'université
   MS 6
      Tancred. *Apparatus to 1 Comp.* 1st rec.
Modena, Biblioteca Estense
   MS lat. 968
      Ricardus Anglicus. *Apparatus to 1 Comp.*
      Bernardus Compostellanus antiquus. *Collectio Romana, una cum glossis.*
Munich, Staatsbibliothek
   Clm 3879
      Ricardus Anglicus. *Apparatus to 1 Comp.*
      Johannes Galensis. *Apparatus to 3 Comp.*
   Clm 6352
      Ricardus Anglicus. *Apparatus to 1 Comp.*
   Clm 14024
      Johannes Teutonicus. *Glossa ordinaria to Decretum.*
Oxford, Bodleian Library
   MS Tanner 8

Bernardus Compostellanus antiquus. *Collectio Romana.*
Padua, Biblioteca Antoniana
    MS 35
        Tancred. *Apparatus to 1 Comp.* 2nd rec.
        Johannes Teutonicus. *Apparatus to 3 Comp.*
Paris, Bibliothèque Mazarine
    MS 1318
        Alanus Anglicus. *Apparatus to Decretum.* 2nd rec.
Paris, Bibliothèque nationale
    MS lat. 3967
        Vincentius Hispanus. *Apparatus to Decretales Gregorii IX.*
    MS lat. 3968
        Vincentius Hispanus. *Apparatus to Decretales Gregorii IX.*
    MS 15402
        Goffredus da Trani. *Apparatus to Decretales Gregorii IX.*
    MS 15393
        Alanus Anglicus et al. *Apparatus to Decretum.* 2nd rec.
St. Gall, Stiftsbibliothek
    MS 697
        Vincentius Hispanus. *Apparatus to 3 Comp.*
Salzburg, St. Peter's Archabbey
    MS a.ix.18
        Ricardus Anglicus. *Apparatus to 1 Comp.*
    MS a.xii.9
        Glossa Palatina to Decretum.
Seo de Urgel, Biblioteca Capitular
    MS 113 (2009)
        Alanus Anglicus. *Apparatus to Decretum.* 1st rec.
Syracuse, University Library
    MS 1
        Bernardus Compostellanus Junior. *Apparatus to Novella Innocentii IV.*
        Bernardus Parmensis. *Glossa ordinaria to Decretales Gregorii IX.*
Tours, Bibliothèque municipale
    MS 565
        Zoen. *Apparatus to 5 Comp.*
Vatican City, Biblioteca Apostolica Vaticana
    MS lat. 1367
        Johannes Teutonicus. *Glossa ordinaria to Decretum.*
    MS lat. 1377
        Tancred. *Apparatus to 2 Comp.*
        Tancred. *Apparatus to 3 Comp.*
    MS lat. 1378
        Vincentius Hispanus. *Apparatus to 3 Comp.*
    MS lat. 1446
        Henricus de Segusio. *Apparatus to Decretales Gregorii IX.*
    MS lat. 2280
        Huguccio. *Summa.*
    MS lat. 2509

Tancred. *Apparatus to 3 Comp.*
MS lat. 2546
Henricus de Segusio. *Apparatus to Decretales Gregorii IX.*
MS lat. 12111
Gesta Innocentii III.
MS Palatina lat. 658
Glossa Palatina to Decretum.
MS Reg. lat. 977
Glossa Palatina to Decretum.
MS Ross. lat. 595
Alanus Anglicus. *Apparatus to Decretum.* 2nd rec.
Vienna, Nationalbibliothek
MS lat. 2113
Petrus de Sampsone. *Lectura to Decretales Gregorii IX.*
MS lat. 2197
Goffredus da Trani. *Apparatus to Decretales Gregorii IX.*
Zwettl, Stiftsbibliothek
MS 30
Johannes Galensis. *Apparatus to 3 Comp.*

PRINTED CANONISTIC AND PAPAL SOURCES

Aegidius de Fuscarariis. *Ordo iudiciarius.* Ed. Ludwig Wahrmund. Quellen zur Geschichte des romischen-kanonischen Prozesses im Mittelalter 3.1. Innsbruck: 1916.
Anselm of Lucca. *Collectio canonum.* Ed. Friedrich Thaner. Innsbruck: 1906–15 (reprinted Aalen: 1965).
Bartholomaeus Brixiensis. *Quaestiones. Tractatus universi iuris.* Vol. 17. Lyon: 1549.
———. *Glossa ordinaria in Decretum Gratiani. Corpus iuris canonici.* Vol. 1. Rome: 1582.
Bernard de Montmirat. *In libris decretalium aurei commentarii uidelicet Abbatis antiqui, Bernardi Compostellani, Guidonis papae, Ioannis a Capistrano.* Venice: 1588.
Bernardus Compostellanus antiquus. *Collectio Romana.* Ed. Heinrich Singer. Sitzungsberichte der kaiserlichen Akademie der Wissenschaften phil. -hist. Klasse, Wien. Vol. 171. Vienna: 1914.
Bernardus Papiensis [of Balbi]. *Summa decretalium.* Ed. E. A. T. Laspeyres. Regensburg: 1860 (reprinted Graz: 1956).
Bernardus Parmensis. *Glossa ordinaria in Decretales Gregorii noni. Corpus iuris canonici.* Vol. 2. Rome: 1582.
Boniface VIII. *Les registres de Boniface VIII.* Vol. 3. Paris: 1921.
Bonizo of Sutri. *Liber de vita Christiana.* Ed. Ernst Perels. Texte zur Geschichte des römischen und kanonischen Rechts im Mittelalter 1. Berlin: 1930.
Burchard of Worms. *Decretum.* PL 140.
Collectio canonum. *Collectio canonum Remedio Curiensi episcopo perperam ascripta.* Ed. Herwig John. MIC, Series B, vol. 2. Città del Vaticano: 1976.
Compilatio quinta. *Compilatio quinta epistolarum decretalium.* Ed. J. A. Riegger. Vienna: 1761.

Corpus iuris canonici. 3 vols. Rome: 1582.
Corpus iuris canonici. Ed. Emil Friedberg. 2 vols. Leipzig: 1879–81 (reprinted Graz: 1959).
Councils, general. *Conciliorum oecumenicorum decreta.* Ed. G. Alberigo et al. 3rd ed. Bologna: 1972 (= COD).
Damasus Ungarus. *Apparatus in constitutiones concilii quarti Lateransis* (see García y García).
García y García, Antonio. *Constitutiones Concilii quarti Lateranensis una cum Commentariis glossatorum.* MIC, Series A, vol. 2. Città del Vaticano: 1981.
Goffredus da Trani. *Summa super titulis decretalium.* Lyon: 1519 (reprinted Aalen: 1969).
Gregory VII. *Das Register Gregors VII.* Ed. Erich Caspar. MGH Epistolae selectae. Berlin: 1920.
Guilielmus Durandus. *Tractatus de modo generalis concilii celebrandi.* Paris: 1671 (reprinted London: 1963).
Henricus de Segusio. *In primum—quintum decretalium librum Commentaria.* 5 vols. Venice: 1581 (reprinted Torino: 1965).
———. *Apparatus in Novellam Innocentii quarti. In sextum librum decretalium Commentaria.* Venice: 1581.
———. *Summa aurea.* Venice: 1570 and 1586.
Innocent III. *Acta Innocentii PP. III (1198–1216).* Ed. T. Haluščynskyj. Città del Vaticano: 1944.
———. *Regestum Innocentii III papae super negotio Romani imperii.* Ed. Friedrich Kempf. Miscellanea Historiae Pontificiae 12. Rome: 1947.
———. *The Letters of Pope Innocent III (1198–1216) Concerning England and Wales.* Ed. Mary and Christopher Cheney. Oxford: 1967.
Innocent IV. *Apparatus super quinque libris decretalium.* Frankfurt: 1570 (reprinted Frankfurt: 1968).
———. *Les registres d'Innocent IV.* 4 vols. Paris: 1884–1911.
Ivo of Chartres. *Decretum.* PL 161.
———. *Panormia.* PL 161.
Jesselin de Cassagnes. *Apparatus in Extravagantes Johannis XXII. Corpus iuris canonici.* Vol. 3. Rome: 1582.
Johannes Teutonicus. *Apparatus in Compilationem quartam.* Ed. Antonio Agustín. Ilerdae: 1576 (also printed in Agustín's *Opera omnia* [Lucca: 1769]).
———. *Glossa ordinaria in Decretum Gratiani. Corpus iuris canonici.* Vol. 1. Rome: 1582.
———. *Apparatus in constitutiones concilii quarti Lateransis* (see García y García).
———. *Apparatus glossarum in Compilationem tertiam.* Ed. Kenneth Pennington. MIC, Series A, vol. 3. Città del Vaticano: 1981.
Papal letters. *Acta pontificum Romanorum inedita.* Ed. Julius von Pflugk-Harttung. 3 vols. Stuttgart: 1881–86 (reprinted Graz: 1958).
———. *Epistolae pontificum Romanorum ineditae.* Ed. S. Löwenfeld. Leipzig: 1885.
———. *Papsturkunden in Frankreich.* Vol. 7: *Nördliche Ile-de-France und Vermandois.* Ed. Dietrich Lohrmann. Göttingen: 1976.
———. *Papsturkunden in Portugal.* Ed. Carl Erdmann. Berlin: 1927.
Pseudo-Isidore. *Decretales Pseudo-Isidorianae et Capitula Angilrammi.* Ed. Paul Hinschius. Leipzig: 1863 (reprinted Aalen: 1963).

Quinque compilationes antiquae. Ed. Emil Friedberg. Leipzig: 1882 (reprinted Graz: 1956).

Rainer of Pomposa. *Collectio decretalium.* PL 216.

Raymond of Pennafort. *Summa de iure canonico.* Ed. Xaverio Ochoa and Aloisio Diez. Universa biblioteca iuris 1.1. Rome: 1975.

———. *Summa de Paenitentia.* Ed. Xaverio Ochoa and Aloisio Diez. Universa biblioteca iuris 1.2. Rome: 1976.

———. *Summa de matrimonio.* Ed. Xaverio Ochoa and Aloisio Diez. Universa biblioteca iuris 1.3. Rome: 1978.

Rolandus Bandinelli. *Summa.* Ed. Friederich Thaner. Innsbruck: 1874 (reprinted Aalen: 1962).

Rufinus. *Die Summa decretorum des magister Rufinus.* Ed. Heinrich Singer. Paderborn: 1902 (reprinted Aalen: 1963).

Seventy-Four Titles. *Diversorum patrum sententie sive Collectio in LXXIV titulos digesta.* Ed. John Gilchrist. MIC, Series B, vol. 1. Città del Vaticano: 1973.

Stephen of Tournai. *Die Summa über das Decretum Gratiani.* Ed. Johann F. von Schulte. Giessen: 1891 (reprinted Aalen: 1965).

Summa Coloniensis. *Summa "Elegantius in iure divino seu Coloniensis."* Ed. Gérard Fransen and Stephan Kuttner. MIC, Series A, vol. 1. New York—Città del Vaticano: 1969–78.

Summa Parisiensis. *The Summa Parisiensis on the Decretum Gratiani.* Ed. Terence P. McLaughlin. Toronto: 1952.

Vincentius Hispanus. *Apparatus in constitutiones concilii quarti Lateransis* (see García y García).

HISTORICAL AND THEOLOGICAL SOURCES

Thomas Aquinas. *Super Evangelium S. Matthaei lectura.* Ed. Raphael Cai. Rome: 1951.

———. *Super Evangelium S. Ioannis lectura.* Ed. Raphael Cai. Rome: 1952.

———. *Catena aurea in quatuor Evangelia.* Ed. Angelico Guarienti. Turin-Rome: 1953.

———. *Summa theologiae.* 4 vols. Torino: 1952–62.

Arnold of Lisieux. *Sermones.* PL 201.

Arnold of Lübeck. *Chronica Slavorum.* Ed. I. M. Lappenberg. MGH, Scriptores in usum scholarum 14. Hannover: 1868.

St. Augustine of Hippo. *In Iohannis Evangelium tractatus CXXIV.* Ed. D. R. Willems. CC 36. Turnholt: 1954.

Battle Abbey. *The Chronicle of Battle Abbey.* Ed. and trans. Eleanor Searle. Oxford: 1980.

Domenico de' Domenichi. *De potestate pape et termino eius.* Ed. Heribert Smolinsky. Münster: 1976.

Evesham. *Chronicon abbatiae de Evesham ad annum 1418.* Ed. W. D. Macray. RS 29. London: 1865.

Ferrara. *Chronica parva ferrariensis.* Ed. L. Muratori. *Rerum Italicarum Scriptores* 8. Milan: 1726.

Gerhoh of Reichersberg. *De investigatione antichristi.* MGH, Libelli de lite 3. Hannover: 1897.

Gervase of Canterbury. *The Chronicle of the Reigns of Stephen, Henry II., and Richard I.* Ed. William Stubbs. RS 73. London: 1879.

Gilbert Foliot. *The Letters and Charters of Gilbert of Foliot.* Ed. Z. N. Brooke, A. Morey, and C. N. L. Brooke. Cambridge: 1967.

Henry Bracton. *On the Laws and Customs of England.* Ed. and trans. Samuel Thorne. 4 vols. Cambridge, Mass.: 1968–77.

Henry Knighton. *Chronicon.* Ed. J. R. Lumby. RS 92. London: 1889.

Huguccio of Pisa. *Agiographia.* Ed. Giuseppe Cremascoli. Spoleto: 1978.

Innocent III. *De sacro altaris mysterio libri sex.* PL 217.

Innocent III. *Gesta Innocentii papae III.* PL 214.

Innocent III. *Opera.* PL 214–17.

Isidore of Seville. *Etymologiarum sive originum libri XX.* Ed. W. M. Lindsay. Oxford: 1966.

James of Viterbo. *De regimine Christiano (1301–1302): Etude des sources et édition critique.* Ed. H. -X. Arquilliere. Paris: 1926.

John of Naples. *Quaestiones variae Parisiis disputatae.* Neapoli: 1618.

John of Paris. *De confessionibus audiendis (Quaestio disputata Parisius de potestate papae).* Ed. Ludwig Hödl. München: 1962.

John of Salisbury. *Policraticus.* Ed. C. C. J. Webb. Oxford 1909. Translated by John Dickinson in *The Statesman's Book of John of Salisbury.* New York: 1927.

Lanfranc of Bec. *The Letters of Lanfranc Archbishop of Canterbury.* Ed. and trans. Helen Clover and Margaret Gibson. Oxford: 1979.

Odorico Raynaldo. *Annales ecclesiastici.* Vol. 15. Coloniae Agrippinae: 1694.

Optatus Afer. *De schismate Donatistarum.* PL 11.

Otto of Freising. *Gesta Friderici I. imperatoris.* Ed. Georg Waitz and B. von Simson. 3rd ed. MGH. Hannover-Leipzig 1912.

Peter Cantor. *Verbum abbreviatum.* PL 205.

Peter Damian. *Opuscula.* PL 145.

Petersberg. *Chronicon montis sereni.* Ed. E. Ehrenfeuchter. MGH, Scriptores 23. Hannover: 1874.

Portugal. *Portugaliae monumenta historica.* Scriptores 1. Lisbon: 1856.

Ralph de Diceto. *Ymagines historiarum.* Ed. William Stubbs. RS 68. London: 1876.

Robert Grosseteste. *Epistolae.* Ed. Henry R. Luard. RS 25. London: 1861.

Salimbene de Adam. *Cronica.* Ed. O. Holder-Egger. MGH, Scriptores 32. Hannover: 1905–13.

Thomas Becket. *Materials for the History of Thomas Becket.* Ed. James C. Robertson. RS 67. London: 1875–85.

Vetera monumenta Slavorum meridionalium historiam illustrantia. Ed. Augustin Theiner. Rome: 1863.

Vincent of Beauvais. *Speculum historiale.* Duaci: 1624 (reprinted Graz: 1965).

William of Ockham. "Octo quaestiones de potestate papae." *Opera politica.* Ed. H. S. Offler. 2nd ed. Manchester: 1974.

SECONDARY WORKS

Abel, H. F. O. *König Philipp.* Berlin: 1852.

Alberigo, Giuseppe. *Lo sviluppo della dottrina sui poteri nella chiesa univer-*

sale: Momenti essenziali tra il XVI e il XIX secolo. Rome-Freiburg-Vienna: 1964.

———. *Cardinalato e collegialità: Studi sull' ecclesiologia tra l'XI e il XIV secolo.* Firenze: 1969.

Amiet, Louis. *Essai sur l'organisation du chapitre cathédral de Chartres (du XIe au XIIIe siècle).* Chartres: 1922.

Arveiler-Ferry, Monique. *Catalogue des actes de Jacques de Lorraine, évêque de Metz 1239–1260.* Metz: 1957.

Baron, Hans. *The Crisis of the Early Italian Renaissance.* Princeton: 1966.

Barraclough, Geoffrey. *Papal Provisions: Aspects of Church History, Constitutional, Legal and Administrative in the Later Middle Ages.* Oxford: 1935 (reprinted Westport, Conn.: 1971).

———. *The Origins of Modern Germany.* New York: 1963.

Benson, Robert L. "Plenitudo potestatis: Evolution of a Formula from Gregory IV to Gratian." *Collectanea Stephan Kuttner.* SG 14: 195–217. Bologna: 1967.

———. *The Bishop-Elect: A Study in Medieval Ecclesiastical Office.* Princeton: 1968.

Bernini, F. "Innocenzo IV et il suo parentado." *Nuova rivista storica* 24 (1940): 178–99.

Bertram, Martin. "Die Abdankung Papst Cölestins V. (1294) und die Kanonisten." ZRG Kan. Abt. 56 (1970): 1–101.

Borch, Leopold, von. *Geschichte des kaiserlichen Kanzler Konrad, Legat in Italien und Sicilien, Bischof von Hildesheim und Wirzburg.* Innsbruck: 1882.

Boyle, Leonard E. "The Compilatio quinta and the Registers of Honorius III." BMCL 8 (1978): 9–19.

———. "Robert Grosseteste and the Pastoral Care." *Medieval and Renaissance Studies: Proceedings of the Southeastern Institute of Medieval and Renaissance Studies* (Summer 1976), 3–51. Ed. Dale B. J. Randall. Medieval and Renaissance Series 8. Durham, N.C.: 1979.

Brentano, Robert. *Two Churches: England and Italy in the Thirteenth Century.* Princeton: 1968.

———. "Localism and Longevity: The Example of the Chapter of Rieti in the Thirteenth and Fourteenth Centuries." *Law, Church, and Society: Essays in Honor of Stephan Kuttner,* 293–310. Ed. Kenneth Pennington and Robert Somerville. Philadelphia: 1977.

Brundage, James. *Medieval Canon Law and the Crusader.* Madison-Milwaukee: 1969.

———. "The Creative Canonist: His Role in Church Reform." *The Jurist* 31 (1971): 301–18.

———. "The Ethics of the Legal Profession: Medieval Canonists and their Clients." *The Jurist* 33 (1973): 237–48.

Buisson, Ludwig. *Potestas und Caritas: Die päpstliche Gewalt im Spätmittelalter.* Köln-Graz: 1958.

Burdach, Konrad. "Der Kampf Walters von der Vogelweide gegen Innozenz III. und gegen das vierte lateranische Konzil." *Zeitschrift für Kirchengeschichte* 55 (1936): 445–522.

Caron, Pier G. *La rinuncia all'ufficio ecclesiastico nella storia del diritto canonico dalla età apostolica alla riforma cattolica.* Milano: 1946.

Cheney, Christopher R. *Pope Innocent III and England.* Päpste und Papsttum 9. Stuttgart: 1976.

Chodorow, Stanley. *Christian Political Theory and Church Politics in the Mid-Twelfth Century: The Ecclesiology of Gratian's Decretum.* Berkeley-Los Angeles-London: 1972.

——— . "Dishonest Litigation in the Church Courts, 1140–98." *Law, Church, and Society: Essays in Honor of Stephan Kuttner,* 187–206. Ed. Kenneth Pennington and Robert Somerville. Philadelphia 1977.

Congar, Yves-M. "Cephas-cephale-caput." *Revue du moyen âge Latin* 8 (1952): 5–42.

——— . "Quod omnes tangit ab omnibus tractari et approbari debet." *Revue historique de droit français et étranger* 35 (1958): 210–59.

——— . "Aspects ecclésiologiques de la querelle entre mendiants et séculaires dans la seconde moitie du XIIIe siécle et le début du XIVe." *Archives d'histoire doctrinale et littéraire du moyen âge.* 25 (1961): 35–151.

——— . *L'ecclésiologie du haut Moyen Age: De saint Grégoire le Grand à la désunion entre Byzance et Rome.* Paris: 1968.

——— . *L'Eglise de saint Augustin à l'époque moderne.* Paris: 1970.

——— , and Dupuy, B. -D., ed. *La collégialité épiscopale: Histoire et théologie.* Unam Sanctam 52. Paris: 1965.

Constable, Giles. *Monastic Tithes from Their Origins to the Twelfth Century.* Cambridge: 1964.

——— . "The Substructure of Medieval Society According to the Dictatores of the Twelfth Century." *Law, Church, and Society: Essays in Honor of Stephen Kuttner,* 253–67. Ed. Kenneth Pennington and Robert Somerville. Philadelphia: 1977.

Cortese, Ennio. *La norma giuridica.* Milan: 1964.

——— . "Norma Giuridica, Storia." *Enciclopedia del diritto* 28 (1978): 393–412.

Cremascoli, Guiseppe. "Uguccione da Pisa: Saggio bibliografico." *Aevum* 42 (1968): 123–68.

D'Avray, D. L. "A Letter of Innocent III and the Idea of Infallibility." *The Catholic Historical Review* 66 (1980): 417–21.

——— . "Origins of the Idea of Infallibility: A Rejoinder to Professor Tierney." *The Catholic Historical Review* 67 (1981): 60–69.

David, Marcel. *La souveraineté et les limites du pouvoir monarchique du IXe au XVe siècle.* Paris: 1954.

Dawson, James D. "William of Saint-Amour and the Apostolic Tradition." *Mediaeval Studies* 40 (1978): 223–38.

De Brys, J. *De dispensatione in iure canonico praesertim apud decretistas et decretalistas usque ad medium saeculum decimum quartum.* Bruges: 1925.

De Luca, Luigi. "L'accettazione popolare della legge canonica nel pensiero di Graziana e suoi interpreti." SG 3 (1955): 193–276.

De-Mauri, L. *Regulae iuris.* 11th ed. Milan: 1976.

Diplovatatius, Thomas. *De claris iuris consultis.* Ed. F. Schulz, H. Kantorowicz, and G. Rabotti. SG 10. Bologna: 1968.

Dufeil, M. -M. *Guillaume de Saint Amour et la polémique universitaire parisienne.* Paris: 1972.

Duggan, Anne. *Thomas Becket: A Textual History of his Letters.* Oxford: 1980.

————, and Duggan, Charles. "Ralph de Diceto, Henry II, and Becket." *Authority and Power: Studies on Medieval Law and Government presented to Walter Ullmann, 59–81*. Ed. Brian Tierney and Peter Linehan. Cambridge: 1980.

Edwards, Kathleen. *The English Secular Cathedrals in the Middle Ages: A Constitutional Study with Special Reference to the Fourteenth Century.* 2nd ed. New York: 1967.

Elze, Reinhold. "Die päpstliche Kapelle im 12. und 13. Jahrhundert." ZRG Kan. Abt. 36 (1950): 145–204.

Eubel, Conrad. *Hierarchia catholica medii aevi.* 2 vols. Monasterii: 1913–23 (reprinted Padua: 1960).

Fasolt, Constantin. "A New View of William of Durant the Younger's 'Tractatus de modo generalis concilii celebrandi.'" *Traditio* 37 (1981): 291–324.

Feine, Hans Erich. *Kirchliche Rechtsgeschichte.* 1: *Die katholische Kirche.* 5th ed. Köln-Wien: 1972.

Figgis, John Neville. *Political Thought from Gerson to Grotius: 1414–1625.* New York: 1960.

Figueira, Robert Charles. "The Canon Law of Medieval Papal Legation." Unpublished dissertation, Cornell University: 1980.

Foreville, Raymonde. *L'Eglise et la royauté en Angleterre sous Henri II Plantagenet (1154–1189).* Paris: 1943.

Fransen, Gérard. "Les diverses formes de la Compilatio prima." *Scrinium Lovaniense: Mélanges historiques Etienne Van Cauwenberg,* 235–53. Louvain: 1961.

Freed, John B. *The Friars and German Society in the Thirteenth Century.* Cambridge, Mass.: 1977.

Fuhrmann, Horst. *Deutsche Geschichte im hohen Mittelalter.* Göttingen: 1978.

————. "Das Papsttum und das kirchliche Leben im Frankenreich." *Nascita dell'Europa ed Europa Carolingia: Un'equazione da verificare,* 419–56. Settimane di studio del Centro italiano di studi sull'alto medioevo 27. Spoleto: 1981.

Gallagher, Clarence. *Canon Law and the Christian Community: The Role of Law in the Church According to the "Summa aurea" of Cardinal Hostiensis.* Analecta Gregoriana 208. Rome: 1978.

Gams, P. B. *Series episcoporum ecclesiae catholicae.* Regensburg: 1873–86.

García y García, Antonio. *Laurentius Hispanus: Datos biográficos y estudio crítico de sus obras.* Madrid-Rome: 1956.

————. "La Canonística Ibérica (1150–1250) en la investigación reciente." BMCL 11 (1981). 41–75.

Ganzer, Klaus. *Papsttum und Bistumsbesetzungen im der Zeit von Gregor IX. bis Bonifaz VIII.: Ein Beitrag zur päpstlichen Reservationen.* Köln-Wien-Graz: 1968.

Gaudemet, Jean. "Utilitas publica." *Revue historique de droit français et étranger* 29 (1951): 465–99.

————. *L'église dan l'empire Romain (IVe–Ve siècles).* Histoire du droit et des institutions de l'église en Occident 3. Paris: 1958.

————. *Le gouvernement de l'église à l'époque classique.* II: *Le gouvernement local.* Histoire du Droit et des Institutions de l'Eglise en Occident 8.2. Paris: 1979.

Gibbs, M., and Lang, J. *Bishops and Reform, 1215–1272: With Special Reference to the Lateran Council of 1215.* London: 1934.

Gibson, Margaret. *Lanfranc of Bec.* Oxford: 1978.

Gillet, Pierre. *La personnalité juridique en droit ecclésiastique, spécialement chez les décrétistes et les décrétalistes et dans le Code de droit canonique.* Malines: 1927.

Gillmann, Franz. "Die Resignation der Benefizien: Historisch-dogmatisch dargestellt." AKKR 80 (1900): 50–79, 346–78, 503–69, 665–708 and 81 (1901): 223–42, 433–60.

———. *Des Laurentius Hispanus Apparat zur Compilatio III. auf der Staatlichen Bibliothek zu Bamberg.* Mainz: 1935.

Gray, J. W. "Canon Law in England: Some Reflections on the Stubbs-Maitland Controversy." *Studies in Church History,* 3:48–68. London: 1966.

Hackett, J. "State of the Church: A Concept of the Medieval Canonists." *The Jurist* 23 (1963): 259–90.

Hageneder, Othmar. "Mandatum und Praeceptum im politischen Handeln Papst Innocenz' III." *Proceedings of the Sixth International Congress of Medieval Canon Law, Berkeley.* Ed. Stephan Kuttner, Robert Somerville, and Kenneth Pennington. MIC, Series C, 7. Città del Vaticano: 1984.

Heckel, Rudolf, von. "Die Dekretalensammlung des Gilbertus und Alanus nach den Weingartener Handschriften." ZRG Kan. Abt. 29 (1940): 116–357.

Herde, Peter. "Römisches und kanonisches Recht bei der Verfolgung des Fälschungsdelikts im Mittelalter." *Traditio* 21 (1965): 291–362.

———. *Cölestin V. (1294): (Peter vom Morrone), der Engelpapst.* Päpste und Papsttum 16. Stuttgart: 1981.

Herrmann, Horst. "Fragen zu eninem päpstlichen Amtsverzicht." ZRG Kan. Abt. 56 (1970): 102–23.

Hess, H. *The Canons of the Council of Sardica A.D. 343: A Landmark in the Early Development of Canon Law.* Oxford: 1958.

Hödl, Ludwig. "Dienst und Vollmacht der Presbyter im mittelalterlichen Ringen um das theologische Verständnis der Kirchenverfassung." *Collectanea Stephan Kuttner.* SG 11: 529–54. Bologna: 1967.

Hoeflich, Michael. "The Concept of Utilitas Populi in Early Ecclesiastical Law and Government." ZRG Kan. Abt. 67 (1981): 37–74.

Holtzmann, Walther. "Die Register Papst Alexanders III. in den Händen der Kanonisten." QF 30 (1940): 69–80.

Honoré, Tony. *Emperors and Lawyers.* London: 1981.

Honsell, Thomas. "Gemeinwohl und öffentliches Interesse im klassischen römischen Recht." ZRG Rom. Abt. 95 (1978): 93–137.

Hoppe, Willy. "Erzbischof Wichmann von Magdeburg." *Geschichtsblätter für Stadt und Land Magdeburg* 43–44 (1908–9): 134–294.

———. *Die Mark Brandenburg, Wettin und Magdeburg: Ausgewählte Aufsätze.* Ed. Herbert Ludat. Köln-Graz: 1965.

Horst, Uwe. *Die Kanonessammlung Polycarpus des Gregor von S. Grisogono: Quellen und Tendenzen.* MGH, Hilfsmittel 5. München: 1980.

Hourlier, Jacques. *L'âge classique (1140–1378): Les religieux.* Histoire du Droit et des Institutions de l'église en Occident 10. Paris: 1971.

Hüls, Rudolf. *Kardinäle, Klerus und Kirchen Roms, 1049–1130.* Tübingen: 1977.

Izbicki, Thomas. *Protector of the Faith: Cardinal Johannes de Turrecremata and the Defense of the Institutional Church.* Baltimore: 1981.

Kantorowicz, Ernst. "Inalienability: A Note on Canonical Practice and the English Coronation Oath in the Thirteenth Century." *Speculum* 29 (1954): 488–502.

——. *The King's Two Bodies: A Study in Mediaeval Political Theology.* Princeton: 1957.

——. "Kingship under the Impact of Scientific Jurisprudence." *Twelfth-Century Europe and the Foundations of Modern Society,* 89–111. Ed. M. Clagett, G. Post, and R. Reynolds. Madison: 1961.

——. "The Sovereignty of the Artist: A Note on Legal Maxims and Renaissance Theories of Art." *Essays in Honor of Erwin Panofsky,* 267–79. Ed. Millard Meiss. New York: 1961.

Kay, Richard. *Dante's Swift and Strong: Essays on Inferno XV.* Lawrence, Kans.: 1978.

Kempf, Friedrich. "Ein zweiter Dictatus papae? Ein Beitrag zum Depositionsanspruch Gregors VII." *Archivum Historiae Pontificiae* 13 (1975): 119–39.

Kern, Fritz. *Kingship and Law in the Middle Ages.* Trans., S. B. Chrimes. New York: 1956.

Kessler, P. J. "Untersuchungen über die Novellengesetzgebung Papst Innocenz IV." ZRG Kan. Abt. 31 (1942): 142–320; 32 (1943): 300–383; 33 (1944): 56–128.

Knowles, David. "The Growth of Monastic Exemption." *Downside Review* 50 (1932): 201–31, 396–436.

——. *The Monastic Order in England: A History of Its Development from the Times of St. Dunstan to the Fourth Lateran Council (940–1216).* 2nd ed. Cambridge: 1963.

Kuttner, Stephan. "Sur les origines du terme 'droit positif.' " *Revue historique de droit francaise et étranger* 15 (1936): 728–40.

——. *Repertorium der Kanonistik (1140–1234): Prodromus corporis glossarum.* Studi e testi 71. Città del Vaticano: 1937.

——. "Die Konstitutionen des ersten allegemeinen Konzils von Lyon." *Studia et documenta historiae et iuris* 6 (1940): 70–131.

——. "Bernardus Compostellanus antiquus: A Study in the Glossators of the Canon Law." *Traditio* 1 (1943): 277–340.

——. "Johannes Teutonicus, das vierte Laterankonzil, und die Compilatio quarta." *Miscellanea Giovanni Mercati.* Studi e Testi 125, 608–34. Città del Vaticano: 1946.

——. "The Barcelona Edition of St. Raymond's First Treatise on Canon Law." *Seminar* 8 (1950): 52–67.

——. "Zur Entstehungsgeschichte der Summa de casibus poenitentiae de hl. Raymond von Penyfort." ZRG Kan. Abt. 39 (1953): 419–34.

——. "Pope Lucius III and the Bigamous Archbishop of Palermo." *Medieval Studies Presented to Aubrey Gwynn,* 409–54. Dublin: 1961.

——. "Johannes Teutonicus, Glossator des kanonischen Rechts, 1. Halfte 13. Jahrhundert." *Neue Deutsche Biographie* 10 (1974): 571a–573a.

——. "A Forgotten Definition of Justice." *Mélanges Gérard Fransen.* SG 20: 75–109. Rome: 1976.

——. *The History of Ideas and Doctrines of Canon Law in the Middle Ages.* London: 1980.

———— . *Medieval Councils, Decretals and Collections of Canon Law: Selected Essays.* London: 1980.

———— . "Universal Pope or Servant of God's Servants: The Canonists, Papal Titles, and Innocent III." *Revue de droit canonique* 32 (1981): 109–49.

Kyer, Clifford I. "*Legatus* and *Nuntius* as Used to Denote Papal Envoys: 1245–1378." *Mediaeval Studies* 40 (1978): 473–77.

Landau, Peter. "Zum Ursprung des 'Ius ad rem' in der Kanonistik." *Proceedings of the Third International Congress of Medieval Canon Law.* Ed. Stephan Kuttner. MIC, Series C, 4: 81–102. Città del Vaticano: 1971.

———— . *Ius Patronatus: Studien zur Entwicklung des Patronats im Dekretalenrecht und der Kanonistik des 12. und 13. Jahrhunderts.* Köln-Wien: 1975.

———— . "Papst Lucius III. und das Mietrecht in Bologna." *Proceedings of the Fourth International Congress of Medieval Canon Law.* Ed. Stephan Kuttner. MIC, Series C, 5: 511–22. Città del Vaticano: 1976.

Larner, John. *Italy in the Age of Dante and Petrarch 1216–1380.* London-New York: 1980.

Laufs, Manfred. *Politik und Recht bei Innozenz III.: Rekuperationspolitik Papst Innozenz' III.* Köln-Wien: 1980.

Le Bras, Gabriel. "Bernard de Pavia." DDC 2: 782–89. Paris: 1937.

———— . "Le droit romain au service de la domination pontificale." *Revue historique de droit français et étranger* 27 (1949): 377–98.

———— . *Institutions ecclésiastiques de la Chrétienté médiévale.* Histoire de l'église depuis les origines jusqu'à nos jours 12. Paris: 1959–64.

————, Lefebvre, Charles, and Rambaud, J. *L'âge classique 1140–1378: Sources et théorie du droit.* Histoire du droit et des institutions de l'Eglise en Occident 7. Paris: 1965.

Lecuyer, J. *Etudes sur la collégialité épiscopale.* Le Puy-Lyon: 1964.

Lefebvre, Charles. "Hostiensis." DDC 5: 1211–27. Paris: 1953.

Leibniz, Gottfried Wilhelm. *Scriptores rerum Brunsvicensium.* Hanover: 1710.

Lenherr, Titus. "Der Begriff 'executio' in der Summa Decretorum des Huguccio." AKKR 150 (1981): 5–44, 361–420.

Leonardi, Corrado. "La vita e l'opera di Uguccione da Pisa, decretista." SG 4: 45–120. Bologna: 1956.

Lerner, Robert. "Joachim of Fiore as a Link between St. Bernard and Innocent III on the Figural Significance of Melchisedech." *Mediaeval Studies* 42 (1980): 471–76.

Letonnelier, Gaston. *L'abbaye exempte de Cluny et le saint-siège: Etude sur le développement de l'exemption clunisienne des origines jusqu'à la fin du XIIe siècle.* Paris-Ligugé: 1923.

Lindner, D. *Die Lehre vom Privileg nach Gratian und den Glossatoren des Corpus iuris canonici.* Regensburg: 1917.

McCready, William D. "Papal *Plenitudo potestatis* and the Source of Temporal Authority in Late Medieval Hierocratic Theory." *Speculum* 48 (1973): 654–74.

———— . "Papalists and Antipapalists: Aspects of the Church/State Controversy in the Later Middle Ages." *Viator* 6 (1975): 241–73.

————, ed. *The Theory of Papal Monarchy in the Fourteenth Century: Guillaume de Pierre Godin Tractatus de causa immediata ecclesiastice potestatis.* Studies and Texts 56. Toronto: 1982.

McCurry, Charles. "*Utilia Metensia:* Local Benefices for the Papal *Curia, 1212–c. 1370.*" *Law, Church, and Society: Essays in Honor of Stephan Kuttner,* 311–23. Ed. Kenneth Pennington and Robert Somerville. Philadelphia 1977.

Maccarrone, Michele. *Vicarius Christi: Storia del titolo papale.* Rome: 1952.

Maffei, Domenico. *La donazione di Costantino nei giuristi medievali.* Milan: 1969.

Maleczek, Werner. "Ein Brief des Kardinals Lothar von ss. Sergius und Bacchus (Innocenz III.) an Kaiser Heinrich VI." DA 38 (1982): 564–76.

Manselli, Raoul. "Federico II ed Alatrino, diplomatico pontificio del secolo XIII." *Studi Romani* 6 (1958): 649–58.

Mansilla, Demetrio. "Obispados exentos de la iglesia española." *Hispania sacra* 32 (1980): 287–321.

Marrone, John. "The Ecclesiology of the Parisian Secular Masters, 1250–1320." Unpublished Ph.D. dissertation, Cornell University: 1972.

———. "The Absolute and the Ordained Powers of the Pope: An Unedited text of Henry of Ghent." *Mediaeval Studies* 36 (1974): 7–27.

Melville, G. "Zur Abgrenzung zwischen Vita canonica et Vita monastica: Das Überstrittsproblem in kanonistischer Behandlung von Gratian bis Hostiensis." *Secundum regulam vivere: Festschrift für P. Norbert Backmund O. Praem.* Ed. G. Melville. Windberg: 1978: 205–44.

Michaud-Quantin, Pierre. *Universitas: Expressions du mouvement communautaire dan le moyen âge latin.* Paris: 1970.

Miethke, Jürgen. "Geschichtsprozess und Zeitgenössisches Bewusstsein—Die Theorie des monarchischen Papats im hohen und späteren Mittelalter." *Historische Zeitschrift* 226 (1978): 564–99.

———. "Die Rolle der Bettelorden im Umbruch der politischen Theorie an der Wende zum 14. Jahrhundert." *Stellung und Wirksamkeit der Bettelorden in der städtischen Gesellschaft,* 119–53. Ed. Kaspar Elm. Berliner Historische Studien 3. Berlin: 1981.

Mollat, G. *La collation des bénéfices ecclésiastiques à l'époque des papes d'Avignon (1305–1378).* Paris: 1921.

Mordek, Hubert. "*Proprie auctoritates apostolice sedis:* Ein zweiter Dictatus papae Gregors VII.?" DA 28 (1972): 105–32.

Morey, Adrian, and Brooke, C. N. L. *Gilbert Foliot and His Letters.* Cambridge: 1965.

Morrall, John B. *Gerson and the Great Schism.* Manchester: 1960.

Morsdorf, K. "Die Regierungsaufgaben des Bishofs im Lichte der kanonischen Gewaltenunterscheidung." *Episcopus: Studien über das Bishofsamt,* 257–77. Regensburg: 1949.

Muller, Léo. "La notion canonique d'abbaye nullius." *Revue de droit canonique* 6 (1956): 115–44.

Munz, Peter. *Frederick Barbarossa: A Study in Medieval Politics.* London: 1969.

Nörr, Knut W. "Der Apparat des Laurentius zur Compilatio III." *Traditio* 17 (1961): 542–43.

———. "Päpstliche Dekretalen und römisch-kanonischer Zivilprozess." *Studien zur europäischen Rechtsgeschichte,* 53–65. Ed. H. Coing. Frankfurt a/M: 1972.

Oakley, Francis. "Jacobean Political Theology: The Absolute and Ordinary Powers of the King." *Journal of the History of Ideas* 29 (1968): 323–46.

————. "Figgis, Constance and the Divines of Paris." *The American Historical Review* 75 (1969): 368–86.

Ober, L. "Die Translation der Bischöfe im Altertum." AKKR 88 (1908): 209–29, 441–65, 625–48; 89 (1909): 3–33.

Ochoa Sanz, Javier. *Vincentius Hispanus canonista boloñes del siglo XIII.* Madrid-Rome: 1960.

Ohnsorge, W. *Die Legaten Alexanders III. im ersten Jahrzehnt seines Pontifikats (1159–1169).* Berlin: 1928.

Pacaut, M. "Les légats d'Alexandre III (1159–81)." *Revue histoire ecclésiastique* 50 (1955): 821–38.

Padoa Schioppa, Antonio. "Sul principio della representanza diretta nel Diritto canonico classico." *Proceedings of the Fourth International Congress of Medieval Canon Law,* 107–31. Ed. Stephan Kuttner. MIC, Series C, 5. Città del Vaticano: 1976.

Paravicini Bagliani, Agostino. *Cardinali di curia e "familiae" cardinalizie dal 1227 al 1254.* Padua: 1972.

Pennington, Kenneth. "The Legal Education of Pope Innocent III." BMCL 4 (1974): 70–77.

————. "The French Recension of *Compilatio tertia.*" BMCL 5 (1975): 53–71.

————. "The Canonists and Pluralism in the Thirteenth Century." *Speculum* 51 (1976): 35–48.

————. "Cum causamque: A Decretal of Pope Innocent III." BMCL 7 (1977): 100–103.

————. "Pope Innocent III's Views on Church and State: A Gloss to *Per venerabilem.*" *Law, Church and Society: Essays in Honor of Stephan Kuttner,* 49–67. Ed. Kenneth Pennington and Robert Somerville. Philadelphia: 1977.

————. "Pro peccatis patrum puniri: A Moral and Legal Problem of the Inquisition." *Church History* 47 (1978): 137–54.

————. "The Making of a Decretal Collection: The Genesis of Compilatio tertia." *Proceedings of the Fifth International Congress of Medieval Canon Law,* 67–92. Ed. S. Kuttner and K. Pennington. MIC, Series C, 6. Città del Vaticano: 1980.

————. "*Epistolae Alexandrinae:* A Collection of Pope Alexander III's Letters." *Studi senesi* (1983).

Perrin, J. W. "Legatus, the Lawyers and the Terminology of Power in Roman Law." *Collectanea Stephan Kuttner,* 461–89. SG 11. Bologna: 1967.

Peters, Edward. *The Shadow King: Rex inutilis in Medieval Law and Literature, 751–1327.* New Haven: 1970.

Pfaff, Volkert. "Der Vorgänger: Das Wirken Coelestins III. aus der Sicht von Innozenz III." ZRG Kan. Abt. 60 (1974): 121–67.

Pitz, Ernst. *Papstreskript und Kaiserreskript im Mittelalter.* Tübingen: 1971.

————. "Die römische Kurie als Thema der vergleichenden Sozialgeschichte." QF 58 (1978): 216–359.

Post, Gaines. *Studies in Medieval Legal Thought: Public Law and the State, 1100–1322.* Princeton: 1964.

————. "Copyists' Errors and the Problem of Papal Dispensations 'Contra statutum generale ecclesiae' or 'Contra statum generalem ecclesiae' According to the Decretists and Decretalists circa 1150–1234." SG 9: 359–405. Bologna: 1966.

————. "Bracton as Jurist and Theologian on Kingship." *Proceedings of the Third International Congress of Medieval Canon Law,* 113–30. Ed. Stephan Kuttner. MIC, Series C, 4. Città del Vaticano: 1971.

————. "Vincentius Hispanus, 'Pro ratione voluntas,' and Medieval and Early Modern Theories of Sovereignty." *Traditio* 28 (1972): 159–84.

Prosdocimi, Luigi. "La 'Summa Decretorum' di Uguccione da Pisa: Studi preliminari per una edizione critica." SG 3: 350–74. Bologna: 1955.

Queller, Donald. *The Office of the Ambassador in the Middle Ages.* Princeton: 1967.

Renna, Thomas J. "Kingship in the *Disputatio inter clericum et militem.*" *Speculum* 48 (1973): 675–93.

Riesenberg, Peter. *Inalienability of Sovereignty in Medieval Political Thought.* New York: 1956.

Ríos Fernández, M. "El primado del romano pontifice en el pensamiento de Huguccio de Pisa decretista." *Compostellanum* 6 (1961): 47–97; 7 (1962): 97–149; 8 (1963): 65–99; 11 (1966): 29–67.

Robinson, I. S. "Gregory VII and the Soldiers of Christ." *History* 58 (1973): 169–92.

————. " 'Periculosus homo': Pope Gregory VII and Episcopal Authority." *Viator* 9 (1978): 103–31.

Ryan, J. Joseph. *Saint Peter Damiani and his Canonical Sources: A Preliminary Study in the Antecedents of the Gregorian Reform.* Toronto: 1956.

Saltman, Avrom. *Theobald of Canterbury.* London: 1956.

Sayers, Jane. "Centre and Locality: Aspects of Papal Administration in England in the Later Thirteenth Century." *Authority and Power: Studies on Medieval Law and Government Presented to Walter Ullmann,* 115–26. Ed. B. Tierney and P. Linehan. Cambridge: 1980.

Schannat, J. F. *Vindemiae literariae.* 2 vols. Fulda: 1723–24.

Schatz, Klaus. "Papsttum und partikularkirchliche Gewalt bei Innocenz III. (1198–1216)." *Archivum Historiae Pontificiae* 8 (1970): 61–111.

Schmutz, R. "Medieval Papal Representatives: Legates, Nuncios, and Judges Delegate." *Post Scripta.* SG 15: 441–63. Rome: 1972.

Schnackenburg, Rudolph. *Das Johannesevangelium.* 1. Teil: *Einleitung und Kommentar zu Kap.* 1–4. 2nd. ed. Freiburg-Basel-Wien: 1967.

Schreiber, Georg. *Kurie und Kloster im 12. Jahrhundert.* 2 vols. Stuttgart: 1910.

Schubert, Ernst. *König und Reich: Studien zur spätmittelalterlichen deutschen Verfassungsgeschichte.* Göttingen: 1979.

Schulte, Johann F., von. "Johannes Teutonicus (Semeca, Zemeke)." *Zeitschrift für Kirchenrecht* 16 (1881): 107–32.

Schwaiger, G. "Der päpstliche Primat in der Geschichte der Kirche." *Zeitschrift für Kirchengeschichte* 82 (1971): 1–15.

Schwarz, Brigide. *Die Organisation kurialer Schreiberkollegien von ihrer Entstehung bis zur 15. Jahrhunderts.* Tübingen: 1972.

Searle, Eleanor. "Battle Abbey and Exemption: The Forged Charters." *English Historical Review* 83 (1968): 449–80.

————. *Lordship and Community: Battle Abbey and Its Banlieu, 1066–1538.* Toronto: 1974.

Singer, Heinrich. *Die Dekretalensammlung des Bernardus Compostellanus antiquus.*

Sitzungsberichte der kaiserlichen Akademie der Wissenschaften phil.-hist. Klasse, Wien 171.2. Vienna: 1914.

Somerville, Robert. *Alexander III and the Council of Tours.* Berkeley-Los Angeles-London: 1977.

Southern, Richard. *Western Society and the Church in the Middle Ages.* Harmondsworth: 1970.

Stickler, Alfons M. *Sacerdotium et Regnum nei decretisti e primi decretalisti.* Torino: 1953.

———. "Alanus Anglicus als Verteidiger des monarchischen Papsttums." *Salesanium* 21 (1959): 346–406.

———. "Uguccio de Pise." DDC 7: 1355–62. Paris: 1965.

———. "Il decretista Laurentius Hispanus." SG 9: 461–549. Bologna: 1966.

———. "La 'Sollicitudo omnium ecclesiarum' nella canonistica classica." *Communio* 13 (1972): 547–86.

———. "Papal Infallibility—A Thirteenth-Century Invention? Reflections on a Recent Book." *The Catholic Historical Review* 60 (1974): 427–41.

Strayer, Joseph. *The Reign of Philip the Fair.* Princeton: 1980.

Sweeney, James Ross. "The Problem of Inalienability in Innocent III's Correspondence with Hungary: A Contribution to the Study of the Historical Genesis of Intellecto." *Mediaeval Studies* 37 (1975): 235–51.

———. "The Decretal Intellecto and the Hungarian Golden Bull of 1222." *Album Elemér Mályusz,* 91–96. Brussels: 1976.

Tangl, G. *Die Teilnehmer an den allgemeinen Konzilien des Mittelalters.* Köln-Graz: 1969.

Tarrant, Jacqueline. "The Life and Works of Jesselin de Cassagnes." BMCL 9 (1979): 37–64.

Thils, Gustave. *Primauté pontificale et prérogatives épiscopales.* Louvain: 1961.

Thomson, W. R. *Friars in the Cathedral: The First Franciscan Bishops, 1226–1261.* Toronto: 1975.

Tierney, Brian. "Some Recent Works on the Political Theories of the Medieval Canonists." *Traditio* 10 (1954): 594–625.

———. *Foundations of the Conciliar Theory: The Contribution of the Medieval Canonists from Gratian to the Great Schism.* Cambridge: 1955.

———. "Grosseteste and the Theory of Papal Sovereignty." *Journal of Ecclesiastical History* 6 (1955): 1–17.

———. "Pope and Council: Some New Decretists Texts." *Mediaeval Studies* 19 (1957): 157–218.

———. "Bracton on Government." *Speculum* 38 (1963): 295–317.

———. " 'The Prince Is Not Bound by Law': Accursius and the Origins of the Modern State." *Comparative Studies in Society and History* 5 (1963): 378–400.

———. *The Crisis of Church and State, 1050–1300.* Englewood Cliffs, N.J.: 1964.

———. "Ockham, the Conciliar Theory, and the Canonists." *The Journal of the History of Ideas* 15 (1964): 40–70.

———. "Medieval Canon Law and Western Constitutionalism." *The Catholic Historical Review* 52 (1966): 1–17.

———. *Origins of Papal Infallibility, 1150–1350: A Study on the Concepts of Infallibility, Sovereignity and Tradition in the Middle Ages.* Leiden: 1972.

————. "Hostiensis and Collegiality." *Proceedings of the Fourth International Congress of Medieval Canon Law.* MIC, Series C, 5: 401–9. Città del Vaticano: 1976.

————. " 'Only the Truth has Authority': The Problem of 'Reception' in the Decretists and in Johannes de Turrecremata." *Law, Church and Society: Essays in Honor of Stephan Kuttner,* 69–96. Ed. Kenneth Pennington and Robert Somerville. Philadelphia: 1977.

————. *Church, Law, and Constitutional Thought in the Middle Ages.* London: 1979.

————. *Religion, Law and the Growth of Constitutional Thought, 1150–1650.* Cambridge: 1982.

Tillmann, Helene. *Papst Innocenz III.* Bonn: 1954.

Torrell, Jean-Pierre. *La théologie de l'épiscopat au premier concile du Vatican.* Paris: 1961.

Ullmann, Walter. *Origins of the Great Schism.* London: 1948.

————. *Medieval Papalism: The Political Theories of the Medieval Canonists.* London: 1949.

————. "Eugenius IV, Cardinal Kemp, and Archbishop Chichele." *Medieval Studies Presented to Aubrey Gwynn, S.J.,* 359–83. Ed. John A. Watt et al. Dublin: 1961.

————. *The Growth of Papal Government in the Middle Ages: A Study in the Ideological Relation of Clerical to Lay Power.* 2nd. ed. London: 1962.

————. "The Bible and Principles of Government in the Middle Ages." *Settimane di studio del Centro italiano di studi sull'alto medioevo,* 10:183–227. Spoleto: 1963.

————. *The Church and Law in the Earlier Middle Ages.* London: 1975.

————. "John Baconthorpe as a Canonist." *Church and Government in the Middle Ages: Essays presented to C.R. Cheney,* 223–46. Ed. C. N. L. Brooke et al. Cambridge: 1976.

————. *The Papacy and Political Ideas in the Middle Ages.* London: 1976.

Van Hove, Alphonse. *De privilegiis <et> de dispensationibus.* Rome: 1935.

Van de Kerckhove, Martinien. "La notion de juridiction chez les décrétistes et les premiers décrétalistes (1140–1250)." *Etudes franciscaines* 49 (1937): 420–55.

Vodola, E. F. "Legal Precision in the Decretist Period: A Note on the Development of Glosses on 'De consecratione' with Reference to the Meaning of 'Cautio sufficiens.' " BMCL 6 (1976): 55–63.

————. "Fides et culpa: The Use of Roman Law in Ecclesiastical Ideology." *Authority and Power: Studies on Medieval Law and Government Presented to Walter Ullmann,* 83–97. Ed. Brian Tierney and Peter Linehan. Cambridge: 1980.

Walf, Knut. *Die Entwicklung des päpstlichen Gesandtschaftswesens in dem Zeitabschnitt zwischen Dekretalenrecht und Wiener Kongress 1159–1815.* Munich: 1966.

Walther, Hans. *Proverbia sententiaeque latinitatis medii aevi.* 5 vols. Göttingen: 1963–67.

Warren, W. L. *Henry II.* Berkeley-Los Angeles: 1973.

Watt, John A. "The Early Medieval Canonists and the Formation of the Conciliar Theory." *The Irish Theological Review* 24 (1957): 13–31.

——— . The Theory of Papal Monarchy in the Thirteenth Century: The Contribution of the Canonists. London: 1965.

——— . "The Use of the Term 'Plenitudo potestatis' by Hostiensis." Proceedings of the Second International Congress of Medieval Canon Law. Ed. Stephan Kuttner and J. Joseph Ryan. MIC, Series C, 1: 161–87. Città del Vaticano: 1965.

——— . "The Constitutional Law of the College of Cardinals: Hostiensis to Johannes Andreae." Mediaeval Studies 23 (1971): 127–57.

——— . "Hostiensis on Per venerabilem: The Role of the College of Cardinals." Authority and Power: Studies on Medieval Law and Government Presented to Walter Ullmann, 99–113. Ed. Brian Tierney and Peter Linehan. Cambridge: 1980.

Weigand, Rudolf. Die Naturrechtslehre der Legisten und Dekretisten von Irnerius bis Accursius und von Gratian bis Johannes Teutonicus. Munich: 1968.

Weiss, Roberto. The Renaissance Discovery of Classical Antiquity. Oxford: 1969.

Wendehorst, Alfred. Das Bistum Würzburg. I: Die Bischofsreihe bis 1254. Germania Sacra 1. Berlin: 1962.

Wilks, Michael. The Problem of Sovereignty in the Later Middle Ages: The Papal Monarchy with Augustinus Triumphus and the Publicists. Cambridge: 1964.

Winter, F. "Erzbischof Wichmann von Magdeburg." Forschungen zur deutschen Geschichte 13 (1873): 111–55.

Wright, J. Robert. The Church and the English Crown 1305–1334: A Study Based on the Register of Archbishop Walter Reynolds. Toronto: 1980.

Zuckerman, Charles. "Some Texts of Bernard of Auvergne on Papal Power." Recherches de théologie ancienne et médiévale 49 (1982): 174–204.

INDEX

Abbas Antiquus. *See* Bernard de Montmirat
abdication of bishops. *See* bishop(s), renunciation
Accursius, 25
Aegidius de Fuscarariis, 73–74
Alanus Anglicus, 53, 105n.97, 124, 135; *Collectio decretalium*, 15; emperor has his sword from the pope, 61–62; episcopal renunciations, 103–4; papal provisions disobeyed, 121–22; bishop may judge exempt cleric, 179
Alatrino, 150–52
Albert, archbishop of Magdeburg, 64
Albrecht the Bear, 91
Alexander III, pope, 90, 93, 97, 102, 121, 161, 174, 176; prebends for clerics, 117–20; privileges of exemption, 155–56; exemptions for monastic chapels, 167; heretics lose papal privileges, 177–78
Alexander IV, pope, 63
Ambrose, St., 70
Anaclet, pope, 55
Anastasius IV, pope, 92
Anastasius, emperor, 158
Andrea dei Mozzi, bishop of Florence, 100n.79
Andrea Fieschi, 149–50
Anselm of Lucca, 80n.16, 86
Anterius, pope, 86, 92
Aquinas, Thomas, 1, 6, 52, 108
archbishop(ric)s. *See* bishop(ric)s
Arnold of Lisieux, 57n.45
Augustinus Triumphus, 7, 55
Ausculta fili, 115–16
Azo VII of Ferrara, 36

Baldwin, archbishop of Canterbury, 94
Barraclough, Geoffrey, 116
Bartholomaeus Brixiensis, 124n.37, 145; exemptions for monastic chapels, 172–74
Battle Abbey, 76, 157–59
Becket, Thomas, 3, 93, 158–59
benefice(s), 115–53; provisions in the twelfth century, 117–20; papal mandates for, 121–23; pluralism, 134–47; simple, 136, 145; in two different bishoprics, 141; without the care of souls, 143; and custom, 143; provisions in the thirteenth century, 148–53
Benson, Robert, 4, 80
Bermudo, bishop of Coimbra, 168
Bernard of Balbi (of Pavia), bishop of Faenza, 77, 90, 102; translation of, 96–98; significance of translation of, 100
Bernard of Montmirat, 146
Bernardus Compostellanus antiquus, 126; *Collectio Romana* of, 15, 24
Bernardus Compostellanus Junior, 186
Bernardus Parmensis, 20, 26, 28, 30, 146, 186; mendicants must have permission of local priests to hear confessions, 5, 187
Bernered, cardinal bishop of Palestrina, 117
Bible, citations to: Isaiah 14:14, 111; Matthew 16:18, 49–54, 139; Matthew 16:18–19, 113; Matthew 18:18, 50; Matthew 19:6, 112; John 1:42, 48–56, 57n.45, 62; John 3:8, 107; John 21:15–17, 51; John 21:17, 113; 2 Cor. 3:17, 107
bishop(ric)s (archbishop[ric]s): Aachen, 151; Antioch, 99; Bamberg, 31; Canterbury, 94; Chartres, 148, 150; Chichester, 150,

INDEX OF MANUSCRIPTS

Full citations of abbreviated entries in this index may be found in the bibliography.

INDEX OF LEGAL CITATIONS

THE MIDDLE AGES
Edward Peters, General Editor